The Race Controversy in American Education

The Race Controversy in American Education

Volume 1

LILLIAN DOWDELL DRAKEFORD, PhD, EDITOR

Racism in American Institutions
Brian D. Behnken, Series Editor

 PRAEGER™

An Imprint of ABC-CLIO, LLC
Santa Barbara, California • Denver, Colorado

Library of Congress Cataloging-in-Publication Data

The race controversy in American education / Lillian Dowdell Drakeford, editor.
    pages cm. — (Racism in American institutions)
    Includes bibliographical references and index.
    ISBN 978-1-4408-3263-5 (alk. paper) — ISBN 978-1-4408-3264-2
1. Critical pedagogy—United States.   2. Minorities—Education—United States.
3. Children with social disabilities—Education—United States.   I. Drakeford, Lillian Dowdell.
    LC196.5.U6R33   2015
    379.2'6—dc23   2015001775

ISBN: 978-1-4408-3263-5
EISBN: 978-1-4408-3264-2

19 18 17 16 15   1 2 3 4 5

This book is also available on the World Wide Web as an eBook.
Visit www.abc-clio.com for details.

Praeger
An Imprint of ABC-CLIO, LLC

ABC-CLIO, LLC
130 Cremona Drive, P.O. Box 1911
Santa Barbara, California 93116-1911

This book is printed on acid-free paper ∞

Manufactured in the United States of America

Contents

III. Race and Racialization in Schools and Curriculum

IV. Race and "Cost" Debate in School Reform

V. Beyond High School

Series Foreword

Brian D. Behnken

The Race Controversy in American Education is the second two-volume collection to be published in Praeger Publisher's series, Racism in American Institutions (RAI). The RAI series focuses on the ways in which racism has become, and remains, a part of the fabric of many American institutions. For example, while the United States may have done away with overtly racist acts such as extralegal lynching, racism still affects many of America's established institutions from public schools to corporate offices. While the media discarded many of its most racist practices and characters years ago, stereotypical depictions of people of color remain with us. Schools were supposed to be integrated after 1954, yet today many American schools remain one-race schools. This open-ended series of one-volume works examines the problem of racism in established American institutions. Each book in the RAI Series traces the prevalence of racism within a particular institution throughout the history of the U.S. and explores the problem in that institution today, looking at ways in which the institution has attempted to rectify racism, but also the ways in which it has not.

The Race Controversy in American Education explores the critically important subject of racism in American schools. Institutional racism within schools should surprise no one, given the long history of school segregation and educational inequities in the U.S. The multiple scholars in 33 well crafted, analytical chapters expand our viewpoint by looking at many of the historic and contemporary manifestations of racism in education. Take for instance zero tolerance policies, which unfortunately tend to target and affect students of color, debilitating young learners and, in some ugly cases, criminalizing them for relatively minor infractions. Those zero tolerance policies have also led to another problem in American education, the school or cradle to prison pipeline. In an oddly reminiscent policy move, educators have in essence enacted a new form of "tracking," one that tracks students of color from schools to prisons.

The authors in these two volumes do not simply address problems in the American educational arena. They also offer novel and important recommendations for how we might work to solve these problems. One solution that education experts have advanced for decades is the restructuring of the curriculum to more fully reflect the diversity of the U.S. That restructuring could also work to target specific groups who are underrepresented in certain fields, from students of color is science or engineering to female students in math. Other authors in this volume seek to correct problems in leadership in schools or emphasize the ways unrecognized groups, or focus on management issues as a corrective measure.

Taken together, these 33 chapters go far in explaining institutionalized racism in education and offering solutions to these problems. This is the goal of the RAI series. Editor Lillian Dowdell Drakeford has skillfully brought these volumes together. As a lifelong educator she is well suited and uniquely experienced for this project. *The Race Controversy in American Education* touches on not just an important subject, but one that profoundly impacts the lives of millions of young Americans on daily basis.

Brian D. Behnken
Iowa State University
Ames, Iowa

Preface

Still Troubled after All These Years

Not everything that is faced will change, but nothing will change until it is faced.[1]

Ever since I grew old enough to reflect, I have been deeply troubled by the insidious persistence of racism and inequality of opportunity in America's public schools. At various junctures throughout my life, I have had the occasion to contemplate the impact of growing up black in America.

I Remember . . .

In 1962, I was one of 60 black children crammed into a partitioned second-grade classroom. There were two teachers, Mrs. Hart and Mrs. Lyle. My teacher was Mrs. Lyle. We did not know we were overcrowded because everybody acted like they had good sense, for the most part, so there were no major distractions, of which we were aware, to teaching and learning. We all knew one another from the neighborhood, we were sure that our teachers loved us, and we learned what we needed to learn to be ready for third grade. That was all that mattered. It was not until I became old enough to reflect on the situation that I realized the inequity of our circumstances. I later learned that our school was overcrowded, but across town, classes in the all-white schools had only 20 students.

It was not until I became a teacher that I realized that there had to have been numerous caveats to teaching and learning from Mrs. Hart and Mrs. Lyle's perspective: caveats like not being able to give individual attention to those students who probably needed it most; having to insist on absolute order, discipline, and control when a little unorthodox active learning might have occasionally better suited the learning environment; and being forced to teach to the middle in deference to the infamous bell curve, which automatically discounts children who appear as outliers in the larger spectrum. In retrospect, I wondered what happened to the much-anticipated reform that was supposed to follow the *Brown v. Board of Education* (1954) victory. At the time, however, in my innocence, I knew nothing of the *Brown* decision, segregation, or the interest that fueled. My world was black and it felt and looked pretty good to me.

I first felt the sting of racism in the seventh grade. I was one of a select group of African American students bused across town to integrate an all-white middle school in Gary, Indiana. While some students were unfriendly, it was not their unfriendliness that bothered me the most. It was not a personal prejudice that I felt; it was more of systematic, institutionalized, collusion of lifelong perceptions of being marginalized because of my color. What troubled me most was a nagging sense of self-doubt. It was a self-doubt borne out of being ignored and feeling diminished in the white environment—ignored at lunch, ignored in class, and rarely asked for my opinion. It was a feeling of doubt that my dad may have unknowingly nurtured as I often heard him lament "if you're black, you have to be perfect and then improve." What a tall order! I doubt that it is possible.

At any rate, I began to second-guess my intellect and ability alongside the majority population of white students. Suddenly, everybody seemed smarter than I was just because they were not black. It was a very unfamiliar feeling because I was accustomed to being one of the smartest students in the class. I did not realize that I still may have been one of the smartest students in the class even if the class was full of white people. Despite loving parents, both of whom were career educators, and numerous positive black role models within my family, church, and neighborhood, the ravaging effects of institutional racism in American society had managed to teach me that white was naturally right and better and that being black made me not quite good enough.

I came home and announced that I just did not feel as smart as the white kids. "They're smarter than I am," I cried. It took a stern talking from my father, one I will never forget, to jolt me out of this destructive self-talk. His words hit me like a splash of cold water on the face. "Don't ever doubt yourself or what you can do. You are just as good, just as smart as anybody else. Keep your eyes on the prize." I took his words to heart, consecrating them in my memory, and have, since then, often culled great strength from their remembrance at critical junctures throughout my life. In one sense, I have never looked back, that is to say, I rarely doubt my capacity to achieve great things. Yet, in another vein, I am constantly reflecting on the why of that lived experience. Several niggling questions come to mind.

How is it that such effects are learned and through what everyday mechanisms? How do the pedagogical dimensions of overt white supremacy differ from the more covert expressions of white dominance in the alleged raceless or color-blind contemporary era, and what effect do they have on black youth? Do children of color still learn from school and society that they are inept and if so, to what degree? Do they learn this differently and if so, how? What happens to children who rarely hear positively affirming words? What happens to children who accept the negative identity frequently ascribed to them? What happens to them?

I fear that many children die inside, and our whole society, even if unknowingly, dies a little bit right along with them. Without a language of hopeful possibility, children become fatalistic about their future, grow cynical, and become what society tells them they are. They become low achievers. All too often, in the midst of progress in more privileged school districts and wealthy suburbs, many African Americans attend substandard schools with substandard resources and substandard teachers who race to beat the children out of the doors at the close of the school day. Of course, this is not the case everywhere, but if it is the case anywhere, that is one case too many.

Some Time in 1979 . . .

Still troubled, I found myself struggling to explain the how and why of racism and naively contemplated what might be done to get rid of the irksome problem once and for all. I wrote an essay back in 1979 on racism and whether black history courses can eradicate racism. I did not believe then (and do not believe now) that racism has much at all to do with ignorance. To the contrary, I argued that racism is caused by insecurities inherent to the human experience and exacerbated to varying degrees by unfulfilled yearnings for security and belonging wrought by society. I wrote:

> All of us, at birth, become detached from our original oneness with nature and truth. We are forced to attune ourselves to a foreign and contradictory human existence. Thus, each step we take into this new existence brings with it fear, insecurity, and the challenge to fuse the perfection of our pre-birth existence with the imperfection of our lived experiences. If we succeed in meeting this challenge, we find truth and become productive and creative individuals. If we fail, we find deception and remain insecure and afraid. The extent to which we fail or succeed in this endeavor is largely determined by the nature of the society into which we are born.

I have since learned that I was not alone in these views. Author and scholar, James Baldwin expressed a similar stance:

> Everyone really knows how long the Blacks have been here. Everyone knows on what level Blacks are involved with the American people and in American life. These are not secrets. It is not a question even of the ignorance of White people. It is a question of the fears of White people. . . . So that's what makes it all so hysterical, so unwieldy, and so completely irretrievable. Reason cannot reach it. It is as though some great, great wound is in the whole body, and no one dares to operate: to close it, to examine it, to stitch it.[2]

In my not so scholarly treatise, I also pondered an unsettling connection between racism, inequality, education, and the larger society:

> Our society, because of its capitalistic and highly industrialized nature, makes it difficult for us to meet this challenge [winning the battle over insecurity during separation from the womb]. The ideals of capitalism and industrialization negate the value of truth and existence. These ideals of merciless competition, technological progress, efficiency, and material accumulation negate the value of truth because they encourage us to outsmart each other and nature. We are rewarded for giving the appearance of truth. These ideals negate the value of our existence because they remind us that we can always be replaced by machines. . . . Thus, we are constantly afraid and insecure. . . . We make technology, efficiency, and the almighty dollar our means, our ends, and our gods. . . . Our passivity has resulted in a number of deceptions. . . . Justice has become the interest of the wealthy. . . . White Americans, who came to this country in search of its traditional values and a new identity, have lost sight of who they are or where their lives are headed. They are sure of nothing except their contrived superiority over black people. . . . Therefore, if the schools are to actively debase racism, then we, as educators, must restore the traditional ideals upon which our country was founded. We must revitalize the quest for truth and our bond with nature. . . . We must determine, for ourselves, what ideals we will teach. Foremost among these ideals must be high intellectual standards, balance and harmony, and truth and justice.

While today, I might pick some parts of this passage apart, it demonstrates my enduring interest in what schools should teach, the role of racism in school and society, and the negative impact of a capitalistic society more concerned with money and human efficiency than basic human worth and dignity. I continue to ponder how schools might function differently to unseat the arrogance of power, perception, and privilege in education.

Over the Next 30 Years . . .

Still deeply troubled, it seemed that I was at my wits end after years of teaching in a public urban school district and watching reform after reform fail to appreciably effect sustained change or eradicate persistent racial inequality of educational opportunities and outcomes. Between 1976 and 2006, I saw a number of educational reforms come and go, some more than once. Across the United States and in my district, I witnessed a myriad of educational reforms, all of which aimed to close the racial achievement gap, raise standards for all students, and promote excellence with equity. In every case, the unspoken impetus behind reform revolved around the controversy of race.

I remember the popular magnet school reform of the late 1970s and early 1980s. The overt appeal of magnet schools stemmed from the assertion that magnet schools provided parents and students with curricular choices while also providing a more diverse student population. "These schools emphasized the performing arts, math or science, or other curricular themes or approaches in an attempt to attract students voluntarily, without coercion from school boards or court edicts."[3] Promoted as a means of democratizing opportunity, magnet schools aimed to subtly maintain integration without mentioning race and also appease both the lower and middle classes. Unfortunately, there are at least two historical problems with increasing democracy in education. First, serving two masters—the interests of the privileged and the interests of the marginalized—has yet to work. Those in power rarely give up power and when they do, it is almost never without struggle. Second, throughout America's history whenever schools have become more inclusive and democratic, traditionally privileged Americans have rushed to the assumption that "more equality meant more mediocrity."[4] Hence, magnet schools ended up serving the privileged, for example, the children most likely to succeed anyway, without magnet schools. In my district, the magnet schools of real quality and in the greatest demand grew increasingly selective by establishing exclusionary admission criteria. Very few of the most needy children reaped the benefits of attending quality magnet schools. In time, the magnet movement waned as it became pretty obvious that magnet schools neither effectively stopped whites from leaving the city and abandoning public schools nor closed the racial achievement/opportunity gap.

Amid the push for magnet schools, I recall a brief resurgence of counterculturals who argued in favor of reforms such as "schools without walls, open classrooms, and more learning pods, electives, and student freedom."[5] Like other schools across the United States, we tried things like "schools without walls, open classrooms, and more learning pods, electives, and student freedom,"[6] but when these gimmicks failed to bring about change, they were replaced with calls for back-to-basics curricula, increased accountability, and a myriad of reform plans, such as performance contract learning, behavioral objectives, and other schemes.

By the 1980s, in fact, mainstream legislators, lawmakers, parents, and educators had grown very anxious about the perceived democratization of schools. They were alarmed by the alleged rise of low standards, soft curriculum, social promotion, and lack of discipline, all of which were covertly attributed to integration and the democratization of schools. I remember parents and teachers lamenting that schools were no longer fulfilling the "old republican promise that America was a land of opportunity where merit alone conferred distinction in a fluid social order."[7] In response to the call for change, schools spent the next decade trying some of everything to increase excellence in the schools, hence came the dawning of minimum competency-based testing.

It caught on like wildfire everywhere, and my district was no exception. Many of the early competency-based tests were quite rigorous. I remember, however, when it became apparent that the wrong students (e.g., the historically *good* students) would not be able to pass the tests, the tests got less rigorous, which, of course, defeated the original purpose of the minimum competency testing. More important, the tests did little, if anything, to address racial inequality or inequity. In fact, because students of color and poverty fared even more poorly than their white counterparts on the exams, the tests actually exacerbated racialized assumptions about their ability and desire to learn. Lackluster improvement in student achievement and persistence of the "achievement gap" between advantaged and disadvantaged youngsters prompted educators and policy makers to shift their focus away from the big picture to little picture reform. Schools set their sites on restructuring schools and making classroom improvements.

Reforms emphasized quality improvement at the school sites. Increasingly, problems confronting schools were seen as a systems problem; consequently, reformers believed a bottom-up approach to change might be more effective. My district tried employing Baldrige to promote and improve the classroom learning system as well as the system at the district level. Grounded in the business principles of Total Quality Management, Baldrige in education views change as a planned event.[8,9] It is a way of doing things and a mind-set that has the potential to transform a stagnant, learning-impoverished school culture into an adaptive, continuously improving, learning-enriched school culture. When Baldrige works as it should, whole school systems align their goals and objectives across and within every subsystem involved in the processes of educating and schooling, teaching and learning. I actually became a Baldrige trainer for the district, and I still strongly assert that it has great merit for facilitating continuous improvement. But, in time for reasons too complex to explain in this discussion, support for Baldrige almost disappeared, except for the proven Plan-Do-Study-Act improvement cycle. What followed across the country and in my district was a myriad of reforms, all of which aimed to close the racial achievement gap, raise standards for all students, and promote excellence with equity.

I taught through a parade of reforms that included Effective Schools, Success for All, specialized academies, smaller learning communities, schools-within-a-school, site-based administration, professional learning communities, academic teams, coaching teams, NCLB, high-stakes testing and increased accountability, design teams, and a lot of "Working on the Work."[10] Heck, I frequently led the band! Through it all, I found this much to be true. Racial inequality of opportunity and outcomes persists. The system fights to stay the same. It protects the privileged. And testing is here to stay.

June 2006 . . .

Still troubled, I enrolled in the PhD in Leadership and Change Program at Antioch University. Convinced that the persistent problem of inequality in education stemmed from the absence of the ethic of care in teachers and school leaders, I hoped to better understand how I might emulate the ethic of care in my profession, live and inspire the moral obligation of education, and help others understand the power of caring in the change process. Decisions grounded in the ethic of care require us to *know* those we teach and serve them well. We must love the children not only for who they are but also for who they can and want to be. Carol Noddings postulated that "the first job of schools is to care for our children."[11] Hence, I devoted a lot of time to reading the literature on the ethic of caring but found myself continually drawn to the haunting problem of race in America. At the root of the reason for a lack of caring and moral obligation was race. Simply put, what I discovered was that race and racialized assumptions determine how deeply and sincerely teachers and leaders care about how *some* children learn. If each of us is honest with ourselves, we don't care the same for everyone. I took a good look at myself, and the role of race in my own consciousness.

I examined the eye through which I process information, the lens through which I construct reality, the means by which I determine my actions, and the possible consequences of those actions. I learned that I am irrevocably influenced by my lived experiences, and growing up black in America is first and foremost among them. I discovered that I, too, must strive to function within an anti-oppressive framework.

We all are a product of our lived experiences, and each of us grapples with making sense of our humanity. When one adds the stain of the proverbial color line, the pernicious race question in America, and the determinative power associated with race to the extant trials of the human condition, the result is a mutually imprisoning human dilemma. "Who is the slave and who is free?"[12] Indeed, it is difficult to discern. We all suffer from the human construction of race and the bondage of racism. I wrestled with questions about the role schools play in perpetuating the bondage, and the role schools should play in eradicating it. I asked:

> What ideologies and epistemologies dictate the order of modern society? What do schools teach? What should schools teach? What do we learn and why? Who benefits from the order of society and education today? What are the possibilities for fruitful intervention in contemporary conflicts? How can education change the nature of society?

I looked for answers from scholars, philosophers, and theorists and became intrigued with critical pedagogy, resistance theory, and critical race theory. Everything I read led me to want to explore the concept of allegedly colorblind, raceless educational reform and its historical significance in the ongoing struggle to provide equity in education. Hence, the central question of my dissertation was, how have allegedly race-less, color-blind educational reform agendas in the post-*Brown* era, intentionally or unintentionally, affected racial inequality of educational opportunity and outcomes in America's public schools? The answers were both simple and complex.

Let it suffice to say that I grew even more convinced that race matters, racism endures, and, to the extent that schools are training grounds for how people view themselves and the world, if we ever intend to achieve equity and equality in schools and society, we must not feign blindness to that which ails us.

October 2013

Still troubled, I was recently retired from my district but eager to effect change, and make a difference. Lo and behold, an old contact led to a new opportunity! I was blessed with the chance to plan, edit, and contribute to this amazing two-volume collection: *The Race Controversy in American Education.*

I believe in the transformational power of education, intellectualism, and writing. I see this work as a change agent. As the seminal author, James Baldwin explained: "The paradox of education is precisely this—that as one begins to become conscious one begins to examine the society in which he is being educated. . . . You write in order to change the world . . . if you alter, even by a millimeter, the way people look at reality, then you can change it."[13]

Notes

1. http://www.goodreads.com/author/quotes/10427.James_Baldwin.
2. Mead and Baldwin 1971, p. 1.
3. Reese 2005, p. 248.
4. Ibid., p. 219.
5. Ibid., p. 309.
6. Ibid.
7. Ibid., p. 287.
8. Mukhopadhyay 2005.
9. Maurer and Pedersen 2004.
10. Schlechty 2002.
11. Noddings 1992, p. xiv.
12. Conklin 2013, p. 127.
13. http://www.goodreads.com/author/quotes/10427.James_Baldwin.

Bibliography

Conklin, T. 2013. *The House Girl.* New York: HarperCollins Publishers.

Edmonds, R. 1982. "Programs of School Improvement: An Overview." http://www.eric.ed.gov/ERICWebPortal/search/detailmini.jsp?_nfpb=true&_&ERICExtSearch_SearchValue_0=ED221536&ERICExtSearch_SearchType_0=no&accno=ED221536.

Maurer, R.E., and S.C. Pedersen 2004. *Malcolm & Me: How to Use the Baldrige Process to Improve Your School.* Lanham, MD: Scarecrow Education.

Mead, M., and J. Baldwin. 1971. *A Rap on Race.* Philadelphia, PA: J.B. Lippincott.

Mukhopadhyay, Marmar. 2005. *Total Quality Management.* 2nd ed. Thousand Oaks, CA: Sage Publications.

Noddings, C. 1992. *The Challenge to Care in Schools: An Alternative Approach to Education.* New York: Teachers College Press.

Reese, W.J. 2005. *America's Public Schools: From the Common School to "No Child Left Behind."* Baltimore, MD: Johns Hopkins University Press.

Schlechty, P.A. 2002. *Working on the Work: An Action Plan for Teachers, Principals, and Superintendents.* San Francisco, CA: Jossey-Bass.

Success for All. 1993. Number 5, August 1993. https://www2.ed.gov/pubs/OR/ConsumerGuides/success.html.

Introduction to Volume 1

This two-volume edited collection features 33 essays written by scholars and practitioners on an array of topics around the controversy of race in American education.

Section I in Volume 1, entitled "The Face of Racism and Color Blindness in American Education," features three chapters. The first chapter, written by Evelyn Young, provides a general overview of the literature in critical race theory (CRT) in both law and educational research. Through the lens of CRT, Young discusses the endemic nature of racism and investigates the interplay of racism in curriculum and instruction, educational policy, school finance, assessment, and educational leadership. She also offers suggestions for how CRT can be used in educational practice to tackle the persistent issues of race, power, and privilege in schools. In the second chapter, Lillian Dowdell Drakeford uses a historical, race-critical lens to analyze the impact of the ideology of color blindness and color-blind educational reform on racial inequality in America's public schools. Drakeford traces the ascendance of the ideology of color blindness from the *Plessy v. Ferguson* (1896) decision to the present and describes the pathological effect it has had on American consciousness and the educational system. She suggests race-critical, counterhegemonic educational reform as an alternative to color-blind school improvement strategies. The third and final chapter in this section, written by Ayana Allen et al., illuminates the historical evolution of race as a human-made social construct of far-reaching proportions, specifically in the ways in which institutional structures of racism have seeped into U.S. schools. Grounded in a critical race theoretical standpoint, they provide a historical examination of how race has been manipulated to enforce systems of categorization, exclusion, and oppression and pinpoint four ways in which schools serve as conduits and harbors of racial inequality. Research-based recommendations are provided to foster democracy and equity in education.

Section II, "The Crackdown," tackles the disturbing school-to-prison pipeline, also referred to as the prison industrial complex. In the first chapter of this section (Chapter 4), Alexi Freeman explores the role of school discipline, policies and practices in the school-to-prison pipeline, paying particular attention to the intersection of race and discipline. She uses research data to highlight the scope and effect of the crisis and also shares positive outcomes that occur when community-based organizations become engaged and empowered to advocate for positive change and reform in school discipline. Chapter 5, written by Nancy A. Heitzeg, investigates the racialization of student behavior and school discipline. She describes how the school-to-prison pipeline criminalizes disruptive behaviors of black and brown children while medicalizing the disruptive behaviors of white youth. Heitzeg raises questions about the extent to which current school disciplinary policies are meant to steer black and brown students toward "careers" as prisoners. Suggestions are provided for ending the school-to-prison pipeline. Mei-Ling Malone and Hui-Ling Malone explore the pipeline a bit further in Chapter 6. They expand and deepen the discussion on the school-to-prison pipeline by explicitly highlighting its role in supporting the prison industry, the segregation of schools, and the American legacy of white supremacy and capitalism as established during slavery. Using California as an example, they provide historical context that documents the relationship between rapid prison expansion and the continued racial segregation of housing and public schools. The chapter ends with recommendations for permanently dismantling the school-to-prison pipeline and creating a more democratic society. In Chapter 7, Tennisha Riley, Aysha Foster, and Zewelanji Serpell illustrate how teachers' expectations are linked to and exacerbated by specific school policies and related reforms; in particular zero tolerance policies and achievement standards based on race/ethnicity. They cite evidence that reveals how teachers' appraisals of student behavior are informed by stereotyped perceptions and racialized judgments that contribute to the overrepresentation of students of color in disciplinary referrals, expulsion, and suspension. They conclude by offering strategies that will deter racial exclusion and advance racial equity in education. The final chapter in Section II (Chapter 8) focuses on the school-to-prison pipeline and its relationship to race and children with special needs. Subini Ancy Annamma uses disability critical race theory (DisCrt) to examine the overrepresentation of students of color in special education. She argues that this overrepresentation is the result of a social construction based on race. Annamma posits further that special education status is correlated with higher rates of disciplinary actions, arrest, and incarceration and recommends specific alternatives to the labeling and incarceration of youth of color.

Section III of Volume 1 is entitled "Race and Racialization in Schools and Curriculum." In the first chapter of this section (Chapter 9), Eileen Carlton Parsons and Dana N. Thompson Dorsey analyze Next Generation Science Standards (*NGSS*) through the lens of critical race theory (CRT). They employ the tenets of CRT to determine if science, technology, engineering, and mathematical (STEM) reforms are fulfilling the goals of *NGSS* and propose suggestions for what educators can do to meet these goals. In the second chapter (Chapter 10), Joi A. Spencer and Victoria M. Hand explore the racialized curriculum of mathematics education within the STEM domain. They critique the grand narrative of black failure and white success in mathematics education and analyze persistent disparities between dominant and nondominant racial, ethnic, and linguistic group within the context of racism and extant notions of racial hierarchy and inferiority. Spencer and Hand explain how mathematics curriculum is racialized from the ground up through students' classroom experiences, school structures, and whole school systems policies. The third and final chapter in this section (Chapter 11), written by Donald Easton-Brooks, documents the need for the greater diversity in teacher education programs. He presents quantitative data that suggests race influences teacher attitudes and perceptions, and supports the premise that teachers of color have a positive impact on the academic performance of students of color. Easton-Brooks provides suggestive strategies to close the diversity gap within the workforce in U.S. public schools.

Funding, like race, is a frequent source of controversy and contention in American education. Section IV of Volume 1, entitled "Race and 'Cost' Debate in School Reform," investigates how school systems and leaders and other stakeholders make decisions about the appropriation of monies for schools and educational reform programs. The first chapter (Chapter 12), written by Theresa Saunders, provides an overview of the School Improvement Grant (SIG) federally funded grant program and explains its purpose, operational structure, and implementation outcomes in general, within two initial national cohorts, and more specifically in one individual state. Saunders presents a perspective on education that privileges the rights of children, develops human capital, and advances equitable school funding. She also makes recommendations for substantive change in the design and implementation of federal school improvement grants. In the Chapter 13, Sabrina Zirkel asserts that although educators may think policy decisions are based on "what works," they are often grounded in racialized assumptions about merit, worth, and deservedness. Zirkel examines three public forums to discern the role race and ethnicity play in determining who deserves what and why with respect to educational funding and access to opportunity, resources, and care. Ramon M. Griffin et al. in Chapter 14 explore "cost" from a different perspective. In the third chapter of this section, they investigate what they call the racial opportunity cost (ROC) of choice for children of color, and position ROC as a theoretical lens to explore the relationship between students of color and their school environment—and the costs incurred by students of color and their families as a consequence of negotiating this terrain. The authors apply the ROC framework to analyze pertinent educational issues of school choice and parental involvement. They also provide implications for future research, policy, and practice.

Section V of Volume 1 is entitled "Beyond High School." It includes three chapters. In the first chapter (Chapter 15), Julie A. Helling explores the concept of "affirmative action" in higher education as envisaged by the U.S. Supreme Court in *Grutter v. Bollinger* (2003), *Gratz v. Bollinger* (2003), and *Fisher v. University of Texas* (2013). She contends that the concept of affirmative action cannot be adjudged monolithically but must be measured within specific context. Helling asserts that the vision of affirmative put forth by the Supreme Court actually benefits white students and does little to remedy past and present racial discrimination. Chapter 16, written by F. Erik Brooks, traces the evolution of historically black colleges and universities (HBCUs), paying special attention to their assets and liabilities. He reviews the historical, present-day, and future significance of HBCUs and calls attention to the many challenges confronting these institutions, specifically in regard to funding, recruitment, retention, branding, and academic success. Brooks provides suggestions for ways to preserve the beauty and tackle the burdens of HBCUs. In the final chapter of this section (Chapter 17), Ronald C. Williams and Adriel A. Hilton advocate for programs that mentor African American male college students attending primarily white institutions. They provide qualitative and quantitative data that identifies best practices in the development and management of mentoring programs that lend social support and may promote degree completion and academic persistence among African American men.

Part I

The Face of Racism and Color Blindness in American Education

Chapter 1

Legal and Educational Foundations in Critical Race Theory

Evelyn Young

Over the past half century, U.S. education has undergone substantial progress toward the elimination of the achievement gap through efforts of desegregation, Title I, Head Start, Early Head Start, school finance reform, and affirmative action. However, much of the legal and historical precedence in addressing the topic of educational equity, opportunity, and achievement has centered around the issue of socioeconomic disparity, not racial inequality. Even today as the Obama administration pushes for higher achievement, more rigorous standards, greater accountability, and more innovative solutions to turn around underperforming schools, what continues to be missing from the discourse is the presence of racism in educational ideologies, policies, and practices. Although education researchers and scholars have long recognized the existence of the racial achievement/opportunity gap, only since the mid-1990s have we begun to use critical race theory (CRT) as the lens by which we examine the systemic roots of racism in U.S. schools. This chapter provides a general overview of the literature in CRT in both law and educational research. In particular, it utilizes a CRT perspective to examine the interplay of racism in the areas of curriculum and instruction, educational policy, school finance, assessment, and educational leadership, as well as how CRT can be used in educational practice to confront issues of race, power, and privilege in schools.

Critical Race Theory in Law

Central to CRT's scholarship in law is Antonio Gramsci's theory of hegemony. Briefly, Gramsci defined hegemony as (1) "the 'spontaneous' consent given by the great masses of the population to the general direction imposed on social life by the dominant fundamental group"; and (2) "the apparatus of state coercive power which 'legally' enforces discipline on those groups who do not 'consent' either actively or passively."[1] In other words, the theory of hegemony posits that in every facet of life, the ideology of the dominant class exerts control over the subordinate masses. The elites' beliefs, attitudes, and traditions became "normalized" into mainstream consciousness such that the formations of law, language, and customs are patterned after the constructs of the ruling class.

Hegemony plays out in the public sphere as a silent plague. To *see* hegemony at work, one would have to envision the sociopolitical sphere turned upside down. *What if* instead of whites filling over 450 seats in the House and Senate and minorities filling a total of roughly 80 seats that the reverse was true? Would the debates on minimum wage increase and universal health care carry the same tone? Would immigration reform be as heated a topic as it is today? Would hate crimes against ethnic minorities in the United States be as prevalent? *What if* we displaced all of the families that live in suburbia and had them switch jobs, schools, and homes with families that live in the inner city for even a day? Would it cause a greater sense of urgency to raise the quality of living, education, and health care for families living in the inner city?

From the outset, critical race theorists placed "race and racism . . . as central pillars of hegemonic power."[2] They posited that oppression was rooted in racism and that "race consciousness . . . must be taken into account in efforts to understand hegemony and the politics of racial reform."[3] CRT legal scholars centered the analysis of law through "fiction, personal experiences, and the stories of people on the bottom [to] illustrate how race and racism continued to dominate our society."[4] Matsuda, Lawrence, Delgado, and Crenshaw framed CRT around six central themes: (1) racism is endemic to American life; (2) legal claims of neutrality, color blindness, and meritocracy are to be viewed with skepticism; (3) racism is rooted in a contextual and historical analysis of the law; (4) experiential knowledge of the oppressed is fundamental in analyzing the existing legal and social structures; (5) CRT is interdisciplinary and eclectic; and (6) CRT works toward eliminating racial oppression as well as ending all forms of oppression.[5] Each of the themes is discussed in greater depth here.

Theme 1: Critical Race Theory Recognizes That Racism Is Endemic to American Life

For the majority of whites in America, it is difficult for them to conceptualize the meaning of whiteness. The reason for this is that whiteness is a taken-for-granted privilege. Frankenberg argues, "Whiteness makes itself invisible precisely by asserting its normalcy, its transparency, in contrast with the marking of others on which its transparency depends."[6] Harris associates whiteness as a property right that anyone in possession of it is guaranteed membership into society's upper caste. One is freely given unmerited deference and benefits solely on account of his or her whiteness. One also has access to schools, employment, housing, and public facilities that are restricted to minorities, even though most companies and institutions today contain a policy of nondiscrimination and equal opportunity. Harris writes,

> Being white automatically ensure[s] higher economic returns in the short term, as well as greater economic, political and social security in the long run. . . . Becoming white increase[s] the possibility of controlling critical aspects of one's life rather than being the object of others' domination. . . . [Furthermore], whites have come to expect and rely on these benefits, and over time these expectations have been affirmed, legitimated, and protected by the law.[7]

Recognizing the privileges bestowed on her as a result of her whiteness, McIntosh laments, "I have come to see white privilege as an invisible package of unearned assets which I can count on cashing in each day, but about which I was 'meant' to remain oblivious."[8] Among these unspoken privileges are the freedom to associate with people of her own race without question or glare, the assurance of being able to feel safe in public places, the opportunity to see people of her race represented in school curriculum, media, and high-status jobs, and the certainty that people would not assume that her accomplishments were the result of affirmative action practices.

One privilege that I, as an Asian female, find that McIntosh fails to mention is the right to speak against racism without sounding like someone who has blown race out of proportion. When whites attack an image, speech, or action as defamatory and racist, others look upon them as righteous, politically correct, if not downright heroic. However, when people of color accuse whites of employing racist speech or practices, the whites' reaction is to dismiss the allegation and regard the accusers as "overreacting." In fact, some will turn the accusation around and claim that the real racists are those who see everything in racial terms. This places minorities in a double-bind position: to vocalize their objection is to risk being targeted as hyper-racists; to remain silent is to submit to their own oppression. The constitutional provision of "freedom of speech" is a privilege that is reserved for the dominant group. People in the minority groups who choose to exercise that privilege must use it at their own discretion.

Theme 2: Critical Race Theory Expresses Skepticism toward Dominant Legal Claims of Neutrality, Objectivity, Color Blindness, and Meritocracy

America in the 1970s witnessed a surge of opposition to the civil rights movement, as neoconservatives attacked race-based policies as antithetical to the fundamental values of democracy. They advocated for a color-blind interpretation of constitutional and judicial analysis, and they sought to dismantle affirmative action programs by heralding the principles of equal opportunity. As overt racist practices began to wane in the wake of the post–civil rights era, the majority of whites increasingly believed that discrimination had become a thing of the past. As a result, it became more difficult to prove discriminatory practices, as seemingly "neutral" standards masked the underlying motives for the denial of housing, employment, health care, and equal schooling.

Sharply criticizing the viewpoint of neutrality, Gotanda argues that "[a] color-blind interpretation of the Constitution legitimates, and thereby maintains, the social, economic, and political advantages that whites hold over other Americans."[9] Nonrecognition of race protects the property interest of whites and denies the historical and social context of white domination. Had the Founding Fathers adopted a color-blind approach when drafting the Constitution, it might have been possible to interpret it from such a viewpoint today. But the reality is that the Constitution was never intended to be color-blind: the Three-Fifth Compromise sealed the fate for a life of oppression and denigration for generations of African Americans to come. No verbiage for the equality of all races was ever written in the Constitution, nor was the right to life, liberty, and the pursuit of happiness meant for all. The Constitution was racially biased from the outset, and its effects continue to run its due course. We cannot absolve the decisions of the Founding Fathers by suddenly turning a blind eye to color.

Race consciousness is necessary to reverse the trends of neutrality and color blindness. Only by proactively recognizing and affirming race would the blatancy of prejudice seep into the consciousness of the perpetrators.

CRT advocates also regard meritocracy as symptomatic of the persistence of racism. Merit alone is incapable of earning a minority his or her position in the dominant group, and neither can it overcome the deep-seated belief of white superiority. The flaws behind the idea of meritocracy are twofold: One, it assumes that everyone starts out on equal footing in life; and two, it assumes that everyone faces the same opportunities and/or obstacles along life's journey. Supporters of meritocracy also embrace the standpoint of equal opportunity, yet no one knows better than the oppressed that equal opportunity favors whites more than it favors non-whites. An "equal opportunity" employer boasts of the fact that he or she selects candidates not by the color of one's skin but rather by one's merit. Yet as already mentioned, one's ability to merit success is intricately tied to one's race and one's social background. In fact, not only does the rhetoric of equal opportunity discriminate against minorities on the basis of merit, but it also works against them on the basis of "reverse discrimination."

In "Is Affirmative Action Reverse Discrimination?" Cullen argued that the election of the United States' first black president, Barack Obama, the appointment of the first Latina to serve on the U.S. Supreme Court, Sonia Sotomayor, and the appointment of Colin Powell and Condoleezza Rice as secretaries of state have given rise to criticisms that highly qualified white men are being passed over on the basis of reverse discrimination. To make her point that claims of reverse discrimination are merely making a mountain out of a molehill, she wrote, much in the style of a counternarrative:

America's Favorite Pastime

White vs. Black

The white team is allowed to field three times the numbers of players than the black team.

Instead of three outs, the white team gets six outs.

The umpires are employed by the white team and use to be members of the white team.

All the games are played at the white team's home stadium where they are cheered and supported while the black team is booed and taunted.

The white team has all of the latest and greatest equipment while the black team has to settle for the white team's discards.

The white team grew up playing baseball in organized leagues and attending private baseball camps.

All of the previous 43 commissioners of baseball have been from the white team. Now the first black commissioner is attempting to appoint a black umpire. Yet the white team is claiming it is unfair.

> Discrimination is discrimination no matter which direction it is pointed. However, it would appear that the only time many whites condemn such behavior is when the bus is backing up on them. Racism in America still results in a disproportionate number of white people getting on base because they were walked while many people of color were hit by a pitch. The end result is the same, but one is much more painful.[10]

If discrimination goes in one direction 90 percent of the time, any effort to stop the momentum is simply that: to resist being completely run over by the dominant group. What whites see as reverse discrimination, people of color see as resistance. What Whites see as unfair, people of color see as hope.

Theme 3: Critical Race Theory Challenges Ahistoricism and Insists on Contextual/Historical Analysis of the Law

The rationale that the Supreme Court gave in its ruling in *Brown v. Board of Education* was that segregation "has a detrimental effect upon the colored children ... [for] a sense of inferiority affects the motivation of a children to learn."[11] Yet for centuries prior to *Brown*, minority students had been subjected to inferior education in segregated schools and, in many instances, had been denied educational opportunities altogether.[12] Up until 1954, the Supreme Court had no qualms about the psychological impact that illiteracy and inadequate education can have on students of color. Therefore, the unexpected regard for the educational welfare of minority students led scholars of color to question the sincerity of the Court's motives.

Bell argued that the historical context of the day rendered it impossible for the Supreme Court to rule against school desegregation. Furthermore, its interest in overturning *Plessy*[13] lay less in the educational welfare of the colored children, but more in the economic and political advantages that would be afforded to whites as a result of desegregation. Bell (1980) posited three suppositions for the Court's decision: (1) to gain international approval for America's struggle against communism; (2) to assure blacks fighting in World War II that their sacrifice for freedom and liberty was as true at home as it was abroad; and (3) to increase economic productivity by transitioning the South from a rural, plantation society to a capitalistic enterprise. Thus, it could be argued that the decision in *Brown* was not made on the grounds of equality and morality but on the basis of "interest-convergence," or as Bell aptly put it, "the interest of blacks in achieving racial equality will be accommodated only when it converges with the interests of whites."[14]

This theory of interest-convergence explains why there continues to be a disparity in education, health care, employment opportunities, and social status between the haves and the have-nots. As long as it bears no advantages to the dominant class, they see the plight of the oppressed as "not their problem." For example, if one day the millions of undocumented illegal immigrants were to be deported and the effects of their hard labor and contribution to the U.S. economy were to be felt, would the dominant group then take a sudden interest in advocating for immigrants' rights, be they legal or illegal? Would they then take the trouble to understand the immigrants' plight and the risks that they were willing to take to come to the United States? Every immigrant has a backstory, and his or her primary reason for coming to the United States—despite what anti-immigration groups claim—is not to take away jobs from American citizens. But until the interest of the underclass converges with that of the dominant group, it is unlikely that action will be taken to equalize opportunities for minority groups.

Theme 4: Critical Race Theory Insists on Recognition of the Experiential Knowledge of People of Color and Our Communities of Origin in Analyzing Law and Society

As Matsuda reminds us, "Every person . . . has an accent. Your accent carries the story of who you are."[15] Storytelling from the perspective of those "on the bottom" is a technique that is heralded by CRT scholars.[16] It is set in contrast to the formal, legalistic discourse of members of the dominant class. It averts that "members of marginalized groups, by virtue of their marginal status, are able to tell stories different from the ones legal scholars usually hear."[17] The use of personal experiences sheds light on the varied perspectives of individuals, and their purpose is to counter the hegemonic voices of the oppressors.

Scheppele points out the exclusivity of the Founding Fathers in the drafting of the Constitution.[18] In the very assertion "We the people," America's forefathers selectively included those who constituted "we." "We" comprised of the white, male, Protestant, educated landowners. "We" possessed the privilege of writing "our" nation's ordinances into law, and "we" had the right to voice "our" opinions as "we" saw fit. Noticeably absent from the "we" were females, people of color, the poor, the uneducated, and anyone who didn't fit the image of the white, male aristocrat. And as long as there was a "we," there also existed a "they."

Dalton articulates three ways in which minorities are often silenced: one, by education—the more advanced one's education, the more one is able to engage in intellectualized discourse using sophisticated rhetoric and technical knowledge that bars common folks from participation. Two, by displaying the "I don't want to be made to feel like a guilty white male" syndrome.[19] That is, they refuse to see themselves as complicitous to the subjugation of the oppressed by muting them with a simple statement of absolution: "I'm not a racist." The underlying message of that statement is, "Don't blame me for what happened in the past. I'm sorry for what happened to your people, but I'm not at fault for your present situation." And three, by barring people of color from speaking for themselves. Whites speak on behalf of the minorities, advocating for "their" causes, presenting "their" plight, and arguing among themselves about how to remedy "their" problems. Minorities' points of view are assumed, not confirmed by their own testimonies. In such instances, minorities feel talked for and talked about, but not talked to.

The importance of attending to the voices of the oppressed is vital in solving social problems together, rather than one for the other. Without hearing the opinions, the counterhegemonic narratives, and the lived experiences of the underclass, advancements in policies will continue to benefit only the dominant group. Resolution to any problem is a two-way street; it is impossible to resolve a conflict if only one side gets to speak.

Theme 5: Critical Race Theory Is Interdisciplinary and Eclectic

CRT is derived from a number of disciplines, including "liberalism, law and society, feminism, Marxism, poststructuralism, critical legal theory, pragmatism, and nationalism."[20] From these disciplines, critical race theorists have learned to view race and racism as historically and socially constructed and to regard the oppression of the marginalized as a pervasive theme throughout the course of human history. Concurrently, CRT is interdisciplinary not only because of the sources that it has drawn from but also because of the sources that it has contributed to. Stemming from CRT are FemCrit, LatCrit, AsianCrit, TribalCrit, and WhiteCrit. Each of these looks critically at how the legal system represses groups of people based on gender, sexual preference, ethnicity, culture, and social status. Recently, CRT has also moved into the field of education, which will be examined more closely in the next section. As a critique of its own dominant position, critical whiteness studies arose to challenge the illegitimacy of its subjugation of others. Critical white theorists seek to overthrow their own power in an attempt to counter the regimes of racism, sexism, and classism. They argue that "what oppressed people of color need from whites is not sympathy as much as a self- and collective-reflection on their own white privilege in a system of white racism, a system that will remain permanent without a revolutionary transformation of white consciousness."[21]

Crenshaw also warns of the need to look at race, gender, and class theories not in isolation from one another but as an intersection of the multiple layers of oppression.[22] She contends that legal interpretations and critical discourse often adopt a single-axis framework, examining discrimination on the basis of race or gender but not as a combination of both. Such observation fails to account for the compounded effects of the oppression felt by people marginalized on multiple fronts. Crenshaw notes, "The intersectional experience is greater than the sum of racism and sexism, [thus] any analysis that does not take intersectionality into account cannot sufficiently address the particular manner in which Black women are subordinated."[23] Thus, CRT alone is an insufficient lens by which to analyze the discriminations faced by individuals bearing multiple markers. An interdisciplinary understanding of the theories that gave birth to as well as stemmed from CRT is necessary to encapsulate the experiences of those living in intersectional dimensions.

Theme 6: Critical Race Theory Works toward the End of Eliminating Racial Oppression as Part of the Broader Goal of Ending All Forms of Oppression

Critical race theorists recognize that race is only one of many elements that are subject to discrimination. People of color commiserate with other oppressed groups who fall under the umbrella termed as "other." The marginalized understand that as long as a group of people has the power to exert control over the legal, political, social, and economic aspects of society, no other person who falls outside of the circle of the dominant group is safe from oppression. Erick Fromm describes the oppressors' pleasure in subordinating others as such: "The pleasure in complete domination over another . . . is the very essence of the sadistic drive. Another way of formulating the same thought is to say that the aim of sadism is to transform a man into a being, something animate into something inanimate, since by complete and absolute control the living loses one essential quality of life—freedom."[24]

All those who are minorities should be ever conscious of the fact that the fate that awaits us—the absolute loss of life, liberty, and the pursuit of happiness—is the same fate that awaits all marginalized groups if we do not fight against hegemony in a concerted effort. Despite the seeming hopelessness in the fate of the oppressed, critical race theorists adamantly place their faith in the hope that circumstances are not written in stone and that change is possible. In this seemingly contradictory duality of fatalism and optimism, Fanon describes on the one hand the inevitable assimilation of the black folks, yet on the other the belief in the alterability of the human condition. He writes, with an air of concession, "For the black man there is only one destiny. And it is white."[25] Yet a few paragraphs later, he makes this argument, "But society, unlike biochemical processes, cannot escape human influences. Man is what brings society into being. The prognosis is in the hands of those who are willing to get rid of the worm-eaten roots of the structure."[26] In other words, as long as there are those who are willing to resist the oppressive structure that the dominant class has created, there is hope for a counterrevolution.

Freire asserts that a pedagogy of the oppressed is a "pedagogy [that] must be forged *with*, not *for*, the oppressed in the incessant struggle to regain their humanity."[27] The struggle for freedom requires awaking the underclass from their state of oppression as well as conjoining the efforts of the oppressors in "true solidarity" with the oppressed. By true solidarity, Freire means to "enter into the situation of the [oppressed]" and to "fight at their side to transform the objective reality which has made them 'beings for the other.'"[28] As educators, this means going beyond playing the part of the social justice educator and actually being one. The act of saving underprivileged students from their miseducation merely intensifies the power relationship between the haves and the have-nots. It is only through emancipatory discourse and identification with the students that both the oppressed and the oppressors can become liberated from the strongholds of hegemony. Both parties need to name the world together, to critique the forces that contribute to the oppression, and to construct a world that is founded upon hope.[29]

Critical Race Theory in Education

The centrality of race in CRT scholars' examination of legal issues led a similar movement among education scholars a decade later. Dissatisfied with how schools served to perpetuate class differences in society, education scholars employed the ideologies established by critical theory and critical pedagogy to condemn the hegemonic nature of academic institutions. But because critical theory and critical pedagogy failed to stress the prevalence of racism in educational practices, scholars of color began to adopt the ideas of CRT into their analysis of racism in schooling.

In a paper Ladson-Billings and Tate presented at the American Educational Research Association meeting in 1994 entitled "Toward a Critical Race Theory in Education," the authors linked the six tenets of CRT in law to issues of race and equity in academic situations.[30] Since then, many education scholars have utilized the concepts of racial hegemony, counternarratives, whiteness as property, and interest convergence to analyze the racial inequities that persist in education. Furthermore, Ladson-Billings urges school leaders and educators to critically examine how race is played out in the areas of curriculum, instruction, assessment, and school funding, in particular as they relate to the suppression of "intellectual rights" of minority children.

In recent years, a proliferation of CRT scholarship has surfaced in educational research. The majority of the studies have focused on the application of CRT in the areas of *curriculum and instruction, education policy, counternarratives,* and *educational leadership.* Each of these areas will be examined in detail here.

CRT in Curriculum and Instruction

Despite the recent proliferation of studies using CRT to examine the role of racism in educational settings, the use of the theory as a pedagogical tool is still in its infancy. Although much is written about the theoretical underpinnings of CRT, little is offered in terms of guidance to educators on how to implement the ideas into practice. The lack of guidance is even more pronounced in the elementary school setting, since the students are perceived to be too young to understand the forces of oppression and to participate in emancipatory dialogue. Ladson-Billings warned of the possibility of such occurrence when the theory began to gain momentum in educational research in the 1990s. She wrote,

> What, then, might happen to CRT in the hands of educational researchers and school personnel? . . . I doubt if it will go very far into the mainstream. Rather, CRT in education is likely to become the "darling" of the radical left, continue to generate scholarly papers and debate, and never penetrate the classrooms and daily experiences of students of color.[31]

To date, there are but only a few studies that have attempted to integrate CRT as a theoretical framework into an evaluation or a construction of classroom pedagogy.[32,33,34] All of these studies used the CRT lens to challenge the students to wrestle with the presence of white dominance and institutional racism in the classroom curriculum. Moreover, the studies heavily stressed the importance of attending to the students' voices and utilizing their counterstories as starting points to critique and resist the Eurocentric policies and curriculum that bear little to no relevance to the students' daily lives.

For example, in Knaus's work with 20 students in an urban continuation high school, many of whom had been in juvenile halls or probation previously, he noted with irony how meaningless the idea of having to meet proficiency on standardized tests is when his students were often victims of hunger, sexual and physical abuse, and street violence. Through the use of journaling and discourse, Kraus provided the students a forum to "(1) develop and express voice; (2) demonstrate the overwhelming nature of racism, poverty, and violence that shapes everyday life; and (3) develop the tools to survive."[35] Thus, while No Child Left Behind (NCLB) sought to normalize the students' knowledge to reflect the Western canon, Knaus aimed to use the minority students' stories to render such a narrow curricular focus as undemocratic and oppressive.

Moreover, Rogers and Mosley introduced the concept of racial literacy to challenge a group of second graders to recognize whiteness and to critique the practice of color blindness.[36] Using literature such as *The Bus Ride*[37] and *Martin Luther King, Jr. and the March on Washington*,[38] the authors led the children in a critical analysis of how the narratives and illustrations in the texts portrayed stereotypical assumptions of whiteness and blackness. They also pushed the children to confront their own whiteness and to recognize that racism is as prevalent today as it was in the days of the civil rights movement. The authors' conclusion was poignant: we must begin racial discourse at an early age if we as a society are to have any hope of dismantling the systemic roots of racism. A curriculum of silence only serves to reinforce the "practice of colorblindness, denial of racism, and the uncritical reproduction of white privilege."[39] If educators are to disrupt this silence in the elementary school setting, children would more likely be attentive to the presence of privilege and power, the counternarratives of racial minorities, and the efforts of white allies in their resistance to racial oppression throughout their upbringing.

But a radical change in curricular design of this magnitude cannot be enforced or maintained without the backing of the local or state educational agencies. Such then is the need to address systemic change at the administrative and policy levels.

CRT in Education Policy

Over the last decade, a preponderance of literature has arisen utilizing CRT as the epistemological lens to examine the racial overtones that preside over matters of education policy. In particular, CRT scholars have used interest-convergence to focus their analysis of legal and policy issues with regard to desegregation, assessment, and school finance.

Desegregation

The year 2005 marked the 50th anniversary of *Brown v. Board of Education,* and with it came an outpouring of anger from education scholars who lamented over the unfulfilled promises for racial integration and educational equity that *Brown* had proffered to procure. Due to practices of white flight, tracking, busing, and the voucher system, schools today are arguably more segregated on the basis of race than in the pre-*Brown* era. As a result, Saddler argues that "African American youth are not only mis-educated but actually 'de-educated,'" in that they are being "systemically excluded from education system and/or being systematically destroyed within that system."[40]

Many scholars of color support Saddler's claim, citing evidence of ability grouping throughout K-12 schooling as a way to maintain the racial imbalance of students in college preparatory versus vocational programs.[41] Solórzano and Ornelas argue that the common practice of "schools within schools" fulfills the districts' responsibility to meet *Brown's* mandate for racial integration while continuing the practice of racial resegregation within schools.[42] More notably, they highlight how Latina/Latino and African American students are disproportionally excluded from Advanced Placement (AP) courses and how such practices preclude their opportunities to colleges and universities that weigh AP courses in the admissions process.

Furthermore, Beratan contends that continued overrepresentation of minority students in special education programs is enhanced by an intersectionality of institutional ableism and racism. One of the stipulations under the Individuals with Disabilities Education Improvement Act (IDEA) is to provide students who qualify for special education services to be placed in the "least restrictive environment" (LRE) (P.L. 108–446). Using the theory of interest-convergence, he argues that

> the institutional abl[e]ism built into IDEA's LRE clause serves to legali[z]e the discrimination that it was intended to alleviate. With this legal and accessible discrimination at its disposal, the special education system offers the general education system a means of maintaining the discrimination that *Brown v. the Board of Education* made illegal. The disproportionate identification of minority students as disabled becomes the means of transposing disability discrimination in place of racist discrimination. Understanding this makes it easier for us to recognize the explicit connection between the development of special education and white America's interest in recouping its losses from the *Brown* decision.[43]

As these practices show, while *Brown* provided the rhetoric of equal opportunities and racial reform in education, its outcomes have remained more or less the same. De facto segregation continues to dominate all facets of public schooling. As these scholars argue, unless there is an interest for whites to mobilize toward desegregation inside and outside of schools, it is unlikely that full racial integration will be achieved.

Assessment

Since its enactment in 2002, NCLB has been much scrutinized for its poor implementation, putative measures, lack of funding, and unscientifically based methods of remediating failing schools. More specifically, it has been argued that in its attempt to promote educational equity for all students, the statute has had the effect of privatizing education for majority gains, undemocratizing education, and widening the gap between minority and non-minority students.

Gillborn argues that the "assessment game" is a conspiracy set up by the dominant group to legitimize its status as the social and intellectual elites while psychologically manipulating the oppressed to believe that their lack of educational attainment is due to their own laziness, familial dysfunctionalism, or lack of intellectual ability.[44] It is set up such that the only measure of the students' scholastic aptitude is determined by a single paper-and-pencil test while failing to account for the numerous factors leading to the outcome, including the lack of opportunity to learn, poor teacher preparation, inadequate funding, and deficit thinking on the part of the entire educational system. Ladson-Billings argues, "In the classroom, a poor-quality curriculum, coupled with poor-quality instruction, a poorly prepared teacher, and limited resources add up to poor performance on the so-called objective tests. CRT theorists point out that the assessment game is merely a validation of the dominant culture's superiority."[45]

The "game" is not lost upon students either. One of the students in the urban continuation high school in Knaus's study said, "Listen, if I fail a test that asks me questions I have never seen, that judges me based on courses I did not take, is that my fault? Is it my responsibility to learn what a teacher don't teach?. . . then don't test me on things I don't know. I can tell you what I don't know without having to sit through your test."[46]

The rhetoric of NCLB purports to eliminate the racial and economic achievement gap, but its putative measures for failing schools have merely served to sustain, if not widen the gap. Simply because initial reports have indicated an increase in the performance of racial and social minorities, the gap has not been eliminated, and neither is it ever likely to. Systemic oppression will see to it that the status quo is maintained, even while giving a false pretense of care on the part of the dominant group. Gillborn further argues that if in the unlikely event that black students begin to master and outperform whites on the standardized tests, it is probable that another strategy will be concocted to "reengineer" black students' failure.[47] We have seen this done time and again with the ever-changing laws to ensure that escaped slaves are properly returned to their owners, the enactment of literacy requirements to block blacks from their entitled voting rights, and the establishment of a tracked system to re-create a "separate but equal" educational policy in the face of desegregation laws. Is it therefore so impossible to conceive of a conspiracy plot to maintain the racial stratification with the development of assessment tests that are intended to *fail* minority students?

School Funding

Ladson-Billings contends that "no area of schooling underscores inequity and racism better than school funding."[48] Although many legal battles have been fought over the issue of disparate school funding such as *McDuffy v.*

Secretary of the Executive Office of Education (1993) and *San Antonio Independent School District v. Rodriguez* (1973), Darling-Hammond argues that "schools serving large number of low-income students and students of color [continue to] have larger class sizes, fewer teachers and counselors, fewer and lower-quality academic courses, extracurricular activities, books, materials, supplies and computers, libraries and special services."[49] The disparity is even more pronounced in the area of the growing digital divide, as hundreds of thousands of school-aged children are being left behind with the lack of connectivity between school--home technology usage, insufficient teacher training, and inadequate access to cable and Internet providers due to geographic, societal, or economic factors. While technology integration and 1:1 computing device initiatives have swept into schools across the country in recent years, urban and rural schools continue to be the hardest hit since the e-rate fund that they receive in federal subsidy is insufficient to cover the hiring of education technology specialists, the cost of computer maintenance, software, and upgrades, or the bandwidth to access high-speed Internet services.

Alemán uses a CRT framework to examine the racially discriminatory practices built into the Texas school finance policy.[50] Since the 1960s, school finance policy in Texas has been challenged in the courts and legislature. After decades of lawsuits filed against the state for its failure to provide equitable funding to poor districts that was made up mostly of minority students, a more equalized system was finally established in 1995 under Robin Hood. Robin Hood aimed to take all of the property taxes collected by the state and redistribute it equitably across all districts, thereby "robbing" wealthier school districts the funds that they could have collected through local property taxes. Within a few years of the law being in effect, however, the largely wealthy, white, male-dominated legislature in both major political parties fought to eliminate the bill, claiming that the system was inherently unfair and un-American.

Vaught also used CRT to study the racially discriminatory financial system practiced at one large, urban school. Using a practice called "differential student funding," the district sought to provide school choice to students by attaching different amounts of money to different kids. Schools with higher number of English Language Learners, Title I students, and students with special needs, therefore, would have the benefit of receiving more funds than schools with students in regular education. However, as Vaught found out, "[T]he money attached to each child stopped following him or her at the front door of the school. All monies were put into one pot, divided evenly across the number of students enrolled at each school, and reported as the per-pupil dollars."[51]

Thus, the money that had been rightfully entitled to predominantly racial minorities who needed every resource available to meet graduation requirements was often taken by vocal white parents who demanded enrichment and advanced placement programs for their children. According to these parents, each child was entitled to his or her "per-pupil expenditure," regardless of where the money had come from and to whom it actually belonged. In this sense, Vaught argues, "Black children were objectified as currency" who were "owned" by middle-class whites.[52]

Furthermore, NCLB is designed such that the schools serving the neediest students are at the greatest risk of losing federal funds. Although NCLB has since been replaced by the Common Core State Standards (CCSS) in most states, the practice of accountability, high-stakes testing, and merit pay that began with NCLB continues its due course today. Under NCLB, rather than providing more financial support to failing schools, the putative measures under the statute remove the much-needed funding by way of vouchers and extra tutoring services provided by outside educational agencies. Darling-Hammond warns, "[i]f left unchanged, the Act will deflect needed resources for teaching and learning to ever more intensive testing of students, ranking of schools, bussing of students and lawyers' fees for litigating the many unintended consequences of the legislation."[53] If the concept of "robbing from the rich" in the Robin Hood bill is unsettling for politicians, what could explain their condoning the practice of "robbing from the poor"? No one would find such practice legal or ethical, unless, of course, one views the "poor" as inherently undeserving of the services rendered to them in the first place. As Vaught argues, intellectual property is a right reserved for the whites. In the eyes of a white dominant society, the robbing is nothing more than rightly cashing in on what naturally belonged to them.

CRT in Counternarratives

Perhaps the most used strategy in the work of critical race theorists is the telling of counternarratives. In naming one's own reality and attending to the voices of the oppressed, those who are traditionally marginalized in the dominant discourse use storytelling so as to challenge the stereotypical images placed on them. Delgado argues that counternarratives serve a threefold purpose: (1) to debunk the validity of the "rational" and "formulaic" discourse commonly used by Anglo-American scholarship, and the illegitimacy of the "personal" and "experiential" knowledge of racial minorities; (2) to heal the nihilistic wounds of minorities whose perceptions of self and their own culture have been denigrated by the dominant group; and (3) to make the oppressors become aware of their power and their role in perpetuating the oppression of others.[54]

Delgado Bernal argued that "the histories, experiences, cultures, and languages of students of color have been devalued, misinterpreted, or omitted within formal educational settings" and that counternarratives provide a venue for students of color to be recognized as "holders and creators of knowledge."[55] Meanwhile, Howard and Reynolds used the strategy to engage middle-class African American parents in focus group discussions on their and their children's experiences in schools. While all of the parents in their study felt that it was important to be involved in the educational experiences of their children, many of the parents did not feel that their voices were included in the decisions that really mattered, such as the hiring of more teachers and administrators of color, budget issues, disciplinary practices, and the need for more cultural and ethnic diversity in the curriculum.[56]

Counternarratives come in a variety of genre and are used in fictional and nonfictional forms. As nonfictions, they represent a personal account of the stories told by people of color. As fictions, they depict a different reality as seen or imagined by the oppressed. These altered realities are based on actual historical precedents, and they represent the fears and concerns of minorities in present and futuristic terms. For example, through the use of counternarratives, Yosso illustrates a fictional, yet probable, account of a group of Chicana mothers actively involved in critical discourse regarding the educational inequities of the school. Unlike typical Parent–Teacher Association meetings where parents are merely assigned duties to serve the interests of the school, *Madres Por la Educación* fought to change the ways in which knowledge is constructed, questioned the inaccessibility of GATE/ magnet programs to minority students, challenged a curriculum that centered on whiteness, and opposed the uneven distribution of resources across the district. They utilized their own cultural wealth and experiential knowledge as channels of empowerment. The parents in this story did not sit idly by and fatalistically accept the politics of school as inevitable. Instead, they were leaders for change and revolutionists against unjust educational practices. In short, Yosso told this story to envision the potential for engaging minority parents' in a vastly different manner than has been traditionally done. Rather than relegating them to the inconsequential roles of planning multicultural nights and sharing ethnic foods, critical race educators place the voices of minority parents and students at the center of schools' decision-making power, especially when the makeup of the school consists primarily of students of color.[57]

In essence, the underlying question of all those who employ the strategy of counterstories is, "whose voices are heard and whose voices are left out?" The efforts of CRT scholars are therefore to deconstruct the traditional line of insider/outsider knowledge and to make the voices of the marginalized count in the larger discourse.

CRT in Educational Leadership

Although issues of race and achievement have long plagued the field of educational administration, the application of CRT in the work of PreK-12 administrators has been a largely unexplored area. While education leaders are well aware of the racial achievement gap, the proposed solutions have tended to come in the forms of restructuring or providing additional services. Among these commonly used tactics include the offering of in-school Title I services and/or additional after-school tutoring to under-achieving students, collaborating with community agencies that provide comprehensive social services, and referring parents to programs that offer early intervention services. All of these strategies, although well intentioned and beneficial to a certain extent, do not address the deeper presence of racism in the structure of schools. Even detracking, which attempts to dismantle white, middle-class privilege by placing students in heterogeneously grouped classes rather than in classes based on ability, can fall into the perpetrator camp if the ultimate goal is simply to "level the playing field." In all of these situations, the students and parents are deemed as helpless individuals who need the assistance of kindhearted benefactors to raise them out of their oppressed state. Instead of regarding minority parents and students as collaborators of school reform and allies in the effort to uproot racism, administrators and teachers often see them as problems to solve.

For those reasons, Lopez argues that it is essential for students in educational administration preparation programs to engage in "critical dialogue about the role of racism in society."[58] School leaders need to begin employing the perspective of the oppressed and to see the ubiquity of racism in the structure of schools from the worldview of minority students and parents. Since racism occurs on the basis of action *and* inaction, Young and Laible argue that it is imperative that administrators actively promote anti-racism in their school environment.[59] Ladson-Billings and Grant (1997) describe antiracist education as a practice that "challenges the total school environment to understand the ways in which racism is manifested in schools and society. It encourages educators to integrate antiracist concepts into all subject areas. . . . [and it] attempts to reveal the adverse effects of racism on student learning and development."[60]

In other words, educational leaders who are committed to anti-racism cannot stop short at simply discussing the students' state of oppression, change the curriculum to incorporate a more multicultural dimension, or expect respect for human differences from everyone. Instead, they need to engage in self-reflective practices that seek to reject "ideologies and practices steeped in blatantly biased or color-blind traditions [in efforts] to transform schools"[61] Dantley argues that a "spiritual" transformation is in order in urban educational leadership. He means this less so in a religious sense, but more in an overtone of critical consciousness, moral resolve, and hopeful idealism. He writes, "[R]ace-transcending leaders . . . critically reflec[t] on the context within which schools are established and contend with the issues of power that are at work there. They facilitate a learning environment that is not put off by the systemic realities of racist, sexist, and classist behavior. They see it . . . as an opportunity to use the academic and intellectual prowess of the learning community to attack and redirect these practices of inequality and social injustice."[62]

The call for educational administrators to become "race-transcending leaders" is particularly crucial in the 21st century. While the minority student population in U.S. schools is increasingly on the rise, whites continue to make up over 80 percent of individuals in educational leadership positions. The positionality of school leaders wields decision-making power that can adversely or beneficially affect the educational experiences and outcomes of minority students. To construct schools as sites of liberation requires administrators who are committed to continuous self-reflection and who are willing to stand firmly on the principles of anti-racism in the face of opposition from the teachers, the parents, and the community.

From the "Darling of the Radical Left" to the Heart of Teacher Education

To date, much research has been done in the field of teacher education to challenge preservice and inservice teachers to confront their own white racism. Much also has been done in the area of critical whiteness studies to

render whiteness visible and to centralize whites in the position of domination and exploitation. The volume of studies on the power and privilege
of whiteness has been instrumental in forwarding the field of education to
address the deep-seated social and racial inequalities present in American
schooling. At the same time, however, the preponderance of literature written on this topic has also posed several problems.

One is that the unsystematic, highly individualized approaches to raising the race consciousness of educators in teacher preparation programs
or professional developments have engendered a smorgasbord of ideas as
to how to engage educators in difficult conversations about race and racism. Aside from the two underlying premises of making whiteness visible
and unpacking white privilege, there seems to be little consensus as to how
to begin such a politically, emotionally, and racially sensitive conversation;
how to handle resistance from the participants; and how to link this new-
found awareness (if that should come to pass) to social activism. The vague-
ness associated with this type of training has led scholars to caution the
adverse effects that poorly constructed and ill-prepared programs can have
on the participants' psychology. It may lead to guilt, shame, anger, resent-
ment, and greater resistance.[63] It may even embitter whites toward being
victims of reverse discrimination or grow fed up with all of the "white bash-
ing."[64] To avoid such a spectrum of reactions, it would behoove scholars
in this area to conglomerate their wealth of experiences to approach the
task of raising educators' race consciousness in a more cohesive, methodical fashion.

A second problem with the current effort to address white racism is that
racism is considered as an individual pathology. Discourse on racism typically centers on efforts to push whites to come to grips with their own
prejudiced nature. It fails to recognize that racism is a *systemic* problem,
one whose roots are much deeper and more pervasive than getting individuals to become aware of their own racist ideologies. Although present
studies situate the need for race consciousness within a context of structural inequalities and white supremacy, the researchers are wholly satisfied when the participants demonstrate an inkling of recognition of their
own white privilege. There is little analysis of how their privilege is situated
in the legal, social, and historical oppression of racial minorities, or how
a purposeful dismantling of their privilege is necessary in order to effect
systemic change. It is, after all, easy to engage in intellectual, circuitous discourse about race and racism if one's lifestyle is more or less unaffected by
one's awareness of *others'* oppression. It is infinitely harder to bear others'

oppression as one's own, which would inevitably lead one to desire change not merely on an individual level but on a larger, systemic scale.

A third problem is that these studies are predominantly conducted by white researchers, whose primary objective is to raise the race consciousness of white educators. However, white scholars' conceptualization of racism is vastly different from scholars of color's experience with racism, and white participants' understanding of white privilege is incomparable to minority participants' familiarity with racial oppression and ostracization. To engage in discourse about *white* racism when either the researchers or the participants are nonwhite may raise issues of power and positionality. Would students of color in teacher preparation programs amplify their racialized experiences so as to give white instructors what they would like to hear in order to receive a higher grade? Would white teachers trivialize minority scholars' experiences with discrimination on account of their being overly sensitive to race issues? Even in the most ideal of circumstances where all participants reflected on their racial experience with utmost candor, where power and positionality did not influence the dynamics of the discussion, one would still have to acknowledge that a discourse that is centered on "blind racism" or "white privilege" among whites would still be radically different from a discourse that is centered on "systemic racism" and "oppression" between people of color. This is perhaps why scholars of color find the dominant discourse on racism somewhat unsatisfactory. It continues to leave out the voices of the marginalized while glorifying the progress made by whites.

The use of CRT in raising the race consciousness of educators alleviates the problems noted earlier. First, the thematic nature of CRT readily lends itself to addressing the historical, social, and political context of race and racism in a methodical manner. A critique on the "endemic nature of racism" and the "myth of meritocracy" is rooted in legal and historical precedents, not merely on theoretical hypotheses or circumstantial interpretations. Rather than challenging the existence of white privilege as an amorphous entity, CRT provides concrete examples of how whiteness has garnered unmerited benefits throughout U.S. history. Second, CRT emphatically rejects the viewpoint that racism is symptomatic of individual pathology; instead, it unwaveringly positions racism as a systemic condition. CRT scholars seek not only to raise educators' consciousness to their own blind prejudices, but more importantly to the pervasiveness and persistence of racism in society. Third, CRT was a movement created by students of color, who felt a need to center their understanding of legal analysis from a racialized perspective. Their refusal to be taught constitutional law from white, distinguished professors was indicative of their desire to have their marginalized experiences heard and validated, not dismissed or objectified by the traditional interpretation of the law. CRT was and is intended to bring a "colored" perspective to the dominant discourse, not to be sidetracked by discourse on whiteness. While dismantling the invisibility of whiteness is undoubtedly a goal of CRT scholars, the more pressing objective is affirming the lived experiences of minorities in the enduring presence of racial discrimination and oppression.

Conclusion

CRT is by no means the anathema to all of the multifaceted problems related to urban education. However, an appreciation and understanding of the tenets that underlie the theory is paramount if policy and pedagogical changes in education are to occur at a structural, rather than a surface, level. Over the last decade, as state commissioners, superintendents, school administrators, and teachers scrambled to fall into compliance with the NCLB (2002), just as they continue to do so with the Race to the Top initiative (RttT) and the CCSS, one cannot help but wonder what hegemonic forces must be at play to have a league of educators so readily accede to demands of the federal government. Under NCLB, the goals were to by 2014: (1) ensure for "high-quality academic assessments, accountability systems, teacher preparation and training, curriculum, and instructional materials that are aligned [to state standards]"; (2) "[meet] the educational needs of low-achieving children in [the] nation's highest-poverty schools"; and (3) "[close] the achievement gap . . . especially the achievement gaps between minority and nonminority students, and between disadvantaged children and their more advantaged peers."[65] In retrospect, we could perhaps say that the goals were never intended to meet the educational needs of low-achieving children in the nation's highest-poverty schools or to close the achievement gap. If they were, assessment data would have been used to direct money and teacher training to underperforming schools rather than transferring the much-needed funds out of the schools through vouchers and outside supplemental educational agencies. Instead, NCLB was created with the purposeful intention of giving the federal government legal access to the design of a national curriculum and accountability system, along with greater control in managing the teachers' union, teacher preparation programs, and teacher credentialing pathways. The ensuing rhetoric in RttT and the development of CCSS seem to suggest this to be the case. Of the total 500 possible points for the RttT competition, 125 points are allotted to ensure for buy-in from local educational agencies to the state's education reform agenda, 70 points are given to the development, adoption, and implementation of common standards and high-quality assessments, 138 points are given to the development of "great teachers and leaders" through performance-based evaluations and the provision of high-quality (and alternative) pathways for aspiring teachers and principals, and 40 points are given to states that can ensure for successful conditions for the establishment of charter schools and other innovative schools.[66] Meanwhile, turning around the lowest-achievement schools is allotted only 50 points, while making education funding a priority is given a whopping 10 points. With the points so heavily weighted toward reshaping the face of education as we know it today, one can only beg to ask the question: Was it ever about the kids?

From a CRT perspective, we can only begin to surmise why such wide-sweeping reforms are suddenly necessary when U.S. education has been plagued by the problem of the racial and socioeconomic achievement gap since the founding of the country. Whether the real reasons lie in the United States' fear of losing its economic and political dominance in the international sphere in the soon-coming decades or in its interest to move education toward a market-based enterprise, one thing we do know is this: with every effort to standardize curriculum, assessment, and accountability, the United States' educational system also moves increasingly toward centralization (understood as the concentration of power in the hands of a group of individuals). Already we have witnessed what NCLB can do to compel millions of free-thinking educators into servile obedience, whether willingly or unwillingly. We can only imagine how many millions more of the educators', teachers', and students' voices will be silenced under the rhetoric of innovation and reform.

It is precisely for this reason that the time is now ripe to engage school administrators and teachers in CRT discourse. From a strictly academic viewpoint, the CCSS has the potential to drive students toward greater critical thinking, communication, collaboration, creativity, perseverance in problem solving, and technology proficiency; from a CRT perspective, however, what really will CCSS mean for millions of schoolchildren in urban school districts? Will they in fact be more college and career ready, or will the achievement gap widen as a result of the disparity in teacher preparation, school funding, access to technology, and curriculum delivery? While we cannot predict the future of what the CCSS may bring, one thing we do know for certain: the racial achievement gap has existed well before the founding of this country, and it will not be readily solved by standardizing curricular objectives. If we are serious about eliminating the racial achievement gap, educators must be willing to engage in CRT discourse on a national level. Only then will we confront racial inequalities in school settings at its root, and only then will we be able to rebuild the system anew.

Notes

1. Gramsci 1971, p. 12.
2. Crenshaw 1988, p. xxii.
3. Crenshaw 1989, p. 1335.
4. Bell 1992.
5. Matsuda et al. 1993.
6. Frankenberg 1997, p. 6.
7. Harris 1993, p. 1713.
8. McIntosh 1990, p. 10.
9. Gotanda 1991, pp. 2–3.
10. Cullen 2011.
11. *Brown v. Board of Education* 1954, p. 494.
12. Bell 1980.
13. *Plessy v. Ferguson,* 163 U.S. 537, 539 (1896).
14. Ibid., p. 523.
15. Matsuda 1991, p. 1329.
16. Matsuda 1987.
17. Delgado 1990, p. 95.
18. Scheppele 1989.
19. Dalton 1987, p. 442.
20. Matsuda 1993, p. 6.
21. Allen 2002, p. 32.
22. Crenshaw 1989.
23. Ibid., p. 140.
24. Fromm 1966, p. 32.
25. Fanon 1967, p. 10.
26. Ibid., p. 11.
27. Freire 1970/2005, p. 48.
28. Ibid., p. 49.
29. Freire 1994.
30. Ladson-Billings 1998.
31. Ibid., p. 22.
32. DeCuir-Gunby 2007.
33. Knaus 2009.

34. Young 2010.
35. Knaus 2009, p. 145.
36. Rogers and Mosley 2006.
37. Miller 1998.
38. Ruffin 2001.
39. Rogers and Mosley 2006, p. 484.
40. Saddler 2005, p. 44.
41. Oakes 2008.
42. Solórzano and Ornelas 2004.
43. Beratan 2008, pp. 348–349.
44. Gillborn 2008.
45. Ladson-Billing 2004, p. 60.
46. Knaus 2009, p. 38.
47. Gillborn 2008.
48. Ladson-Billings 1998, p. 12.
49. Darling-Hammond 2007, p. 247.
50. Alemán 2006.
51. Vaught 2009, p. 552.
52. Ibid., p. 559.
53. Darling-Hammond 2007, p. 247.
54. Delgado 1989.
55. Delgado Bernal 2002, p. 105.
56. Howard and Reynolds 2008.
57. Yosso 2006.
58. Lopez 2003, p. 76.
59. Young and Laible 2000.
60. Ladson-Billings and Grant 1997, p. 20.
61. Cooper 2009, p. 695.
62. Dantley 2005, p. 670.
63. Tatum 1992.
64. Gillespie, Ashbaugh, and DeFiore 2002.
65. U.S. Department of Education 2001.
66. U.S. Department of Education 2010.

Bibliography

Alemán, Enrique. 2006. "Is Robin Hood the 'Prince of Thieves' 1 or a Pathway to Equity?: Applying Critical Race Theory to School Finance Political Discourse." *Educational Policy* 20 (1): 113–142.

Allen, Richard L. 2002. "Whiteness as Territoriality: An Analysis of White Identity Politics in Society, Education, and Theory." Unpublished doctoral dissertation. Los Angeles: University of California, Los Angeles.

Anyon, Jean. 1997. *Ghetto Schooling: A Political Economy of Urban Educational Reform*. New York: Teachers College Press.

Bell, Derrick A. 1980. "*Brown v. Board of Education* and the Interest-Convergence Dilemma." *Harvard Law Review* 93 (3): 518–533.

Bell, Derrick A. 1992. *Faces at the Bottom of the Well: The Permanence of Racism*. New York: Basic Books.

Beratan, Gregg D. 2008. "The Song Remains the Same: Transposition and the Disproportionate Representation of Minority Students in Special Education." *Race Ethnicity and Education* 11 (4): 337–354.

Borkowski, John W., and Maree Sneed. 2006. "Will NCLB Improve or Harm Public Education?" *Harvard Educational Review* 76 (4): 503–525.

Brown v. Board of Education. 1954. 347 U.S. 483.

Cooper, Camille W. 2009. "Performing Cultural Work in Demographically Changing Schools: Implications for Expanding Transformative Leadership Frameworks." *Educational Administration Quarterly* 45 (5): 694–724.

Crenshaw, Kimberlé. 1988. "Race, Reform, and Retrenchment: Transformation and Legitimation in Antidiscrimination Law." *Harvard Law Review* 101 (7): 1331–1397.

Crenshaw, Kimberlé. 1989. "Demarginalizing the Intersection of Race and Sex: A Black Feminist Critique of Antidiscrimination Doctrine, Feminist Theory and Antiracist Politics." *University of Chicago Legal Forum* 140: 139–167.

Cullen, Maura. 2011. "Is Affirmative Action Reverse Discrimination?" Accessed August 27, 2014. http://www.mauracullen.com/wp-content/uploads/2011/09/Is-Affirmative-Action-Reverse-Discrimination.pdf.

Dalton, Harlon L. 1987. "The Clouded Prism." *Harvard Civil Rights-Civil Liberties Law Review* 22 (2): 435–448.

Dantley, Michael E. 2005. "African American Spirituality and Cornel West's Notions of Prophetic Pragmatism: Restructuring Educational Leadership in American Urban Schools." *Educational Administration Quarterly* 41 (4): 651–674.

Darling-Hammond, Linda. 2006. "Highly Qualified Teachers for All." *Educational Leadership* 64 (3): 14–20.

Darling-Hammond, Linda. 2007. "Race, Inequality, and Educational Accountability: The Irony of 'No Child Left Behind.'" *Ethnicity & Education* 10 (3): 245–260.

DeCuir-Gunby, Jessica T. 2007. "Negotiating Identity in a Bubble: A Critical Race Analysis of African American High School Students' Experiences in an Elite, Independent School." *Equity & Excellence in Education* 40 (1): 26–35.

Delgado, Richard. 1989. "Storytelling for Oppositionists and Others: A Plea for Narrative." *Michigan Law Review* 87 (8): 2411–2441.

Delgado, Richard. 1990. "When a Story Is Just a Story: Does Voice Really Matter?" *Virginia Law Review* 76 (1): 95–111.

Delgado Bernal, D. 2002. "Critical Race Theory, Latino Critical Theory, and Critical Raced-Gendered Epistemologies: Recognizing Students of Color as Holders and Creators of Knowledge." *Qualitative Inquiry* 8 (1): 105–126.

Emery, Kathy. 2007. "Corporate Control of Public School Goals: High-Stakes Testing in Its Historical Perspective." *Teacher Education Quarterly* 34 (2): 25–44.

Fanon, Frantz O. 1967. *Black Skin, White Masks.* New York: Grove Press.

Feagin, Joe R. 2006. *Systemic Racism: A Theory of Oppression.* New York: Routledge.

Frankenberg, Ruth, ed. 1997. *Displacing Whiteness.* Durham, NC: Duke University Press.

Freire, Paulo. 1970/2005. *Pedagogy of the Oppressed.* New York: Continuum.

Freire, Paulo. 1994. *Pedagogy of Hope: Reliving Pedagogy of the Oppressed.* New York: Continuum.

Fromm, Erich S. 1966. *The Heart of Man: Its Genius for Good and Evil.* New York: Harper & Row.

Gay, Geneva. 2007. "The Rhetoric and Reality of NCLB." *Race Ethnicity and Education* 10 (3): 279–293.

Gillborn, David. 2008. *Racism and Education: Coincidence or Conspiracy?* New York: Routledge.

Gillespie, Diane, Leslie Ashbaugh, and JoAnne DeFiore. 2002. "White Women Teaching White Women about White Privilege, Race Cognizance and Social Action: Toward a Pedagogical Pragmatics." *Race Ethnicity and Education* 5 (3): 237–252.

Gotanda, Neil. 1991. "A Critique of 'Our Constitution Is Color-Blind.'" *Stanford Law Review* 44 (1): 1–68.

Gramsci, Antonio. 1971. *Selections from the Prison Notebooks.* New York: International Publishers.

Harris, Cheryl I. 1993. "Whiteness as Property." *Harvard Law Review* 106 (8): 1707–1791.

Howard, Tyrone, and Rebecca Reynolds. 2008. "Examining Parent Involvement in Reversing the Underachievement of African American Students in Middle-Class Schools." *Educational Foundations* 22 (1/2): 79–98.

Hursh, David. 2005. "The Growth of High-Stakes Testing in the USA: Accountability, Markets and the Decline in Educational Quality." *British Educational Research Journal* 31 (5): 605–622.

Knaus, Christopher B. 2009. "Shut Up and Listen: Applied Critical Race Theory in the Classroom." *Race Ethnicity and Education* 12 (2): 133–154.

Ladson-Billings, Gloria J. 1998. "Just What Is Critical Race Theory and What's It Doing in a *Nice* Field Like Education?" *Qualitative Studies in Education* 11 (1): 7–24.

Ladson-Billings, Gloria J. 2004. "New Directions in Multicultural Education: Complexities, Boundaries, and Critical Race Theory." In *Handbook of Research on*

Multicultural Education, eds. James A. Banks and Cherry M. Banks. (2nd ed.) (pp. 50–65). San Francisco: Jossey-Bass.

Ladson-Billings, Gloria J., and Carl A. Grant. 1997. *Dictionary of Multicultural Education.* Phoenix: Oryx Press.

Leonardo, Zeus. 2002. "The Soul of White Folk: Critical Pedagogy, Whiteness Studies, and Globalization Discourse." *Race Ethnicity and Education* 5 (1): 29–50.

Lopez, Gerardo R. 2003. "The (Racially Neutral) Politics of Education: A Critical Race Theory Perspective." *Educational Administration Quarterly* 39 (1): 68–94.

Matsuda, Mari J. 1987. "Looking to the Bottom: Critical Legal Studies and Reparations." *Harvard Civil Rights-Civil Liberties Law Review* 22 (2): 323–399.

Matsuda, Mari J. 1991. "Voices of America: Accent, Antidiscrimination Law, and a Jurisprudence for the Last Reconstruction." *Yale Law Journal* 100 (5): 1329–1408.

Matsuda, Mari J., Charles R. Lawrence, Richard Delgado, and Kimberlé Crenshaw. 1993. *Words That Wound: Critical Race Theory, Assaultive Speech, and the First Amendment.* Boulder, CO: Westview Press, Inc.

McDuffy v. Secretary of the Executive Office of Education. 1993. 415 Mass. 545.

McIntosh, Peggy. 1990. "White Privilege: Unpacking the Invisible Knapsack." *Independent School* 49 (2): 31–35.

Miller, William. 1998. *The Bus Ride.* New York: Lee & Low Books.

National Center for Education Statistics. 2008. "Table 2. Number of School Principals and Percentage Distribution of School Principals, by Race/Ethnicity, School Type, and Selected School Characteristics: 2007–08." Accessed December 31, 2009. http://nces.ed.gov/pubs2009/2009323/tables/sass0708_2009323_p12n_02.asp.

No Child Left Behind Act. 2002. P.L. 107–110.

Oakes, Jeannie. 2008. "Keeping Track: Structuring Equality and Inequality in an Era of Accountability." *Teachers College Record* 100 (3): 700–712.

Roediger, David R. 1991. *The Wages of Whiteness.* London: Verso.

Rogers, Rebecca, and Melissa Mosley. 2006. "Racial Literacy in a Second-Grade Classroom: Critical Race Theory, Whiteness Studies, and Literacy Research." *International Reading Association* 41 (4): 462–495.

Ruffin, Frances E. 2001. *Martin Luther King, Jr. and the March on Washington.* New York: Grosset & Dunlap.

Saddler, Craig A. 2005. "The Impact of *Brown* on African American Students: A Critical Race Theoretical Perspective." *Educational Studies* 37 (1): 41–55.

San Antonio Independent School District v. Rodriguez. 1973. 411 U.S. 1.

Scheppele, Kim L. 1989. "Foreword: Telling Stories." *Michigan Law Review* 87 (8): 2073–2098.

Sleeter, Christine E. 2008. "Teaching for Democracy in an Age of Corporatocracy." *Teachers College Record* 110 (1): 139–159.

Solórzano, Daniel G., and Armida Ornelas. 2004. "A Critical Race Analysis of Latina/o and African American Advanced Placement Enrollment in Public High Schools." *The High School Journal* 87 (3): 15–26.

Starratt, Robert J. 2003. "Opportunity to Learn and the Accountability Agenda." *Phi Delta Kapan* 85 (4): 298–303.

Tatum, Beverly D. 1992. "Talking about Race, Learning about Racism: The Application of Racial Identity Development Theory in the Classroom." *Harvard Educational Review* 62 (1): 1–24.

U.S. Department of Education. 2001. "Title I: Improving the Academic Achievement of the Disadvantaged." Accessed March 17, 2014. http://www2.ed.gov/policy/elsec/leg/esea02/pg1.html.

U.S. Department of Education. 2010. "Appendix B: Scoring Rubric." Accessed July 21, 2011. http://www2.ed.gov/programs/racetothetop/scoringrubric.pdf.

Vaught, Stephanie. E. 2009. "The Color of Money: School Funding and the Commodification of Black Children." *Urban Education* 44 (5): 545–570.

Yosso, T.J. 2006. *Critical Race Counterstories along the Chicana/Chicano Educational Pipeline.* New York: Routledge.

Young, Evelyn. 2010. "Challenges to Conceptualizing and Actualizing Culturally Relevant Pedagogy: How Viable Is the Theory in Classroom Practice?" *Journal of Teacher Education* 61 (3): 248–260.

Young, Michelle D., and Julie Laible. 2000. "White Racism, Anti-racism, and School Leadership Preparation." *Journal of School Leadership* 10: 374–415.

Chapter 2

The Pathology of Color Blindness: A Historical Account

Lillian Dowdell Drakeford

[We] ought not sit back and wish away, rather than confront, the racial inequality that exists in our society. It is this view that works harm, by perpetuating the facile notion that what makes race matter is acknowledging the simple truth that race does *matter. (italics added)*

—Justice Sonia Sotomayor[1]

The problem of the 21st century in America is the problem of the color line. If this sounds hauntingly familiar, it should! More than a century ago, notable scholar and historian, W.E.B. DuBois declared, "The problem of the 20th century is the problem of the color-line . . . the relation of the darker to the lighter races of men in Asia and Africa, in America and the islands of the sea. It was a phase of this problem that caused the Civil War."[2] In this 21st century, we may not be fighting a military Civil War, but we are fighting a mighty moral and psychological war within ourselves as a nation, the object of which centers on something we refuse to confront: the conundrum of race.

The refusal of Americans to honestly tackle the enigma of race, race relations, and racism is nothing new. The inequities wrought by the U.S. cowardice and hypocrisy on the issue of race gnaw at our consciousness and integrity as individuals. They challenge our sense of decency and uprightness as a nation that claims the title of Leader of the Free World. Currently, Americans are embroiled in a destructive cover-up and an irrational disavowal of the continuing significance of race in American schools and society. Despite concrete and unrelenting evidence to the contrary, we stubbornly uphold systems, policies, and practices predicated on the fantasy that we have somehow closed the racial divide, conquered racism, and eradicated the collective, systematic, systemic, and institutional causes of racial inequality. Our schools, places of employment, service providers, and courthouses pretend to be race-neutral, operating as though race no longer matters as a determinant of one's life chances and experiences. While acknowledging the inarguable history of racism in the United States, far too many Americans, particularly those in decision-making positions, refute the extant role race plays in their own thoughts, attitudes, and decisions as well as the racialized consciousness of the United States as a whole.

When overt and extreme acts of racism occur, they are quickly condemned and categorized as aberrant and an individual problem that can be remediated by the enforcement of long-standing antidiscriminatory legislation. Hence, racism tends not to be a problem of general concern. Indeed, a blind eye is often turned to the institution of racism. We treat the cancerous disease of racism as though it is in permanent remission. Those who attempt to raise consciousness of the persistence of racism and the role race plays in society and its institutions are frequently silenced, ridiculed, dismissed, and accused of "playing the race card" and "race-baiting." Moreover, some purport to be "beyond race," living in a "post-racial era," even color-blind. But do we really believe that we have transcended the race problem or have we simply perfected the cowardly art of self-deception? Are we truly color-blind? Should we aspire to be color-blind? Do we even know what it means to be color-blind or understand its ramifications? I think not.

In this chapter, I elucidate the pathology of color blindness. By taking a race-critical historical view of American education and society, I demystify the ideology of color blindness, uncover the pattern of denial about racism that color blindness encourages, and expose why and how color blindness operates to the detriment of all Americans. Because it is not possible to fully comprehend the mystery of color blindness without first clarifying the meaning and influence of race and racism throughout American history, I begin with a brief discussion of the construction of race and the development of the United States as a racial state. Next, I trace the evolution and effects of ideology of color blindness in America's schools and society. Finally, I conclude with recommendations for race-critical, counterhegemonic educational reform in American education.

Race and the United States as a Racial State

What is race? Prior to the turn of the century, biological explanations of race and racial inferiority and superiority prevailed. It took 100 years for scholars to replace these perceptions with an approach that regards race as a social concept.[3] Most scholars now concur that there is no solid biological foundation for race and that race is a social construction. Omi and Winant (1994) proposed that "race is a concept which signifies and symbolizes social conflicts and interests by referring to different types of human bodies."[4] They contended that we should think of race "as an element of social structure rather than as an irregularity within it; we should see race as a dimension of human representation rather than an illusion."[5] Essed (1991) theorized:

> Racism must be understood as ideology, structure, and process in which inequalities inherent in the wider social structure are related, in a deterministic way, to biological and cultural factors attributed to those who are seen as a different "race" or "ethnic" group.[6]

In her view, "race is an ideological construction, not just a social construction because the idea of race is never outside of a framework of group interest."[7] Goldberg (2002) defined race as "a social or cultural significance assigned to or assumed in physical or biological markers of human beings, including the presumed physical or physiognomic markers of cultural attributes, habits, or behaviors."[8] What all of these definitions have in common is an understanding of race as a human-made construct predicated on social, cultural, and ideological beliefs aimed at ordering, categorizing, defining, and determining the place of certain others in society. Racism, different from race, is the deployment of the ideological and social construct of race—the race-based institutionalization and structuration of the power over others (e.g., the privileging of some and the depriving of others).

Traditionally, the focus of racism in the United States has most often been limited to a black–white experience. Manning Marable (1992), however, positioned racism within a broader context and defined racism as "a system of ignorance, exploitation, and power used to oppress African-Americans, Latinos, Asians, Pacific Americans, American Indians, and other people on the basis of ethnicity, culture, mannerisms, and color."[9] Lorde (1992) emphasized the relation between power (e.g., feelings of superiority and dominance) and racism. She defined racism as "the belief in the inherent superiority or dominance of one race—in particular, Whites—over others."[10] Fredricksen (2002), in *Racism: A Short History,* alleged that a defining characteristic of racism is the assumption on the part of a superior group of the inferiority of others who are deemed to manifest some immutable difference.[11] Embedded within these definitions are the following characteristics of racism:

(1) Racism involves the belief of the dominant group that it is superior.
(2) Racism involves the enactment of power.
(3) Racism affects a wide range of racial and ethnic groups.

These determinants suggest that "racism is about institutional power, a form of power that people of color—that is, non-Whites, in the United States have never possessed."[12]

Goldberg (2009) argued, however, that racism is more than the presumption of inferiority or superiority. It "is more broadly that racial difference warrants exclusion of those so characterized from elevation into the realm of protection, privilege, property, or profit."[13] Racism becomes institutionalized, structured, and reproduced in what Goldberg (2002) called the racial state. He theorized that the processes by which privilege and deprivation, freedom and unfreedom, liberty and oppression, and opportunity and denial are structured become normalized in the racial state. Goldberg explained:

> States are racial more deeply because of the structural position they occupy in producing and reproducing, constituting and effecting racially shaped spaces and places, groups and events, life worlds, and possibilities, accesses and restrictions, inclusions and exclusions, conceptions and modes of representation. They are *racial* by virtue of their modes of population definition, determination, and structuration. And they are racist to the extent such definition, determination, and structuration operate to exclude or privilege in or on racial terms, and in so far as they circulate in and reproduce a world whose meanings and effects are racist. This is a world we might provocatively identify as a *racist world order*. (italics added)[14]

According to Goldberg (2002), there are five ways in which racial states manage racial groups. First, they define, regulate, govern, manage, and mediate racial matters by fashioning racially identifiable groups, for example, census taking, laws, and policy making.[15] Second, racial states *regulate* social, political, economic, legal, and cultural relations between those between white citizens and others (nonwhites), the consequences of which often aggravate racial tension within and between racial groups who must compete for the advantages that whites enjoy. Third, "racial states *govern* populations identified in explicitly racial terms."[16] In simple terms, what this means is that in the racial state those groups regarded as either naturally substandard or historically underdeveloped are managed, controlled, and watched. Fourth, "racial states *manage* economic life and structure the opportunities or possibilities of economic access and closure."[17] Segregated educational practices in the United States are one example. "Finally, racial states not only regulate but also claim to *mediate* relations between those (self)-identified as 'White' or 'European' and those declared 'non-White' or 'Native.'"[18] Despite claims of neutrality, the racial state historically reproduces a system of entitlement for whites. In short, the racial state is driven to control others by perpetuating their subjugation through racial categorization and structuration. "Race appears in this scheme of things as a mode of crisis management and containment, as a mode mediating that tension, of managing manufactured threats and of curtailing while alienating the challenge of the unknown."[19] Goldberg believed that racial states exist to restrict heterogeneity. Racism is a means of "securing political, cultural, and racial homogeneity."[20] I posit further that fear of instability and the displacement of white privilege essentializes the racial state and mandates subsequent modes of subjugation, hegemony, and racism. The unspoken objective of the racial state is to maintain white privilege.

Whites in America are privileged in three primary ways. First, they enjoy a structural advantage in the form of racial privilege because most institutions are founded by and for white people. Second, they profit from a standpoint advantage that allows them to view themselves more favorably than they view nonwhites. Third, they benefit from a cultural advantage. White culture is regarded as the norm and the standard by which other cultures are measured.[21] White is not viewed as a race; it is simply normal.

While most whites are taught about prejudice, discrimination, and racism, they are often oblivious to whiteness and white privilege because, "unlike discrimination, which is a conscious act against another person, White privilege requires that no decisions be made, no premeditated actions taken."[22] It is so pervasive and commonplace that it becomes an unconscious habit for many whites.[23] The phenomenon of white privilege perpetuates the permanence of racism and is central to understanding racial paradigms in American history.

Omi and Winant (1994) identified three historical racial paradigms that have dominated the formation of racial theory in America since the turn of the century: ethnicity, class, and nation. The ethnicity model, which has enjoyed theoretical primacy for the last 60 years, has experienced three major stages:

> A pre-1930s stage in which the ethnic group view was an insurgent approach, challenging the biologistic (and at least implicitly racist) view of race which was dominant at the time; a 1930s to 1965 stage, during which the paradigm operated as the progressive/liberal "common sense" approach to race, and during which two recurrent themes—assimilationism and cultural pluralism—were defined; and a post-1965 phase, in which the paradigm has taken on the defense of conservative (or "neoconservative") egalitarianism against what is perceived as the radical assault of group rights.[24]

In the years since *Brown* and civil rights, the ideology of color blindness has achieved political and educational hegemony in the United States. But Americans have been toying with the idea of color blindness for decades.

The Evolution of the Ideology of Color Blindness

Color-blindness is not simply a new strategy in this fight, enabling the ongoing theft of Black gifts in the name of anti-racism. It operates as an unconscious defense device that allows White people to avoid recognizing themselves as non-White people often see them: as "sheer malevolence."[25]

The eagerness with which contemporary society does away with racism, replacing this recognition with evocations of pluralism and diversity that further mask reality is a response to the terror [of Whiteness]. It has also become a way to perpetuate the terror by providing a cover, a hiding place.[26]

Present commitments to state racelessness (e.g., color blindness, the death of race, and the end of racism) insist that "Race is a politically irrelevant category yet make appeals to universal values and interests allied with Whiteness."[27] Consequently, we see attempts to eradicate difference through assimilation, for example, turning difference into sameness. Color blindness and the implication of race-transcendence are evidenced in the form of universals that are equated with whiteness and perpetuated to preserve white privilege.

The problem is that preservation of white privilege and the belief that one race is superior to another contradict the very principles on which the United States was founded, for example, freedom, meritocracy, equal opportunity, and justice for all. Herein lies the moral dilemma with which Americans have wrestled since the nation's birth. Living with the dilemma has required persistent delusion. How does a nation, heralded as Leader of the

Free World, make sense of the paradox and hypocrisy? America has done so by crafting a perpetually evolving ideology that overtly seeks one end but covertly achieves another. Bonilla-Silva (2003) elaborated,

> Ideologies are about "meaning in the service of power." They are expressions at the symbolic level of the fact of dominance. As such, the ideologies of the powerful are central in the production and reinforcement of the status quo. They comfort rulers and charm the ruled much like an Indian snake handler. Whereas rulers receive solace by believing they are not involved in the terrible ordeal of creating and maintaining inequality, the ruled are charmed by the almost magical qualities of a hegemonic ideology.[28]

Indeed, the ideology of color blindness operates in this fashion. It exacerbates what it purports to eradicate by feeding persistent delusion about the role of race in schools and society. It is much easier to deny the significance of race than it is to admit that race matters. Hence, color blindness represents the most recent mutation of the ongoing U.S. racial discourse to gain political hegemony, yet it was first conceived in the 19th century. We need examine only a few of the landmark legal cases in the racial history of the United States to unearth the evolution of the ideology of color blindness.

Plessy v. Ferguson, 1896: Separate but Equal

In the aftermath of the Reconstruction Era (1865–1877), legislators in Southern states initiated a vicious legal backlash with the passage of Jim Crow laws aimed at ensuring the separation of the races and guaranteeing the second-class citizenship of blacks. The Reconstruction Era was a period in which the country hoped to heal the ravages of a war that had freed almost 4 million slaves, but destroyed cities and homes, dismantled the plantation-based economy, and dislocated thousands of blacks and whites alike. During these years, blacks acquired some degree of social leadership, sought assistance from able and appropriate groups, and strove to obtain enough knowledge to "teach themselves wisdom and the rhythm of united effort."[29] Among the greatest achievements were the advancement of the black in education and the training of black teachers. This era of progress, however, was short lived.

Determined to put a halt to the progress of the Jim Crow laws, whites in the South enacted legislation that mandated strict segregation of the races in all public places. The goal was to maintain white privilege and suppress the advancement of blacks toward true social, economic, political, and educational quality. Suppression of black progress toward equality found support, not only in Southern state courthouses but also in the highest court of the land: the U.S. Supreme Court. The *Plessy v. Ferguson,* 1896, decision is one of the most infamous examples of the U.S. government's promotion of racism.

In 1890, the Louisiana legislature passed a law requiring railroads to segregate passengers on the basis of race. Trains with two or more passenger cars were required to designate separate seating/cars for blacks and whites. One-car trains had to divide the races by a curtain or some other physical partition. Failure to comply with these stipulations resulted in a fine of $25 or up to 20 days in jail.[30] Citizen groups across the South organized in protest of the laws. In 1896, Howard Plessy, acting on behalf of such a citizens' group in Louisiana, intentionally refused to sit in the "colored" section of the train as requested. Plessy, who ironically was seven-eighths white and one-eighths black, considered an "octoroon"[31] and looked like a white man, was arrested and charged. He petitioned the Louisiana Supreme Court for a writ against the trial court judge, the Honorable John H. Ferguson, to stop the proceedings against him, but the court refused his request. Determined, Plessy then appealed to the Supreme Court of the United States. Central to his case were questions involving the Thirteenth and Fourteenth Amendments to the Constitution. The Thirteenth Amendment, ratified in 1865, essentially abolished slavery. The source of numerous unforeseen legal challenges, the Fourteenth Amendment (1868) was a bit more complex. Key provisions in the Fourteenth Amendment included the following:

(1) State and federal citizenship for all persons regardless of race both born or naturalized in the United States was reaffirmed.
(2) No state would be allowed to abridge the "privileges and immunities" of citizens.
(3) No person was allowed to be deprived of life, liberty, or property without "due process of law."
(4) No person could be denied "equal protection of the laws."[32]

In a 7–1 decision, the U.S. Supreme Court ruled that, in spite of the fact that the Fourteenth Amendment decreed "absolute equality of the two races before the law,"[33] such equality pertained only to political and civil rights (e.g., voting and serving on juries), not social rights (e.g., sitting in a railway car one chooses). As Justice Henry Brown put it, "If one race be inferior to the other socially, the constitution of the United States cannot put them upon the same plane."[34] Moreover, the Court maintained that the Thirteenth Amendment applied only to the burden of slavery and nothing else.

Several other long-standing precedents were set in the *Plessy* decision. The Court refuted Plessy's claim that the law stigmatized blacks "with a badge of inferiority,"[35] by asserting that equal facilities were provided for blacks and whites alike and both races were equally subject to the same legal penalty for failure to comply. Absolving the Louisiana law of any ill intent, the Court argued further that there was no basis for the allegation that enforced separation of the two races branded the "colored" race with a badge of inferiority except if the colored race chose to make that assumption. Employing a rationale that would shape political debate and Court opinion for years to come, Justice Brown wrote, "Legislation is powerless to eradicate racial instincts or to abolish distinctions based upon physical differences."[36] In other words, legislation cannot change public attitudes, "and the attempt to do so can only result in accentuating the difficulties of the present situation."[37] The best-known declaration in the decree was that segregation was legal and constitutional as long as "facilities were equal."[38] Thus evolved the "separate but equal doctrine" that would keep America divided along racial lines for over half a century.[39]

Justice John Harlan expressed the only dissenting voice on the high court. It was in Harlan's epic dissenting argument that the term "color-blind" first appeared. He rebuked the notion of separate but equal on the basis that the Constitution of the United Sates was color-blind. The statement most frequently quoted from Harlan's decision read as follows:

> But in the view of the Constitution, in the eye of the law, there is in this country no superior, dominant, ruling class of citizens. There is no caste here. Our Constitution is color-blind and neither knows nor tolerates classes among citizens.[40]

Critical analysis of Harlan's full dissent reveals, however, an unsettling opacity about not only the reality of a color-blind Constitution but also the appropriateness of a color-blind interpretation of the Constitution. The unabridged paragraph is alarmingly duplicitous:

> *The White race deems itself to be the dominant race in this country. And so it is, in prestige, in achievements, in education, in wealth, and in power. So, I doubt not, it will continue to be for all time if it remains true to its great heritage and holds fast to the principles of constitutional liberty* [emphasis added]. But,

in view of the Constitution, in the eye of the law, there is in this country no superior, dominant, ruling class of citizens. There is no caste here. Our Constitution is colorblind and neither knows nor tolerates classes among citizens.[41]

Harlan alleged, on the one hand, the constitutional equality of blacks while simultaneously acknowledging the permanent superiority of white race. A former slave owner himself, Harlan epitomizes the hypocrisy of the United States. Although credited with being ahead of his contemporaries in his perspectives on the race question, he held enduring assumptions predicated on racialized and racist beliefs that were actually quite prevalent among his peers.

Closer scrutiny of Harlan's dissent reveals more about the complicated issue of race in America:

> The recent amendments of the Constitution, it was supposed, had eradicated these principles from our institutions. But it seems that we have yet, in some of the States, a dominant race—a superior class of citizens, which assumes to regulate the enjoyment of civil rights, common to all citizens, upon the basis of race. The present decision, it may well be apprehended, will not only stimulate aggressions, more or less brutal and irritating, upon the admitted rights of colored citizens, but will encourage the belief that it is possible, by means of state enactments, to defeat the beneficent purposes which the people of the United States had in view when they adopted the recent amendments of the Constitution, by one of which the blacks of this country were made citizens of the United States and of the States in which they respectively reside, and whose privileges and immunities, as citizens, the States are forbidden to abridge. Sixty millions of whites are in no danger from the presence here of eight millions of blacks. The destinies of the two races in this country are indissolubly linked together, and the interests of both require that the common government of all shall not permit the seeds of race hate to be planted under the sanction of law.[42]

In this passage, Harlan recognized the shared destiny of the whites and blacks and understood that the prosperity of the United States depended on peaceful coexistence between the races. He worried that segregated seating on a public transportation would enflame the race problem and incite aggressive attitudes and behaviors between the races. Perhaps, eager to move beyond the problem of race, Harlan seemed hopeful that the passage of the beneficent privileges provided for in the Thirteenth and Fourteenth Amendments had resolved the issue of race equality under the law. As if to reassure the "dominant" white race of the permanence of their position, he reasoned that giving a relative few blacks equal access to seating on public transportation should not pose a threat to whites. Little attention has been given to the incongruent and paradoxical statements in Harlan's opinion. Instead, his assertion of a color-blind Constitution has continued to provide the basis for the ideology of color blindness and enactment of color-blind policies that directly influenced education in America's public schools and society. The issue of segregation in education, however, came to a head with the landmark case—*Brown v. Board of Education.*

Brown v. Board of Education, 1954: A Dream Deferred

Color blindness, now as a century ago, is adopted as the easy resolution of issues of race with which the nation would rather not wrestle, much less try seriously to resolve. . . . Brown v. Board of Education *was a dramatic instance of remedy that promised to correct deficiencies in justice far deeper than the Supreme Court was able to understand.*[43]

As far back as the mid-19th century, Americans had challenged the policy of racially segregated public schools. By the early 1930s, the National Association for the Advancement of Colored People (NAACP) had structured a concentrated effort to fight segregation in the courts. Strategies were devised to combat segregation not only in schools but also throughout society as a whole. Public schools, however, presented "a far more compelling symbol of the evils of segregation and far more vulnerable target than railroad cars, restaurants, and restrooms."[44] With the help of the NAACP and the prestigious cadre of attorneys affiliated with the organization, blacks continued to contest the denial of their admission to white schools on the grounds that the black schools were inadequately staffed or resourced, or as was the case in many petitions involving higher education, black colleges and universities did not offer the same certain postgraduate-level opportunities. Finally, in 1952, five great cases were combined into one case known as *Brown v. Board of Education,* named for the first of the five cases.

Prosecutors argued:

1. In *Plessy v. Ferguson,* the Supreme Court had misinterpreted the equal protection clause of the 14th Amendment. Equal protection of the laws did not allow for racial segregation. The Constitution was indeed, color-blind.
2. The 14th Amendment allowed the government to prohibit any discriminatory state action based on race, including segregation in schools.

3. The 14th Amendment did not specify whether the states would be allowed to establish segregated education.
4. Psychological testing demonstrated the harmful effects of segregation on the minds of African American children.[45]

Conversely, defense attorneys for the Topeka, Kansas Board of Education, argued:

1. The Constitution did not require White and African American children to attend the same schools.
2. Social separation of Blacks and Whites was a regional custom; the states should be left free to regulate their own social affairs.
3. Segregation was not harmful to Black people.
4. Whites were making a good faith effort to equalize the two educational systems. But, because Black children were still living with the effects of slavery, it would take some time before they were able to compete with White children in the same classrooms.[46]

In the end, *Brown* symbolically overturned the pernicious *Plessy* decision and, by many traditional historical accounts, vindicated the rights of black Americans. In presumably denouncing the caste system of racialized classifications and segregated practices in the nation's schools, the *Brown* ruling adhered to a jurisprudence of color blindness that helped destroy the legality of racial taxonomy and overt racial discrimination. Hopeful Americans, black and white, believed that the *Brown* decision would be instrumental in diminishing the significance of race, leveling the playing field between blacks and whites, even resolving problems caused by racism.

The truth of the matter, however, is that in the aftermath of the cacophonous reaction to *Brown,* the victories the civil rights advocates managed to win in the fight for racial justice were offset by consistent efforts of the American legal system to deradicalize the impact of the racial freedom movement.[47] One effective means of taking the teeth, so to speak, out of *Brown* and thwarting the impending civil rights movement that would follow in the 1960s was to frame the post-*Brown* antidiscrimination and antidefiance legislation *within* the perpetrator's perspective.

To clarify, between 1954 and 1965 Americans were consumed with great uncertainty caused by a barrage of post-*Brown* antidiscrimination and antidefiance legislation, most of which was rooted in a perpetrator perspective as opposed to a victim perspective.

From the victim's perspective, racial discrimination describes those conditions of actual social existence as a member of a perpetual underclass. This perspective includes both the objective conditions of life (lack of jobs, lack of money, lack of housing) and the consciousness associated with those objective conditions (lack of choice and lack of human individuality in forever being part of a group rather than as an individual). The perpetrator perspective sees racial discrimination not as conditions but as actions, or series of actions, inflicted on the victim by the perpetrator. The focus is more on what particular perpetrators have done or are doing to some victims than on the overall life situation of the victim class.[48]

The perpetrator perspective recognizes no system of oppression—no racism, classism, or sexism. Viewed in an ahistorical light, racial discrimination is then seen as an isolated or specific action committed by specific or particular actors, devoid of any systematic, systemic, or institutional structure. Operating from this perspective, it stands to reason that the world affords equal opportunity to everyone, except those who, for some innate reason, are undeserving or fail to meet the mark. Hence, there is support for belief in objective truth and inevitability, a certain sense of resignation about life that has nothing to do with anything systematic or institutional. In other words, the natural order is that there will be winners and losers, and the losers are responsible (e.g., at fault) for their fate on account of natural causes. In addition, the perpetrator perspective advances "twin notions"[49] of fault and causation that work in concert to absolve the perpetrator of responsibility.

Fault implies intention; consequently, the law addresses only intentional acts. Causation places the burden of proof on the victim. In the *Brown* case, the Court was more concerned with identifying wrongdoers than confronting the larger issues implicated by the victims or remedying the larger problems like the problem of racism. Tackling the problem of racism would necessitate acknowledging the historical significance of race and race relations in America, assuring equal protection under the law for African Americans, and eliminating conditions associated with discrimination and unequal treatment. It was and continues to be easier to invoke the ideology of color blindness.

"To explain [the meaning of] *Brown* by invoking the slogan that the 'Constitution is color-blind' reflects a means-oriented view of the equal protection clause"[50] and is predicated on the assumption that race and racial classification are irrational and unrelated to any valid government purpose. The problem is that, based on the initial assumption, color blindness in its purest form would have to discount racial classification, no matter the context. Answers to racial questions would be quite simple as long as the theory remained separate from the reality of race relations. This is precisely what Justice Harlan unsuccessfully tried to do. He argued for a color-blind Constitution while acknowledging actual inequality between the races. And, if we look at *Brown* as a precursor to the evolving color-blind ideology, we see that in merely invalidating the practice of segregation and identifying segregation as "wrong," *Brown* emphasized specific wrongdoing rather than remedying conditions, "with a consequent inability to deal with ostensibly neutral practices."[51] Since *Brown,* the ideology of color blindness has steadily gained momentum.

Civil Rights and Color Blindness: Strange Bedfellows

The civil rights movement profoundly changed America, bringing a measure of racial justice and hope to people of color. Barely 40 years later, racial justice has ceased to be a priority, and in some instances, the gains of the 1960s and 1970s have been reversed.[52]

With the passage of the Civil Rights and Voting Rights Acts of 1964 and 1965, respectively, President Lyndon Baines Johnson and most Americans hoped to finally right the historical wrong of blatant racial discrimination against African Americans in America or at least bury the ugly past of racial injustice. Eager to set the problem of race aside, Johnson set out to build what he called a Great Society fashioned around a rhetoric that espoused a new liberalism. Johnson hoped to awaken an indifferent American people to the potentially fatal social ills of poverty, racial injustice, and inequality of educational opportunity. He viewed education as the panacea for poverty.

Americans did not need to be convinced that education could cure society's ills, as this was an assumption ingrained in the American psyche by pioneers in education. Horace Mann, the pioneer of the common school, perceived education as "the balance wheel of the social machinery" and "the great equalizer of the conditions of men."[53] Johnson believed, as did Horace Mann, that education could "uplift the poor, protect the property and wealth of the successful, and obliterate factitious distinctions in society."[54] However sincere his intentions, Johnson found poverty, a condition experienced by blacks and whites, more approachable than overtly attacking racism. Consequently, Johnson used his political muscle to push for a series of color-blind legislation that targeted economic considerations. At his urging, Congress adopted the Economic Opportunity Act of 1964, which laid the groundwork for the historic Elementary and Secondary Education Act (ESEA) of 1965.

The ESEA, the cornerstone educational legislation of the Johnson era, significantly increased the role of the federal government in K-12 education. Prior to the passage of the ESEA, local and state authorities had controlled education and schooling in America. Several factors worked in concert to ensure that Congress passed the ESEA, not the least of which being the diminished significance of race in the legislation. In the aftermath of *Brown* and enactment of the Civil Rights Act, especially the provision of Title VI that withheld federal dollars to schools that refused to desegregate, black and white Americans hoped the issues of race (and racism) were well on their way to being resolved. Legislators agreed that the federal government should and would address poverty and the quality of education for children of all races. The ESEA might be considered the first modern-day color-blind educational reform. Indeed, expectations ran high, but enduring inequalities produced sobering realities.

Three misleading assumptions undermined the anticipated far-reaching effectiveness of civil rights legislation and the ESEA. The first was the false premise that desegregating the schools would automatically eliminate racial inequalities in the schools, erase the harm caused by historical racism, and enhance the cognitive and affective development of black children. The second erroneous assumption was that the punitive consequence of withholding federal dollars from schools that continued to practice discriminatory practices, as mandated by Title VI of the Civil Rights Act, would force compliance and, thus, rid the nation of discrimination in school and society based on race, color, and national origin. The third misconception was that increased spending of federal dollars for compensatory programs under the provisions of Title I of the ESEA would remedy the principal ills of society. In time, the fallacy of these suppositions would become evident, but for all the wrong reasons.

As time went on, Americans demanded proof that the educational reforms fueled by civil rights legislation and Johnson's ideological Great Society were actually producing the results they set out to accomplish. Several research projects were commissioned to investigate the effectiveness of the reforms, the results of which cast serious doubt on the merit of compensatory educational programs and the ability of schools to close the racial achievement gap in the nation's schools.[55,56] Controversial, yet highly respected educational research literature during the 1960s and early 1970s[57,58] suggested inferiority of black intellectual capacity and dysfunctional black family culture were responsible for the enduring inequalities of educational outcomes, thus reigniting old prejudices and stereotypes.

In addition, while allegedly moving toward a more egalitarian society, the bedeviling issue of race and refusal to confront it head on resulted in a series of racialized reactions. Many blacks became increasingly outraged with the persistent lack of racial justice. School desegregation proved not to be the cure-all for injustice. Poverty persisted. Americans grew increasingly disillusioned and conflicted. The mounting discord did not have as much to do with the explicitly declared War on Poverty as it did the implicit "elephant in the room"—race.

Regardless of intent, the civil rights movement, desegregation, and compensatory educational reforms of the Great Society did little to confront the *institution* of racism in America. Perhaps the most disturbing and ironic outcome of this era is how effectively the United States deceived itself about the race problem. Amid a period in the nation's history wrought with heightened race consciousness and unresolved interracial and intra-racial conflict, Americans, true to tradition, grew even more determined to deal with the race problem by ignoring its existence and embracing the deception of color blindness.

A Nation at Risk: Playing Politics with Fear, Race, and Education

A new mood of "social meanness" pervaded the U.S., and many Americans resented having to provide for the "underprivileged." Indeed many felt that far from being the victims of deprivation, racial minorities were unfairly receiving "preferential treatment" with respect to jobs and educational opportunities.[59]

Disenchanted with the lackluster results of the Great Society and the seemingly unappreciative, even violent response, of some blacks, many liberals and politically moderate whites who had supported the civil rights movement and Johnson's agenda were growing increasingly fed up. "It was time," conservatives argued with increasing popular support, to stop "throwing away good money after bad."[60]

Several factors contributed to this growing sentiment. Conservatives ascribed many of society's ills to America's fastest-growing population: poor minorities living in female-single-dominated homes. Increasingly, Americans were reminded in school reform literature of "dramatic growth in Black and Hispanic populations."[61] The data indicated that the "most significant changes in America are considered to be the nation's changing racial and ethnic composition."[62]

Omi and Winant (1994) explained:

> The far right, the new right, and neoconservatism reopened the 1960s de-
> bates about racial identity and racial inequality, and questioned once more
> the role of racial issues in the democratic political process. The effectiveness
> of a right-wing challenge to ideals promoted by the racial minority move-
> ment of the 1960s hinged on its ability to rearticulate the meaning of race in
> contemporary American society.[63]

This rearticulation advanced a color-blind ideology that fashioned a deter-
ministic model of race, one that greatly refuted the significance of historical
inequalities wrought by patterns of racial injustice. Previous efforts alleged
to promote respect for cultural difference (e.g., multiculturalism), remediate past racial injustices (e.g., affirmative action), and initiate social welfare
programs were viewed as the cause, not the solution, to the myriad of problems confronting schools and society.

Neoconservatives, under the leadership of President Ronald Reagan, introduced a new approach to domestic social policies. "Instead of employing
the traditional classical/libertarian Republican party solutions, this New
Right coalition called for a much more centrally controlled, activist federal
government to provide the framework for renewed national supremacy."[64]
Shea, Kahane, and Sola (1989) elaborated:

> The New Federalism was conceived as a political arrangement whereby fed-
> eral level policy experts were empowered to prescribe the "consensus goals,"
> whereas individual states, school systems, and local business groups were
> delegated to compete between and among themselves over the most ef-
> ficient means to implement these natural goals. . . . There was a commit-
> ment to achieve these goals not through liberal "give-away" programs, but
> rather through a series of federal level *incentive* programs in the areas of tax,
> trade, antitrust policies, etc. . . . On the state level, therefore, the principles of
> the New Federalism worked to play off one state economy against another,
> thereby extracting tax breaks and labor concessions in order to attract large,
> multinational, corporate industry and huge Pentagon-controlled defense
> production plants.[65]

Reagan's "New Federalism" employed a novel approach that was actually
aimed at keeping things the same and essentially maintaining the status
quo. Once again, the established racial state would be preserved.

The grand narrative persisted. That is to say, the well-publicized correlation between low school achievement and poverty among African

Americans along with the inferred causal relationship between female-single-headed households and misplaced family or lack of family values revitalized familiar and comfortable assumptions of black inferiority. Such assumptions downplayed the role that racism plays in adversely affecting educational opportunities and outcomes for African Americans. In fact, neoconservatives effectively shifted the national conversation away from race as a significant determinant of one's life chances and the concept of color blindness reemerged. As Goldberg (2009) explained:

> Colorblindness accordingly materialized fully first as a characteristic expression of the civil rights regime and then as a reaction to its commitment to affirmative action. One was not supposed to judge intellectual or moral competence, or for that matter physical prowess, by the color of a person's skin.
>
> Colorblindness—or racelessness more generally—claimed to judge people according to individualized merit and ability. *Where members of a racially identified group were generally and repeatedly judged to fail, or to be less qualified, it would be attributed to cultural deficiencies of the group, historically developed, rather than as naturalistically, biologistically determined* [emphasis added].[66]

The *new* racism caught on because it seemed less obvious, less offensive, and less racist than the biological racism of old. In reality, it merely camouflaged racism. The consequences of racism for black children remained the same: low expectations and unequal educational opportunities. In addition, the nuanced racial climate worsened because the United States was becoming increasingly black, brown, and poor. I suggest, as do other scholars,[67,68,69] that conservatives grew increasingly fearful of and alarmed about the state of education in America. They responded by manufacturing a sense of urgency about the need to improve the overall quality of education in the nation's schools.

Conservatives, historically critical of public schools, targeted public school reform as a means of reclaiming the nation and its future. If Americans doubted that the nation and its schools were at risk, their skepticism was put to rest in the historic report, *A Nation at Risk,* 1983. This report focused on education as a tool to enhance economic competitiveness, rather than having at its center the development of an informed and engaged citizenry. Reaction to *A Nation at Risk* resulted in a propensity for color-blind educational reform focused on excellence and accountability. The report invigorated furor over multiculturalism and political correctness and enlisted the defense of familiar "standards" and "values" predicated on "universalism" and "common culture" from liberals and conservatives.[70] What emerged was a common call for replacing the allegedly more liberal social welfare programs with policies that promoted personal responsibility. Once again, American politics had successfully rearticulated the tenets of the racial state. The neoconservative movement of the 1980s paved the way for a neoliberal political ideology that achieved dominance in the 1990s.

Neoliberal Ideology: The Rise of Color Blindness

[The neoliberal agenda], in its quest to avoid the potentially divisive aspects of racial politics by rearticulation, by learning from the enemy, neoliberalism has quite deliberately fostered neglect issues of race. It has, in effect, buried race as a significant dimension of its politics. It has attempted to close the Pandora's box first opened—in contemporary terms—during the 1960s. At best, it advances a "hidden agenda" which seeks to improve the lot of racial minorities while avoiding race-baiting from the right. But such a perspective, although ostensibly premised on creating community and avoiding divisive political conflicts, misses the depth and degree to which competing definitions of race continue to structure and signify politics in the U.S.[71]

By the 1990s, a new kind of Democrat was ushered in with the election of Bill Clinton—the neoliberal. Contrary to what its name implies, there is really nothing new about neoliberalism. Since the beginning of the 17th century, liberalism has continued to exert a commanding influence on philosophical, political, and economic theory. The tenets of classic liberalism have always been plagued by paradox. The principles of liberalism provided the foundation for the American Revolution and the U.S. Constitution. They also informed the practices of colonialism, imperialism, slavery, Jim Crow, *Brown,* the Civil Rights Act, and the emergence of neoconservatives.

Racial politics in the 1990s advanced the neoliberal agenda and reshaped classic liberalism. Rather than extending the precepts of previous democratic liberal practices, neoliberalism expands on classic liberalism's belief in the individual as a rational chooser within the free market. Neoliberalism does not *overtly* hold claim to color blindness, but it does significantly downplay the significance of race and racism. Pivoting away from race and group-specific policies of reform, neoliberals cleverly asserted that any attempt to decrease social, economic, educational inequalities would more benefit the most needy. It was better, they resolved, to address racism by ignoring race, hence followed a renewed push for standards-based education that would ostensibly benefit all children. It resembled a "trickle down" education theory, and according to Clinton, technology would then serve as the "great equalizer" in American education.[72]

Needless to say, technology did not prove to be the great equalizer nor did standards-based education obliterate racial inequality of opportunity or outcomes in our schools. To the contrary, standards-based education, aimed at raising the bar of excellence and accountability for all schools and school children, has fallen short of bringing equity (and excellence) in education for historically marginalized. Yet, neoliberal values and color-blind strategies for change remain the driving force in educational reform.

NCLB and the Neoliberalism: Marketing Color-Blind Education

One of the best-known examples of color-blind, neoliberal educational reform was the once-famous, perhaps now infamous, No Child Left Behind (NCLB) legislation.[73] "Educational neoliberal reforms are based on an *economic model of educational policy* (emphasis added)."[74] A variety of free-market principles undergird the neoliberal model of educational reform: "rationalization and cost-cutting, declining investments, a limited selection of curricular options, privatization, the specter of school choice."[75]

NCLB openly adhered to the following script:

> Because schools bear much of the responsibility for the economic decline in America, they must do a better job of aligning their policies and practices with the goals and objectives of the postindustrial labor market and the new global economy. As the demand for jobs that require lower skills decreases, almost all jobs in the current era of restructured globalization will require a new kind of knowledge—a set of minimum competencies that schools must provide. Curricula needs, then, to be focused on productivity, entrepreneur-ism, multi-skilling, and mastering the "right" knowledge. Standardized tests provide the best means for measuring progress, maintaining accountability, and making sure school curricula are aligned with the needs of the global economy. Furthermore, competition from charter and private schools and punishment in the form of failing report cards, withdrawal of federal funds, and the threat of parent vouchers and school closings are believed to be the best medicine for ailing public schools.[76]

High bipartisan expectations preceded the implementation of NCLB. The law promised 100 percent success of children in U.S. schools by 2014. Well, 2014 has come and gone, and now states are feverishly applying for waivers from the NCLB mandates while new market-based, neoliberal color-blind reform initiatives struggle to right the wrongs of NCLB. The Race to the Top (RttT) Grant Program, for example, rewards states for creating conditions conducive to innovative school reform, significantly improving student achievement outcomes and achievement, closing the achievement gap, raising graduation rates, and ensuring that students are prepared to succeed in college or the workplace.[77] Often times, however, the appeal of the money tied to the RttT compromises the integrity of school reform and student gains, and the ideological underpinnings of NCLB endure.

NCLB originated "from within the historical condition of color-blindness."[78] Although the reform rhetoric professes to erase the color line in education by no longer refusing to account for the achievement of children from all racial, ethnic, and economic subgroups as well as special education students, what it really does is redraw the color line.[79] While ostensibly giving all schools an equal opportunity (e.g., the language of abstract liberalism) to meet the government-prescribed standards, NCLB gives whiteness the exclusive right to label schools and students of color as failing. Because NCLB is informed by an ideology of whiteness, it thrives on perpetuating racial differences as part of a natural difference, rather outcome. With little or no regard for structural, societal, or historical causes for inequalities in school performance, NCLB exacerbates a different, more nuanced racism, a "color-blind racism," by perpetuating the notion that the achievement gap is the result of natural and/or cultural differences, rather than social outcomes.[80]

Race is both minimized and maximized. It is minimized because the historical and structural accumulations of advantage and/or disadvantage caused by race and racism are not considered to be factors that affect teaching or learning. All students are expected to meet the same expectations at the same time regardless of their point of origin. Race is maximized because racial groups are clearly delineated as determinants in how a school is evaluated. Because poor students, nonwhite students, and special education students historically do not test as well as middle-class whites, schools with high populations of these students are disproportionately rated as failing. Schools that want high ratings are, thus, encouraged to be as white and homogeneous as possible. Hence, an inevitable snowballing of negative consequences has unfolded.

Without ever mentioning race, schools are again profoundly resegregated and unequal. Persistent underachievement of traditionally marginalized children is used to legitimize historical racism, thus reigniting familiar fears of and age-old criticisms about diversity in public education. The heightened threat of race and diversity legitimizes zero tolerance for dress, behavior, language, and almost anything that is deemed deviant (non-white). Renewed talk of a new crisis in education energizes the push for privatizing education under the guise of choice as evidenced by the explosion of charter schools. Fear of the Unites States losing the global race in education justifies the implementation of a new set of standards, the Common Core, which arguably merely dump "new standards on old inequalities."[81] Children of color and difference are disproportionately targeted, labeled as criminal, and unfairly funneled into what is commonly known as the school-to-prison pipeline. As Charles Payne (2008) so aptly put it, we have seen "so much reform, so little change."[82] The ideology of color blindness bears great responsibility for ongoing racial inequalities in American education.

Trick or Trick? The Ideology of Color Blindness

I find little, if any, merit in the intent or impact of the ideology of color blindness. If the intent was to somehow bring about racial equality, it failed miserably. If the intent was to whitewash race by denying its influence on the lived experiences of black and white Americans, it did not succeed. If the intent was to squelch animosity and tension between the races, it was unsuccessful. The very idea of color blindness is, in and of itself, hopelessly ill-fated and can come to no good. The ideology of color blindness is, by nature, pathological and deceptive for several reasons.

First of all, the term is misleading. People who profess to be color-blind frequently make statements like "I don't even see color (e.g., race), all I see is the human being" or "I don't have a racist bone in my body." Contrary to the literal interpretation of the word, color blindness has nothing to do with not seeing race or skin color. As Leonardo (2009) clarified,

> Color-blindness is not actually "the inability to see race" and is an imperfect term. In the USA, color-blind people cannot fail to see race, but they can choose to see it in a particular way. In asserting that race should not matter in either social policy or transactions, color-blind people—especially whites— experience what psychologists call cognitive dissonance. Color-blindness prevents them from dealing with the racial conditioning of their behavior, which is considered as incidental rather than causal. Racial consequences may then be dismissed as unintentional or the common refrain that actions or words have been "taken out of context."[83]

The practical meaning of the term refers more to race and color-avoidance rather than color blindness. Avoiding the problem of racism will not make it go away.

Second, the ideology of color blindness falsely professes to stand on high ethical ground and claims victory over the moral dilemma of race in America. It supports, in theory, the belief that all Americans should be treated fairly and equally. Who would argue with that? The problem lies in the meaning of fair and equal. Color-blind ideology purports that fair means not taking race or its legacies into account, particularly for racial groups. "Race should not be seen, talked about, and race-talk should not be heard with too attentive of an ear because it is tantamount to victimology: see no race, speak no race, hear no race."[84] The meaning of equal is even trickier. Despite all of the rhetoric about equality, and "one America, indivisible,"[85] color-blind ideology is not committed to creating an egalitarian society, which would constitute the highest form of equality and, by necessity, be committed to equality of outcomes.[86] As stated previously, the ideology of color blindness only ensures a formal guarantee of equality before the law and draws attention, primarily, to ideals of rugged individualism, the myth of meritocracy, and the belief that people will rise and fall according to their own abilities rationalizes the inevitability of inequality.[87] Color-blind ideology would have us believe that while theoretically all men are created equal, inherent inequalities exist between and within racial groups that make inequity and inequality of outcomes unavoidable. If that sounds like double-talk, that is because it is!

Color-blind ideology is misleading in a third way. Proponents of color blindness would have us believe that the ideology revitalizes traditional liberalism.[88,89,90] But this is a fallacy. Color blindness does not so much revive the tenets of classical liberalism as it rearticulates those principles into a racial ideology designed to rationalize racially unfair situations.[91] Racial ideology, defined by Bonilla-Silva (2003), is "the racially based frameworks used by actors to explain and justify (dominant race) or challenge (subordinate race or races) the racial status quo,"[92] which is bundled into four frames that work conterminously as a color-blind racism or racism without racists. A brief description of each frame is provided here:

(1) Abstract liberalism involves using ideas associated with political liberalism (e.g., "equal opportunity," the idea that force should not be used to achieve social policy) and economic liberalism (e.g., choice, individualism) in an *abstract* manner to explain racial matters. Examples include framing

race-related issues in the language of liberalism to oppose affirmative action, claim moral high ground, and sanction individual choices that oppress or disadvantage others and justifying the right to segregated education.

(2) Naturalization is a frame that allows whites to explain away racial phenomena by suggesting they are natural occurrences. For example, denying *any* relationship between segregation and racism by claiming that it is natural for people to "gravitate toward likeness."

(3) Cultural racism is a frame that relies on culturally based arguments such as "Mexicans do not put much emphasis on education" or "Blacks have too many babies" to explain the standing of minorities in society.

(4) Minimization of racism is a frame that suggests discrimination is no longer a central factor affecting minorities' life chances ("It's better now than in the past" or "There is discrimination but there are plenty of jobs out there"). This frame allows whites to accuse minorities of being "hypersensitive," of using race as an "excuse," or of "playing the race card."[93]

By bundling these frames, whites get away with saying things like "I am all for equal opportunity, that's why I oppose affirmative action" or "I support integration, but I do not believe in forcing people to do anything they do not want to do." In short, the ideology of color blindness "explains contemporary racial inequality as the outcome of non-racial dynamics."[94] The result is an under-the-radar racism without racists: a color-blind, born-again racism.[95,96]

Fourth, the ideology of color blindness is not only self-deceiving and maybe even disingenuous, but also pathological. The free reign of color-blind racism has opened the floodgate for related racial diseases that adversely affect perpetrators as well as victims. I call attention to dysconscious racism and internalized racism, in particular, for two reasons: (1) Both negatively impact the quality and outcomes of teaching and learning, and (2) There is little hope of eradicating either of them as long as the racial ideology of color blindness prevails.

Perpetrators of color-blind racism often suffer unknowingly from a general dysconsciousness that leads to dysconscious racism. Dysconsciousness is "an uncritical habit of mind (including perceptions, attitudes, assumptions, and beliefs) that justifies inequity and exploitation by accepting the existing order of things as given."[97] When applied to attitudes and beliefs about race, Joyce E. King (1991) postulated,

> Dysconscious racism is not the *absence* of consciousness (that is, not unconsciousness) but an *impaired* consciousness or distorted way of thinking about race as compared to, for example, critical consciousness. Uncritical ways of thinking about racial inequity accept certain culturally sanctioned assumptions, myths, and beliefs that justify the social and economic advantages

White people have as a result of subordinating diverse others (Wellman, 1977). Any serious challenge to the status quo that calls this racial privilege into question challenges the self-identity of White people who have internalized these ideological justifications.[98]

Dysconscious racism is the "hallmark of racism" in general[99] and particularly injurious in educational settings. When combined with a racial ideology of color blindness, teachers whose conscious understanding is based on the faulty and uncritical thinking of dysconscious racism will continue to act in ways that stigmatize and oppress children who are not white. Likewise, everyday people will deny racism at all cost, which I believe is one reason why we are now witnessing racism with no racists. Victims of racism are often psychologically harmed by the ideology of color blindness as well.

Blacks (and to a lesser degree other racialized groups) frequently suffer from internalized racism. A number of black co-counselors and participants in black caucuses and black workshops devoted to reevaluation counseling studied internalized racism and its effects on African Americans. The consensus of these groups was that internalized racism is the primary means by which blacks have unconsciously perpetuated and participated in their own oppression. They alleged that "patterns of internalized oppression severely limit the effectiveness of every existing Black group" and, furthermore, that "no Black person in this society is spared."[100] As part of their liberation work, they identified what they call *chronic distress patterns* that describe the ways in which internalized racism operates within the black culture. The following is a description of how these patterns are manifested. The wording of each pattern has not been altered; therefore, the descriptions are in first person (i.e., I, we, us). The group is essentially "naming their voice"—and "naming own reality"[101] as black people fighting for the liberation of their people. Lipsky (2009) wrote:

What are some of the ways patterns of internalized racism operate among us?

- Individual relations—patterns of internalized feelings of rage, fear, indignation, frustration, and powerlessness are directed at each other— at other Black people—often those closest to us.
- Our children—we invalidate our children with fierce criticism and fault-finding, intending to "straighten them out," but in the process, destroying their self-confidence.
- Group effort—patterns of internalized racism cause us adults [*sic*] to find fault, criticize, and invalidate each other. This invariably happens when we come together in a group to address some important problem

or undertake some liberation project. What follows is divisiveness and disunity leading to despair and abandonment of the effort.

- Leadership—patterns of internalized oppression cause us to attack, criticize, or have unrealistic expectations of any one of us who has the courage to step forward and take on leadership responsibilities.

- Isolation from other Blacks—patterns of internalized racism have caused us to be deeply hurt by our brothers and sisters. We often develop defensive patterns of fear, mistrust, withdrawal, and isolation from other Blacks. The isolation which results from internalized racism can become so severe that a Black person may feel safer with and more trustful of White people than of Blacks.

- Internalized stereotypes—patterns of internalized racism have caused us to accept many of the stereotypes of Blacks created by the oppressive majority society. We have been taught to be angry at, ashamed of, anything that differs too much from a mythical ideal of the middle class of the majority culture—skin that is "too dark," hair that is "too kinky," dress, talk, and music that is "too loud."

- Narrowing of Black culture—internalized oppression leads us to accept a narrow and limiting view of what is "authentic" Black culture and behavior. Blacks have been ridiculed, humiliated, attacked, and isolated because they excelled in school; because they did or did not talk in a particular way.

- Mistrusting our thinking—institutionalized racism and the internalized racism which results from it have given rise to patterns which cause us to mistrust our own thinking.

- Needing to feel good right now—the patterns of powerlessness and despair that result from this "impossible" situation give rise to still another pattern common among us, which I will call the "feel good now" pattern. Drugs, alcohol, and other; addictions; compulsive and hurtful sexual behaviors; flashy consumerism; irrational use of money; all kinds of elaborate street rituals, games, posturing and pretenses that waste our energies—these are all related to patterns of internalized and racism and oppression.

- Survival—internalized oppression is a major factor in the perpetuation of so-called "getting by" or "survival behaviors." Learning to silently withstand humiliation by practicing on one another is an example—e.g., playing "the dozens." In order to survive we have learned also not to show our feelings ("cool" patterns) or to disguise them ("tough" patterns)— particularly feelings of tenderness, love, and zest.[102]

Based on my experiences and observations as a black woman, I propose that these interpretations represent the experiential knowledge of many other black voices. At first glance, some of these phenomena appear to mirror the claims of whites who blame racial inequality on the alleged pathology of black culture; however, there is one major difference. Those who have written about the "diseased" black culture marginalize the significance of race and dehistoricize racism and its impact on black Americans. Indeed, that is precisely what the ideology of color blindness would have us do. There can be no progress toward achieving sustained racial quality of educational opportunity and an egalitarian society in America as long as we remain psychologically crippled by the pathology of color blindness.

Have We Learned Anything?

One of my goals for writing this chapter was to illuminate the historical denial of the significance of race in America. To that end, I chose to open my discussion with a quote by Justice Sonia Sotomayor, the first Supreme Court justice of Hispanic heritage in American history. To review, Justice Sotomayor wrote:

> [We] ought not sit back and wish away, rather than confront, the racial inequality that exists in our society. It is this view that works harm, by perpetuating the facile notion that what makes race matter is acknowledging the simple truth that race *does* matter.[103]

This statement is an excerpt from Sotomayor's epic dissent in the 2014 Supreme Court decision in the *Schuette v. Coalition to Defend Affirmative Action*, Integration, and Immigration Rights and Fight for Necessary Equality by Any Means Necessary (BAMN) et al., case that upheld the state of Michigan's 2006 ban on affirmative action. I did not debate the specifics of affirmative action in this chapter but was intrigued by the fact that more than 100 years after the *Plessy* case, the U.S. Supreme Court continues to rearticulate the Fourteenth Amendment and that, in spite of the reality of persistent, even heightened, racial tension in the Obama era, and ongoing racial inequality of opportunity and outcome, the prevailing opinion in the highest court in the land supports a color-blind interpretation of the Constitution that ignores the legacy and significance of race in America. I was disturbed to see the the most influential judges in the nation perpetuate the notion that we are somehow beyond race. I was disheartened by their lingering fears and denials surrounding the race controversy. The Schuette case was not even allowed to be about the merit or constitutionality of affirmative action or race-conscious policies. Rather, the justices considered only if and how voters could prohibit states from exercising their otherwise available discretion to consider race in college and university admissions.

Writing for the plurality in the *Schuette* case, Justice Anthony Kennedy reasoned,

> democracy has the capacity—and the duty—to learn from its past mistakes; to discover and confront persisting biases, and by respectful, rationale deliberation to rise above the flaws and injustices. It is demeaning to use the democratic process to presume the voters are not capable of deciding such an issue of this sensitivity on decent and rational grounds.[104]

Kennedy suggested further that in spite of obvious racial tension, Americans have overcome the legacy of racism, yet he worried that race-based policies might aggravate racial tensions and revitalize racial stereotypes. Justice Antonin Scalia also feared that race-conscious admission considerations could further divide the United States along racial lines but may have been more concerned that such policies would compromise the equal protection rights of *all* under the Fourteenth Amendment. He advocated for a color-blind interpretation of the Constitution.[105] Drawing on a bit of history, Scalia wrote,

> As Justice Harlan observed over a century ago, "[o]ur Constitution is color-blind, and neither knows nor tolerates classes among citizens." Plessy v. Ferguson, 163 U.S. 537, 559 (91896) (dissenting opinion). The people of Michigan wish the same for their governing charter. It would be shameful for us to stand in the way.

These fundamental sentiments, rooted in fear and delusion, implied that acknowledging the enduring significance of race and racial inequality in American society is actually what makes race matter. In other words, race will matter less (or maybe eventually not at all) if we just stop talking about it. This twisted logic is misguided and disconcerting. Yet, it has far-reaching implications. The floodgates are now open for voters to take similar actions in states across the United States and the legal and political hegemony of the ideology of color blindness is likely fortified for years to come.

So, I ask: have we learned anything? The lessons have been there, and so have opportunities to learn from them, but I am afraid that we, as a nation, have chosen not to learn very much at all about race and racism that will actually aid us in confronting and resolving the race controversy in American schools and society. Many Americans, black and white, remain trapped in a tangled web of deception that has been and continues to be exacerbated by the pathology of color blindness. From the lessons of *Plessy v.*

Ferguson to the present, what we have chosen to learn is how to avert the race controversy, avoid honest, race-critical dialogue and antiracist action, and mask the fear and moral dilemma of racial inequality that plagues the United States.

I would argue that what we should have learned, and still need to learn, are at least four critical lessons.

(1) Race influences the lived experiences and life trajectories of black and white people.
(2) Racism still exists, and is a multifaceted, deep-seated, frequently taken-for-granted aspect of power relations in America.
(3) The enigma of race is not caused by talking about race, but rather by structural inequalities in our society, and the refusal to admit and address those inequalities.
(4) Racism is an inevitable part of the fiber of this nation; thus, it is futile to try to "whitewash race" and entertain "the myth of a color-blind society."[106]

I do not think, however, that the situation is hopeless.

Where Do We Go from Here?

A hopeful path forward will require a radical and far-reaching shift in how we conceptualize the role of race in education and politics. Americans must confront "the defence (and extension) of race inequity," "the question of racism and intentionality," and "the taken-for-granted routine privileging of white interests that goes unremarked in the political mainstream."[107] Furthermore, there must be some admission that, even though race inequity may not be the intended goal of education policy, neither is it accidental. "The patterning of racial advantage and inequity is structured in domination and its continuation represents a form of *tacit intentionality* on the part of white powerholders and policy-makers."[108] These are unsettling realities that Americans must acknowledge and challenge if the nation is to seriously shift toward an agenda that produces social justice and racial equity in education, in particular, and society, more generally.

Schools can drive this change, but only if we repurpose education. The aims of education must extend beyond neoliberal, color-blind goals. The primary ambition of education can no longer be to simply produce workers who will support the status quo and all of its inevitable inequities. Education must seek first to produce a nation of citizens critically aware of cultural politics and the "specific cultural rationality of social inequity in modern American society."[109] Teachers and leaders must focus their efforts on achieving common political interests through counterhegemonic, race-critical strategies. The repurposing of education, then, needs to occur not only in schoolhouses but also in higher education and teacher education programs.

Educational leaders must embrace and employ a liberatory pedagogical approach in teacher education that requires would-be teachers to take a more critical perspective of the social order and challenges them to examine their worldviews. Educators must be given opportunities to "recognize and evaluate the ideological influences that shape their thinking about schooling, society, themselves, and diverse others."[110] Practicing this kind of rigorous analysis and self-examination will enable teachers to guide students in the same just cause.

The path ahead will not be easy or comfortable, but few things worth doing are. The rewards, however, will be immeasurable.

Notes

1. *Schuette v. BAMN,* 572 U.S.___(2014) (Justice Sonia Sotomayor dissenting).
2. DuBois 1994, p. v.
3. Omi and Winant 1994.
4. Ibid., p. 55.
5. Ibid.
6. Essed 1991, p. 43.
7. Ibid.
8. Goldberg 2002, p. 118.
9. Marable 1992, p. 5.
10. Lorde 1992, p. 496.
11. Fredricksen 2002.
12. Solorzano, Ceja, and Yossi 2000, p. 61.
13. Goldberg 2009, p. 5.
14. Goldberg 2002, p. 104.
15. Ibid., p. 110.
16. Ibid.
17. Ibid.
18. Ibid., p. 111.
19. Giroux 2006, p. 13.
20. Omi and Winant 1994, p. 19.
21. Frankenberg 1993.
22. Donnelly et al. 2005, p. 7.
23. Sullivan 2006.

24. Omi and Winant 1994, p. 14.

25. Sullivan 2006, p. 127.

26. hooks 1998, p. 51.

27. Giroux 2006, p. 14.

28. Bonilla-Silva 2003, pp. 25–26.

29. DuBois 1969, p. 637.

30. *Plessy v. Ferguson.* 1896. Accessed June 7, 2015. http://www.ourdocuments .gov/doc.php?flash=true&doc=52.

31. *Plessy v. Ferguson Supreme Court of the United States* 163 U.S. 537. May 18, 1896. Accessed June 7, 2015. http://law2.umkc,edu/faculty/projects/ftrials/conlaw/ plessy.html.

32. http://americanhistory.about.com/od/usconstitution/a/14th-Amendment-Summary.htm.

33. Ibid.

34. Ibid.

35. http://www.ourdocuments.gov/doc.php?flash=true&doc=52&page= transcript.

36. Ibid.

37. Ibid.

38. Ibid.

39. Ibid.

40. http://chnm.gmu.edu/courses/nclc375/harlan.html (Harlan dissent).

41. Ibid.

42. Ibid.

43. Bell 2004, pp. 9–10.

44. Crenshaw et al. 1995, p. 6.

45. Smithsonian National Museum of American History (n.d.b.), p. 1.

46. Smithsonian National Museum of American History (n.d.a.), p. 1.

47. Crenshaw et al. 1995, p. xv.

48. Ibid., p. 29.

49. Ibid., p. 30.

50. Ibid., p. 31.

51. Ibid., p. 32.

52. Brown et al. 2003, p. vii.

53. Mann 1957, p. 87.

54. Reese 2005, p. 28.

55. Coleman et al. 1966.

56. Ciracelli 1969.

57. Jensen 1969.

58. Herrnstein 1971.

59. Omi and Winant 1994, p. 113.

60. Ibid., p. 116.

61. Shea, Kahane, and Sola 1989, p. 8.
62. Ibid.
63. Omi and Winant 1994, p. 116.
64. Shea, Kahane, and Sola 1989, p. 16.
65. Ibid., p. 330.
66. Goldberg 2009, p. 330.
67. Berliner and Biddle 1995.
68. Pincus 1984.
69. Shea, Kahane, and Sola, 1989.
70. Omi and Winant 1994, p. 148.
71. Ibid., p. 152.
72. National Education Summit 1996, p. 11.
73. Ravitch 2010.
74. Torres 2005, p. 67.
75. Lund and Carr 2008, p. 9.
76. Drakeford 2010, pp. 208–209.
77. Race to the Top Executive Summary 2009, p. 2.
78. Leonardo 2009, p. 134.
79. Freeman 2005.
80. Leonardo 2009.
81. Darling-Hammond 2004, p. 12.
82. Payne 2008.
83. Leonardo 2009, p. 188.
84. Ibid., p. 131.
85. Thernstrom and Thernstrom 1997, p. 530.
86. Michaels 2006.
87. Brown et al. 2003.
88. Jacoby 1998.
89. Sleeper 1997.
90. Thernstrom and Thernstrom 1997.
91. Bonilla-Silva 2003.
92. Ibid., p. 9.
93. Ibid., pp. 28–29.
94. Ibid., p. 2.
95. Ibid.
96. Ibid., p. 13.
97. King 1991, p. 135.
98. Ibid.
99. Ibid.
100. Lipsky 2009, p. 1.
101. Dixson and Rousseau 2006, p. 20.

102. Lipsky 2009, pp. 2–4.
103. *Schuette v. BAMN,* 572 U.S.___(2014) (Justice Sonia Sotomayor dissenting).
104. Ibid.
105. Ibid.
106. Gillborn 2005, p. 485.
107. Ibid.
108. Ibid.
109. King 1991, p. 143.
110. Ibid.

Bibliography

Bell, D. 2004. Silent Covenants: *Brown v. Board of Education and the Unfulfilled Hopes of Racial Reform.* Oxford, UK: University Press.

Berliner, D.C., and B.J. Biddle. 1995. *The Manufactured Crisis: Myths, Fraud, and the Attack of America's Public Schools.* New York: Basic Books.

Bonilla-Silva, E. 2003. *Racism without Racists: Colorblind Racism and the Persistence of Racial Inequality in the United States.* New York: Rowman & Littlefield.

Brown, M.K., M. Carnoy, T. Currie, T. Duster, D.B. Oppenheimer, M.M. Schultz, and D. Wellman. 2003. *The Myth of a Color-Blind Society.* Los Angeles, CA: University of California Press.

Ciracelli, V. 1969. *The Impact of Head Start: An Evaluation of the Effects of Head Start on Children's Cognitive and Affective Development (Ohio Report to the Office of Economic Opportunity).* Washington, DC: Clearinghouse for the Federal Scientific and Technical Information.

Coleman, J.S., E.Q. Campbell, C.J. Hobson, J. McPartland, A.M. Mood, F.D. Weinfeld and R.L. York. 1966. *Equality of Educational Opportunity.* Washington, DC: U.S. Office of Education, National Center of Educational Statistics.

Crenshaw, K., N. Gotanda, G. Peller, and K. Thomas. 1995. *Critical Race Theory: The Key Writings That Formed the Movement.* New York: The New York Press.

Darling-Hammond, L. 2004. "From 'Separate but Equal' to 'No Child Left Behind': The Collision of New Standards and Old Inequalities." In *Many Children Left Behind: How the No Child Left Behind Act Is Damaging Our Children and Our Schools,* eds. D. Meier and G. Wood (pp. 3–32). Boston, MA: Beacon Press.

Dixson, A.D., and C.K. Rousseau, eds. 2006. *Critical Race Theory in Education: All God's Children Got a Song.* New York: Routledge.

Donnelly, D.A., K. Cook, D. Van Ausdale, and L. Foley. 2005, January. "White Privilege, Color Blindness, and Services to Battered Women." *Violence against Women* 11 (1): 6037.

Drakeford, L.D. 2010. "What's Race Got to Do with It: A Historical Inquiry into the Impact of Color-Blind Racism on Racial Inequality in America's Public Schools." Available from ProQuest Information and Learning (AAT 3475944).

DuBois, W.E.B. 1969. *Black Reconstruction in America, 1860–1880.* New York: Atheneum (original work published 1935).

DuBois, W.E.B. 1994. *The Souls of Black Folk.* New York: Dover (original work published 1903).

Essed, P. 1991. *Everyday Racism: An Interdisciplinary Theory.* London, UK: Sage. 14th Amendment Summary. http://americanhistory.about.com/od/usconstitution/a/14-Amendment-Summary.htm.

Frankenberg, R. 1993. *White Women, Race Matters: The Social Construction of Whiteness.* Minneapolis: University of Minnesota.

Fredricksen, G.M. 2002. *Racism: A Short Story.* Princeton, NJ: University Press.

Freeman, A.D. 1995. "Legitimizing Racial Discrimination through Antidiscrimination Law: A Critical Review of Supreme Court Doctrine." In *Critical Race Theory: The Key Writings That Formed a Movement,* eds. K. Crenshaw, N. Gotanda, G. Peller, and K. Thomas (pp. 29–46). New York: New Press.

Freeman, J. 2005. "No Child Left Behind and the Denigration of Race." *Equity & Excellence in Education* 38: 190–199.

Gillborn, David. 2005, July. "Education Policy as an Act of White Supremacy: Whiteness, Critical Race Theory and Educational Reform." *Journal of Education Policy* 20 (4): 485–505.

Giroux, S.S. 2006. "On the state of race theory: A conversation with David Theo Goldberg." http://uchri.org/media/images/about-david-theo-goldberg/goldberg_jac_2006.pdf.

Goldberg, D.T. 2002. *The Racial State.* Oxford, UK: Wiley-Blackwell.

Goldberg, D.T. 2009. *The Threat of Race: Reflections on Racial Neoliberalism.* Oxford, UK: Wiley-Blackwell.

Herrnstein, R. 1971. "IQ." *Atlantic Monthly,* 43–64.

hooks, b. 1998. "Representations of Whiteness in the Black imagination." In *Black and White Writers on What It Means to Be White,* ed. D.R. Roediger (pp. 38–53). New York: Schocken Books.

Jacoby, T. 1998. *Someone Else's House: America's Unfinished Struggle for Integration.* New York: Free Press.

Jensen, A.R. 1969. "How Much Can We Boost I.Q. and Scholastic Achievement?" *Harvard Educational Review* 33: 1–123.

King, J. 1991. "Dysconscious Racism: Ideology, Identity, and the Miseducation of Teachers." *The Journal of Negro Education* 60 (2): 133–146.

Leonardo, Z. 2009. *Race, Whiteness, and Education.* New York: Routledge.

Lipsky, S. 2009. "Reevaluation Counseling." http://www.rc.org/publications/journals/Black_reemergence/br2/br2_5_sl.html.

Lorde, A. 1992. "Age, Race, Class, and Sex: Women Redefining Difference." In *Race, Class, and Gender: An Anthology,* eds. M. Anderson and P.H. Collins (pp. 495–502). Belmont, CA: Wadsworth.

Lund, D., and P.R. Carr, eds. 2008. *Doing Democracy: Striving for Political Literacy and Social Justice.* New York: Peter Lang.

Mann, H. 1957. *The Republic and the School: Classics in Education, No. 1,* ed. L.A. Cremin. New York: Teacher's College Press. Twelfth Annual Report (1948).

Marable, M. 1992. *Black America.* Westfield, NJ: Open Media.

Michaels, W.B. 2006. *The Trouble with Diversity: How We Learned to Love Diversity and Ignore Inequality.* New York: Henry Holt.

National Education Summit. 1996. "A Review of the 1996 National Education Summit." http://www.scribd.com/doc/29608185/A-Review-of-the-1996-National-Education-Summit.

Omi, M., and H. Winant. 1994. *Racial Formation in the United States: From the 1960s to the 1990s.* 2nd ed. New York: Routledge.

Payne, C.M. 2008. *So Much Reform, So Little Change: The Persistence of Failure in Urban Schools.* Cambridge, MA: Harvard University Press.

Pincus, F.L. 1984, Winter. "From Equity to Excellence: The Rebirth of Educational Conservatism." *Social Policy,* 50–56.

Plessy v. Ferguson, 163 U.S. 537 (1896). Primary source document: Judge Harlan's Dissent. http://chnm.gmu.edu/courses/nclc375/harlan.html.

Plessy v. Ferguson, U.S 163 U.S. 537 (1896). http://americanhistory.about.com/od/usconstitution/a/14th-Amendment-Summary.htm.

Race to the Top Executive Summary. 2009, November. Washington, DC: U.S. Department of Education. http://www.docstoc.com/docs/16011856/Race-to-the-Top-Program-Executive-Summary-Rules-November-2009.

Ravitch, D. 2010. *The Death and Life of the Great American School System: How Testing and Choice Are Undermining Education.* New York: Basic Books.

Reese, W.J. 2005. *America's Public Schools: From the Common School to "No Child Left Behind."* Baltimore, MD: Johns Hopkins University Press.

Shea, C., E. Kahane and P. Sola, eds. 1989. *The New Servant of Power: A Critique of the 1980s School Reform Movement.* New York: Greenwood Press.

Sleeper, J. 1997. *Liberal Racism: How Fixating on Race Subverts the American Dream.* New York: Penguin Books.

Smithsonian National Museum of American History. n.d.a. "The Integrationists' Argument in the Decision: A Landmark in American Justice, Separate Is Not Equal." http://americanhistory.si.edu/brown/history/5-decision/integration-argument.html.

Smithsonian National Museum of American History. n.d.b. "The Segregationists' Argument in the Decision: A Landmark in American Justice, Separate Is Not Equal." http://americanhistory.si.edu/brown/history/5-decision/segregation-argument.html.

Solorzano, D., M. Ceja, and T. Yosso. 2000. "Critical Race Theory, Racial Microaggressions, and the Campus Racial Climate: The Experiences of African American College Students." *The Journal of Negro Education* 69 (1/2): 60–73.

Sullivan, S. 2006. *Revealing Whiteness: The Unconscious Habits of Racial Privilege.* Bloomington, IN: Indiana University Press.

Thernstrom, A., and S. Thernstrom. 1997. *America in Black and White: One Nation, Indivisible.* New York: Simon & Schuster.

Torres, C.A. 2005. "No Child Left Behind: A Brainchild of Neoliberalism and American Politics." *New Politics* 10 (2), 1–13.

Transcript of *Plessy v. Ferguson.* 1896. http://www.ourdocuments.gov/doc.php?flash=true&doc=52&page=transcript.

Chapter 3

Schools as Conduits of Racism: How Mind-Sets, Policies, and Practices Impact Historically Marginalized Students

*Ayana Allen, Marcia Watson,
Cherese D. Childers-McKee, Laurie Garo,
and Chance W. Lewis*

Introduction

Race has seeped into American schools through various systems of institutional and inferential racism (underlying "belief of power, privilege, and representation that reconfirms the White hegemonic order").[1] In this vein, race has been manipulated to enforce systems of categorization, exclusion, and oppression of students of historically marginalized groups. Schools are microcosms of the society at large and serve as conduits and harbors of perpetual racial inequality. Bearing this in mind, our discussion is three part in nature. First, we highlight the historical context of race and racism in society as a whole, the justice system in part, and education in particular. Second, rooted in a critical race theoretical paradigm, our discussion illuminates the ways in which schools often directly and indirectly impact the social/emotional and academic identity development of students. Third, we demonstrate the ways in which schools perpetuate racial inequality through deficit ideologies and the hidden curriculum, color blindness, and disproportional discipline policies and practices. Recommendations are presented to encourage more equitable, democratic schools which are epicenters of social justice and achievement.

The Historical Context

Social scientists and anthropologists alike declare race as a social construct. Yet, the dichotomous relationships between racial groups are authentic and well documented throughout history. As early as the ninth century AD, there are historical evidences of racial exclusion. Hamitic hypothesis, which originates from the recorded conflict between Hebrews and Canaanites, undergirds racial conflict even today. In fact, this theory was used to justify the enslavement of Africans in the 18th and 19th centuries and was residually adapted to other historical moments of disenfranchisement thereafter—like Jim Crow. Using this hypothesis, the idea of African inferiority solidified.

During the 19th and 20th centuries, scientific inquiry and discovery became paramount to understanding human relations, interactions, and hierarchy. Using the same tales of biblical and ethnic superiority, the 20th century experienced brash intersections of religious beliefs and racist research. Sociology and anthropology became avenues for the propagation of these Hamitic claims, which created long-lasting effects on racial concepts. As Sanders explains, "Historians who began to compile histories of Africa wrote with an unconscious racial bias, and accepted the dicta of the discoverers of the continent indisputable proven facts and presented them as historical explanations of African past."[2] Even prior to transatlantic slavery, blacks were seen as inferior and oppositional to whites. Once enslaved, this inferiority theory also seeped deeply into the American judicial system. Legislation from these key court cases altered the status of racial inclusion, educational attainment, and social opportunity for minorities.

Court cases of the 19th century determined the trajectory of race relations in the United States. Most notably, there are three seminal cases that crystallized racial hierarchies on the basis of racial origin and skin color. Decisions from these cases helped ferment social stratification that impacted many confounding factors of education, equality, and accessibility. *People v. Hall* (1854) codified racial groupings and introduced a white versus nonwhite racial binary. This landmark case helped to solidify the correlation between whiteness and citizenry. The *Dread Scott v. Sandford* (1856) case, most known for the "Dred Scott decision," declared African Americans as noncitizens for whom the Bill of Rights did not apply. This constitutionalized the subjugation of African Americans, even several decades post-emancipation. Last, the ruling from the *Plessy v. Ferguson* (1896) case deemed "separate but equal" conditions as constitutional for African American citizens.[3] The compilation of these cases forcibly confirmed the connection between race and citizenship. In result, those who were considered ethnically or phenotypically descendants of Europe had an increased chance of social mobility.

Situating each of the aforementioned court cases in the context of education, James Anderson (1988) suggests that education has long been used as a tool for social mobility for those racially underprivileged. This is despite the unwelcoming environment many minorities inhabited in post-emancipation. In the 20th century, African Americans expressed the need for educational equality and desegregation. The 1954 *Brown v. Board of Education* case spawned from a dissatisfaction of unequal educational conditions. The 1965 *Civil Rights Act* initiated significant desegregation efforts through changed legislation. Despite eventually obtaining racial desegregation, the gloomy survey of U.S. history unveils a tumultuous past, based on racism and inaccurate theory.

As stated, the idea that race is biological has irreversibly altered the course of U.S. history. As noted by the American Anthropological Association, "Ultimately 'race' [is] an ideology about human differences, [which] was subsequently spread to other areas of the world."[4] Alongside judicial cases, which socially prevented racial equality, this ideology was also pervasively used in research during the 19th and 20th centuries. Intelligence (IQ) testing, for example, was considered a reliable measure of human cognitive capacity in the 20th century. Lewis Terman, who is considered the father of psychological intelligence, repeatedly tested the difference of intelligence between racial groups. In turn, psychologists alike documented scientific evidence of racial—and moral—intelligence quotas. Compounding on Terman's studies, researchers Richard Hernstein and Charles Murray released *The Bell Curve: Intelligence and Class Structures in American Life* in 1994, which dangerously defined black and white cognitive abilities. Studies such as these have permanently demarcated nonwhites as inferior. With the latter study published only 20 years ago, this leaves the American racial landscape still delicately unsettled. These damages have direct implications on teacher education, teacher perceptions, and classroom culture, because of the long-lasting misnomers of racial hierarchy.

Within the 21st century, race still carefully tarries between past and present. Today's transnational world positions race in many nuanced "post" contexts.[5] These contexts each codified in trendy terms—like racial progressivism, post-racialism, and color blindness—continuously ignore the historical qualms of racism. The naive ideology of post-racialism and the implementation of color blindness in many teacher education programs, for example, converges two very conflicting views of diversity. These racially progressive models often fail to address structural impediments that prohibit organic progressivism. Although structural racism is arguably less overt than blatantly racist policies and practices, it is no less harmful. These are conditions that post-racialism—and color-blind theories—cannot capacitate thoroughly. When considering over 80 percent of public education teachers are white,[6] the need to critically examine the intersections of racial dissonance and consonance in today's classrooms is paramount.

Critical Race Theory

Our exploration of race in education is situated within a critical theoretical paradigm. Critical race theory (CRT) has been used extensively to describe the experiences and perspectives of people of color. CRT interrogates the impact and influence of the pervasiveness of race on U.S. society. CRT has been defined as a "framework that can be used to theorize, examine and challenge the ways race and racism implicitly and explicitly impact social structures, practices and discourses."[7] CRT is based on the following tenets: (1) the permanence of racism; (2) a challenge to dominant ideology; (3) the importance of narratives, storytelling, and counternarratives; (4) the social constructedness of race; (5) the critique of liberalism and a belief in interest convergence; and (6) the importance of critical race praxis or the idea that ending racial oppression will contribute to the end of other oppression. CRT, although it originated in legal studies, was popularized in educational circles following the publication of Ladson-Billings and Tate's (1995) influential article, *Toward a Critical Race Theory of Education*. In the decades that followed, CRT has been used as a framework to discuss a variety of educational issues. For example, Ladson-Billings contends that an analysis of class and gender alone fails to adequately account for pervasive educational inequality. CRT represents a powerful vehicle by which to theorize inequality in schools. It works to deconstruct stock stories that serve to oppress and marginalize students of color by putting forth the idea of "naming one's own reality"[8] and enabling students to create counterstories that speak back to oppressive mainstream narratives. Such liberation from oppression is best understood within the framework of social interaction and environmental context.

Social Constructivism and Environmental Contextual Impact

Interpretive theory views schools as spaces by which meaning is constructed through the social interaction of people within the setting. Interpretivism "emphasizes micro level qualitative analysis of interactions within schools and classrooms . . . students are engaged in the process of constructing culture through daily interactions."[9] Human beings respond to each other and to their surroundings not so much on the basis of any objective or inherent meanings but out of meanings assigned to people and settings by the people within those settings. An individual's reality is created via social interactions with others within the social, institutional, or organizational environments in which they live, work, attend school, as well as within the context of race, class, and gender. Interaction and the assignment of meaning are affected by people's past experiences and beliefs, their current experiences in the given setting, and what they come to believe as interaction unfolds. This process is called the social construction of meaning.

Human behavior can be studied within the context of a person's past and current history, including family influences and experiences, demographic details (race/ethnicity, gender, socioeconomic status), schooling, peer group(s), employment, and, where applicable, interactions with the criminal justice system or other type of institution. These varied components of individual behavioral development also influence the opinions of others within social and institutional settings, thus impacting the way others treat the individual. In school, for example, teacher opinions of students may influence teacher expectation and degree of fairness in academic and disciplinary matters. Group dynamics among like-minded youth (peers) or youth belonging to the same social network may likewise provide structure and normative behaviors for youth to follow, rules to live by, and ways to interpret their world, including the school setting. Educators may also view the social constructivist perspective as a way to encourage collaborative learning and as a vehicle for social transformation. Just as students take social cues from one another, they may develop new learning behaviors through transformative pedagogy.

Schools are social contexts that have a direct impact on the self-perception and identity development of students. "A dissonant context is one in which a salient characteristic of the individual is at variance with that of the predominant group in a given social context, particularly in the case of school."[10] Verna and Runion contend that the effects of dissonance are mediated by whether the dissonant context involves immersion into a social group more or less highly regarded than one's own. In this vein, the experiences of historically marginalized groups of students' engagement in contextual dissonant environments such as school greatly impact student sense of self and development of self-concept as "school climate mediates the effects of contextual dissonance."[11] Gray-Little and Carels discussed the influence of social dissonance as it relates to students' self-evaluation and school performance which is illuminated through three specific areas: (1) racial composition, (2) socioeconomic dissonance, and (3) the impact of the reference group.[12] Gray-Little and Carels's findings demonstrated that the association of racial dissonance with academic self-evaluation and achievement among different age racial groups suggest that racial composition can contribute to understanding variations in self-esteem and achievement:

> Dissonance is concerned with social contexts which include level of social support, the opportunities for friendship, and the number of people with a shared value system. These features of the social setting affect the appraisals that one receives from others, as well as the comparisons that are made between the self and others. The study of dissonance most frequently has centered on the school environment because the school is such an important and powerful social setting for them.[13]

Identity formation is an important factor as it is often impacted by the environmental context of schools. Brittian (2012) defined identity formation as a developmental process which includes an individual's contribution to his or her sense of self and the given context's actions to activate, hinder, or foster the process of establishing identity. Students must manage and navigate their own development within the given context to create their social identities. Social identities encompass understanding social categorization, assessing the potential for group membership to make a positive contribution to positive social identity, and then integrating, altering, or discarding components of the social category into self-concept. Chavous et al. contended: "African American youths' beliefs about self and race relate to their educational and social development through their attitudes and self-evaluations around education."[14] If contextual supports are lacking (dissonant contexts), negative identity formation can occur for historically marginalized racial groups. Moreover, schools often serve as harbors of racist and exclusionary policies and practices that maintain dissonant environmental contexts.

Schools as Conduits of Racism and Racial Inequality

Deficit Ideology

Historically, deficit ideology has been linked to race- and class-based oppression and provided support for the belief in the intellectual and genetic inferiority of people of color. Although scholars have debunked emerging deficit-based theories as racist and not empirically sound, deficit-based models have continually resurfaced in the guise of new theories and approaches. In educational settings, proponents of deficit theory suggest that students' failure in school occurs as a result of internal deficits that cause "limited intellectual ability, linguistic shortcomings, lack of motivation to learn, and immoral behavior."[15] Schools populated by students of color are filled with deficit-based policy and instructional approaches that vilify students' race and culture and perpetuate negative perceptions of them rather than interrogating inequality, inadequate resources, and deficit beliefs held by teachers.

Solorzano and Yosso describe examples of deficit and racist ideologies that can be viewed in the informal language in education. They identify common stereotypes used in the media to describe blacks and Latinos such as "dumb," "dirty," or "lazy" and suggest that in education, coded language such as "uneducable" or "lack motivation" is often used to describe students of color in similar ways.[16] In delineating the underlying deficit nature of the commonly used terms, "at risk" and "culture of poverty," Margonis suggests "at risk" is often more "palatable" to educators because it does not immediately imply an idea that is race, class, or culturally based as did the term "culture of poverty" and that "the apparent neutrality is the concepts greatest ideological strength: a deficit conception with egalitarian pretensions."[17] The term "at-risk" continues to be used frequently in educational circles to describe students, usually poor and/or black or Latino/Latina, who presumably have some individual or familial characteristics that prevent them from being successful in school.

Ladson-Billings's reframing of the achievement gap further illustrates the deficit ideas that influence the education of students of color. Ladson-Billings asserts, "We do not have an achievement gap, we have an education debt" which is no surprise considering the "historical, economic, sociopolitical, and moral decisions and policies that characterize our society." Yet these forces that are at work in teacher perceptions and students' beliefs about themselves are often invisible or not readily apparent. For example, Ladson-Billings describes experiences of working with preservice teachers in which "culture is randomly and regularly used to explain everything" and is frequently used by teachers as "one of the primary explanations for everything from school failure to problems with behavior management and discipline."[18] She attributes this tendency to three main components: teacher education's heavy emphasis on psychological theory as opposed to anthropology and other social sciences, teachers' feeling of discomfort at discussing issues of race which make it easier to fall back on the culture argument, and the tendency to explain student failure as an individual deficit rather than as a symptom of school culture. Ladson-Billings also suggests that white teachers view themselves as "just normal" and without culture, thus suggesting that culture is a "code word" for "difference" and "deviance."[19] Similarly, in a study of a group of white preservice teachers, Marx found that teachers viewed themselves as normal, antiracist, and not prejudiced, while simultaneously viewing students of color as deficit in language, intelligence, and culture. Perry, Steele, and Hilliard view deficit ideology as "so deeply embedded in society's beliefs about the achievement potential of students of color, particularly African American students, that both students and teachers need powerful counternarratives to challenge that ideology."[20]

Deficit ideology about students of color is upheld and fostered through the workings of the hidden curriculum of schools. Described as the implicit messages that students receive about values, beliefs, and acceptable behavior, the hidden curriculum consists of the unspoken, taken-for-granted components of the school environment. Although the hidden curriculum was traditionally seen as a mechanism to maintain class hierarchies, it also interacts with common racial stereotypes and controlling images. The influences of racist narratives and controlling images on teacher and student behavior become especially dangerous when normalized and systematized as a part of the hidden curriculum. Furthermore, as urban schools become increasingly segregated, the hidden curriculum, operating through racialized lenses, contributes to the overwhelmingly negative characterizations that plague the urban schools' settings of many students of color.

While the deficit ideologies that underlie the hidden curriculum influence teacher perception of students, they also influence the ways in which students perform their raced and gendered identities. The hidden curriculum shapes and influences student behaviors through implicit messages about what is normal, respectable, and valued. In conceptualizing the notion of the "looking glass self," Sensoy and DiAngelo suggest that students negotiate perceptions of themselves based on how they are perceived by others and how they perceive themselves in relation to others They suggest that "the looking glass self includes the concept that the process of learning to know who we *are* is shaped by learning who we are *not*."[21] Students of color confront negative media stereotypes about themselves, potentially tense interaction with teachers in the school environment, and through the hidden curriculum implicitly learn that they are outside of the acceptable norm. Therefore, because behaviors of students of color are often pathologized and seen as barriers to success, a more strengths-based approach would view student behaviors as acts of agency in response to oppression. Scholars have argued that there must be a more complex and nuanced analysis of individual and collective agency in resisting oppression.[22] Therefore, a greater understanding of the ways in which students of color attempt to resist oppression in schools holds implications for creating educational settings that are safer, more empowering, and more transformative.

Although deficit understandings of the education of students of color have been insidious and ongoing, educators have challenged these notions with counter discourses of strength and resilience. Brown and Brown define counter discourses as "knowledge, theories, and histories that emerge as a direct challenge to commonly held deficit-oriented beliefs about racial groups and social phenomenon."[23] Through theories of culturally relevant pedagogy, critical youth studies, and other strengths-based approaches, scholars have attempted to disrupt pervasive deficit depictions of students of color. For example, Milner presents counternarratives of teachers who counter deficit ideas about their urban students through a variety of strategies, including immersing themselves in students' lives, viewing the influences of race and culture in students' lives, and developing critical consciousness of privilege and oppression. Further, it is argued that much of traditional research on youth has been characterized by universalizing and deficit-based portrayals in which youth appear at risk, delinquent, troubled, and completely susceptible to the control of societal forces. In contrast, critical youth scholars advocate for research that displays the nuances and complexities of youth agency and their potential for resistance. Akom, Cammarota, and Ginwright claim that critical youth studies "goes beyond traditional pathological approaches to assert that young people have the ability to analyze their social context, to collectively engage in critical re-search, and resist repressive state and ideological institutions."[24]

Color Blindness

The color-blind approach, metaphorically exemplified in the "melting pot" model, glorifies group similarities and ignores racial differences. In essence, color-blind multiculturalism is a tenet of assimilation, which mystifies ra-cial phenotypes and naively seeks solidarity and intergroup unification. Rattan and Ambady suggest that the origins of color blindness stem from efforts to increase racial equality. More simplistically, the color-blind per-spective is known as a "point of view [that] sees racial and ethnic group membership as irrelevant to the ways individuals are treated."[25] Supporters of color blindness attribute student *similarities*—versus differences—as the litmus for identification.

Coupled in views of post-racialism and "post-Obamaism," color blind-ness provides a one-dimensional, binary view of multicultural education. Truthfully, several white citizens and people of color alike believe racial discrimination is a dated phenomenon and not reflective of the current political landscape. This belief relies heavily on the beauty of Ameri-can individualism and self-efficacy, which is rooted in white privilege. Hartmann and Gerteis (2005) warn about the intersections of political views and multiculturalism and posit that beliefs regarding multiculturalism are overwhelmingly viewed as inseparable to political affiliation. For example, color blindness and assimilation—as approaches to multiculturalism—are associated with *conservative* political viewpoints. Proponents of more vis-ible diversity, on the other hand, are overwhelmingly considered *liberal* in political affiliation. Within education, district and state approaches to mul-ticulturalism are usually influenced by political stances and contemporary nuances. Researchers discovered the adaptation of color-blind ideologies often stems from a need for "political correctness." Usually, this derives from the need to appear unprejudiced and avoid topics of oppressive history.[26]

Naively, many teacher education programs posit substantive moral bonds of the school and classroom culture, which are taught to supersede cul-tural and racial differences. Although seemingly harmless in theory, the de-structiveness of this concept manifests when put into practice. The fictional ability to implement organic color blindness is documented in a study by Ito and Urland. Here, researchers found that complete color blindness in-volving ignoring descriptive identification about group identity is virtually impossible. This is due to the obligatory, and often unconscious, tendency to rely on race for descriptive purposes. From here, it is almost impossible not to categorize certain groups based on race.

More practically, Milner suggests that teacher perceptions, especially regarding race and color, come with automatic assumptions and misnomers. He warns that often teachers consider some students as a liability on the basis of race, which contaminates the learning environment in the classroom. These perceptions eventually eradicate the utility, and abstractness, of true color blindness. Thus, when the theory of color blindness meets the classroom, the utopian ideal of "oneness" diverges.[27] In saying so, pragmatically, color blindness fails to respond to classroom diversity.

Within the context of schooling, more assertive forms of multiculturalism are needed. It is imperative for teachers to avoid color blindness and embrace a more encompassing perspective on race and diversity. As a solution, we suggest "color consciousness" in American schooling.[28] This effective step in multiculturalism confronts delicate topics, such as race and privilege. Moreover, color consciousness debunks the hegemonic, monolithic, and dismissive perspectives of current policies that often dilute the value of student culture in the classroom. For teachers and teacher education programs, a more encompassing approach to multiculturalism is critically important for the vitality of culturally competent educators. The application of color consciousness and multiculturalism is a strong tool by which to strategically address discipline disproportionality among students of color and their white counterparts. Furthermore, these tools offer a lens by which to examine often harmful policies such as zero tolerance and the school-to-prison pipeline.

Zero Tolerance, Discipline Disproportionality, and the School-to-Prison Pipeline

The use of "zero tolerance" policies by schools can be dated back to the 1980s, a period of prolific state and federal law enforcement on the "War on Drugs."[29] Zero tolerance is a policy that involves swift punishment for what amounts to minor offenses in attempted efforts to deter crime and reduce the likelihood of reoccurrence. As youth arrests for violent crime rose steadily between 1980 and 1994, zero tolerance became the widespread practice in public schools and ultimately led to the 1994 Gun-Free Schools Act passed by Congress in efforts to "get tough on crime."[30] With this act, students found with a weapon in school received automatic expulsion for at least one year. While youth violence declined steadily after 1994, the zero tolerance approach was increasingly applied to minor school disciplinary policies and practices whereby students were suspended for up to 10 days for such trivial infractions as profanity, fighting, smoking, truancy, and behaviors that disrupt classroom order and learning but are not against the law. As a result, annual short-term suspensions have nearly doubled from 1.7 million in 1974 to 3.1 million in 2001.[31]

Zero tolerance policies set the precedence for police presence on school campuses and often the police took over the disciplinary role once held solely by school administrators. In consequence, there have been significant increases in student arrests and referrals to juvenile court, which has led to the "school-to-prison pipeline" phenomenon. Teske and Huff stated, "Zero tolerance policies contribute to the existing racial and ethnic disparities in discipline within public education. These inequalities more often than not produce lower graduation rates among minority youth, which contributes to higher rates of criminality among these youth."[32] Others have noted have noted that African American students, students who are economically disadvantaged, and special education students are groups that are disproportionately suspended. Out-of-school suspensions for minor discipline infractions serve to marginalize students who tend to fall behind academically while suspended. Marginalized students are at greater risk for school failure, dropping out, and falling into criminal activity for economic survival.

Practitioners of zero tolerance seldom assess reasons for disruptive student behavior and/or develop interventions relevant to the reasons. Zero tolerance policies, rather, rely on punishment alone for behavior modification, a practice that has proven to be ineffective in changing behavior. Punitive methods of discipline, for example, suspension, expulsion, and/or arrest, are also exclusionary and disproportionately affect marginalized students. In this way zero tolerance policies contribute to disparities in academic outcomes for these students. Disproportionate suspension of black and Latino students leads also to the racial and ethnic disparities in the juvenile justice system, "thereby lending additional support to the 'school-to-prison pipeline' argument; that is, removing students from positive learning environments and criminalizing normative immaturity increases the risk of incarceration."[33] Research also points to significant numbers of adult inmates who dropped out of school lending further evidence of a school-to-prison pipeline. Deficit ideologies and color blindness practices as examined in this discussion may also influence school staff toward the pathological characterization of students and the assignment of other behavior problem–related labels. Many students may well be angered at being viewed as deficit and at having their cultural identity devalued or denied. Their anger may be misinterpreted as insubordinate attitudes which can potentially fuel punishment-oriented discipline. Transformative approaches can empower students to understand the role of hegemonic forces that have shaped their current predicament and assist in liberating them toward a more enriching educational experience. In light of our discussion, we posit recommendations to combat schools' perpetuation of racism and racial inequality.

Recommendations

The following research-based recommendations contribute to fostering more positive school settings that acknowledge the historical influences of race/class oppression and build on students' cultural strengths in order to encourage more equitable, democratic schools which are epicenters of social justice and achievement.

- **Move from deficit ideologies to asset-based approaches**

    It is imperative to center the voices of students of color through collaborative, participatory-style activities in which teachers actively engage students in asking critical questions about their school and community settings. Likewise, schools should promote antiessentialist ways of viewing students of color by highlighting historical and social influences on identity. While adhering to racialized discourses and deficit models is harmful, even positive counternarratives risk essentializing people of color who may have varied social and educational experiences. Lastly, cultivate teacher education and training that centers advocacy, social justice teaching, and awareness of the influences of power, privilege, and oppression on school settings. Through models and descriptions of programs that successfully challenge inequality, educators are able to view practical examples of social justice theory in action.

- **Eradicate beliefs that color blindness is an adequate approach to multiculturalism.**

    Color blindness is simply a masked form of assimilation, which is antithetical to diversity. It is important for researchers and practitioners to identify the dangers of this naive concept, which is damaging for students.

- Promote teacher education programs that cultivate, rather than disregard, student culture. For transformative learning to take place, topics of race are critical to the discussion.
- Encourage educators, practitioners, and researchers to embrace a "color conscious" ideology. Color consciousness critically examines race and promotes diversity. Pragmatically, color consciousness is best cultivated through critical reflection, positive teacher and student relationships, and student-centered classroom environment.

- **Institute fair and consistent disciplinary policy and practice.**

    Disruptive behaviors in school do indeed interfere with teaching and learning and must be addressed. Many schools, however, place an overreliance on zero tolerance methods of school discipline for disruptive behaviors as they are limited in resources to effectively handle disorderly students. Changes must be implemented, however, in school disciplinary policy and practice to reverse the dependence on zero tolerance measures. Toldson and Lewis's recommendations include establishing clear, fair, consistent, and strictly enforced rules that maintain a positive learning environment without disproportionately punishing black males or any other group; providing mentoring, tutoring, and counseling to improve academic engagement for students who are slower learners or who come from stressful life situations and social inequalities that impact behavior and place them at greater risk for delinquency; providing teachers with cultural awareness training to counter "racially prejudiced hegemony"[34] and prioritize healthy and nurturing learning environments of teacher empathy, dignity, and respect, and the belief in the excellence that resides within each and every child.

- **Invoke measures to strengthen students' connection to schooling.**

    Connection to school is a protective factor against the often dissonant environmental contexts that historically marginalized students encounter in schools. Students tend to participate in risky behaviors less frequently, experience decreased emotional distress, demonstrate improved academic performance, and exhibit a greater likeliness to graduate when they feel connected to school. Such connection to schooling is more likely to happen under culturally inclusive curricula and pedagogy and when students feel they are in the presence of school personnel who genuinely care about them. Schools should be places where children and youth feel safe, receive nurturing attention and adult guidance toward healthy development, and connect socially and culturally within the curricula and the school community.

Conclusion

Schools can no longer claim to operate in a "post-Brown"/"post-racial context." Rather, we must examine the ways in which schools serve as institutions that often perpetuate racism and racial disharmony. As demonstrated in this discussion, racism is an evolving construct that must be aggressively combated to ensure that all students have access to opportunities that will greatly benefit their academic and social well-being. Furthermore, schools must become more inclusive spaces that eliminate issues of colorism, deficit ideology, and disproportional acts of discipline to encourage more equitable, democratic schools which are epicenters of social justice and achievement.

Notes

1. Patton 2004.
2. Saunders 1969, p. 502.
3. Rattan and Ambady 2013; Ullucci and Battey 2011.
4. American Anthropological Association 1998.
5. Mittelman 2009; Napolitano 2009.
6. Kunjufu 2002.
7. Yosso 2005, p. 70.
8. Delgado and Stefancic 1993, p. 462.
9. deMarrias and LeCompte 1999, p. 26.
10. Verna and Runion 2001, p. 450.
11. Ibid., p. 451.
12. Gray-Little and Carels 1997.
13. Ibid., p. 109.
14. Chavous et al. 2003, p. 1085.
15. Valencia 1997.
16. Solorzano and Yosso 2001, p. 4.
17. Margonis 1992.
18. Ladson-Billings 2006b.
19. Ladson-Billings 2006a.
20. Sleeter 2004, p. 134.
21. Sensoy and DiAngelo 2012, p. 24.
22. Best 2007.
23. Brown and Brown 2012, p. 11.

24. Akom, Cammarota, and Ginwright 2008, p. 12.
25. Schofield 1997, p. 252.
26. Norton et al. 2006.
27. Ito and Urland 2003; Rattan and Ambady 2013.
28. Ullucci and Battey 2011.
29. Teske and Huff 2011.
30. Kang-Brown et al. 2013.
31. Teske and Huff 2011, p. 88.
32. Ibid., p. 15.
33. Ibid., p. 90.
34. Toldson and Lewis 2012, p. 35.

Bibliography

Aarim-Heriot, Najia. 2003. *Chinese Immigrants, African Americans, and Racial Anxiety in the United States, 1848–1882*. Urbana: University of Illinois.

Akom, A.A., Julio Cammarota, and Shawn Ginwright. 2008. "Youthtopias: Towards a New Paradigm of Critical Youth Studies." *Youth Media Reporter* 2 (4): 1–30.

"American Anthropological Association's Statement on 'Race.'" aaanet.org. Last modified May 17, 1998. http://www.aaanet.org/stmts/racepp.htm.

American Civil Liberties Union (ACLU). 2013. "Handcuffs on Success: The Extreme School Discipline Crisis in Mississippi Public Schools." MS: ACLU, 25 pp.

Anderson, James D. 1988. *The Education of Blacks in the South, 1865–1930*. Chapel Hill: University of North Carolina.

Anyon, Jean. 1980. "Social Class and the Hidden Curriculum of Work." *Journal of Education* 162 (1): 67–92.

Apfelbaum, Evan. A., Michael I. Norton, and Samuel R. Sommers. 2012. "Racial Colorblindness: Emergence, Practice, and Implications." *Current Directions in Psychological Science* 21: 205–209.

Apfelbaum, Evan A., Samuel R. Sommers, and Michael I. Norton. 2008. "Seeing Race and Seeming Racist? Evaluating Strategic Color-Blindness in Social Interaction." *Journal of Personality and Social Psychology* 95: 918–932.

Bell, Derrick. 2004. *Silent Covenants: Brown v. Board of Education and the Unfulfilled Hopes for Racial Reform*. New York: Oxford.

Berry, Theodorea Regina. 2009. "Women of Color in a Bilingual/Dialectal Dilemma: Critical Race Feminism against a Curriculum of Oppression in Teacher Education." *International Journal of Qualitative Studies in Education* 22 (6): 745–753.

Berry, Theodorea Regina. 2010. "Engaged Pedagogy and Critical Race Feminism." *Educational Foundations* 24 (3): 19–26.

Best, Amy L., ed. 2007. *Representing Youth: Methodological Issues in Critical Youth Studies*. New York: New York University Press.

Bonilla-Silva, Eduardo. 2010. *Racism without Racists: Color-Blind Racism and the Persistence of Racial Inequality in the United States*. Lanham: Rowman & Littlefield.

Braz, Rose, and Myesha Williams. 2011. "Diagnosing the Schools-to-Prison Pipeline: Maximum Security, Minimum Learning." Chapter 5 in *Challenging the Prison Industrial Complex: Activism, Arts & Educational Alternatives*, ed. Stephen J. Hartnett. Urbana, Chicago: University of Illinois Press.

Brittian, Aerika. 2012. "Understanding African American Adolescents' Identity Development: A Relational Developmental Systems Perspective." *Journal of Black Psychology* 38 (2): 172–200.

Brown, Keffrelyn D., and Anthony L. Brown. 2012. "Useful and Dangerous Discourse: Deconstructing Racialized Knowledge about African-American Students." *Educational Foundations* 26: 11–26.

Cammarota, Julio, and Michelle Fine, eds. 2008. *Revolutionizing Education: Youth Participatory Action Research in Motion*. New York: Routledge.

Carlson, Dennis. 2004. "Narrating the Multicultural Nation: Rosa Parks and the White Mythology of the Civil Rights Movement." In *Off White: Readings on Power, Privilege, and Resistance*, eds. Michelle Fine, Lois Weis, Powell Pruitt, and April Burns (pp. 302–311). New York: Routledge.

The Center for Civil Rights Remedies. 2013. "A Summary of New Research—Closing the School Discipline Gap: Research to Policy." The Civil Rights Project, LA: UCLA. 8 pp.

Chavous, Tabbye M., Debra H. Bernat, Karen Schmeelk-Cone, Cleopatra H. Caldwell, Laura Kohn-Wood, and Marc A. Zimmerman. 2003. "Racial Identity and Academic Attainment among African American Adolescents." *Child Development* 74 (4): 1076–1090.

Collins, Patricia Hill. 2009. *Black Feminist Thought: Knowledge, Consciousness, and the Politics of Empowerment*. New York: Routledge.

Corsaro, William A. 2005. *The Sociology of Childhood*. Thousand Oaks, CA: Pine Forge Press.

Delgado, Richard, and Jean Stefancic. 1993. "Critical Race Theory: An Annotated Bibliography." *Virginia Law Review* 79 (2): 461–516.

deMarrais, K. B., and M. LeCompte. 1999. *The Way Schools Work: A Sociological Analysis of Education*. White Plains, NY: Longman.

Dixson, Adrienne D., and Celia K. Rousseau, eds. 2006. *Critical Race Theory in Education: All God's Children Got a Song*. New York: Routledge.

Federal Interagency Forum on Child and Family Statistics. 2013. *America's Children: Key National Indicators of Well-Being, 2013*. Washington, DC: U.S. Government Printing Office. 203 pp.

Ferber, Abby L. 2012. "The Culture of Privilege: Color-Blindness, Postfeminism, and Christonormativity." *The Society for the Psychological Study of Social Issues* 68 (1): 63–77.

Filkins, Kathleen M. 1998. "Revisiting the Bell Curve: Refuting Classism, Racism, and Elitism." *Educational Forum* 62 (2): 188–189.

Fox, Madeline, and Michelle Fine. 2013. "Accountable to Whom? A Critical Science Counter-Story about a City That Stopped Caring for Its Young." *Children & Society* 27 (4): 321–335.

Gray-Little, Bernadette, and Robert A. Carels. 1997. "The Effects of Racial and Socioeconomic Dissonance on Academic Self-Esteem and Achievement in Elementary, Junior High, and High School Students." *Journal of Research on Adolescence* 7: 109–131.

Harrison, Faye. 1995. "The Persistent Power of 'Race' in the Cultural and Political Economy of Racism." *Annual Review of Anthropology* 24: 47–74.

Hartigan, John. 2010. *Race in the 21st Century: Ethnographic Approaches.* New York: Oxford.

Hartmann, Douglass, and Joseph Gerteis. 2005. "Dealing with Diversity: Mapping Multiculturalism in Sociological Terms." *Sociological Theory* 23 (2): 218–240.

Herrnstein, Richard J., and Charles Murray. 1994. *The Bell Curve: Intelligence and Class Structure in American Life.* New York: Free Press Paperbacks.

Hytten, Kathy, and Silvia C. Bettez. 2011. "Understanding Education for Social Justice." *Educational Foundations* 25 (1): 7–24.

Irons, Jenny. 2010. *Reconstituting Whiteness: The Mississippi State Sovereignty Commission.* Nashville, TN: Vanderbilt University Press.

Ito, Tiffany. A., and Geoffrey R. Urland. 2003. "Race and Gender on the Brain: Electrocortical Measures of Attention to the Race and Gender of Multiply Categorizable Individuals." *Journal of Personality and Social Psychology* 85: 616–626.

Jay, Michelle. 2003. "Critical Race Theory, Multicultural Education, and the Hidden Curriculum of Hegemony." *Multicultural Perspectives* 5 (4): 3–9.

Kang-Brown, Jacob, Jennifer Trone, Jennifer Fratello, and Tarika Daftary-Kapur. 2013. "A Generation Later: What We've Learned about Zero Tolerance in Schools." Vera Institute of Justice, Center on Youth Justice. Issue Brief, December 2013. New York. www.vera.org.

Kunjufu, Jawanza. *Black Students Middle Class Teachers.* Chicago: African American Images, 2002.

Ladson-Billings, Gloria. 1994. *The Dreamkeepers: Successful Teachers of African American Children.* San Francisco: Jossey-Bass.

Ladson-Billings, Gloria. 1995. "Toward a Theory of Culturally Relevant Pedagogy." *American Educational Research Journal* 47: 465–491.

Ladson-Billings, Gloria. 1998. "Just What Is Critical Race Theory and What's It Doing in a Nice Field like Education?" *International Journal of Qualitative Studies in Education* 11 (1): 7–24.

Ladson-Billings, Gloria. 2006a. "It's Not the Culture of Poverty, It's the Poverty of Culture: The Problem with Teacher Education." *Anthropology and Education Quarterly* 37 (2): 104–109.

Ladson-Billings, Gloria. 2006b. "From the Achievement Gap to the Education Debt: Understanding Achievement in US Schools." *Educational Researcher* 35 (7): 3–12.

Ladson-Billings, Gloria. 2009. "Critical Race Theory in Education." *Routledge International Handbook of Critical Education* 110: 110–122.

Ladson-Billings, Gloria, and William Tate, W. 1995. "Toward a Critical Race Theory of Education." *Teachers College Record* 97 (1): 47–68.

Lemert, Charles. 2004. *Social Theory: The Multicultural and Classic Readings.* 4th ed. Boulder, CO: Westview Press.

Margonis, Frank. 1992. "The Cooptation of 'At Risk': Paradoxes of Policy Criticism." *Teachers College Record* 94 (2): 343–364.

Menchaca, Martha. 1997. "Early Racist Discourses: The Roots of Deficit Thinking." In *The Evolution of Deficit Thinking: Educational Thought and Practice,* ed. R. Valencia (pp. 13–40). Oxon, OX: RoutledgeFalmer.

Milner, Richard. 2006. "But Good Intentions Are Not Enough: Theoretical and Philosophical Relevance in Teaching Students of Color." In *White Teachers/ Diverse Classrooms,* eds. Julie Landsman and Chance Lewis (pp. 79–90). Sterling: Stylus.

Milner IV, Richard. 2008. "Disrupting Deficit Notions of Difference: Counter-Narratives of Teachers and Community in Urban Education." *Teaching and Teacher Education* 24 (6): 1573–1598.

Mittelman, James H. 2009. "The Salience of Race." *International Studies Perspectives* 10: 99–107.

Morris, Edward. 2007. "'Ladies' or 'Loudies': Perceptions and Experiences of Black Girls in Classrooms." *Youth & Society* 38 (4): 490–515.

Napolitano, Andrew. 2009. *Dred Scott's Revenge: A Legal History of Race and Freedom in America.* Nashville, TN: Thomas Nelson.

Nieto, Sonia. 1992. *Affirming Diversity: The Sociopolitical Context of Multicultural Education.* White Plains, NY: Longman.

Norton, Michael I., Samuel R. Sommers, Evan A. Apfelbaum, Natassia Pura, and Dan Ariely, 2006. "Color Blindness and Interracial Interaction: Playing the Political Correctness Game." *Psychological Science* 17 (11): 949–953.

Patton, Tracy. 2004. "Reflections of a Black Woman Professor: Racism and Sexism in Academia." *Harvard Journal of Communications* 15: 185–200.

Plaut, Victoria C. 2010. "Diversity Science: Why and How Difference Makes a Difference." *Psychological Inquiry* 21: 77–99.

Plaut, Victoria C., Flannery G. Garnett, Laura E. Buffardi, and Jeffrey Sanchez-Burks. 2011. "What about Me? Perceptions of Exclusion and Whites' Reaction to Multiculturalism." *Journal of Personality and Social Psychology* 101 (2): 337–353.

Plaut, Victoria C., Kecia M. Thomas, and Matt J. Goren. 2009. "Is Multiculturalism or Color Blindness Better for Minorities?" *Psychological Science* 20 (4): 444–446.

Pratt-Clarke, Menah A. 2010. *Critical Race, Feminism, and Education: A Social Justice Model.* New York: Palgrave Macmillan.

Rattan, Aneeta, and Nalini Ambady. 2013. "Diversity Ideologies and Intergroup Relations: An Examination of Colorblindness and Multiculturalism." *European Journal of Social Psychology* 43: 12–21.

Richards, Graham. 1998. "Reconceptualizing the History of Race Psychology: Thomas Russell Garth (1872–1939) and How He Changed His Mind." *Journal of the History of the Behavioral Sciences* 34 (1): 15–32.

Richeson, Jennifer A., and Richard J. Nussbaum. 2004. "The Impact of Multiculturalism versus Colorblindness on Racial Bias." *Journal of Experimental Social Psychology* 40: 417–423.

Richman, Alyssa. 2007. "The Outsider Lurking Online: Adults Researching Youth Cybercultures." In *Representing Youth: Methodological Issues in Critical Youth Studies,* ed. A. L. Best (pp. 182–202). New York: New York University Press.

Rogers, Karen B. 1996. "What the Bell Curve Says and Doesn't Say: Is a Balanced View Possible?" *Roeper Review* 18 (4): 252–256.

Rosenberg, Pearl. 2004. "Colorblindness in Teacher Education: An Optical Delusion." In *Off White: Readings on Power, Privilege, and Resistance,* eds. Michelle Fine, Lois Weis, Powell Pruitt, and April Burns (pp. 257–272). New York: Routledge.

Saunders, Edith. 1969. "The Hamitic Hypothesis: Its Origins and Functions in Time Perspective." *Journal of American History* 10 (4): 521–532.

Schofield, Janet. 1997. "Causes and Consequences of the Colorblind Perspective." In *Multicultural Education: Issues and Perspectives,* eds. James A. Banks and Cherry McGee Banks (pp. 251–271). Needham Heights, MA: Allyn & Bacon.

Scott, Robert, and Miguel Saucedo. 2012. "Mass Incarceration, the School-to-Prison Pipeline, and the Struggle over 'Secure Communities' in Illinois." *Journal of Educational Controversy* 7 (1): 1–20.

Sears, David O., and Victoria. 2006. "The Political Color Line in America: Many 'Peoples of Color' or Black Exceptionalism?" *Political Psychology* 27 (6): 895–924.

Sensoy, Özlem, and Robin DiAngelo. 2012. *Is Everyone Really Equal?: An Introduction to Key Concepts in Social Justice Education.* New York: Teachers College Press.

Sleeter, Christine. 2004. "Context-Conscious Portraits and Context-Blind Policy." *Anthropology & Education Quarterly* 35 (1): 132–136.

Sleeter, Christine. 2012. "Confronting the Marginalization of Culturally Responsive Pedagogy." *Urban Education* 47 (3): 562–584.

Small, Mario Luis, David J. Harding, and Michèle Lamont. 2010. "Reconsidering Culture and Poverty." *The Annals of the American Academy of Political and Social Science* 629 (6): 6–27.

Solorzano, Daniel. 1997. "Images and Words That Wound: Critical Race Theory, Racial Stereotyping, and Teacher Education." *Teacher Education Quarterly* 24: 5–19.

Solorzano, Daniel, and Tara Yosso. 2001. "From Racial Stereotyping and Deficit Discourse: Toward a Critical Race Theory in Teacher Education." *Multicultural Education* 9 (1): 1–8.

Teske, Steven C. 2011. "A Study of Zero Tolerance Policies in Schools: A Multiintegrated Systems Approach to Improve Outcomes for Adolescents." *Journal of Child and Adolescent Psychiatric Nursing* 24: 88–97.

Teske, Steven C., and J. Brian Huff. 2011. "When Did Making Adults Mad Become a Crime?: The Courts Role in Dismantling the School to Prison Pipeline." *Juvenile and Family Justice Today* Winter: 14–17.

Thomas, Anita J., Denada Hoxha, and Jason D. Hacker. 2013. "Contextual Influences on Gendered Racial Identity Development of African American Young Women." *Journal of Black Psychology* 39 (1): 88–101.

Todd, Andrew R., and Adam D. Galinsky. 2012. "The Reciprocal Link Between Multiculturalism and Perspective-Taking: How Ideological and Self-Regulatory Approaches to Managing Diversity Reinforce Each Other." *Journal Experimental Social Psychology* 48: 1394–1398.

Toldson, Ivory A., and Chance W. Lewis. 2012. *Challenge the Status Quo: Academic Success among School-Aged African American Males.* Washington, DC: Congressional Black Caucus Foundation, Inc.

Trueba, Enrique T., and Lilia I. Bartolomé, eds. 2000. "Beyond the Politics of Schools and the Rhetoric of Fashionable Pedagogies: The Significance of Teacher Ideology." In *Immigrant Voices: In Search of Educational Equity,* eds. E.T. Trueba and L.I. Bartolomé (pp. 277–292). Lanham, MD: Rowman & Littlefield.

Ullucci, Kerri, and Battey, Dan. 2011. "Exposing Color Blindness/Grounding Color Consciousness: Challenges for Teacher Education." *Urban Education* 46 (6): 1195–1225.

United States District Court Southern District of Mississippi. 2012. Case 4:12-cv-00168-HTW-LRA: United States of America vs. City of Meridian. http://www.justice.gov/crt/about/spl/documents/meridian_complaint_10-24-12.pdf.

Valencia, Richard. 1997. "Conceptualizing the Notion of Deficit Thinking." In *The Evolution of Deficit Thinking: Educational Thought and Practice,* ed. R. Valencia (pp. 1–12). Oxon, OX: Routledge Palmer.

Verna, Gary., and Keith B. Runion. 2001. "The Effects of Contextual Dissonance on the Self-Concept of Youth from a High versus Low Socially Valued Group." *Journal of Social Psychology* 125 (4): 449–458.

Vorauer, Jacquie D., Annette Gagnon, and Stacey J. Sasaki. 2009. "Salient Intergroup Ideology and Intergroup Interaction." *Psychological Science* 20: 838–845.

Williamson, Joy A., Lori Rhodes, and Michael Dunson. 2007. "A Selected History of Social Justice in Education." *Review of Research in Education* 31 (1): 195–224.

Wing, Adrien. K. 1997. *Critical Race Feminism: A Reader.* New York: New York University Press.

Wing, Adrien. K., ed. 2000. *Global Critical Race Feminism: An International Reader.* NYU Press.

Yosso, Tara. 2005. "Whose Culture Has Capital? A Critical Race Theory Discussion of Community Cultural Wealth." *Race, Ethnicity, and Education* 8 (1): 69–91.

Part II

The Crackdown

Chapter 4

Classrooms, "Crimes," Color, and the Power of Community Resistance

Alexi Freeman

No one wants safe schools more than we do, but getting arrested for writing your name on a desk doesn't make us feel safe. It makes us feel like we aren't even human—like we are animals. Being treated like this in a place where our dreams are supposed to be supported only breaks our spirits down.[1]

A 13-year-old is arrested after passing gas in class. A five-year-old arrives home in a police car after wearing shoes that violate the dress code. A middle schooler is suspended after holding the door open for someone whose hands were full. A charter school network serving low-income black and brown students collects $400,000 in disciplinary fines. A seventh grader faces a 180-day suspension for stretching and accidentally bumping her teacher.

These examples of school discipline gone awry represent the harsh reality for students—particularly students of color—in America's schools. For the past two decades, when students engage in behavior that, in many cases, is completely innocent and harmless and, other times, is typical of what young people have always done, we respond quickly, harshly, and unapologetically. We have little sympathy for mistakes and trial and error. These knee-jerk reactions result in students being suspended, expelled, shuffled to alternative schools, and even arrested.

Students are not suspended or expelled, frequently, if much at all, for possessing weapons or drugs, the types of offenses that prompted the proliferation of discipline policies that emphasized removing students from the classroom. Instead, these overly harsh measures are being used to respond mostly for minor misconduct that does not threaten safety, such as talking back, failing to follow directions, and engaging in minor pushing and shoving.

With the influx of school police, students are now also arrested for these behaviors. The lines between what is a school discipline matter to be handled by school officials and a criminal matter to be handled by police have blurred and students receive a double dose of punishment.

This approach of "zero tolerance"—where there are no second chances—and "exclusionary discipline practices"—which remove the student from the classroom and sometimes the school entirely—is a main feeder into a larger crisis known as the "school-to-prison pipeline."[2] The school-to-prison pipeline refers to the cocktail of policies and practices that push young people, especially young people of color, out of classrooms and schools and into the juvenile and criminal justice systems.[3]

While there are many reasons why students get caught in the pipeline, since the early 1990s, schools have been increasingly using exclusionary disciplinary measures to respond to minor student misconduct. This is in spite of the fact that "by nearly every measure, safety has improved and violence has dropped for students and teachers."[4]

This chapter explains the role of school discipline policies and practices in the school-to-prison pipeline by focusing on the experience for students of color. I highlight two community-based organizations—Padres y Jóvenes Unidos (PJU) in Denver, Colorado, and VOYCE (Voices of Youth in Chicago Education) in Chicago, Illinois—paying particular attention to the intersection of race and discipline. I then briefly provide an overview of the racial underpinnings of this crisis and the research that has unequivocally proven the detrimental effects of harsh school discipline. I return to the community-based organizations to demonstrate how activated communities of color can demand—and win—sweeping school discipline reforms. While this chapter spends time explaining research around this issue, it intends to inspire engagement with those most impacted by the overuse and misuse of punitive discipline policies. Communities of color have long been victims of this crisis, but they have begun to flip the switch—using their traumatic experiences to advocate for concrete, sustainable, and progressive reforms—and we need to respond.

Harsh School Discipline in Action

When kids are pushed out of school, they're more likely to get in trouble. . . . My brother wasn't allowed to go anywhere . . . he said he hated school and didn't think he wanted to go back. He wondered why he should even try.[5]

          —Dionna Hudson, PJU Youth Leader, Denver

Fernando Lara was a 10th grader in Denver when he was caught tagging on the bathroom stall. Police stationed at the school took him to the office and informed him that he would be going to jail to have his mug shot taken. He was summoned to court twice. He was frustrated and admittedly slacked off by not attending court the second time. Three years later, he was pulled over. His identification showed a warrant existed for his arrest. He was brought in, again, subjected to handcuffs on his legs and feet, and held for a week. Fernando managed to graduate, but he still has permanent physical—and likely emotional—scars from the ordeal.[6]

Moui Lim cannot discuss her son Johnny's experience as a student at one of the Chicago-based Noble Network of Charter School's high schools without crying. What started as a detention for losing a shirt button ultimately led to Johnny receiving countless demerits and detentions, 10-day suspension, and an expulsion—a mother's worst nightmare. When Johnny was late to detention, he was punished with more detentions. When he used the word "hell" after leaving detention, he was suspended. Each time he received a detention or suspension, it also cost money. The school actually charged Johnny and his classmates in addition to doling out the punishment. Having a Sharpie marker, eating Cheetos, and so on, these "offenses" warranted fines and punishments in his school. Johnny, like many other students enrolled in this charter school network who never make it past freshman year, found it impossible to follow these impossibly stringent and arguably offensive rules.[7]

Fernando's and Johnny's individual experiences are forever etched in their minds. While they cannot change their lives, they speak out because their stories are not isolated incidents. A broader community-led movement in each of their respective cities exists, and these movements have been successfully pushing back against overly harsh school discipline practices—the same practices that derailed Fernando's and Johnny's lives.

In Denver, Fernando partnered with PJU, a multi-issue organization led by parents and youth of color. PJU began organizing over two decades ago to demand school reforms to end the pushout crisis and racial inequities in student achievement in Denver Public Schools (DPS). Moui, Johnny's mother, met with VOYCE, a Chicago-based citywide youth organizing collaborative comprised of leaders from six organizations. Its mission is to "advance education justice through youth-led policy reforms that increase the graduation rates and college readiness of Chicago Public Schools (CPS) students."[8]

What does the school-to-prison pipeline look like and mean to these groups? More telling than any statistic, their day-to-day experiences depict the harsh, invasive realities of life as students of color in a policed school state. Feeling under constant surveillance, they face significant trauma:

> You're telling me I'm going to be a criminal instead of seeing that I'm trying to do good now.[9]
>
> As a parent, I felt let down and disheartened about the way my daughter was treated.[10]
>
> . . . there was a fight going on between two girls. One of the police officers tried to get one of the girls off the other. When they finally separated them apart, the girl kept talking, so they tasered her. . . . What if I was the one who had gotten tasered?[11]
>
> But what they did made me feel like this is what you are going to do throughout your whole life. You're going to become a criminal. That's how they made me feel.[12]
>
> One thing I don't like about my high school is the hall sweeps [where guards sweep the hallways for any students in the halls after the bell rings. Any student caught in a hall sweep automatically gets a detention, or worse]. . . . They would put on the intercom, "Hall Sweep!" and then teachers will lock their doors and then they'll sweep everyone on the floor and give them detention. I got caught when I was trying to get my books out of my locker.[13]
>
> . . . I cut class one day . . . but I got caught by a teacher and he sent me to the disciplinary office. . . . They said they were gonna suspend me for two days. I had never been suspended before. But then the assistant principal came in. . . . She saw my grades were low, my attendance was kind of bad. She said, "OK, let's drop him." So they dropped me.[14]
>
> My experience with being targeted by a teacher and suspended made me feel frustrated that my school created a negative school climate. I felt angry that I could not learn because I missed schoolwork, and unsupported and discouraged by what was happening around me.[15]
>
> When my classmates were suspended, they would disappear for days and when they were kicked out, they would disappear even for weeks.[16]

The statistics in these districts concretizes these experiences. Denver, which had 6,000 suspensions this past academic year, has the seventh highest suspension rate among Colorado's 20 largest school districts.[17] Despite years of progress prompted by PJU, racial disparities in school discipline continue to plague the district. A student of color is *189 percent* more likely than a white student to be suspended, expelled, or referred to law enforcement.[18] In fact, the disparities between both black and Latino students and white students are far greater than neighboring districts, despite DPS overall having fewer suspensions or expulsions.[19] In Chicago, where progress has been slower, 25 public school students are arrested each day.[20] Eighty-four percent of arrests are for misdemeanors, and black students account for 75 percent of the arrests—even though they are not even half of student enrollment.[21] The data on suspensions and expulsions is similarly staggering. Black students are 30 times more likely to be expelled than white students.[22] The district issued an average of 386 out-of-school suspensions per day, which amounted to students losing 173,000 instructional days.[23] In Chicago's public charter schools, the data is even starker. Charters expelled 61 of every 10,000 students while the district-run schools expelled just 5 of every 10,000 students.[24] Some charter schools expel students at a rate of 15 times that of traditional public schools.[25]

This is unfortunately the status quo for communities of color across the country. In recent years, over 3 million students have been suspended at least once; schools suspend and expel students at a rate more than double that in 1974.[26] Almost half of all public schools have assigned police; at least 17,000 sworn officers are detailed from police or sheriffs' departments to schools, which omits districts with their own police departments.[27]

Nationwide, youth of color disproportionately bear the brunt of such practices too. They receive significant, disproportionate punishments for insignificant behaviors. Black students are three times as likely to be suspended and expelled as white students,[28] and black and Latino students are over 80 percent more likely to be arrested in school than their white peers.[29] These disparities start as early as preschool.

The "Conundrum" of Color and Race

I think that schools need to throw out the assumption that young people are all dangerous or a threat.[30]

—Edward Ward, Youth Leader, Chicago

Racial disparities in school discipline are present in almost every community. In fact, the "racial gap" in suspensions has exploded over time, almost tripling in 30 years.[31] The question that plagues us is, why? Why is there such a disproportionate effect? Do students of color act out more or engage in behaviors that warrant more serious consequences? Is it merely coincidence?

First, we know that schools with higher enrollments of students of color are more likely to use harsh and exclusionary school discipline measures, have increased security measures (e.g., surveillance cameras, metal detectors, etc.), and involve court and police in school discipline matters.[32] Unsurprisingly, these schools also have the highest dropout (or pushout[33]) rates.

If students of color were simply the "bad apples"—the students who act out more and then obviously receive greater and/or harsher punishments— we would be less troubled. But numerous studies have shown that there is no evidence that racial disparities in discipline are due to higher rates of misbehavior by students of color. If anything, these students are punished more severely for engaging in *less serious* behaviors than their peers. Research also shows that Latino and black students receive more serious consequences when they engage in the same offenses as white students. So, for example, a student of color caught fighting in the hallway may be suspended out of school for 10 days or more, or even arrested; a white student similarly caught is more often than not given a less severe consequence, like a detention, or something actually productive, like conflict resolution classes. If students receive the same disciplinary consequence, students of color often receive a punishment of longer duration. A white student's out- of-school suspension may last three days, but the suspension for the student of color will last longer, perhaps five or more days. These inequities are particularly common when student misconduct is considered soft, subjective, or intangible, such as defiance or disruption.

While many studies examining racial disparities in discipline focus on black students, new research indicates that other students of color, such as Latino and Native American students face similar predicaments.[34] Intersectional marginalized identities cause even greater problems for students. For example, a student who identifies as black, male, and gay is likely to face harsher punishments than a student who identifies as black, male, and straight. The situation is similar for students with documented disabilities. More than one in four black boys with disabilities is suspended out of school and nearly one in five girls of color with disabilities is suspended out of school[35]—these odds are worse than for students of color and students with disabilities alone. As best explained by researchers who have examined intersectional identities, identities are "additive"[36] within school discipline.

Even with this evidence, misconceptions about the role that poverty plays in comparison to race within the school discipline context persist. Many people believe that poverty explains these disparities, not race. They think black and brown students are more likely to be poor so the challenges that come with being poor cause disproportionate discipline. Research, however, consistently shows that black students are more likely to be suspended than their white peers of the same socioeconomic status—at all income levels.[37] Race is more indicative than factors of poverty, an unstable home environment, or a violent neighborhood.[38] While these factors impact behavior and success in school, research repeatedly shows that race trumps.

If individual behavior or poverty is not to blame, but exclusionary discipline practices are rampant in schools with students of color, the question shifts. We have to ask, is everyone just *racist*?

Structural Racism and Implicit Bias

There is no doubt that historical inequalities in our country—and within our education system—influence how institutions and individual people within them, including educators, principals, police officers, and others in the school community, think about, label, and treat students of color.[39] "Structural racism" refers to the "system in which public policies, institutional practices, cultural representations, and other norms work in various, often reinforcing ways to perpetuate racial group inequity. It identifies dimensions of our history and culture that have allowed privileges associated with 'whiteness' and disadvantages associated with 'color' to endure and adapt over time."[40] Within the education context, structural racism is the "system's built-in tendency to make minority students feel unintelligent, despised or marginalized."[41]

This plays out in many different ways—and each way has an indirect or direct effect on school discipline. For example, many schools that students of color attend are far from ideal—they have suffered from few resources for far too long, have overcrowded classrooms, and hire far too many inexperienced teachers. In these schools, teachers and students alike recognize the inadequacy and become disengaged, frustrated, ashamed, and discouraged. Conversely, schools with unlimited access to endless resources and/or schools where parents feel empowered to demand high-quality education, both of which often go hand in hand, usually offer interactive classrooms, field trips, and arts and music curriculum. Teachers have flexibility; they are less focused on test results and instead can care about creating life-long learners, providing hands-on experience, and fostering critical thinking. When this is the academic environment, intuitively, it would seem that school discipline matters are minimized. Unsurprisingly, research shows that school discipline referrals are drastically lower in schools where students are engaged, eager to learn, and enthusiastic about their schoolwork.[42] The problem is that because of our nation's history, housing patterns, political power or lack thereof by certain communities, and the like, the schools with such robust educational environments are overwhelmingly white.

There are other, more subtle, ways in which race matters. "Implicit bias" refers to the "attitudes or stereotypes that affect understanding, actions, and decisions in an unconscious manner."[43] It is "the mental process that causes us to have negative feelings and attitudes about people based on characteristics like race, ethnicity, age, and appearance. Because this cognitive process functions in our unconscious mind, we are typically not consciously aware of the negative racial biases that we develop over the course of our lifetime."[44] In other words, while individuals and entities may not intend to discriminate or perceive someone or something in certain negative ways, they still may do so because of ingrained stereotypes they have about a particular group.

And that phenomenon has certainly been true in schools. To be clear, most educators and school officials join the profession with noble intentions to help all students succeed. But, even with good intentions, we may still perpetuate harm and inequities. Within school discipline, we know that our opinions and biases on race matter—more than anything else.

According to the Kirwan Institute for Race and Ethnicity (the Kirwan Institute), "implicit racial bias often supports the stereotypical caricature of Black youth—especially males—as irresponsible, dishonest, and dangerous."[45] This stereotype is furthered by the media. For example, research found that "the black underclass appears as a menace and a source of social disorganization in news accounts of black urban crime, gang violence, drug use, teenage pregnancy, riots, homelessness, and general aimlessness . . . poor blacks (and Hispanics) signify a social menace that must be contained."[46]

We can picture these stereotypes on television; this is nothing new. But we cannot imagine such biases playing out in schools. We become ignorant to the fact that when educators and school-based police walk into a school building, they do not suddenly become immune to stereotypes that have permeated our society for centuries.

Indeed, research shows that police officers are less likely to see black youth as "innocent" and more likely to see them as being older, and more culpable, than their white counterparts.[47] White educators find black students to be more threatening than white students, and students who "displayed a Black walking style (i.e., 'deliberately swaggered or bent posture, with the head slightly tilted to the side, one foot dragging, and an exaggerated knee bend')" were perceived by teachers as being "highly aggressive" and performing worse academically.[48]

Teachers also have been shown to have lower expectations for students of color in comparison to white students. Oftentimes, students of color are counseled into certain classes and out of others. Some are even counseled out of school entirely—as one administrator in Connecticut noted, "If you are in the business to eradicate your school of all 'wrongdoing'—and that's interpreted as you gotta get rid of that 3% that's causing the problems—you can find a way to do that."[49] Pressured to be recognized as a high-performing school or be rated as a high-performing teacher, an educator's unconscious bias comes out even stronger.

All of this, in turn, affects how school leaders may react to, or perceive, student conduct. And, in some cases, these dynamics can actually cause different—and maybe worse—behavior by students of color. The stereotypes and lowered expectations can morph into reality—students of color may actually end up acting out more. Known as stereotype threat, essentially, students of color may play into their stereotypes and engage in more disruptive behavior because that is what they believe, unconsciously or consciously, is expected of them.[50]

Cultural Mismatches

A lack of understanding or familiarity about cultural norms is an easy gateway into the misuse of school discipline. Research shows that "teachers' implicit biases may be further amplified by a cultural mismatch that exists between White teachers and their students of color, and this mismatch can lead to teachers misinterpreting student behavior."[51] For example, in some cultures, it is not appropriate to look an adult in the eye. But students at a Noble Network Charter High School in Chicago receive demerits if they fail to track the teacher with their eyes. A demerit easily leads to detentions and fines.[52] If you grew up being told repeatedly to lower your eyes with adults—as a sign of respect—then you are easily confused and ultimately subjected, perhaps unfairly, to punitive consequences.

As another example, consider cultures in which public displays of affection are encouraged. A student who is raised learning that hugging, for example, is an appropriate way to express feelings is shocked when he or she is suspended or even arrested for "inappropriate displays of affection." In many schools across the country, any sort of physical contact, including something as innocent as hugging, is often prohibited and failing to abide by the rule can result in removal from school.[53]

It has long been documented that students of color also encounter few adults who are of the same race or color as them in their schools.[54] We know that schools with more diverse teachers and teachers who are representative of the student body are less likely to have discipline disparities. Students may act out to express frustration with such dynamics.

The effect of having inclusive school curriculum has also been widely studied; incorporating race in a meaningful way matters. The link of cultural relevance in classwork to school discipline, however, may not be as obvious. Research shows that "when students' identities and cultures are reflected back to them,"[55] they feel safer and report less victimization and discrimination. This promotes improved relationships and connections between students and school staff, which has a direct impact on discipline. In fact, the research is abundantly clear that students feel safest when they trust their teachers; it is these connections that make all the difference.[56]

While all students may not be able to initially identify by name what they see in schools as structural racism or implicit bias, for example, they still often internalize their existence and feel their effects. Students may begin to feel hopeless and discouraged, as the system seems designed against them. This is where community organizations like PJU and VOYCE fill a critical void. They help students better understand how these factors affect school dynamics. They work to build student power, reminding students that they not only have a valid and valuable voice to share but their voices can shape school culture and policy, and change even the most long-standing and destructive of practices.

So What?

Nationally, as many as 95 percent of out-of-school suspensions are for nonviolent offenses such as disruption, disrespect, tardiness and dress code violations. . . . I must ask: Is putting children out of school the best solution, the best remedy, for those problems?

—Arne Duncan, U.S. Secretary of Education

The overuse and misuse of school discipline has been devastating for students of color, and its impact is not coincidental; its roots are deep-seated. What happens to these students, however, actually presents grave consequences for *all* students and schools as a whole, in both the short- and long terms.

In 2006, a task force of the American Psychological Association found that harsh school discipline does not improve school safety.[57] According to the study, "Schools are not any safer or more effective in disciplining students than they were before zero-tolerance policies were implemented. On the contrary, schools with higher rates of school suspension and expulsion have less satisfactory ratings of school climate," which broadly refers to the norms and values of the school, and the experiences members of the school community, including families, have.[58]

Removing a student from school has negative effects on future behavior. There is no evidence that, after receiving a suspension or expulsion, students will be deterred from acting out or being disruptive again.[59] Instead, harsh discipline policies "make students feel less 'connected' to school, which is linked to increased likelihood of engaging in risky behaviors, violence, and alcohol or substance abuse."[60]

Harsh school discipline also has a negative impact on academic performance, for both the affected student and the overall school. The suspended student falls behind after missing class. Studies show that students who miss fewer days of school tend to earn better grades[61] and that students "suspended in the past year score three grades levels behind their peers in reading skills after one year, and almost five years behind after two years."[62] Students are also more likely to drop out or not graduate on time if they are suspended.[63] One study showed that "students suspended three or more times by the end of their sophomore year of high school are five times more likely to drop out than students who have never been suspended."[64] Schools with high suspensions and expulsion rates have lower schoolwide achievement overall.[65]

When security measures, police, and the power to arrest come into the picture, consequences ratchet up. What may seem insignificant or commonplace for police is traumatic for youth. Youth attending schools with security guards and metal detectors actually feel *less* safe; students become more fearful and are more likely to be worried about crime in these schools.[66] As one student recalled, "I had to take off my shoes and they searched me like I was a real criminal . . . [after that] I was making up every excuse not to go to school."[67] Students like this—or worse, students actually arrested—alienate themselves from school and from others.[68] They are scarred for life. This sets the stage for a pattern of negative interaction with the justice system. One study showed that one in three families of incarcerated youth reported that their child's first arrest took place at school.[69] Indeed, since law enforcement invaded our schools, arrests and referrals to the juvenile and criminal justice systems increased.[70]

Once arrested, odds of being successful in school plummet. In one survey, 69 percent of families of incarcerated youth shared that it was difficult to get their child back in school post-release.[71] This is consistent with national data. After encounters with police in schools, students become twice as likely to drop out and more likely to be incarcerated in the future.

Students who drop out "are more than eight times as likely to be incarcerated as those who graduate."[72] Another study found that "80 percent of youth incarcerated in a state facility had been suspended and 50 percent had been expelled from school prior to incarceration."[73] Students who face run-ins with police and/or are arrested in schools face barriers far into the future, experiencing difficulty applying for college, military, and employment.[74]

Progress Comes from People *Not* in Power

I am grateful for the work of our students and to Padres y Jóvenes Unidos. . . . As a result of this partnership . . . we have reduced the number of expulsions in DPS by two thirds in the last two years, and out-of-school suspensions this year are on pace to be reduced by nearly one half compared to three years ago. . . . We are fortunate to have students . . . express their views so thoughtfully, take leadership, and help create the campus climates that provide the safest environment and the best learning opportunities possible.[75]

—Tom Boasberg, Superintendent, Denver Public Schools

PJU and VOYCE have each achieved tangible victories, resulting in local abandonment of zero tolerance and attention to racial disparities. Their victories teach us about the power of building change from the ground up. Through a variety of multipronged strategies, PJU and VOYCE brought attention to school discipline and race. They staged protests, analyzed and shared quantitative data, interviewed countless youth and parents, engaged other stakeholders, and researched viable alternatives to exclusionary practices. Their tireless efforts resulted not only in changed policy but also in changed culture. They have proven that when those most impacted are leading the charge for discipline reform, such reform is more likely to be sustainable and grounded in reality.

Padres y Jóvenes Unidos

After six years of organizing strategic campaigns aimed at reducing the reliance on exclusionary school discipline practices and reducing racial disparities, PJU achieved a triumvirate of victories. In 2008, it became the first community group in the country to win new progressive discipline policies; its reforms focused on keeping students in school, introduced restorative justice as an alternative, and emphasized progressive and tiered discipline strategies.[76] For the first time, the discipline policy included the term structural racism.[77] This kept the focus on racial disparities, helping to restore the relationship between the community and school leadership and give credence to those with lived experiences.

Reductions in expulsions and out-of-school suspensions were witnessed almost right away. Since PJU began its campaign, district-wide suspensions decreased 60 percent.[78] Eighty-five percent of elementary schools have at least one teacher or members trained in *restorative* justice, an alternative that makes students accountable not by punishment but by repairing the harm done by student misconduct.[79]

This victory put PJU and Denver on the forefront of discipline reform, paving the way for others to follow suit.[80] It also helped lay the groundwork for future reform in Colorado. Four years later, with allies, PJU led the passage of Colorado's Smart School Discipline Law, which was one of the first and most comprehensive state bills to reform school discipline.[81] PJU built momentum for this win because of its results on the local level.

At the same time, PJU continued to place pressure on local decision makers. While pleased with the progress made, PJU remained concerned about police tickets and student arrests. It then returned to one of its earlier goals, engaging in reform with the police department. In 2013, ironically right after the tragedy in Newtown, a new intergovernmental agreement with the Denver Police Department was adopted, restricting police involvement and decriminalizing student misbehavior.[82] When countless people across the country, including federal officials and former allies, were calling for more school-based police,[83] stakeholders in Denver finalized policies that "policed those same police." Once again, PJU allowed the unthinkable to happen at an unbelievably challenging time for school discipline reform.

PJU continues to push school leadership to reevaluate and readjust its approach to school discipline. Each year, it releases a community accountability report card detailing where the district has made improvements and where it continues to fall short.[84] The two now identify potential solutions and approaches for reform together.

Voices of Youth in Chicago Education (VOYCE)

VOYCE's creative organizing tactics[85] and participatory-based research have made a dent in school discipline within the city of Chicago—a school district that is notorious for being one of the worst offenders of zero tolerance. Their first significant victory came in 2012 when the Chicago Board of Education approved a new Student Code of Conduct that namely eliminated mandatory two-week suspensions for minor offenses and allowed for the use of in-school suspensions instead of out-of-school suspensions for some offenses.[86] More recently, the district finally released to the public expulsion data for traditional and charter schools and released student suspension data for every school.[87] While Chicago schools still have a long way to go, these reforms certainly are doing more to keep students in school.

VOYCE has also been successful in slowing chipping away at the particularly rigid discipline policies within charter schools in Chicago—schools that are not required to abide by the district's discipline policy. In 2013, the Noble Network of Charter Schools, which fined students for failing to abide by its set of draconian rules and retained those who did not pay the fines, altered its policy so that students could no longer be held back for failure to pay such fines. Feeling increased pressure, one year later the charter network went even further, releasing a statement that claimed it would no longer issue disciplinary fines.[88] Given the support for charters in the city, and particularly this one, this was quite a win.

Throughout all of its work, VOYCE worked tirelessly to engage the large and influential Chicago Teachers Union (CTU) and its members, understanding that if educators were not behind their campaign, change would be incremental and short lived at best.[89] Supporting each other, VOYCE and CTU evolved into a powerful force that demonstrated the power of collaboration and coalition among those most directly affected by school and district policies.

While VOYCE monitors work in Chicago, it is now leading the charge on a state legislative campaign to eliminate the overuse and misuse of suspensions, expulsions, arrests, and fines across the state for all schools, whether in traditional public schools or charter schools. In the 2014 legislative cycle, one of the bills they spearheaded passed. The new law requires schools to make public suspension and expulsion data and for some to develop a school discipline improvement plan to address racial disparities.

Taking Victories to Scale

Each of these victories has laid the groundwork for change on the national level. A number of alliances and coalitions have sprung up, as more and more communities, educators, and others join together to push for school discipline reform. Together, this has raised the profile of the school discipline crisis.

In early 2014, the administration unveiled a number of major efforts related to ending the overuse of suspensions and expulsions, particularly for students of color. In February, the president announced "My Brother's

Keeper," a community engagement initiative focused on men of color, given that "for decades, opportunity has lagged behind" for them.[90] This announcement came on the heels of two others by the federal government. A few months earlier, the president created the White House Commission on Educational Excellence for African Americans, aimed at improving educational opportunities for black students. Among its directives:

> reducing the dropout rate of African American students and helping African American students graduate from high school prepared for college and a career, in part by promoting a positive school climate that does not rely on methods that result in disparate use of disciplinary tools, and by supporting successful and innovative dropout prevention and recovery strategies that better engage African American youths in their learning.[91]

Some weeks after that, the U.S. Department of Education and the U.S. Department of Justice issued long-awaited[92] guidance documents on administering discipline in compliance with civil rights laws.[93] The guidance advocated for abandoning "overly zealous discipline policies that send students to court instead of the principal's office." It went so far as to declare that the "significant and unexplained racial disparities in student discipline give rise to concerns that schools may be engaging in racial discrimination that violates the Federal civil rights laws."[94]

Conclusion

In the beginning, I wasn't thinking this would ever happen. . . . But there are so many people in support of us, I knew there was something we can do for the students and the community.[95]

—Delia Lozano, Student, Denver Public Schools

Led by communities of color, much progress has been made to make the school-to-prison pipeline a household name. Community campaigns have not just realized reforms on the local level but have also helped to make school discipline a national priority. Their work has affected the lives of hundreds of thousands of young people, and we should applaud that success. While progress warrants celebration, we are a far distance from reversing the havoc that harsh school discipline policies have had or from addressing the underlying roots of this crisis.

What we know is this: the quality of relationships between students and staff, and between staff and parents, as opposed to the overuse and misuse of suspensions and expulsions, or the presence of police, creates safe schools.[96] Such trustful relationships can begin when our schools acknowledge underlying issues affecting our perceptions and understandings of race, and how race plays out in society and the school setting. If our schools then address biases with ongoing targeted interventions and trainings, perhaps we can understand the roots of disparities in discipline and begin to chip away at them.[97]

For reform to be sustainable, those most affected, like the members of PJU and VOYCE, need to have not just a seat at but be at the front and center of the decision-making table. Schools must be proactive and pay attention to the concerns of communities of color, as these communities have been marginalized and in many cases shut out of educational decisions, for far too long. Educators' willingness to prioritize these concerns and confront race head-on can go a long way toward reform that benefits educators, the school, and students alike.

With voice, comes victory.

Notes

1. VOYCE 2011, p. 1.
2. According to the American Psychological Association (APA), zero tolerance is "a philosophy or policy that mandates the application of predetermined consequences, most often severe and punitive in nature, that are intended to be applied regardless of the seriousness of behavior, mitigating circumstances, or situational context." Skiba et al. 2006, p. 2.

This essay considers official zero tolerance policies with overly harsh and exclusionary school discipline policies as the same.

3. See, for example, "Understanding the Issue" 2014; "What Is the School-to-Prison Pipeline," American Civil Liberties Union 2014; and "School to Prison Pipeline" 2014.
4. United States Department of Education, National Center for Education Statistics 2013.
5. Jones 2012.
6. This story comes from a video produced by Advancement Project, New Media Advocacy Project, and Padres y Jóvenes Unidos. As a lawyer at Advancement Project during that time, I assisted on the development of this video.
7. This story comes from a video produced by VOYCE during its campaign to end harsh school discipline in all publically funded schools. When I was a lawyer at Advancement Project, I supported this campaign.
8. "About Us," VOYCE 2014.
9. VOYCE 2011, p. 7.

10. Padres y Jóvenes Unidos 2011, p. 16.

11. VOYCE 2011, p. 11.

12. Ibid., p. 20.

13. Ibid., p. 12.

14. Ibid., p. 17.

15. "Denver Public Schools Show Progress, But Racial Disparities Persist in Punishment" 2014.

16. Ending the School to Prison Pipeline Hearing before the Senate Judiciary Subcommittee on the Constitution, Civil Rights, and Human Rights. "Testimony of Edward Ward," p. 19.

17. Padres y Jóvenes Unidos 2014, p. 7.

18. Ibid., p. 4.

19. Colorado Department of Education 2014.

20. Harris 2012.

21. Ibid.

22. Cox 2014.

23. Data on file with author.

24. Ahmed-Ullah and Richards 2014.

25. Perspective Charter School is one such example. See, for example, VOYCE, "Fact Sheet: Civil Rights, Transparency, and Accountability at Chicago Charter Schools."

26. "What Is School Pushout" 2014.

27. Raymond 2010.

28. United States Department of Education, Office for Civil Rights 2014

29. Ibid.

30. Ending the School to Prison Pipeline Hearing before the Senate Judiciary Subcommittee on the Constitution, Civil Rights, and Human Rights. "Testimony of Edward Ward."

31. St. George 2014.

32. Torres and Stefkovich 2009.

33. While the research cited uses the term "dropout," "pushout" may be more appropriate. The term "pushout" is specifically used to shift the burden and blame. As perhaps best stated by the youth organizing group Youth United for Change, "The term 'dropout' points the finger at an individual in a negative way. The term 'dropout' suggests that people leave school because of individual mistakes and poor decisions; the term neglects the larger, systemic problems that lead to young people leaving school. We chose the term 'pushout' because it focuses on the school-based factors that lead to young people leaving school." Youth United for Change, "Pushed Out." According to the Dignity in Schools Coalition, a national multi-stakeholder coalition of youth, parents, educators, advocates, organizers, grassroots groups, lawyers, and policy groups, "school pushout" refers to the numerous systemic factors that prevent or discourage young people from remaining on track to complete their education and has severe and lasting consequences for students,

parents, schools, and communities. These factors include the failure to provide essential components of a high-quality education, lack of stakeholder participation in decision making, overreliance on zero tolerance practices and punitive measures such as suspensions and expulsions, overreliance on law enforcement tactics and ceding of disciplinary authority to law enforcement personnel, and a history of systemic racism and inequality. These factors have an impact on all students but have a disproportionate impact on historically disenfranchised youth. "Mission" 2014.

34. Skiba, Arredondo, and Rausch 2014. This is in addition to students with disabilities and students who identify as lesbian, gay, bisexual, transgender, or queer.

35. United States Department of Education, Office for Civil Rights 2014.

36. Skiba, Arredondo, and Rausch 2014.

37. Skiba and Williams 2014, p. 2.

38. Skiba, Arredondo, and Rausch 2014, pp. 2–3.

39. "School to Prison Pipeline" 2014.

40. The Aspen Institute Roundtable on Community Change 2004.

41. Kuznia 2009.

42. Gregory, Bell, and Pollock 2014, p. 4.

43. Staats 2013, p. 6.

44. Rudd 2014, p. 3.

45. Ibid.

46. Jenkins 2007.

47. McDonough 2014.

48. Ibid.

49. McCargar 2011, p. 20.

50. Stereotype threat occurs "when a person's social identity is attached to a negative stereotype, that person will tend to underperform in a manner consistent with the stereotype . . . the underperformance . . . [is attributed] to a person's anxiety that he or she will conform to the negative stereotype. The anxiety manifests itself in various ways, including distraction and increased body temperature, all of which diminish performance level." "Steele Discusses Stereotype Threat."

51. Staats 2013, p. 33.

52. See Noble Network of Charter Schools, discipline policy, on file with author.

53. See, for example, Gray 2007; Wallace 2013; and Youth United for Change 2011, p. 23.

54. Hanssen 1998, p. 694.

55. Gregory, Bell, and Pollock 2014, p. 5.

56. Skiba, Arredondo, and Rausch 2014, p. 3.

57. Skiba et al. 2006.

58. Ibid., p. 4.

59. Skiba et al. 2006, p. 5; Tobin, Sugai, and Colvin 1996, pp. 82–94.

60. Blum and Reinhart 2001.

61. Balfanz and Byrnes 2012, p. 4.

62. "What Is School Pushout" 2014.

63. Blum and Reinhart 2001.

64. National Center on Education Statistics 2006.

65. Skiba et al. 2006, p. 5.

66. Bachman, Randolph, and Brown 2011; Schreck and Miller 2003.

67. Advancement Project 2010, p. 14.

68. Advancement Project 2005, p. 12.

69. Justice for Families 2012, p. 7.

70. Carter, Fine, and Russell 2014, p. 3.

71. Justice for Families 2012, p. 9.

72. "What Is School Pushout" 2014.

73. Ibid.

74. Advancement Project 2005, p. 12.

75. Boasberg 2013.

76. "History and Accomplishments."

77. Denver Public Schools 2014.

78. Padres y Jóvenes Unidos 2014, p. 4.

79. Ibid., p. 8.

80. For example, as an attorney at Advancement Project, I, along with my colleagues, worked with Baltimore City Public Schools and Buffalo Public Schools to reform their respective discipline policies. Both were inspired by, and used, Denver Public Schools' discipline policy as a model.

81. "Colorado School Expulsions Drop Because of Law" 2014.

82. Advancement Project 2013.

83. Elliot 2013; Bezalher 2013.

84. Padres y Jóvenes Unidos 2014.

85. VOYCE's use of imagery and creativity to expose quantitative data has set them apart and has helped them get media attention. For example, when the mayor of Chicago heralded a charter network as having the "secret sauce" to education, despite their use of disciplinary fines as punishment, VOYCE youth marched to the mayor's office wearing chef hats. Just this past year in a press conference, to symbolize the 25 students who are arrested each day in Chicago Public Schools, 25 VOYCE youth each held signs with pictures of students who were arrested, along with what they had aspired to be. And, when working alongside the teacher's union to protest over-testing (and testing's link to the school-to-prison pipeline), VOYCE youth carried thousands of pencils linked together to represent the 11,700 hours of testing students experience. Rossi 2012; Harris 2012; and Street 2012.

86. Chicago Public Schools 2012.

87. "Publish School Suspension and Expulsion Rates" 2014.

88. Ahmed-Ullah 2014.

89. See, for example, CTU Communications 2014 (describing a shared coalition on discipline).

90. The White House, Office of the Press Secretary 2014.

91. The White House, Office of the Press Secretary 2012.

92. The guidance documents were released over two years after both of the departments came together to create the Supportive School Discipline Initiative. The goals of the Supportive School Discipline Initiative were to build consensus for action among federal, state, and local education and justice stakeholders; collaborate on research and data collection that may be needed to inform this work, such as evaluations of alternative disciplinary policies and interventions; develop guidance to ensure that school discipline policies and practices comply with the nation's civil rights laws and to promote positive disciplinary options to both keep kids in school and improve the climate for learning; and promote awareness and knowledge about evidence-based and promising policies and practices among state judicial and education leadership. United States Department of Justice, Office of Public Affairs, "Attorney General Holder, Secretary Duncan Announce Effort to Respond to School-to-Prison Pipeline by Supporting Good Discipline Practices."

93. United States Department of Education. Office for Civil Rights and United States Department of Justice: Civil Rights Division 2014. For example, the three points of emphasis were on (1) taking deliberate steps to create the positive school climates that can help prevent and change inappropriate behaviors; (2) ensuring that clear, appropriate, and consistent expectations and consequences are in place to prevent and address misbehavior; and (3) understanding civil rights obligations and striving to ensure fairness and equity for all students by continuously evaluating the impact of discipline policies and practices on all students using data and analysis. The document went into much greater detail on each of these points of emphasis, explaining why they were important and offering ideas for how to follow through with each of them. United States Department of Education, Office for Civil Rights, "Guiding Principles: A Resource Guide for Improving School Climate and Discipline."

94. United States Department of Education, Office for Civil Rights and United States Department of Justice: Civil Rights Division 2014. The guidance's overview opened with the following: The Civil Rights Data Collection (CRDC), conducted by OCR, has demonstrated that students of certain racial or ethnic groups tend to be disciplined more than their peers. For example, African American students without disabilities are more than three times as likely as their white peers without disabilities to be expelled or suspended. Although African American students represent 15 percent of students in the CRDC, they make up 35 percent of students suspended once, 44 percent of those suspended more than once, and 36 percent of students expelled. Further, over 50 percent of students who were involved in school-related arrests or referred to law enforcement are Hispanic or African American.

95. Simpson 2012.

96. A school principal's perspective on discipline and achievement significantly affects disparities in discipline and school safety issues; for example, a principal

who acknowledges the racial impact of the crisis is more likely to address it and ultimately lead a school with fewer discipline disparities. Steinberg, Allensworth, and Johnson 2011. In turn, schools with positive school climates are associated with lower rates of student misconduct. Bickel and Qualls 1980, pp. 79–86; and Welsh 2003, pp. 346–368.

97. Now, more and more, school officials and educators are seeking out programming and professional development on implicit bias. For more information on implicit bias, see, for example, Arredondo and Williams 2014; "Project Implicit" 2011; Teaching as Leadership; and Teaching Tolerance.

Bibliography

"About Us," VOYCE. Accessed June 5, 2014. http://voyceproject.org.

Achilles, G.M., M.J. Mclaughlin, and R.G. Croninger. 2007. "Sociocultural Correlates of Disciplinary Exclusion among Students with Emotional, Behavioral, and Learning Disabilities in the SEELS National Dataset." *Journal of Emotional and Behavioral Disorders* 15 (1): 33–45.

Advancement Project. "Education on Lockdown: The Schoolhouse to Jailhouse Track." March 2005, 12. http://www.advancementproject.org/reports/FINALE-OLrep.pdf. http://www.advancementproject.org/resources/entry/education-on-lockdown-the-schoolhouse-to-jailhouse-track.

Advancement Project. "Summary of 2013 Intergovernmental Agreement between DPS and DPD." 2013. http://b.3cdn.net/advancement/e746ea2668c2ed19b3_urm6iv28k.pdf.

Advancement Project. "Test, Punish and Pushout: How Zero Tolerance and High-Stakes Testing Funnel Youth into the School-to-Prison Pipeline." March 2010, 9–10. http://b.3cdn.net/advancement/d05cb2181a4545db07_r2im6caqe.pdf.

Ahmed-Ullah, Noreen S. 2012. "Parent, Student Groups Criticize Charter Schools' Student Fines." *Chicago Tribune* (February 14). http://articles.chicagotribune.com/2012-02-14/news/ct-met-charter-fines-20120214_1_student-groups-troubled-students-charter-schools.

Ahmed-Ullah, Noreen S. 2014. "Charter School Drops Controversial Discipline Fee." *Chicago Tribune* (April 11). http://articles.chicagotribune.com/2014-04-11/news/chi-charter-school-drops-controversial-discipline-fee-20140411_1_charter-school-noble-network-student-discipline.

Ahmed-Ullah, Noreen S., and Alex Richards. 2014. "CPS: Expulsion Rate Higher at Charter Schools." *Chicago Tribune* (February 26). http://articles.chicagotribune.com/2014-02-26/news/ct-chicago-schools-discipline-met-20140226_1_charter-schools-andrew-broy-district-run-schools.

American Civil Liberties Union. Accessed June 2, 2014. https://www.aclu.org/racial-justice/what-school-prison-pipeline.

Arredondo, M., and N. Williams. "Annotated Bibliography: Possible Contributions of Bias to the School-to-Prison Pipeline." The Equity Project at Indiana
University. March 2014. http://www.indiana.edu/~atlantic/wp-content/up-
loads/2013/06/Implicit-Bias-Annotated-Bibliography.pdf.

The Aspen Institute Roundtable on Community Change. "Structural Racism and
Community." June 2004, 11. http://www.aecf.org/upload/publicationfiles/re36
22h650.pdf.

Association of Schools of Journalism and Mass Communication. "Diversity in the
Curriculum." Accessed March 6, 2015. http://www.asjmc.org/resources/diver
sity_booklet/5_curriculum.pdf.

Bachman, R., A. Randolph, and B.L. Brown. 2011. "Predicting Perceptions of Fear
at School and Going to and from School for African American and White Students: The Effects of School Security Measures." Youth & Society 43: 705–726.

Balfanz, R., and V. Byrnes. "The Importance of Being in School: A Report on
Absenteeism in the Nation's Public Schools." May 2012. https://ct.global.ssl
.fastly.net/media/W1siZiIsIjIwMTQvMDgvMTUvMjE1dnkya3BzOF9G
SU5BTENocm9uaWNBYnNlbnRlZWlzbVJlcG9ydF9NYXkxNi5wZGY
iXV0/FINALChronicAbsenteeismReport_May16.pdf.pdf?sha=ffcb3d2b.

Balfanz, R., and N. Legters. "Locating the Dropout Crisis." Center for Research on
the Education of Students Placed at Risk. September 2004. http://www.csos
.jhu.edu/crespar/techReports/Report70.pdf.

Bezalher, L. 2013. "Why Do Democrats Want More Police in Schools." The Nation (January 11). http://www.thenation.com/article/172173/why-do-demo
crats-want-more-police-schools.

Bickel, F., and R. Qualls. 1980. "The Impact of School Climate on Suspension
Rates in the Jefferson County Public Schools." The Urban Review 12: 79–86.

Blum, R.W., and P.M. Reinhart. 2001. "Reducing the Risk: Corrections That Make
a Difference in the Lives of Youth." The National Longitudinal Study of Adolescent Health. http://www.cpc.unc.edu/projects/addhealth/faqs/addhealth/
Reducing-the-risk.pdf.

Boasberg, T. 2013. "Keeping Our Schools Safe." Denver Public Schools Newslet-
ter. http://archive.constantcontact.com/fs151/1110617542386/archive/11125
30423050.html.

Carter, P., M. Fine, and S. Russell. "Discipline Disparities: An Overview." The
Equity Project at Indiana University. March 2014, 3. http://www.indiana
.edu/~atlantic/wpcontent/uploads/2014/04/Disparity_Overview_040414.pdf.

"Causes of Pushout." Dignity in Schools Campaign. Accessed June 5, 2014. http://
www.dignityinschools.org/pushout-factors.

Chicago Public Schools. "Board of Education Approves Student Code of Conduct
to Foster Positive, Safer Learning Environments and Limit Removal of Students from Schools." Accessed June 27, 2012. http://www.cps.edu/News/Press_
releases/Pages/06_27_2012_PR3.aspx.

Colorado Department of Education. "Suspension/Expulsion Statistics for 2012–13." 2014. http://www.cde.state.co.us/cdereval/suspend-expelcurrent.

"Colorado School Expulsions Drop Because of Law." *USA Today* (March 26, 2014). http://www.usatoday.com/story/news/nation/2014/03/28/colorado-school-expulsions-drop/7026457/.

Cox, Ted. 2014. "CPS Discipline Racially Biased, Says Student Group." *DNA Info Chicago* (March 24). http://www.dnainfo.com/chicago/20140324/loop/cps-discipline-racially-biased-says-student-group.

CTU Communications. "CTU Statement on Obama Administration's New Guidelines on School Discipline." Chicago Teachers Union. January 9, 2014. http://www.ctunet.com/blog/ctu-statement-obama-school-discipline.

Denver Public Schools. "Policy JK-R-Student Conduct and Discipline Procedures." 2014. http://ed.dpsk12.org:8080/policy/FMPro?-db=policy.fp3&-format=detail.html&-lay=policyview&File=JK&-recid=32967&-find=.

"Denver Public Schools Show Progress, But Racial Disparities Persist in Punishment." Padres y Jóvenes Unidos press release. April 22, 2014, on the Padres y Jóvenes Unidos website. Accessed March 6, 2015. http://padresunidos.org/pressroom/release-denver-public-schools-show-progress-racial-disparities-persist-punishment.

Elliot, P. 2013. "NRA Calls for Armed Police Officer in Every School." *Associated Press.* (December 21). http://news.yahoo.com/nra-calls-armed-police-officer-every-school-162851713.html.

Ending the School to Prison Pipeline Hearing before the Senate Judiciary Subcommittee on the Constitution, Civil Rights, and Human Rights, 112th Cong. 3 (2012) (testimony of Julie Woestehoff, Executive Director, Parents United for Responsible Education). http://pureparents.org/wp-content/uploads/2012/12/PURE testimony12–10–12.pdf.

Ending the School to Prison Pipeline Hearing before the Senate Judiciary Subcommittee on the Constitution, Civil Rights, and Human Rights, 112th Cong. 3 (2012) (testimony of Edward Ward). https://www.youtube.com/watch?v=WVmw_uYlUMI.

Gray, S. 2007. "Where Students Can't Hug." *Time* (November 13). http://content.time.com/time/nation/article/0,8599,1683668,00.html.

Gregory, A., J. Bell, and M. Pollock. "How Educators Can Eradicate Disparities in School Discipline: A Briefing Paper on School-Based Interventions." The Equity Project at Indiana University. March 2014, 4. http://www.indiana.edu/~atlantic/wp-content/uploads/2014/03/Disparity_Interventions_Full_031214.pdf.

Hanssen, E. 1998. "A White Teachers Reflects on Institutional Racism." *Phi Delta Kappan* 79 (9): 694. Accessed June 3, 2014. http://public.hcesc.org/resources/Culturally%20Responsive%20Practice/Awhiteteacherreflects.pdf.

Harris, Rebecca. 2012. "Students, CPS Spar over School Arrests." *Catalyst Chicago* (April 24). http://www.catalyst-chicago.org/notebook/2012/04/24/20052/students-cps-spar-over-school-arrests.

"History and Accomplishments." Padres y Jóvenes Unidos. Accessed March 6, 2015. http://www.padresunidos.org/history-accomplishments.

Jenkins, A. 2007. "Inequality, Race, and Remedy." *The American Prospect* (April 22). http://prospect.org/article/inequality-race-and-remedy.

"Je'Terra Bowie, 7th Grader, Faces 180-Day Suspension for Yawning, Accidentally Touching Teacher." *Huffington Post* (November 22, 2011). http://www.huffingtonpost.com/2011/11/22/7th-grader-faces-180-day-suspension_n_1108241.html.

Jones, Rebecca. 2012. "Zeroing Out School Zero-Tolerance Policies." *Chalkbeat Colorado* (August 30). http://co.chalkbeat.org/2012/08/30/zeroing-out-school-zero-tolerance-policies/#.U5C2iyjLPTw.

Justice for Families. "Families Unlocking Futures: Solutions to the Crisis in Juvenile Justice." 2012, 7. http://www.justice4families.org/download-report/.

Kuznia, R. 2009. "Racism in Schools: Unintentional but No Less Damaging." *Pacific Standard* (April 8). http://www.psmag.com/navigation/books-and-culture/racism-in-schools-unintentional-3821/.

McCargar, L. "Invisible Students: The Role of Alternative and Adult Education in the Connecticut School-to-Prison Pipeline." A Better Way Foundation. December 2011, 20. http://www.abwfct.org/wp-content/uploads/2013/01/InvisibleStudents-Laura-McCarger.pdf.

McDonough, K. 2014. "Study: Police See Black Children as Less Innocent and Less Young Than White Children." *Salon* (March 11). http://www.salon.com/2014/03/11/study_police_see_black_children_as_less_innocent_and_less_young_than_white_children/.

McGee, K. "How Cultural Differences May Affect Student Performance." Great Schools. 2008. http://www.greatschools.org/special-education/support/704-cultural-differences-student-performance.gs.

"Middle School Student Suspended for Opening Door." *Tidewaternews.com* (February 26, 2011). http://www.tidewaternews.com/2011/02/26/middle-school-student-suspended-for-opening-door/.

"Mission." Dignity in Schools. Accessed June 3, 2014. http://www.dignityinschools.org/about-us/mission.

Padres y Jóvenes Unidos. "100 Days of Colorado Stories—Day 1: Father and Daughter." *YouTube* video, 3:16. October 5, 2011. https://www.youtube.com/watch?v=uwsyUtxhUio.

Padres y Jóvenes Unidos. "3rd Annual Community Accountability Report Card." April 2014, 7. https://s3.amazonaws.com/s3.documentcloud.org/documents/1146135/2013-dps-report-card-final-web-eng.pdf.

"Project Implicit." 2011. https://implicit.harvard.edu/implicit/; National Center for State Courts. "Strategies to Reduce the Influence of Implicit Bias."

http://www.ncsc.org/~/media/Files/PDF/Topics/Gender%20and%20
Racial%20Fairness/IB_Strategies_033012.ashx.

"Publish School Suspension and Expulsion Rates." *Chicago Sun Times* (May 14, 2014). http://www.suntimes.com/opinions/27440303-474/publish-school-sus pension-and-expulsion-rates.html#.U4jXYijLNrk.

Raymond, B. "Assigning Police Officers to Schools." *Center for Problem-Oriented Policing,* 2010. http://www.popcenter.org/responses/school_police/.

Rossi, R. 2012. "'Flaming Hot' Chips, Gum, Other 'Infractions' Costly at Some Schools." *Chicago Sun Times* (March 15). http://www.suntimes.com/news/ed ucation/10626363-418/flaming-hot-chips-gum-other-infractions-costly-at-some-schools.html.

Rudd, T. "Racial Disproportionality in School Discipline." The Kirwan Institute for the Study of Race and Ethnicity. February 2014, 3. http://kirwaninstitute .osu.edu/racial-disproportionality-in-school-discipline-implicit-bias-is-heav ily-implicated/.

"School Climate." National School Climate Center. Accessed May 31, 2014. http:// www.schoolclimate.org/climate/.

"School Pushout Story Bank." Dignity in Schools. Accessed June 8, 2014. http:// www.dignityinschools.org/our-work/school-pushout-story-bank.

"School to Prison Pipeline." NAACP Legal Defense and Education Fund. Accessed June 1, 2014. http://www.naacpldf.org/case/school-prison-pipeline.

Schreck, C.J., and J.M. Miller. 2003. "Sources of Fear of Crime at School: What Is the Relative Contribution of Disorder, Individual Characteristics and School Security?" *Journal of School Violence* 2: 57–79.

Silva, M. "Best Ways to Reach Out and Understand the Latino Culture." *NAMI NJ En Español,* 5. http://www.nami.org/Multicultural/Reaching_out_and_La tino_culture.pdf.

Simpson, K. 2012. "DPS Students Continue to Be Heard on School Discipline Issue." *Denver Post* (September 16). http://www.denverpost.com/ci_21553841/ dps-students-continue-be-heard-school-discipline-issue.

Skiba, R., et al. "Are Zero Tolerance Policies Effective in the Schools? An Eviden-tiary Review and Recommendations." *A Report by the American Psychological Association Zero Tolerance Task Force.* August 9, 2006. https://www.apa.org/ pubs/info/reports/zero-tolerance-report.pdf.

Skiba, R., and N. Williams. "Are Black Kids Worse: Myths and Facts about Racial Disparities in Discipline." The Equity Project at Indiana University. March 2014, 2–3. http://www.indiana.edu/~atlantic/wp-content/uploads/2014/03/ African-American-Differential-Behavior_031214.pdf.

Skiba, R., M. Arredondo, and M. Karega Rausch. "New and Developing Research on Disparities in Discipline." The Equity Project at Indiana University. March 2014, 2. http://www.indiana.edu/~atlantic/wp-content/uploads/2014/04/Dis parity_NewResearch_Full_040414.pdf.

Staats, C. "State of the Science Implicit Bias Review 2013." The Kirwan Institute for the Study of Race and Ethnicity. 2013, 6. http://kirwaninstitute.osu.edu/docs/SOTS-Implicit_Bias.pdf.

"Steele Discusses Stereotype Threat." *College Street Journal* (September 24, 2004). https://www.mtholyoke.edu/offices/comm/csj/092404/steele.shtml.

Steinberg, M., E. Allensworth, and David W. Johnson. "Student and Teacher Safety in Chicago Public Schools: The Roles of Community Context and School Social Organization." Consortium on Chicago School Research. May 2011. https://ccsr.uchicago.edu/sites/default/files/publications/SAFETY%20IN%20CPS.pdf.

St. George, Donna. 2014. "Researchers Point to Racial Disparities in School Suspension, Spotlight New Practices." *Washington Post* (March 14). http://www.washingtonpost.com/local/education/researchers-point-to-racial-disparities-in-school-suspension-spotlight-new-practices/2014/03/14/0017cd98-aaa7-11e3-adbc-888c8010c799_story.html.

"Stories." Suspension Stories. Accessed June 8, 2014. http://www.suspensionstories.com/.

Street, P. "Stories from on the Ground in Chicago." Network of Teacher Activist Groups. September 13, 2012. http://www.teacheractivistgroups.org/ctu-solidarity/page/3/#sthash.xRxVGOwK.dpuf.

Teaching as Leadership. "The 'Knowledge Base' of Self: Uncovering Hidden Biases and Unpacking Privilege." Teach for America. Accessed March 6, 2015. http://teachingasleadership.org/sites/default/files/Related-Readings/DCA_Ch5_2011.pdf.

Teaching Tolerance. The Southern Poverty Law Center. "Test Yourself for Hidden Bias." http://www.tolerance.org/activity/test-yourself-hidden-bias.

"Tell Your Story with Pre-Prison Diaries." Community Rights Campaign, Labor/Community Strategy Center. Accessed June 8, 2014. http://www.thestrategycenter.org/node/879.

Tenants and Workers United. "Obstacles to Opportunity: Alexandria, Virginia Students Speak Out." October 2007, 9–10. http://virginia-organizing.org/sites/default/files/Obstacles2Opportunity-Final.pdf.

"13-Year-Old Student Arrested for 'Passing Gas' in School." *Huffington Post* (November 24, 2008). http://www.huffingtonpost.com/2008/11/24/13-year-old-student-arres_n_146222.html.

Tobin, T., G. Sugai, and D. Colvin. 1996. "Patterns in Middle School Discipline Records." *Journal of Emotional and Behavioral Disorders* 4: 82–94.

Torres, M., and J.A. Stefkovich. 2009. "Demographics and Police Involvement: Implications for Student Civil Liberties and Just Leadership." *Education Administration Quarterly* 45 (3): 450–473.

"Understanding the Issue." Ending the Schoolhouse to Jailhouse: A Project of Advancement Project. Accessed June 7, 2014. http://safequalityschools.org/pages/understanding-the-school-prison-pipeline.

United States Department of Education, National Center on Education Statistics. "The Conditions of Education 2006." 2006. http://nces.ed.gov/pubs 2006/2006071.pdf.

United States Department of Education, National Center for Education Statistics. "Indicators of School Crime and Safety 2013." 2013. http://nces.ed.gov/pro grams/crimeindicators/crimeindicators2013/index.asp.

United States Department of Education, Office for Civil Rights. *2011–2012 Civil Rights Data Collection Data Snapshot: School Discipline,* Issue Brief No. 1. March 2014. http://www2.ed.gov/about/offices/list/ocr/docs/crdc-discipline-snapshot.pdf.

United States Department of Education, Office for Civil Rights. "Guiding Principles: A Resource Guide for Improving School Climate and Discipline." January 2014. http://www2.ed.gov/policy/gen/guid/school-discipline/guid ing-principles.pdf.

United States Department of Education, Office for Civil Rights and United States Department of Justice: Civil Rights Division. "Joint Dear Colleague Letter." January 8, 2014. http://www2.ed.gov/about/offices/list/ocr/letters/col league-201401-title-vi.html.

United States Department of Justice, Office of Public Affairs. "Attorney General Holder, Secretary Duncan Announce Effort to Respond to School-to-Prison Pipeline by Supporting Good Discipline Practices." July 11, 2011. http://www .justice.gov/opa/pr/2011/July/11-ag-951.html.

"Videos." Fix School Discipline. Accessed June 8, 2014. http://www.fixschooldis cipline.org/.

VOYCE. "Fact Sheet: Civil Rights, Transparency, and Accountability at Chicago Charter Schools." *EdWeek.* Accessed March 28, 2015. http://blogs.edweek .org/edweek/District_Dossier/FACT%20SHEET%20no%20embargo .6.11.13%20%281%29.pdf.

VOYCE. "Failed Policies, Broken Futures: The Trust Cost of Zero Tolerance in Chicago." July 2011. https://s3.amazonaws.com/s3.documentcloud.org/docu ments/216318/voyce.pdf.

Wallace, K. 2013. "Student Suspended for Sexual Harassment after Hugging Teacher." *CNN* (December 17). http://www.cnn.com/2013/12/17/living/par ents-student-suspended-sexual-harassment-hugging-teacher/.

Welsh, W.N. 2003. "Individual and Institutional Predictors of School Disorder." *Youth Violence and Juvenile Justice* 1: 346–368.

"What Is School Pushout." Dignity in Schools. Accessed June 1, 2014. http://www .dignityinschools.org/files/Pushout_Fact_Sheet.pdf.

The White House, Office of the Press Secretary. "Executive Order—White House Initiative on Educational Excellence for African Americans." July 26, 2012. http://www.whitehouse.gov/the-press-office/2012/07/26/executive-or der-white-house-initiative-educational-excellence-african-am.

The White House, Office of the Press Secretary. "Fact Sheet: Opportunity for All: President Obama Launches My Brother's Keeper Initiative to Build Ladders of Opportunity for Boys and Young Men of Color." February 27, 2014. http://www.whitehouse.gov/the-press-office/2014/02/27/fact-sheet-opportunity-all-president-obama-launches-my-brother-s-keeper-.

"WTF: Cops Nab 5-Year-Old for Wearing Wrong Color Shoes to School." *Yahoo News,* January 18, 2013. http://news.yahoo.com/wtf-cops-nab-five-old-wearing-wrong-color-203600800.html.

Youth United for Change. "Pushed Out." February 2011, 2. http://ourcity-our schools.org/sites/default/files/Pushed-Out%20—%20Youth%20Voices%20 on%20the%20Dropout%20Crisis%20in%20Philadelphia%20—%20YUC%20 report.pdf.

Youth United for Change. "Zero Tolerance in Philadelphia." January 2011, 23. http://b.3cdn.net/advancement/68a6ec942d603a5d27_rim6ynnir.pdf.

Chapter 5

Criminalization and Medicalization: The School-to-Prison Pipeline and Racialized Double Standards of Disciplinary Control

Nancy A. Heitzeg

Over the past two decades, scholars, educators, activists, and advocates have expressed growing concern over the emergence of a "school-to-prison pipeline." The immediate impetus for the pipeline is "zero tolerance" policies, which, when accompanied by a growing police presence in schools, result in the indirect/direct funneling of millions of youth out of school and on a pathway toward prison. The application of these educational policies is neither neutral nor random. Students of color, especially African Americans, are suspended and expelled at more than three times the rate of their white peers, this despite no documented differences in rates of disciplinary infractions. Research also increasingly indicates that disruptive white youth are medicalized rather than criminalized at school, receiving DSM-V diagnoses for attention-deficit hyperactivity disorder (ADHD) and other disorders rather than suspensions and expulsions, and that the implicit biases of teachers and other school personnel play a key role in this trajectory. Efforts to disrupt the school-to-prison pipeline must take this larger context into account. Eliminating zero tolerance and police in schools is an essential first step, but the underlying tendency—both macro and micro, old and new—toward racialized double standards in social control must be examined and uprooted. In the following, the school-to-prison pipeline and efforts to dismantle it will be examined in light of (1) "color-blind" yet racialized social control that relies on the criminalization of blackness and the medicalization of "whiteness"; (2) educational policies, such as zero tolerance and a police presence at schools, that make the school-to-prison pipeline possible; (3) the racial dynamics of social control in the schools that leads to disproportionate suspension/expulsion of students of color and the corresponding medicalization of white students; and (4) recommendations for ending the school-to-prison pipeline.

The School-to-Prison Pipeline: Racialized and Criminalized Control in an Age of Race-Neutral Policy

Sixty years since *Brown,* the promise of equal educational opportunity remains elusive. The call for desegregation with "all deliberate speed" was stymied at every turn and now has been abandoned by the "race-neutral" language of the post–civil rights era, which has essentially forbidden any consideration of race to balance school enrollments.[1] Separate and unequal continues, characterized now by de facto hyper-segregation by both race and class and by gulfs in both funding and quality.

Further, shifts in educational policy in the past decades have exacerbated the inequities. Decreased funding, high-stakes testing with sanctions for "underperforming" schools, overcrowded class rooms, massive school closures, and a push toward privatization and "charterization" have widened the racial gaps in both opportunity and achievement. Perhaps the most troubling development is the trend toward criminalization of these same students in under-resourced schools. For them, rather than creating an atmosphere of learning, engagement and opportunity, current educational practices have increasingly blurred the distinction between school and jail. The school-to-prison pipeline refers to this growing pattern of tracking students out of educational institutions, primarily via zero tolerance policies, and tracking them directly and/or indirectly into the juvenile and adult criminal justice systems.

While schools have long been characterized by both formal and informal tracks that route students into various areas of the curriculum, tracking students *out* of school and into jail is a new phenomenon. Current policies have increased the risk of students being suspended, expelled, and/or arrested at school. This pattern of "pushout" has become so pronounced that scholars, child advocates, and community activists now refer to it as "the school-to-prison pipeline," the "schoolhouse to jailhouse track," or, as younger and younger students are targeted, "the cradle to prison track."[2]

In part, the school-to-prison pipeline is a consequence of schools that criminalize minor disciplinary infractions via zero tolerance policies, have a police presence at the school, and rely on suspensions and expulsions for minor infractions. What were once disciplinary issues for school administrators are now called crimes, and either students are arrested directly at school or their infractions are reported to the police. Students are criminalized via the juvenile and/or adult criminal justice systems. The risk of later incarceration for students who are suspended or expelled even without arrest is also great. For many, going to school has become literally and figuratively synonymous with going to jail.

The immediate impetus for the pipeline is zero tolerance policies, which, when accompanied by a growing police presence in schools, result in the indirect/direct funneling of millions of youth out of school and on a pathway toward prison. But it is also the result of larger social and political trends. The school-to-prison pipeline is consistent with an increasingly harsh legal system for both juveniles and adults, and the rise of the prison industrial complex, where punishment translates into profit. These policies exactly mirror the "get tough" mandatory minimums associated with the War on Drugs, and the corresponding rise in mass incarceration, a trend that has resulted by a more tenfold increase in incarceration in a period of 40 years.

This in itself has been cause for alarm, but a consistently growing body of research further indicates that the application of these educational policies is neither neutral nor random. The school-to-prison pipeline disproportionately impacts the poor, students with disabilities, and youth of color. Students of color, especially African Americans, are suspended and expelled at more than three times the rate of their white peers, this despite no documented differences in rates of disciplinary infractions. While race is the most significant factor, disparities in suspension/expulsion escalate at the intersections of class, gender, sexual orientation, and ability. Research also increasingly indicates that disruptive middle-class white youth are medicalized rather than criminalized at school, receiving DSM-V diagnoses for ADHD and other disorders rather than suspensions and expulsions. The implicit biases of teachers and other school personnel play a key role in this trajectory.

Supposedly color-blind educational policies that criminalize blackness and mitigate whiteness, especially through medicalization, reflect the larger national context of racialized double standards in social control. Mass incarceration of people of color in the context of the War on Drugs, for example, is made possible by the corresponding rise of the medical model of treatment as an option for the middle class and white. The school-to-prison pipeline continues the flow of black/brown youth into criminal justice, while medicalizing the disruptive behaviors of white youth. And to the extent that schools serve as institutions of socialization toward career pathways, questions must be raised as to the extent that current school disciplinary policies are meant to steer some toward "careers" as prisoners. It is within this larger context of color blindness, mass incarceration, and corresponding medicalization that the school-to-prison pipeline emerges. And it is within this larger context that recommendations for the interruption of this growing pattern of punishing rather than educating America's youth must be made as well.

Color-Blind Racism and Social Control

One of the major challenges of the post–civil rights era involves confronting the notion that racism is now over. White supremacy was removed from its legalized pedestal with the Civil Rights Act of 1964, the Voting Rights Act of 1965, and, finally, the Fair Housing Act of 1968. The law became race-neutral and it now suddenly was illegal to discriminate on the basis of race. Many are content to believe that once de jure segregation ended, everything was magically equal on a now-level color-blind playing field. "Color-blind racism" explains contemporary racial inequality as the outcome of nonracial dynamics and allows whites (others too) to equate racism with prejudice, ignoring the institutionalized and systemic racial structures that sustain and reproduce white racial privilege.

Much racial inequality is now embedded de facto in structural arrangements; it is certainly more invisible. Racism, as both white supremacist ideology and institutionalized arrangement, remains merely transformed with its systemic foundations intact. Segregation in housing and education persists at levels beyond that noted in *Brown v. Board of Education,* racial wealth gaps grow, and racial disparities in criminal injustice proliferate at a pace that has led to the claim that racial caste has again been reinscribed, this time via color-blind criminal justice policies, a.k.a. "The New Jim Crow."[3]

A large body of research documents the paradigmatic shift from overt essentialist racist to color blindness. This style of racism relies heavily on ideological frames and linguistic shifts which allow whites to assert they "do not see race," deny structural racism, claim a level playing field that in fact now victimizes them with "reverse discrimination" and appeals to the "race card," and argue that any discussion of race/racism is in fact racist, serving to foment divisions rather than reflect/redress societal realities. Color-blind racism also creates a set of code terms and frames that implicitly indict people of color without ever mentioning race. There is an emphasis on merit, claims to equal opportunity, natural patterns that explain away institutional discrimination, appeals to cultural racism, and a denial or minimization of the ongoing effects of racism.

These ideological frames are used to justify all sorts of racial arrangements, but play a particularly strong role in providing cover for institutionalized racism in social control, including the criminal justice system and the school-to-prison pipeline. The Black Man as Dangerous is an old idea, now honed and solidified into an archetype that scholars and activists now refer to in aggregate short-hand: The Criminal-Black-Man. The Criminal-Black-Man archetype is the centerpiece of the post–civil rights era's reliance on color blindness. Race needs never be explicitly named, but "high crime neighborhoods," "gangs," "thugs," "ghettos," "hoods," and "hoodies" all evoke a racialized image. All people of color—Latinos/Latinas and Native American especially and the poor, women, the young, the queer—are targets here too—but it is blackness that provides the paradigm. This image is ubiquitous; it offers the framework for both creating and then perversely justifying the demographics of both the prison industrial complex and the school-to-prison pipeline, the medicalization of white deviance, and unnamed double standards of social control.

Prisonization, Medicalization, and Profit

The color-blind frame serves to mask wide racial disparities in social control to create an additional context for the school-to-prison pipeline. White deviance is often framed as individualized sickness that should be via the medical model, while communities of color are most likely to be criminalized. The implications of this are profound. While both medical and criminal labels carry stigma and the possibility of social exclusion, the consequences attached vary dramatically. Those who are medicalized are offered treatment, diminished culpability, and the expectation of a "cure"; those criminalized face the harshest sanctions that U.S. society can mete out, relatively permanent stigma, attenuated opportunities, and civil and, sometimes, literal death.

The post–civil rights era has brought an expansion of the use of criminal justice as the primary mechanism for defining and controlling communities of color. The War on Drugs, with its attendant harsh sentences and reliance on racial profiling, has been the essential vehicle for reinscribing racial inequality. This is the continuation of an old theme: post-slavery, the criminalizing narrative has been a central cultural feature of ongoing efforts at oppression; from convict lease/plantation prison farms to the contemporary prison industrial complex, the control of black bodies for profit has been furthered by the criminal justice system. "Slave Codes" become Black Codes and Black Codes become the War on Drugs with the race-neutral language but racial enforcement of gang legislation, mandatory minimum, and three-strikes sentencing.[4] The result has been an unparalleled explosion in imprisonment, the emergence of the prison industrial complex, and a downward drift in punitive approaches that has created the so-called school-to-prison pipeline as well.

The United States is the world's leader in incarceration, with nearly 2.4 million people currently in prison or jail—a 500 percent increase over the past 30 years.[5] The connection of the prison to the profit motive in the prison industrial complex has led to draconian policies that target juveniles as well as adults via the school-to-prison pipeline and which inhibit reentry of former inmates with a host of collateral consequences that limit access to employment, education, housing, the vote, and other benefits upon release.

The increased rate of incarceration can be traced to the War on Drugs and the rise of lengthy mandatory minimum prison sentences for drug crimes and other felonies. These policies have proliferated, not in response to crime rate or any empirical data that indicates their effectiveness, due to newly found sources of profit for prisons. As Brewer and Heitzeg observe:

> The prison industrial complex is a self-perpetuating machine where the vast profits (e.g. cheap labor, private and public supply and construction contracts, job creation, continued media profits from exaggerated crime reporting and crime/punishment as entertainment) and perceived political benefits (e.g. reduced unemployment rates, "get tough on crime" and public safety rhetoric, funding increases for police, and criminal justice system agencies and professionals) lead to policies that are additionally designed to insure an endless supply of "clients" for the criminal justice system (e.g. enhanced police presence in poor neighborhoods and communities of color; racial profiling; decreased funding for public education combined with zero-tolerance policies and increased rates of expulsion for students of color; increased rates of adult certification for juvenile offenders; mandatory minimum and "three-strikes" sentencing; draconian conditions of incarceration and a reduction of prison services that contribute to the likelihood of "recidivism"; "collateral

consequences"—such as felony disenfranchisement, prohibitions on welfare receipt, public housing, gun ownership, voting and political participation, employment—that nearly guarantee continued participation in "crime" and return to the prison industrial complex following initial release.[6]

These policies disproportionately affect people of color. This trend toward mass incarceration is marred by racial disparity. While 1 in 35 adults is under correctional supervision and 1 in every 100 adults is in prison, 1 in every 36 Latino adults, 1 in every 15 black men, 1 in every 100 black women, and 1 in 9 black men aged 20 to 34 are incarcerated.[7] Nationally, blacks are incarcerated five times more than whites are, and Latinos/Latinas are nearly twice as likely to be incarcerated as whites.[8] These disparities are indicative of differential enforcement practices rather than any differences in criminal participation. This is particularly true of drug crimes, which account for the bulk of the increased prison population. Even though blacks and whites use and sell drugs at comparable rates, African Americans are anywhere from 3 to 10 times more likely to be arrested and in addition likely to receive harsher sentences than their white counterparts.[9]

Correspondingly, the medical model has expanded as well, offering an alternative to incarceration for the white and well to do. It offers a definition of deviance—be it drug use, other criminal activity, or school misbehavior—that allows treatment rather than punishment. The expansion of the medical industrial complex coincides exactly with the emergence of the prison industrial complex. This is not mere historical coincidence. The medical model offers a safety value whereby white middle-class deviants may be diverted from the legal system and offered treatment, escaping both the harsh collective label of criminal and the increasingly punitive treatment associated with the U.S. legal system. One of the key features of the medical model involves mitigating deviant behavior by attributing it to "sickness rather than badness"[10] with a particular focus on the condition rather than the behavior and treatment as opposed to punishment.

Once laden with extreme stigma and images of the publicly funded insane asylum, the treatment of mental illness is now a multibillion-dollar industry, privatized and driven by the widespread use of pharmaceuticals to treat nearly every major affliction. Access to this model requires insurance or sufficient wealth to accommodate psychiatrists, $30,000 stays at private treatment facilities, and psychotropic medications. The expansion of the model was initially sparked by the addiction treatment industry for Substance Use Disorders and now extends far beyond.

The medical model overlaps significantly with the legal system with regard to both Substance Use and Disruptive Behavior Disorders, the two issues most immediately connected to the War on Drugs and the school-to-prison pipeline. The medical model focuses on conditions/illnesses rather than intentional actions and, as such, may offer an alternative to incarceration and/or suspension and expulsion by diverting offenders away from criminal systems/labels and toward treatment. In other words, offenders may be treated for their addictions or attention-deficit disorders or punished for their legal violations or disruptive behavior at school. A growing body of research indicates that race and race as it interacts with class plays a significant role in medicalization versus criminalization of both drug use and school misbehavior.[11]

This is not to say that whites are not criminalized; they are, but class is a key determinate, and it is poor whites, rather than their well-off counterparts, who are disproportionately arrested, charged, and incarcerated. Nor is this to say that communities of color do not receive psychiatric diagnoses. They do but tend to receive the more serious diagnoses that still carry substantial stigma such as schizophrenia or, in the context of educational settings, learning disabilities. Often these diagnoses may come within the context of criminal justice, rather than as a diversion from it, as increasing numbers of mentally ill are incarcerated. Still, the overall of trajectory of social control is now for profit, where medicalization is the preferred response to white deviance and criminalization the label of choice for communities of color, especially blacks. This larger social trend is now reflected in schools as well and shapes both the demand and the flow of students of color into the school-to-prison pipeline.

The School-to-Prison Pipeline: Criminalized Education

The school-to-prison pipeline, and the policies that make it possible, does not exist in isolation. The school-to-prison pipeline is part and parcel of a larger sociopolitical color-blind climate characterized by extensive for-profit and racialized systems of social control. It is consistent with a range of policies associated with mass incarceration, harsh sentences for nonviolent offenses, and an increasingly punitive legal system for both juveniles and adults. Further, the impact of the school-to-prison pipeline is complicated by and correlated with failing schools that are overcrowded, inadequately resourced, heavily pressured by the high-stakes testing originally associated with No Child Left Behind (NCLB) and related initiatives, and highly segregated by both race and class.

The term the "school-to-prison pipeline" began to emerge in the late 1990s as scholars, child advocates, and community activists began to see the results of school policy changes that emerged during that decade. The school-to-prison pipeline describes the growing pattern of tracking students out of educational institutions and sending them on a pathway toward the juvenile and adult criminal justice systems.[12]

Sometimes this push toward prison and jail is indirect; students who are suspended and/or expelled are less likely to return to school, are sent to under-resourced alternative schools, and are, in effective, "pushed out" of the educational system. Increasingly, the school-to-prison pipeline operates in a more direct fashion, as misconduct has become criminalized and as a growing police presence in the schools allows for direct arrests and ticketing, often for minor misconduct that once would have been handled by teachers and school administrators.[13]

Most immediately, the school-to-prison pipeline is the direct result of educational policies and practices that have transformed many schools from sites of opportunity and inclusion into centers of criminalization and exclusion.[14] Over the past two decades, the proliferation of zero tolerance policies and an increased police presence at schools have combined to shape the school-to-prison pipeline via the "criminalization of school discipline."[15] The school-to-prison pipeline is a consequence of schools which criminalize minor disciplinary infractions via zero tolerance policies, have a police and/or security officers' (School Resource Officer [SRO]) presence for enforcement, and rely on suspensions, expulsions, and arrests for minor infractions. While these policies were motivated, in part, by the perceived need to increase "safety" and "security," zero tolerance policies and police in schools have instead blurred the lines between the educational function of schools and the punishment orientation of legal systems.

Zero Tolerance, Police in the Hallways, and Risk

While there is no official definition of the term "zero tolerance," generally the term means that a harsh predefined mandatory consequence is applied to a violation of school rules without regard to the seriousness of the behavior, mitigating circumstances, or the situational context. Violators are suspended, expelled, and increasingly arrested and charged in juvenile court as a result. Zero tolerance rhetoric, which was borrowed from the War on Drugs, became widespread by the mid-1990s, despite school crime/violence rates that were stable or declining. Implementation was achieved by appeals to fears and calls for safety and further enforced by the connection of related policies to both federal and state school funding.

The Gun-Free Schools Act of 1994 (GFSA) provided the initial impetus for zero tolerance policies. The GFSA mandates that all schools that receive federal funding must (1) have policies to expel for a calendar year any student who brings a firearm to school or to school zone and (2) report that student to local law enforcement, thereby blurring any distinction between disciplinary infractions at school and breaking the law. Subsequent amendments to the GFSA and changes in many state laws and local school district regulations broadened the GFSA focus on firearms to apply to many other kinds of weapons.[16]

While the original intent of the GFSA was to require these punishments for serious violations involving weapons and conduct, most schools nationally have adopted zero tolerance policies for a variety of behavioral issues—weapons, alcohol/drugs, threatening behavior, fighting on school premises, and increasingly minor "misconduct" such as tardiness, "defiance," and disorderly conduct.[17] Zero tolerance policies often do not distinguish between serious and nonserious offenses, nor do they adequately separate intentional troublemakers from those with behavioral disorders. And as the name implies, these policies indicate zero tolerance for any infractions, casting a very wide net.

Zero tolerance policies are additionally associated with an increased police presence at school, metal detectors, security cameras, locker and person searches, and all the accoutrements of legal control. The Safe Schools Act of 1994 and a 1998 amendment to the Omnibus Crime Control and Safe Streets Act of 1968 promoted partnerships between schools and law enforcement, including the provision of funding for in-school police forces or SROs.[18] In 1999, the U.S. Department of Justice "COPS in Schools" grant program dramatically increased the use of SROs, in part as a response to the highly publicized Columbine shootings.[19]

The presence of uniformed police officers in schools is now routine. According to Raymond, "An estimated one-third of all sheriffs' offices and almost half of all municipal police departments assign nearly 17,000 sworn officers to serve in schools, and nearly half of all public schools have assigned police officers."[20] Although enhanced security measures were largely inspired by the school shootings in predominately white suburban schools, they have been most readily adopted and enforced in urban schools, where nearly 70 percent report a police presence.[21] It is less common but also possible now for some schools to employ canine units, Tasers, and SWAT team raids for drug and weapons searches.[22]

Zero tolerance and school policing were promoted as policies that would increase the safety and security of students and enhance the orderly delivery of education. In reality, the opposite has occurred. There is little research that documents any correlation between these policies and reduced school violence. A growing body of work, however, documents the myriad risks created for students, including increased rates of suspension/expulsion and dropouts/pushouts, hostile climate, and racial disparities in the application of discipline. It is these very policies that have facilitated the flow of students out of schools and into legal systems, in fact, creating the school-to-prison pipeline.

Under zero tolerance policies, over 3.3 million students are suspended each year and over 100,000 expelled.[23] This number has nearly doubled since 1974, with rates escalating in the mid-1990s as zero tolerance policies began to be widely adopted.[24] Suspension and expulsion rates increased most dramatically immediately following the adoption of No Child Left Behind legislation and related forms of high-stakes testing. Critics have noted that zero tolerance policies have been used to "push out" low-performing students. Since school funding is directly tied to test scores, NCLB (and later Race to the Top and Common Core) gives schools an incentive to get rid of rather than remediate students with low test scores; it is more "efficient" to simply remove the child from class through punitive disciplinary measures and focus on the remaining students.

While zero tolerance was initially intended to address serious offenses such as deadly weapons, assaults, and possession/sale of illegal drugs, the bulk of the suspensions are for minor infractions. Quite typical cases include the following:

- A 17-year-old junior shot a paper clip with a rubber band at a classmate, missed, and broke the skin of a cafeteria worker. The student was expelled from school.
- A nine-year-old on the way to school found a manicure kit with a 1-inch knife. The student was suspended for one day.
- Two 10-year-old boys from Arlington, Virginia, were suspended for three days for putting soapy water in a teacher's drink. The boys were charged with a felony that carried a maximum sentence of 20 years, and were formally

processed through the juvenile justice system before the case was dismissed months later.

- A Pennsylvania kindergartener tells her friends she's going to shoot them with a Hello Kitty toy that makes soap bubbles. The kindergartener was initially suspended for two days, and the incident was reclassified as a "threat to harm others."
- In Massachusetts, a five-year-old boy attending an after-school program makes a gun out of Legos, points it at other students, and mimics the sound of gunfire. He was expelled.[25]

Students who are suspended and/or expelled are deprived of educational services or are, at best, referred to substandard alternative schools. Many states fail to offer any access at all to alternative schools. In fact, only 13 states mandate alternative education for expelled students, and those that do often rely on educational settings that are less resourced than the schools that students were expelled from in the first place. Students are left to fend for themselves, and if they are reinstated, they are now further behind their peers and more likely to be suspended again. In fact, rather than deterring disruptive behavior, the most likely consequence of suspension is additional suspension.

Increased dropout rates are directly related to the repeated use of suspension and expulsion. Students who have been suspended or expelled are more likely to experience poor academic performance and eventually drop out. Additional suspensions increase this likelihood. The National Center for Education Statistics documents this: 31 percent of high school sophomores who dropped out of school have been suspended three or more times, a rate much higher than for those who had not been suspended at all.[26]

Both suspension/expulsion and dropout/pushout rates are highly correlated with future involvement in the juvenile and adult legal systems, creating an indirect pathway out of school and into jail. It is, however, the growing police presence at schools that contributes to the direct flow of youth into the juvenile justice system. Police in schools means more arrests and not necessarily for serious criminal violations. A variety of studies have shown that a police presence significantly increases both arrests and the criminalization of minor misconduct; one three-year study of numerous schools in the same district, for example, found that the schools with police had nearly five times the number of arrests for disorderly conduct as schools without a police presence.

Each year, hundreds of thousands are ticketed and/or arrested at school for minor infraction; research indicates that as many as two-thirds may be for "offenses" such as talking back to teachers, truancy, or disorderly conduct. Typical cases involve tantrums, pushing other students, writing on school desks, and disobeying an officer. The following are indicative examples:

- A five-year-old boy in Queens, New York, was arrested, handcuffed, and taken to a psychiatric hospital for having a tantrum and knocking papers off the principal's desk.
- In St. Petersburg, Florida, a five-year-old girl was handcuffed, arrested, and taken into custody for having a tantrum and disrupting a classroom.
- An 11-year-old girl in Orlando, Florida, was tasered by a police officer, arrested, and faced charges of battery on a security resource officer, disrupting a school function and resisting with violence. She had pushed another student.
- An honors student in Houston, Texas, was forced to spend a night in jail when she missed class to go to work to support her family.
- A 13-year-old from New York was handcuffed and removed from school for writing the word "okay" on her school desk.[27]

This is not a climate conducive to education. The American Psychological Association and the American Academy of Pediatrics have found that extreme discipline, including arrests, predicts grade retention, school dropout, and future involvement in the juvenile and criminal justice systems.[28] Research shows that a first-time arrest doubles the odds that a student will drop out of high school, and a first-time court appearance quadruples the odds. Zero tolerance policies and over-policing are associated with negative outcomes for all youth, academically, socially, emotionally, and behaviorally. This includes a decreased commitment to education in light of perceptions of unfair treatment.[29]

The School-to-Prison Pipeline: Race-Neutral Language, Racialized Results

School policies that insist on zero tolerance and a police presence at school are couched in race-neutral language and appeals to safety and security. Like their legal War on Drugs counterparts, race is unnamed in the policies but central to their enforcement. It is students of color, especially, African Americans, who are the target of enforcement efforts and, ultimately, those disproportionately pushed out of schools and on a pathway to prison. This is made possible in part by the option for medicalizing rather than criminalizing disruptive students, and that is the option most often pursued for white students.

Criminalization of Black Youth

While turning schools into "secure zero tolerance environments" lowers morale and makes learning more difficult for all students, schools that have a high percentage of minority and low-income students bear the brunt.[30] Criminalized education disproportionately impacts the poor, students with disabilities, lesbian, gay, bisexual, and transgender students, and youth of color, especially African Americans, who are suspended, expelled, and arrested at the highest rates, despite comparable rates of infraction. The U.S. Department of Education, Civil Rights Division, documents the disparity. The most recent data indicates that the racial gap is widening, as nationally, black students were three and a half times more likely to be suspended or expelled than their white peers. In some districts, black students are more than six times more likely to be suspended or expelled than their white peers. One in five black boys and more than 1 in 10 black girls received an out-of-school suspension, with the suspension and expulsion rates for black girls surpassing that of boys of other races. The trend starts early, as preschools now play a role in suspension and expulsions. Black children represent 18 percent of preschool enrollment, but 42 percent of the pre-school children suspended once, and 48 percent of the preschool children suspended more than once.[31]

Black students made up only 18 percent of students, but they accounted for 35 percent of those suspended once, 46 percent of those suspended more than once, and 39 percent of all expulsions. In districts that reported expulsions under zero tolerance policies, "Hispanic and black students represent 45 percent of the student body, but 56 percent of those expelled under such policies."[32] In addition, black and Latino students represent over 70 percent of the students arrested or referred to law enforcement at school.[33] This racial overrepresentation then manifests itself in both higher dropout rates for students of color (students from historically disadvantaged minority groups have little more than a 50–50 chance of finishing high school with a diploma) and the racialized dynamic of the legal system.

Black youth, especially males, are additionally at risk due to their over-representation in special education programs for disability.[34] They are nearly twice as likely as any other group to receive services under the Individuals with Disabilities Education Act (IDEA).[35] A substantial body of literature documents that African American boys typically receive the most stigmatizing labels here. They are often mislabeled as mentally retarded; they are nearly three times more likely to receive special education services under IDEA for mental retardation and more than two times more likely to receive services for emotional disturbance than same-age students of all other racial/ethnic groups combined. Students with disabilities are at most risk for suspension/expulsion; one in four black males with a disability is suspended/expelled. In addition, these students are most likely to face seclusion and physical restraint at school.

Since research has found no indication that African American youth violate rules at higher rates than other groups, the persistence of stereotypes of young black males and "cultural miscommunication" between students and teachers is oft cited as one key factor. Eighty-three percent of U.S. teaching ranks are filled by whites, mostly women, and implicit biases with attendant stereotyping can shape the decision to suspend or expel. This is supported by recent research that suggests that young white females in particular view black male children as young as 10 as "criminals" rather than "innocent" children.[36] In fact, the highest rates of racially disproportionate discipline are found in states that have low minority populations, indicating that boys of color are potentially threatening to white teachers, even in small numbers.

Medicalization of White Youth

While students of color are being criminalized for disruptive behaviors at school, white students are medicalized. One of the growth sectors of psychiatry is the diagnosis and treatment of Disorders of Infancy, Childhood and Adolescence (DICA), particularly the Disruptive Behavior Disorders of Attention-Deficit Hyperactivity Disorder, Oppositional Defiant Disorder and Conduct Disorder. These psychiatric labels perfectly overlap with potential educational and legal labels and thus offer an alternative mechanism for parents, school officials, and law enforcement to deal with disciplinary infractions. ADHD in particular has become the diagnosis of choice for addressing issues at school.

Controversy still remains as to whether or not ADHD represents an actual disease or a sociocultural construct. Debate rages too over the use of medication, especially stimulants, as the primary treatment option. Nonetheless, the use of ADHD as a diagnosis for school children has increased dramatically in the past decades, coincidental to the proliferation of zero tolerance policies. Since 1980, ADHD diagnoses have increased 40 percent over the last decade and more than 50 percent over the 25-year period, with medication use rising at a corresponding rate.[37] Currently, nearly one in five high school–age boys in the United States and 15 percent of school-age children overall have received a medical diagnosis of ADHD.[38]

Race/ethnicity, class, and insurance coverage are key indicators of who receives an ADHD diagnosis and medication. While ADHD was largely once a middle-class phenomenon, increases in the use of diagnoses expanded with the inclusion of ADHD in IDEA and the subsequent expansion of Medicaid coverage to pay for medication. These increases in both ADHD diagnoses and medication further correlate with NCLB and pressure for test score accountability that translates into funding. Research shows that states with high rates of ADHD diagnoses correlated closely with state laws that penalize schools when students fail.

While class matters less than it once did with regard to ADHD diagnoses, race continues to be highly correlated. Study after study shows racial disparities in the diagnosis and treatment of ADHD as well as other Disruptive Behavior Disorders, with the indication that teachers were most likely to expect and define ADHD as an issue for white boys. Both black and Latino/Latina students are far less likely than their white peers to receive an ADHD diagnosis; as we have seen, if they are medicalized in the school context at all, it is with more stigmatizing labels of learning disorders that focus on intellectual ability rather than behavior.

ADHD becomes a vehicle for the medicalization of disruptive white students, as well as a perceived panacea in the climate of high-stakes testing. While there is growing concern about overdiagnosis of ADHD, overmedication, and a growing black market for ADHD medications, this medical label is arguably preferable to suspension/expulsion for comparable disruptive behaviors. This diagnosis serves as a barrier to the de facto criminalization experienced by students of color at school, who are suspended, expelled, and/or arrested at school at rates more than three times that of their white classmates.

These double standards of control are consistent with the larger context of for-profit medicalization and criminalization in the post–civil rights era of color blindness. Disproportionately, whites are medicalized, and blacks and other people of color are criminalized, all under the guise of legal, social, and educational policies which, on the face, are race-neutral. So while white deviance is medicated in the hopes that this will further academic success, students of color are funneled out of schools via a very deliberate pipeline and sent on the pathway toward prison.

Beyond the School-to-Prison Pipeline and Double Standards of Disciplinary Control

The school-to-prison pipeline is the racialized result of a sea of contextual troubles, both societal and educational: color-blind racism, mass incarceration and the prison industrial complex, for-profit systems of social control, schools that remain hyper-segregated by both race and class, schools that are underfunded and under pressure, teachers who are overworked, underpaid, and inadequately trained to address the needs of diverse student bodies. Most immediately, the school-to-prison pipeline is made possible by educational policies that have turned schools into pseudo-prisons. The solutions start there.

Decriminalizing Our Schools

The school-to-prison pipeline is most immediately the result of the criminalization of school discipline via zero tolerance policies and a police presence in schools. Sold as a means to "safety and security" and heavily funded at the expense of other educational programming, these policies have been abysmal failures. They have "succeeded" only in creating the pipeline by which students, particularly students of color and especially black males, are pushed out of educational institutions and into legal systems.

A growing chorus of scholars, educators, youth advocates, and youth themselves are challenging the illogic of zero tolerance and policing in schools. There is widespread agreement that the criminalization of school discipline via zero tolerance and school-based policing is the most significant contributor to the pipeline. There are increasing efforts—on the local, state, and national levels—to curtail the impact of debilitating school discipline policies via reform and alternative approaches.

A number of school districts and states have revised their disciplinary policies, distinguishing between minor infractions and more serious violations, offering graduated responses to discipline, reducing the amount of suspension time, and encouraging a nonpunitive commonsense approach to discipline. Even districts that have not entirely abandoned a police presence or zero tolerance have taken steps to mitigate the scope of their impact

and decriminalize minor infractions. These schools have implemented better data collection methods to facilitate the documentation of disparities
in school discipline with an eye toward remedies. Still others have offered
additional training and evaluation for police officers who patrol the hallways, with a particular emphasis on dealing with students who have disabilities or mental health challenges. Most recently and significantly, several
school districts have turned away from a punishment-centered approach
entirely with an emphasis instead on restorative/transformative justice
models and peace circles as means to create a positive school climate and
culture.

Nationally, the U.S. Department of Education and the Civil Rights Division of the U.S. Department of Justice have committed to addressing disparities in the school suspensions and expulsions as a civil rights matter,
first filing suit against the state of Mississippi for operating a school-to-
prison pipeline in Meridian. In December 2012 the first-ever congressional
hearings on the school-to-prison pipeline were held and featured expert
testimony that detailed both the scope of the problem and solutions, including calls for decreased funding incentives for police, increased funding
for counseling, support staff and educational resources, mandatory nationwide data collection on suspension, expulsion and arrests at school, and
support for evidence-based solutions to end the persistent racial disparities
that shape the contours of the pipeline.

In January 2014, the Department of Education and the Department of
Justice issued new guidelines on School Climate and Discipline that, for the
first time in 20 years, advocated a move away from zero tolerance policies
and mandated suspension/expulsion as a last resort. The guidelines in brief
are as follows and include recommended action steps that emphasize collaboration, prevention, and restorative justice measures:

Principle 1: Climate and Prevention: Schools that foster positive school climates can help to engage all students in learning by preventing problem
   behaviors and intervening effectively to support struggling and at-risk students.

Action Steps

(1) Engage in deliberate efforts to create positive school climates.
(2) Prioritize the use of evidence-based prevention strategies, such as tiered
   supports, to promote positive student behavior.
(3) Promote social and emotional learning to complement academic skills and
   encourage positive behavior.

(4) Provide regular training and supports to all school personnel—including teachers, principals, support staff, and school-based law enforcement officers—on how to engage students and support positive behavior.

(5) Collaborate with local mental health, child welfare, law enforcement, and juvenile justice agencies and other stakeholders to align resources, prevention strategies, and intervention services.

(6) Ensure that any school-based law enforcement officers' roles focus on improving school safety and reducing inappropriate referrals to law enforcement.

Principle 2: Expectations and Consequences: Schools that have discipline policies or codes of conduct with clear, appropriate, and consistently applied expectations and consequences will help students improve behavior, increase engagement, and boost achievement.

Action Steps

(1) Set high expectations for behavior and adopt an instructional approach to school discipline.

(2) Involve families, students, and school personnel in the development and implementation of discipline policies or codes of conduct, and communicate those policies regularly and clearly.

(3) Ensure that clear, developmentally appropriate, and proportional consequences apply for misbehavior.

(4) Create policies that include appropriate procedures for students with disabilities and due process for all students.

(5) Remove students from the classroom only as a last resort, ensure that any alternative settings provide students with academic instruction, and return students to their regular class as soon as possible

Principle 3: Equity and Continuous Improvement: Schools that build staff capacity and continuously evaluate the school's discipline policies and practices are more likely to ensure fairness and equity.

Action Steps

(1) Train all school staff to apply school discipline policies and practices in a fair and equitable manner so as not to disproportionately impact students of color, students with disabilities, or at-risk students.

(2) Use proactive, data-driven, and continuous efforts, including gathering feedback from families, students, teachers, and school personnel to prevent, identify, reduce, and eliminate discriminatory discipline and unintended consequences.[39]

These guidelines are only in the earliest stages of implementation, but they clearly reinforce the efforts already under way in many districts to reduce suspensions and expulsion. Rightful concern remains over lack of clear federal guidance on the continued presence of police in schools, and the potential for continued racial dynamics here, but this policy shift is an important first step. The significance of this federal policy shift on school discipline after 20 years of mandated zero tolerance cannot be overstated. It creates an opportunity to open a dialogue about the multitude of educational and societal issues that gave rise to the school-to-prison pipeline.

Remedying the Rest

The flow of children into the school-to-prison pipeline may be slowed by a decreased reliance on zero tolerance, police in the hallways, and criminalized education. But given the larger climate of educational policy, this alone will not be enough. Real change will require deep challenges, not just to the situation of educational policy and practice but to our propensity for excessive and deeply racialized systems of social control.

The school-to-prison pipeline flourishes in schools that are segregated by race and class, under-resourced, and overstressed, with an overworked and underpaid pool of teachers who are demographically and culturally distant from the students that they teach. There are a multitude of specific remedies that could be offered here, but many discussions of "school reform" move in a decidedly different direction. As Bill Ayers observes:

It's part of a larger pattern and an intentional strategy that becomes clearer day by day. This strategy begins by positing education as a product, like a car or a refrigerator, a box of bolts or a screwdriver—something bought and sold in the marketplace like any other commodity—and schools as businesses run by CEOs with teachers taking the role of assembly line workers and students playing the part of the raw materials bumping helplessly along the factory floor as information is incrementally stuffed into their little up-turned heads. In this metaphoric straitjacket it's rather easy to suppose that "downsizing" the least productive units or "outsourcing" and privatizing a space that once belonged to the public is a natural event, that teaching toward a simple, standardized metric and relentlessly applying state-administered (but privately-developed and quite profitable) tests to determine the "outcomes," is a rational proxy for learning, that centrally controlled "standards" for curriculum and teaching are commonsensical, that "zero tolerance" for student misbehavior as a stand-in for child development or justice is sane, and that "accountability," that is, a range of sanctions on students, teachers and schools—but never on lawmakers, foundations or corporations—is logical and levelheaded. This is in fact what a range of noisy politicians, and their chattering pundits in the bought media, call "school reform."[40]

Beyond this, the school-to-prison pipeline is the by-product of a society that thrives on racialized for-profit punishments, under the guise of color-blind, race-neutral policy. The proliferation of the prison industrial complex demands more bodies to sustain endless profits, as does the medical model, always in pursuit of more clients, more consumers of medications. There is no escaping the role of persistent racism here, even in our allegedly "color-blind" post-racial era. White students are medicalized, perhaps too unnecessarily and to their disadvantage, but it is students of color, especially black students, who are de facto criminalized and denied the right to both an education and a childhood.

Sixty years after *Brown,* this separate and unequal treatment must finally end, and we must move toward equity, imagination, critical thinking, and freedom, toward education for democracy. The right to an education for all has long been contested, even amid claims of its centrality to an effective democracy. The right to equal education was and remains a civil rights issue. As W.E.B. DuBois observed:

> Of all the civil rights for which the world has struggled and fought for 5,000 years, the right to learn is undoubtedly the most fundamental. . . . The freedom to learn . . . has been bought by bitter sacrifice. And whatever we may think of the curtailment of other civil rights, we should fight to the last ditch to keep open the right to learn, the right to have examined in our schools not only what we believe, but what we do not believe; not only what our leaders say, but what the leaders of other groups and nations, and the leaders of other centuries have said. We must insist upon this to give our children the fairness of a start which will equip them with such an array of facts and such an attitude toward truth that they can have a real chance to judge what the world is and what its greater minds have thought it might be.[41]

Perhaps challenges to the school-to-prison pipeline will serve as a model for a path forward. Long-standing critiques of the excesses of zero tolerance—from teachers, parents, students, community groups, and advocacy organizations—have finally resulted in the recognition of racialized suspensions/expulsions as, in fact, a civil rights issue. Despite the larger situation of mass incarceration and public support of draconian law and order tactics, the targeting of increasingly young school children for a path to prison seemed, for many, to be shockingly unfair. In addition, resistance to the school–to-prison pipeline has clarified the connections between school pushout, high-stakes standardized testing and school closures. The result has been galvanized opposition and a call to "rethink education."[42] A call to imagine again, in the words of Kozol, schools removed from "the distant kingdom of intimidation and abstraction—lists of 'mandates,' 'sanctions,' and 'incentives' and 'performance standards' and the rest—into the smaller, more specific world of colored crayons, chalk erasers, pencil sharpeners, and tiny quarrels, sometimes tears and sometimes uncontrollably contagious jubilation." A call to imagine schools where learning is centered, difference is celebrated, color-blindness cast off, and stigmatizing labels— be they criminal or medical—are disavowed. As always, in crisis, there is opportunity.

Notes

1. Orfield and Frankenberg 2014.
2. Advancement Project 2005; Children's Defense Fund 2007; NAACP 2005.
3. Alexander 2010.
4. Davis 1997, 2003.
5. Jones and Mauer 2013.
6. Brewer and Heitzeg 2008, p. 637.
7. PEW Center on the States 2008.
8. Sakala 2014.
9. American Civil Liberties Union 2009, 2013.
10. Conrad 2005; Conrad and Schneider 1998.
11. Currie 2005; Hinshaw and Scheffler 2014; Safer and Malever 2000.
12. Advancement Project 2005; Children's Defense Fund 2007; NAACP 2005.
13. Advancement Project 2011.
14. Heitzeg 2014.
15. Hirschfield 2008, p. 79.
16. Birkland and Lawrence 2009.
17. Kim, Losen, and Hewit 2010.
18. Raymond 2010.
19. Addington 2009 p. 143; Birkland and Lawrence 2009.
20. Raymond 2010.
21. Justice Policy Institute 2011; Na and Gottfredson 2011.
22. Birkland and Lawrence 2009.
23. The Schott Foundation for Public Education 2012.
24. NAACP 2005.
25. Advancement Project 2011; Eckholm 2013; Justice Policy Institute 2011.

26. National Center for Education Statistics 2012.

27. Ibid.

28. American Academy of Pediatrics 2013; American Psychological Association 2006; Wildeman 2009, pp. 268–272.

29. Advancement Project 2005; Arum and Preiss 2008; Nolan 2011.

30. Kim, Losen, and Hewit 2010.

31. Lewin 2012; Rios 2011; U.S. Department of Education Office for Civil Rights 2014.

32. Advancement Project 2010; U.S. Department of Education Office for Civil Rights 2012.

33. Eckholm 2013; Nolan 2011.

34. Noecella II and Socha 2014.

35. Skiba et al. 2006, pp. 411–424; U.S. Department of Education Office for Civil Rights 2012.

36. Goff and Jackson 2014.

37. Connor 2011; Hinshaw and Scheffler 2014.

38. Centers for Disease Control and Prevention 2013; Diller 1998; Schwarz 2013; Schwarz and Cohen 2013.

39. Ibid.

40. Ayers 2014.

41. DuBois 1970.

42. Advancement Project 2010; 2011.

Bibliography

Abbott, Jeff. 2014 "Across North America, Teachers Declare: 'No No. 2 Pencils Required!'" *Common Dreams* (June 10).

Addington, L.A. 2009. "Cops and Cameras: Public School Security as a Policy Response to Columbine." *American Behavioral Scientist* 52(10): 1426–1446.

Advancement Project. 2005. *Education on Lockdown: The School to Jailhouse Track.* Washington, DC.

Advancement Project. 2010. *Test Punish and Push-Out: How "Zero Tolerance" and High–Stakes Testing Funnel Youth into the School-to-Prison Pipeline.* Washington, DC.

Advancement Project. 2011. *Federal Policy, ESEA Reauthorization, and the School-to-Prison Pipeline.* Washington, DC.

Advancement Project. 2012. *Testimony of Judith A. Browne Dianis Co-director, Advancement Project Hearing on Ending the School-to-Prison Pipeline before the Subcommittee on the Constitution, Civil Rights, and Human Rights, Senate Committee on the Judiciary.* Washington, DC, Wednesday, December 12.

Advancement Project. 2013. *Police in School Is Not the Answer to the Newton Shootings.* Washington, DC.

Alexander, Michelle. 2010. *The New Jim Crow: Mass Incarceration in the Era of Color-Blindness.* New York: The Free Press.

American Academy of Pediatrics. 2013. "Out-of-School Suspension and Expulsion." *Pediatrics*: 1000–1007.

American Bar Association. 2001. *Zero Tolerance Policy.* Washington, DC.

American Civil Liberties Union. 2009. *The Persistence of Racial and Ethnic Profiling in the United States.* New York: American Civil Liberties Union.

American Civil Liberties Union. 2013. *The War on Marijuana in Black and White.* New York: American Civil Liberties Union.

American Psychological Association. 2006. *Are Zero Tolerance Policies Effective in the Schools? An Evidentiary Review and Recommendations.* Washington, DC: APA.

Arum, Richard, and Doreet Preiss. 2008. "From *Brown* to Bong 'Hits': Assessing a Half Century of Judicial Involvement in Education." *American Enterprise Institute for Policy Research* (October 15).

Ayers, Bill. 2014. "With Teacher Tenure Threatened, Trouble in Every Direction for Education." *Truthout* (June 29).

Bell, Derrick. 1989. *And We Not Saved: The Elusive Search for Racial Justice.* New York: Basic Books.

Birkland, Thomas A., and Regina Lawrence. 2009. "Media Framing after Columbine." *American Behavioral Scientist* 52: 1387.

Bonilla-Silva, Eduardo. 2001. *White Supremacy and Racism in the Post-Civil Rights Era.* Boulder, CO: Lynne Rienner.

Bonilla-Silva, Eduardo. 2013. *Racism without Racists: Color-Blind Racism and the Persistence of Racial Inequality in the United States.* 3rd ed. New York: Rowman & Littlefield.

Brewer, Rose, and Nancy A. Heitzeg. 2008. "The Racialization of Crime and Punishment: Criminal Justice, Color-Blind Racism and the Political Economy of the Prison Industrial Complex." *American Behavioral Scientist* 51: 625. doi:10.1177/0002764207307745.

Brown, Patricia Leigh. 2013. "Opening Up, Students Transform a Vicious Circle." *New York Times* (April 3).

Carroll, Maureen. 2008. "Educating Expelled Students after No Child Left Behind: Mending an Incentive Structure That Discourages Alternative Education and Reinstatement." *UCLA Law Review* 55 (6): 1909.

Centers for Disease Control and Prevention. 2013. *2011–2012 National Survey of Children's Health.* Hyattsville, MD: Centers for Disease Control and Prevention. http://www.cdc.gov/nchs/slaits/nsch.htm.

Children's Defense Fund. 2007. *America's Cradle to Prison Pipeline.* Washington, DC: CDF.

Connor, Daniel F. 2011. "Problems of Overdiagnosis and Overprescribing in ADHD." *Psychiatric Times* (August 11).

Conrad, Peter. 2005. "The Shifting Engines of Medicalization." *Journal of Health and Social Behavior* (March) 46 (1): 3–14.

Conrad, Peter, and J.W. Schneider. 1998. *Deviance and Medicalization: From Badness to Sickness.* Revised Edition. Philadelphia: Temple University Press.

Currie, J. 2005. Health Disparities and Gaps in School Readiness. *School Readiness: Closing Racial and Ethnic Gaps* 15: 1.

Darling-Hammond, Linda. 1998. "Education for Democracy." In *A Light in Dark Times: Maxine Greene and the Unfinished Conversation,* eds. Maxine Greene, William Ayers, and Janet L. Miller (pp. 78–91). New York: Teachers College Press.

Darling-Hammond, Linda. 2010. *Redesigning Schools.* Boston, MA: Boston University.

Davis, Angela. 1997. "Race and Criminalization: Black Americans and the Punishment Industry." In *The Angela Y. Davis Reader,* ed. J. James (pp. 61–73). New York: Blackwell.

Davis, Angela. 2003. *Are Prisons Obsolete?* New York: Seven Stories Press.

Diller, Lawrence. 1998. *Running on Ritalin.* New York: Bantam.

Eckholm, Erik. 2013. "With Police in Schools, More Children in Court." *New York Times* (April 12).

Escobar, Javier I. 2012. "Diagnostic Bias: Racial and Cultural Issues." *Psychiatric Services.* doi:10.1176/appi.ps.20120p847.

Feagin, Joe. 2013. *The White Racial Frame: Centuries of Racial Framing and Counter-Framing.* 2nd ed. New York: Routledge.

Frymer, B. 2009. "The Media Spectacle of Columbine: Alienated Youth as an Object of Fear." *American Behavioral Scientist* 52: 1387.

Fuentes, Anette. 2013. *Lockdown Hugh: When the Schoolhouse Becomes a Jailhouse.* New York: Verso.

Goff, Phillip Atiba, and Matthew Christian Jackson. April 2014. "The Essence of Innocence: Consequences of Dehumanizing Black Children." *Journal of Personality and Social Psychology* 106 (4): 526–545. doi:10.1037/a0035663.

Heitzeg, Nancy A. 2014. "Criminalizing Education: Zero Tolerance Policies, Police in the Hallways, and the School to Prison Pipeline." In *From Education to Incarceration: Dismantling the School to Prison Pipeline,* eds. Anthony J. Noecella II, Priya Parmar, and David Stovall (pp. 11–36). New York: Peter Lang.

Henley, R., S. Ramsey, and R. F. Algozzine. 2008. *Characteristics of and Strategies for Teaching Students with Mild Disabilities.* 6th ed. New York: Pearson.

Hinshaw, Stephan P., and Richard M. Scheffler. 2014. *The ADHD Explosion: Myths, Medication, Money and Today's Push for Performance.* New York: Oxford University Press.

Hinshaw, Stephen P., and Andrea Stier. 2008. "Stigma as Related to Mental Disorders." *Annual Review of Clinical Psychology* 4: 367–393. Doi:10.1146/annurev.clinpsy.4.022007.141245.

Hirschfield, P.J. 2008. "Preparing for Prison? The Criminalization of School Discipline in the USA." *Theoretical Criminology* 12 (1): 79–101.

Jones, Sabrina, and Marc Mauer. 2013. *Race to Incarcerate: A Graphic Retelling*. New York: The Free Press.

Justice Policy Institute. 2011. *Education under Arrest: The Case against Police in Schools*. Washington, DC.

Kim, Catherine, Daniel Losen, and Damon Hewit. 2010. *The School to Prison Pipeline: Structuring Legal Reform*. New York: New York University Press.

Kozol, Jonathan. 2005. *Shame of the Nation: The Restoration of Apartheid Schooling in America*. New York: Three Rivers Press.

Kozol, Jonathan. 2007. *Letters to a Young Teacher*. New York: Three Rivers Press.

Lewin, Tamar. 2012. "Black Students Face More Discipline, Data Suggests." *New York Times* (March 6).

Losen, Daniel J., and Jonathan Gillispie. 2012. *Opportunities Suspended: The Disparate Impact of Disciplinary Exclusion from School*. The Center for Civil Rights Remedies at the Civil Rights Project (August).

Mauer, Marc, and Meda Chesney-Lind, eds. 2003. *Invisible Punishment: The Collateral Consequences of Mass Imprisonment*. New York: The New Press.

Morgan, Paul, P. Staff, M. Hillemeier, G. Farkas, and S. Maczuga. 2013. "Racial and Ethnic Disparities in ADHD Diagnoses from Kindergarten to Eight Grade." *Pediatrics* 132: 85 (July). http://pediatrics.aappublications.org/content/132/1/85.1.full.pdf.

Morgan, Paul, P. Staff, M. Hillemeier, G. Farkas, and S. Maczuga. 2014. Racial/Ethnic Disparities in ADHD Diagnosis by Kindergarten Entry. *Journal of Child Psychology and Psychiatry* (January 24). doi:10.1111/jcpp.12204.

Muhammad, Khaled G. 2010. *The Condemnation of Blackness: Race, Crime, and the Making of Modern Urban America*. Cambridge, MA: Harvard University Press.

Na, Chongmin, and Denise C. Gottfredson. 2011. "Police Officers in Schools: Effects on School Crime and the Processing of Offending Behaviors." *Justice Quarterly* 30 (4): 619–650.

NAACP. 2005. *Interrupting the School to Prison Pipe-line*. Washington, DC.

National Center for Education Statistics. 2012. *The Condition of Education*. Washington, DC.

Noecella II, Anthony J., and Kim Socha. 2014. "The New Eugenics: Challenging Urban Education and Special Education and the Promise of Hip-Hop Pedagogy." In *From Education to Incarceration: Dismantling the School to Prison Pipeline*, eds. Anthony J. Noecella II, Priya Parmar, and David Stovall. New York: Peter Lang.

Nolan, Kathleen. 2011. *Police in the Hallways: Discipline in an Urban High School*. Minneapolis: University of Minnesota Press.

Orfield, Gary, and Erica Frankenberg, with Jongyeon Ee and John Kuscera. 2014. *Brown at 60: Great Progress, a Long Retreat and an Uncertain Future*. Los Angeles, CA: The Civil Rights Project.

PEW Center on the States. 2008. *One in 100: Behind Bars in America 2008*. Washington, DC.

Polakow-Suransky, Sasha. 2001. "America's Least Wanted: Zero Tolerance Policies and the Fate of Expelled Students." In *The Public Assault on America's Children: Poverty, Violence and Juvenile Justice,* ed. Valerie Polakow (pp. 101–139). New York: Teacher's College Columbia University.

Prison Culture. "A Different Approach to School Safety: A Short Film." April 12, 2013. http://www.usprisonculture.com/blog/2013/04/19/a-different-approach-to-school-safety-a-short-film/.

Raymond, Barbara. 2010. *Assigning Police Officers to Schools; Problem-Oriented Guides for Police Response Guides Series Guide No. 10.* Washington, DC: Center for Problem-Oriented Policing, Inc.

Rethinking Schools. 2014. "Editorial: The Gathering Resistance to Standardized Tests." *Rethinking Schools* 28: 3 (Spring).

Rios, Victor. 2011. *Punished: Policing the Lives of Black and Latino Boys.* New York: New York University Press.

Roberts, Dorothy. 2004. "The Social and Moral Cost of Mass Incarceration in African American Communities." *Stanford Law Review* 56 (127): 1271–1305.

Russell-Brown, Kathryn. 2009. *The Color of Crime.* 2nd ed. New York: New York University Press.

Safer, D., and M. Malever. 2000. "Stimulant Treatment in Maryland Public Schools." *Pediatrics* 106 (3): 55.

Sakala, Leah. 2014. *Breaking Down Mass Incarceration in the 2010 Census: State-by-State Incarceration Rates by Race/Ethnicity.* Northampton, MA: Prison Policy Initiative.

The Schott Foundation for Public Education. 2012. *The Urgency of Now: 50 State Report on Black Males and Education.* Cambridge, MA.

Schwarz, A. 2013. "The Selling of Attention Deficit Disorder." *New York Times* (December 14). http://www.nytimes.com/2013/12/15/health/the-selling-of-attention-deficit-disorder.html?hp.

Schwarz, A., and S. Cohen. 2013. "A.D.H.D. Seen in 11% of U.S. Children as Diagnoses Rise." *New York Times* (March 31). http://www.nytimes.com/2013/04/01/health/more-diagnoses-of-hyperactivity-causing-concern.html?pagewanted=1&_r=0&hp.

Skiba, Russell. 2001. *Zero Tolerance, Zero Evidence: An Analysis of School Disciplinary Practice.* Bloomington, IN: Indiana Education Policy Center, Indiana University.

Skiba, Russell, K. Knesting, and L.D. Bush. 2002. "Culturally Competent Assessment: More Than Nonbiased Tests." *Journal of Child and Family Studies* 11 (1): 61–78. doi:10.1023/A:1014767511894.

Skiba, Russell, L. Poloni Staudinger, S. Gallini, A. B Simmons, and R. Feggins Azziz. 2006. "Disparate Access: The Disproportionality of African American Students with Disabilities across Educational Environments." *Exceptional Children* 72 (4): 411–424.

Torrey, E. Fuller, et al. 2010. *More Mentally Ill Persons Are in Jails and Prisons Than Hospitals: A Survey of the States.* Arlington VA: Treatment Advocacy Center.

Urban Strategies Council. 2012. *African American Male Achievement Initiative: A Closer Look at Suspensions of African American Males in OUSD.* Oakland, CA (May).

U.S. Department of Education. 2014. *Guiding Principles for Improving School Climate and Discipline.* Washington, DC: U.S. Department of Education.

U.S. Department of Education Office for Civil Rights. 2012. *Civil Rights Data Collection: Data Snapshot Opportunity Gap.* Washington, DC: U.S. Department of Education Office for Civil Rights.

U.S. Department of Education Office for Civil Rights. 2014. *Civil Rights Data Collection: Data Snapshot (School Discipline).* Washington, DC: U.S. Department of Education Office for Civil Rights, March 21.

Wagner, Peter, and Leah Sakala. 2014. *Mass Incarceration: The Whole Pie.* Northampton, MA: Prison Policy Initiative.

Walker, C. Spohn, and M. DeLone. 2012. *The Color of Justice: Race, Ethnicity and Crime in America.* 6th ed. Belmont, CA: Wadsworth.

Welch, Kathleen. 2007. "Black Criminal Stereotypes and Racial Profiling." *Journal of Contemporary Criminal Justice* 23: 276.

Whitlock, Kay, and Nancy A Heitzeg. 2013. "After Trayvon Martín Revisited." *Critical Mass Progress* (July 3). http://criticalmassprogress.com/2013/07/03/ci-after-trayvon-martin-revisited/.

Wildeman, Christopher. 2009. "Parental Imprisonment, the Prison Boom, and the Concentration of Childhood Disadvantage." *Demography* 46: 265–280.

Witt, Howard. 2007. "School Discipline Tougher on African Americans." *Chicago Tribune* (September 5).

Chapter 6

Housing Segregation and the Prison Industrial Complex: Looking at the Roots of Today's School-to-Prison Pipeline

Mei-Ling Malone and Hui-Ling Malone

Introduction

While the school-to-prison pipeline is a relatively novel term, its negative impact of enforcing racial oppression via segregation and criminalization is age old. This "new" disturbing pipeline, in which school policies and practices are pushing students toward the criminal justice system and away from school, is unfortunately just another symptom of U.S. long-standing legacy of white supremacy and capitalism. In this chapter we will trace the historical development of the pipeline and explain the ways in which to-day's school-to-prison pipeline is actually a manifestation of slavery. In particular, we will focus on describing how America's power structure has consistently used segregation and criminalization as tools to uphold racism and capitalism throughout history, and how our current pipeline is merely a result of this. Without this historical knowledge, educators, reforms and policy makers stand little chance of addressing the school-to-prison pipeline at its roots and risk unknowingly perpetuating the oppression of students of color and the pipeline itself for decades to come.

We begin with a brief explanation of the dynamics of chattel slavery as the starting point for our nation's two-punch segregation and criminalization tactic that is designed to simultaneously empower some while oppressing others. Then we review the history of school segregation and analyze its ties to housing segregation. Next, we examine the evolution of the school-to-prison pipeline in relation to the for-profit prison industry. We will employ these two important trajectories to show how school segregation and the emerging school-to-prison pipeline have negatively supported each other to ultimately uphold the American legacy of white supremacy and capitalism as established during slavery. By the end of this chapter, we hope it will be abundantly clear that our nation's history of injustice has always been rooted in segregating people and criminalizing some while privileging others. Based on this realization we share our vision for permanently dismantling the school-to-prison pipeline and creating a more just and equitable society for all.

Earliest Forms of Segregation and Criminalization

Chattel slavery was undoubtedly one of the first legs of white supremacy and capitalism in America and operated successfully through employing segregation and criminalization. Not only were enslaved Africans separated from Europeans and deemed inferior to be used for physical labor, but they were also negatively portrayed psychologically and emotionally in stark contrast to their European American counterparts, the purpose being to reassert white superiority and African inferiority. European Americans associated themselves with positive characteristics such as intelligence, leadership, sophistication, and order, while defining enslaved Africans as having the negative and opposite traits. Africans were declared unintelligent, savage, and criminal. This black–white binary kept whites in power and blacks oppressed during slavery and beyond, physically, mentally, and emotionally. The persecution and marginalization of blacks did not end with slavery. A study of Alabama prisoners reported that during slavery prisoners were all white; however, after slavery was abolished, prisoners rapidly became all black in the state. This was a telling revelation on the state of race relations. Even post-emancipation proclamation, blacks were still seen as inferior and criminal. In other words, the black–white binary remained, and the segregation and criminalization of blacks were the chief mechanisms by which white supremacy was maintained.

History of Jim Crow Housing Segregation

Given the history of injustice and oppression, it makes sense that housing discrimination continued to be a common practice. "The Case for

Reparations" by Ta-Nehisi Coates, recently published in *The Atlantic*, detailed the severe consequences of housing discrimination and its explicitly racist practices. The booming industrialization in the North brought millions of African Americans from the South during the Great Migration. It was common for whites to flee to the suburbs to avoid the growing African American population during this period. Whites created restrictions to keep blacks out of their neighborhoods. Many housing contracts prohibited the sale of homes to blacks. Coates wrote, "From the 1930s through the 1960s, black people across the country were largely cut out of the legitimate home-mortgage market through means both legal and extralegal. Chicago whites employed every measure, from 'restrictive covenants' to bombings, to keep their neighborhoods segregated."[1]

Individual acts of racism by whites were overtly supported by the U.S. government. The Federal Housing Administration (FHA) helped home-buyers by dropping interest rates and reducing down payments for mortgages. Yet the FHA excluded certain neighborhoods from its backing. The FHA created maps with green areas and red areas. The green areas were neighborhoods that were "in demand" and considered excellent prospects for insurance could often not sold to blacks or foreigners. The red areas, where blacks were allowed to reside, were usually considered ineligible for FHA backing. As Coates noted, "Neither the percentage of black people living there nor their social class mattered."[2] Primarily, where one lives determines where one attends school. The government's role in devising segregated housing practices contributed greatly to segregated schooling and explains the historical inequity that persists in schools today.

Indeed, looking closely into California's history of housing segregation helps us understand the state of segregated schools today. As the numbers of Latinos increase within the state, this demographic is the most segregated within schooling. The article "Strictly in the Capacity of Servant: The Interconnection between Residential and School Segregation in Oxnard, California, 1934–1954" by Garcia and Yosso show how Mexicans were historically segregated in schools and given an inferior education. First, schools segregated Mexicans "under the auspices of culture or language, and subsequently emphasized vocational and Americanization curricula."[3] The city's elementary schools served to push out the majority of Mexican children before high school, making Mexican youth prime targets for a readily available pool of manual laborers for the booming agricultural industry.

The Oxnard, California, school board provides a fine example. Trustees on the Oxnard school board explicitly supported housing segregation.

Garcia and Yosso explained that "Ventura County records show that [board members] sought to maintain separation from Mexicans as their neighbors. Indeed, all of the trustees owned properties bound by racial covenants." The school officials had a vested interest in residential segregation. One trustee, Dockstader, bought property that stated, "Premises shall not, at any time, be sold or conveyed to any person of the Negro, Japanese, or Chinese race, nor to any Mexican or Indian . . . the premises hereby conveyed are part of a subdivision intended to be used exclusively as a first class residence property."4 Many other trustees, principals, school board members, and school teachers owned racially restricted property through the 1970s. In the eyes of school officials and the larger white community, Mexican Americans were tolerated but never seen as equals. They were expected to work in the fields, not to succeed academically. Thus, "the trustees' meticulous plans to segregate students by residence and race in the 1930s helped establish a separate and unequal schooling system in Oxnard. Pressure to maintain racial segregation of children increased as the population grew."5

Eventually the blatant segregation in California schools was challenged. *Mendez v. Westminster* (1946) was the landmark case that contested racial segregation in Orange County schools. Gonzala Mendez, angered that his daughter was rejected from a California "whites only" school, took four schools in Southern California to court, reaching the federal level. This federal case (the court) ruled that segregation of Mexican and Mexican American students was unconstitutional. Similar to *Brown v. Board of Education,* prosecutors argued that segregation resulted in feelings of inferiority among Mexican American children that limited their potential to succeed. Then California governor Earl Warren signed a bill ending school segregation, and California became the first state to officially desegregate its public schools. Eight years later, the Supreme Court ruled in *Brown v. Board of Education* that segregation throughout the United States was unconstitutional. The opinion was written by Chief Justice Earl Warren. Technically, school segregation became illegal, but in reality, racially divided schools persisted. Sixty years later, there is much speculation that the ruling of *Brown* has improved the equality of schools.

The Current Landscape of Segregated Schools (California)

Segregated schooling remains an issue today in the state of California as well as across the nation. Recently, the University of California at Los Angeles (UCLA) released a report "Brown at 60: Great Progress, a Long Retreat and an Uncertain Future," detailing the current state of U.S. educational system. According to the report, black and Latino students are still enrolled in schools with few white students, and Latinos are the most segregated in suburban America. Black students are the most segregated in the inner cities of New York, Illinois, and California. Furthermore, California is the state where Latino students are the most segregated.

According to the California Department of Education, the enrollment of students in California schools is 53.25 percent Latino, 6.16 percent African American, and 25 percent white. At the time *Brown* was decided, California was overwhelmingly white. Now, whites are only the second largest group, following Latinos, who account for 41 percent of students in the region. The black population in the west is only 5 percent, compared to its 8 percent Asian enrollment. These huge changes in racial demographics unfortunately did not result in integrated schooling. To the contrary, segregated education became more pronounced, and profound racial inequalities have been well documented (Figure 6.1).

The UCLA report enables us to take a closer look into a typical classroom in the United States. Nationally, in a classroom of 30 students, the classmates of the average white student are 22 whites, 2 African Americans, 4 Latinos, 1 Asian, and 1 "Other." On the other hand, the average African American or Latino student has 8 white classmates and at least

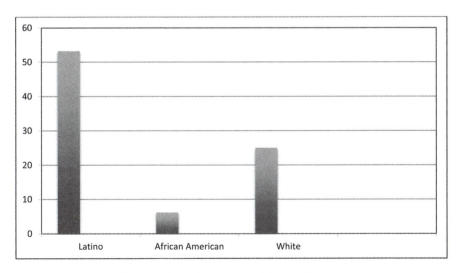

FIGURE 6.1   Enrollment of Students in California by Race

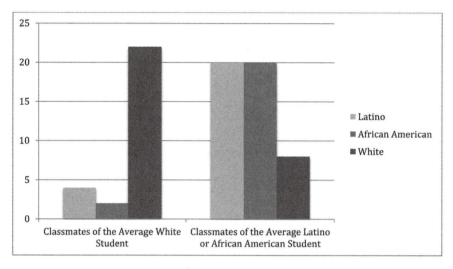

FIGURE 6.2   Classmates of the Average White, African American, and Latino Students

20 African American and/or Latino classmates. It is also important to note that most schools that are predominantly African American or Latino are also predominantly socioeconomically disadvantaged. Clearly, segregation persists for all children. Thus, it goes without saying that not only are African American and Latinos segregated but so are white students (Figure 6.2).

A closer look into three high schools in the Los Angeles area, Beverly Hills High School, George Washington Prep High School, and Fremont High School, presents an equally disturbing picture.

Beverly Hills High School

According to the California Department of Education (CDE), the racial make-up of the Beverly Hills High School is 72.6 percent white, 6.87 percent Latino, and 4 percent African American. It offers 54 Advanced Placement (AP) classes. The graduation rate is at a stellar 96.3 percent. Fifty-eight percent of the graduating class meets the minimal requirements to attend UCLA or California State University (CSU). According to Census data, the surrounding community of Beverly Hills is 82.4 percent white, 2.2 percent black, and 5.7 percent Latino. A total of 58.1 percent of residents have a bachelor's degree or higher and the per capita income is $76,391. Beverly Hills has a concentrated population of higher-income whites.

Washington Prep High School

On the flipside, Washington Prep High School is 0.3 percent white, 43.8 percent Latino, and 54.3 percent African American. The school offers 26 AP classes, which is less than half of what Beverly Hills offers. The graduation rate is 67.9 percent, and only 23.8 percent of the graduates are CSU/UC eligible. Washington Prep is located in the designated "Westmont" area, where the population is 51.1 percent black, 46.7 percent Latino, and 15.8 percent white. The average household income in the surrounding area is $31,110 and only 5.7 percent of residents 25 and older have a four-year degree.

Fremont High School

Fremont High School, located in South Los Angeles, is 90.7 percent Latino, 8 percent African American, and 0.1 percent white. There are just 20 AP courses, and only 28.4 percent of its graduates are UC/CSU eligible. The graduation rate is 62.35 percent. The surrounding community of Fremont High School is 84 percent Latino, 12 percent African American, and 3 percent mixed race. Approximately, 43.6 percent of the population is foreign born, with 100 percent coming from Latin America (primarily Mexico). A total of 89.9 percent of the residents speak Spanish at home (PCS Report). The average adjusted gross income is $22,565, with 30.5 percent of adults and 56 percent of children under the age of 15 living below the poverty level. Only 3.8 percent of the population has a bachelor's degree (Figures 6.3–6.5).

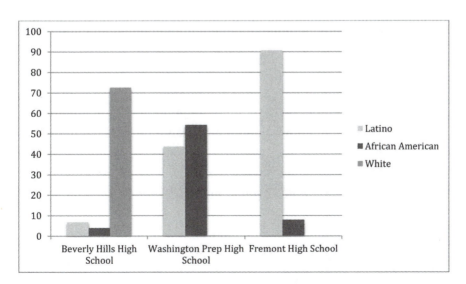

FIGURE 6.3 The Percentage of Students Attending Each High School by Race

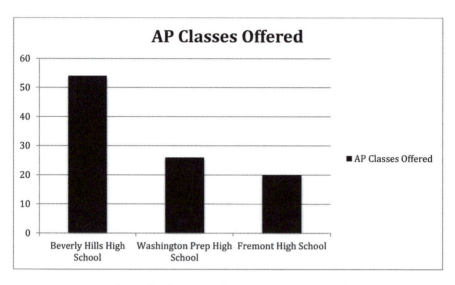

FIGURE 6.4   Number of Advanced Placement Classes Offered by School

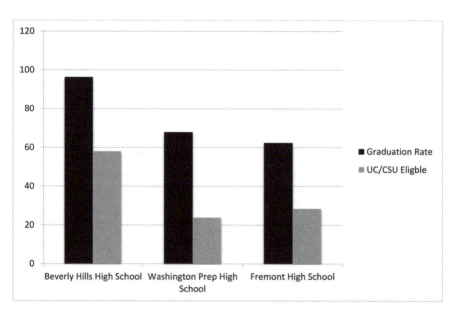

FIGURE 6.5   The Graduation Rate and UC/CSU Eligible Students by Percentage

These three schools provide a snapshot of the segregation that exists in California, but they are not outliers when compared to the racial composition or racial and economic inequalities across the nation and the rest of the country. Poverty is highly saturated in certain areas and African American, Latinos, and, to the greatest extent, whites are explicitly separated. The myriad of challenges surrounding Washington Prep and Fremont high schools account for the low performances of many students in those institutions and can be tied to years of housing segregation and criminalization of black and brown bodies and impoverished minorities that started with slavery in the United States.

The School-to-Prison Pipeline

These trajectories provide the context for understanding the school-to-prison pipeline as manifestation of slavery and consequence of an unjust society that continuously enforces segregation and criminalization of historically marginalized people. The American Civil Liberties Union defines the school-to-prison pipeline is "a disturbing national trend wherein children are funneled out of public schools and into the juvenile and criminal justice systems. Many of these children have learning disabilities or histories of poverty, abuse or neglect, and would benefit from additional educational and counseling services. Instead, they are isolated, punished and pushed out."[6] Progressive educators everywhere concerned about this pipeline generally focus much energy and attention on reforming punitive discipline policies such as the infamous zero tolerance policy.[7] Unfortunately, however, the pipeline's history and connection to the prison industrial complex and white supremacy is often missing from this conversation and as a result reform efforts are limited at best. In collaboration with other scholars we too seek to historically root the pipeline and share this history broadly.

California's Prison Industrial Complex History

San Quentin, California's first state prison, opened in 1852. A total of nine new prisons were constructed in California over roughly a 100-year time period between 1852 and 1955. Between 1962 and 1965, California established the California Rehabilitation Center and two camps. No prisons were opened after the mid-1960s and during all of the 1970s. However, during the 1980s, a massive project of prison construction was initiated. In fact, during the 1980s and 1990s, almost two-thirds of existing California prisons opened. Between the five short years of 1984 and 1989, nine new prisons were opened and thus California prisons doubled in less than a decade, whereas previously it took the state more than a 100 years to create the same number of prisons. In total, from 1982 to 2000, the state of California built 23 new prisons at a cost of $280 million to $350 million apiece, and the state prison population grew at a rate of 500 percent during this time period.

Indeed, the prison system proved to be a powerful and lucrative industry that has served as a means to boost or at least stabilize rural economies. California prisons have been utilized as a "fix" to social, psychological, environmental, political, and economic programs. The popular catch phrase "get tough on crime" ultimately proved to be a harsh reality in California. Prison authorities devoted great effort to enacting excessive crime prevention policies and practices in the 1980s and 1990s with small efforts toward rehabilitation in the 2000s. From 1979 through 1994, 1,100 changes were made to California's penal code, most of which lengthened and toughened prison terms. This shift toward harsher laws aided in the state's prison population explosion. California incarcerated less than 30,000 inmates in the late 1970s. This number soared to over one 126,000 by the 1990s.[8] In short, lawmakers in California spent much of the last few decades locking up more and more people in prison for longer and longer periods of time through punitive criminal policies that have taken an enormous toll on poor communities of color throughout the state.

The history of California reveals many important lessons about the state politics and priorities. Since the 1980s, the state chose to create an unprecedented increase in prison facilities despite no dramatic spike in crime rates. Furthermore, the ensuing growth in incarceration cannot be ethically justified in which African Americans are grossly overrepresented in jails and prisons especially and as Latinos disproportionately make up the majority of the population. The numbers indicate that California now holds the distinction of having the largest prison building program in the world, and over the last few decades, countless punitive criminal laws were passed in the state causing the prison population to explode, increasing by over 450 percent.[9] According to an article from Chicago Alliance Against Racist and Political Repression (CAARPR), today "there are now thirty-three prisons, thirty-eight camps, sixteen community correctional facilities, and five tiny prisoner mother facilities in California," and currently, most California prisoners are nonwhite despite a long history of whites make up the majority of the general population. Latino inmates account for approximately

38 percent of the population, while African American and white inmates each represent about 27 percent of the population. Latinos and blacks are both overrepresented in comparison to the percentage of each group in the overall population of California. The data is even more alarming for black and Latino men. The CAARPR also report that "among adult men in 2005, African Americans were incarcerated at a rate of 5,125 per 100,000 in the population, compared to 1,142 for Latinos, 770 for whites, and 474 for men of other races." With respect to women, racial inequality is also found. "Among women, African Americans were incarcerated at a rate of 346 per 100,000 in the population, compared to 62 for Latinas, 80 for whites, and 27 for women of other races."[10]

Slavery Legacy Lives on in Prisons

It is clear that race plays a central role in perpetuating the legacy of slavery in prisons. The black–white binary, made salient during slavery, serves as the foundation for how the system works. Just as prisons went from all white to all black post-slavery, this legacy of criminalizing of black and brown skin is abundantly evident when studying the impact of the prison industrial complex, with the rapid prison expansion during the 1980s and 1990s and the rapid fire increase in punitive crime laws; this skyrocketed the rate of incarceration for people of color and black people especially. Most important, this growth in imprisoned people of color did not result from an increase in criminality of blacks and Latinos. The rise in numbers of black and brown people in the prison system was due to people of color being disproportionately targeted by law enforcement for drug use, which resulted in alarming rates of imprisonment. Given the history of Black Codes and Jim Crow, the "War on Drugs" unsurprisingly merely continued the criminalization and demonization of people identified as black.

Since the 1980s, increases in imprisonment for drug offenses have been two to three times greater for people of color than for whites despite the fact that whites display greater incidences of illegal-drug abuse problems. Regardless of age, a Californian of color is four to five times more likely to be imprisoned for a drug offense than a white person compared to their rates of drug abuse. Working-class people of color have been hit the hardest by California's "tough on crime" laws by way of heavy policing of communities of color, racial profiling, and racial discrimination throughout the system. The War on Drugs of the 1980s nearly quadrupled prison admissions for blacks in three years and increased steadily until 2000 when it reached a level of more than 26 times the number of admissions in 1983; this is in spite of the fact that blacks make up only 13 percent of our nation's drug users.[11]

In addition to racial discrimination found in law enforcement for drug use, racism was found in police work around gangs. Police often view gang members as primarily urban black and Latino males and target them, while ignoring white gang activity. In fact research indicates that law enforcement gang task forces often label large numbers of youth of color as gang members with little or no evidence of any gang involvement. This racism is further increased by a complete refusal to recognize and address primarily white gangs, even when they clearly meet the provisions of the STEP Act. An extreme example of this racial bias is seen in the Los Angeles County gang database where approximately half of all African American men between the ages of 16 and 24 are listed as gang members or associates. As a result of these racist practices, black and other minority males are disproportionately targeted, arrested, and incarcerated for gang involvement at far higher rates than their actual involvement dictates.

In addition, blacks and Latinos disproportionately endure the brunt of the harsh "three strikes" law. Regardless of circumstances, this law mandates a 25 years to life sentence for people receiving their third conviction. While African Americans made up 6.5 percent of the state's population in 2004, they made up nearly 30 percent of the prison population, 36 percent of second strikers, and 45 percent of third strikers.[12] Unlike blacks and Latinos, whites are underrepresented among those in imprisoned and the "striker" population in California. The three strikes disparities in California centrally results from racial disparities at each stage of the criminal justice system starting at the arrest stage. People of color are arrested at higher rates than whites, and this disproportionality increases as they proceed through the system. Thus, as cases move through the justice system into progressively harsher punishment, the proportion of whites diminishes while the proportion of African Americans increases.

History of Educational Discipline in California

The history of segregated housing and schooling coupled with the increasingly racialized criminalization of blacks was perpetuated in the California public school system. Over time there was a growing presence of and authority given to law enforcement in schools. The implementation of criminal justice tactics dictated discipline and safety practices in state schools, including random searches, gating up schools, and arrests. Ultimately, California's urban school discipline and law enforcement worked collaboratively to enact increasingly punitive policies and practices.

Prior to the 1980s, school districts and law enforcement agencies had little to do with each other. In the spring of 1974, the attorney general and the superintendent of public education convened an Ad Hoc Task Force on "Management of Conflict and Crime in Schools." The catalyst for the meeting grew out of perceived fears around gang activity, increasing acts of violence and assault, and general problems of discipline and control on school campus, especially in Los Angeles schools. The task force concluded that there was "very little coordination between school and criminal justice officials, prevention efforts and crisis planning were non-existent, and that reporting of school-related crime was poor, not uniformly coded, and lacked a statewide mandate."[13] Things began to change in 1980 when the first laws requiring schools to report crime were passed. In fact, since the 1980s, law enforcement, criminal laws, and criminal justice procedures have played an increasingly prominent role in discipline and safety policies in schools across California.

In 1982, Californian voters passed a proposition to amend California Constitution Article I, Section 28, to provide "all students and staff . . . the inalienable right to attend campuses which are safe, secure and peaceful." In support to this, the state superintendent of Public Instruction and the attorney general formed the School/Law Enforcement Partnership the next year in 1983. This partnership licensed law enforcement to play an integral role in school discipline and safety procedures and suggests that law enforcement and schools could and should work together to best serve students. Schools came to be viewed as sites of criminal activity. School authorities and law officials asserted that adequately regulating students' behavior was beyond the capacity of school staff; hence, schools began to rely on the support of law enforcement. The formal working relationship between schools and law enforcement would officially form a merger, in which the goals of the education system and the criminal justice system worked in tandem when it came to matters of discipline.

By the end of the 1980s, criminal justice strategies and tactics had thoroughly permeated the education system. While law enforcement agencies and school systems were once separate and distinct entities, starting in the 1980s, these two institutions struck up a collaborative partnership that would forever change the nature and ideology surrounding school safety policies and practices. Schools' discipline policies became increasingly more punitive and criminal. In fact, in 1989, some school districts in California adopted zero tolerance policies that mandated expulsion for drugs, fighting, and gang-related activity. In general, suspension and expulsion are usually heavier on black and brown students. The CDE revealed that "differences in the rates at which some student groups are suspended. For example, the data show African-American students are 6.5 percent of total enrollment, but make up 19 percent of suspensions. White students are 26 percent of total enrollment, but represent 20 percent of suspensions. Hispanic students are 52 percent of total enrollment, and 54 percent of suspensions."[14]

The trend toward incorporating law enforcement into school discipline and adopting criminal justice practices into California schools continued throughout the 1990s. During this decade, school actors remained preoccupied with drug use and became increasingly worried about gang activity and students bringing weapons to schools. As a result, schools created policies to combat these fears of crime on campus and created more policies and practices resembling punitive criminal justice legislation. During this decade, LAUSD advocated for gating and fencing all schools and supported expanding police and probation officer involvement. Also nationwide, the notorious zero policy was applauded and implemented in schools.

During the 2000s, a growing number of suspensions and expulsions and police abuse in LAUSD prompted concern. A report entitled "Police in LAUSD Schools: The Need for Accountability and Alternatives" documents incidents of misconduct by the Los Angeles School Police Department in LAUSD high schools from 2005 to 2009. Reports of police misconduct were gathered from over 1,500 student surveys from 18 LAUSD high schools collected by the Community Rights Campaign. The report included "incidents of excessive force and restraint, verbal abuse, sexual harassment, intimidation, frequent and indiscriminate use of mace and pepper spray on large numbers of students, racial profiling, handcuffs used on students' whose 'crime' was being late, frequent searches, and more."[15]

Not surprisingly, this criminalization of schools was not a color-blind phenomenon by any stretch of the imagination. Thanks to the long-standing history of white supremacy, housing segregation, and the resulting segregation of schools and prison industrial complex, black and brown schools were deemed sites of criminal activity. Black and Latino children were pepper sprayed, beaten, and arrested by law enforcement at school—the place where they are supposed learn, develop, and grow. Majority black schools like Crenshaw High in South Los Angeles reported that the police were circling the premises at all times. A tiny terrified six-year black girl was arrested in her kindergarten classroom.[16] The black–white binary has worked to humanize white skin and demonize black skin and has had a deep and devastating impact on our school children of color, particularly those hit hardest by poverty.

In short prisons, criminal laws, and school discipline are deeply influenced by and interrelated to each other. Statewide policies in favor of housing and school segregation, for-profit prisons, and a punitive, zero tolerance justice system negatively impact urban schools and contribute to a hostile environment of criminalization for their students. The increasingly harsh discipline in California urban schools has contributed to the proliferation of schools as breeding grounds for prisons.[17]

Piecing It All Together

We presented a great deal of historical information concerning segregation and criminalization. We hope that it is abundantly clear how past policies both in housing and in the prison industry have birthed the ugly school-to-prison pipeline that we see today. It is evident that the way blacks were criminalized and segregated during slavery has endured the test of time. Intentional housing segregation and the resulting segregated schools expose America as promoting a white supremacist social order. The growth of the prison industrial complex and its devastating impact on black and brown families also highlights a culturally and structurally racist nation. Together, housing segregation and our pro-prison power structure naturally has spilled over into schools and contributed to the current school-to-prison pipeline.

We hope that the information from this chapter helps educators, policy makers, reformers, and activists better understand our nation's long-standing legacy of oppression and the central role segregation and criminalization has played in maintaining white supremacy and capitalism. We hope that readers will never again mention the school-to-prison pipeline without mentioning white supremacy, housing segregation, and the criminalization of dark skin. As long as whiteness constitutes superiority and blackness constitutes criminality, our racial arrangement will remain hierarchal and oppressive. As a starting point, the public conversation around race needs to reject the false hegemonic idea of color blindness and instead reflect on reality of white supremacy that continues to reign, even in the absence of slavery and Jim Crow laws, as evidenced by enduring segregation and disproportionately inferior outcomes for people of color. Policy makers, educators, and criminal justice actors must address and work to combat all of the disproportionate adverse outcomes that plague people of color. The overwhelming evidence of racial discrimination in our schools and prisons makes it inexcusable for those in power to largely ignore the racist impact of our state's policies and practices.

It is also evident that if our nation cares about freedom, equality, and rights for all like we claim to, we will take serious measures to disrupt housing segregation. We also need to shift California policy makers away from prison expansion, punitive crime laws, and harsh school policies, in favor of social welfare. California, as representative of national economic policy, is in sore need of a radical redistribution of resources and power to our communities that are most underserved. Capitalism, the prison industrial complex, and the enduring unfairly racialized social arrangement all serve to poison society's ability to extend civil and human rights to all people. Without these basic rights, as guaranteed by the Constitution, people are denied the capacity to enjoy respect, live decently with dignity, and equally access opportunities and resources to make the most of one's life. The current social arrangement does not foster conditions for all people to have decent housing, access to quality health care, education, living wages, and protection under the law.

Instead, capitalism is an economic system based on the private ownership of capital by a few, including the bodies that govern our California Departments of Corrections and education institutions, and is designed to extract as much profit as it possibly can from the vast majority of working-class peoples. Thus, this economic order is inherently inhumane since concerns for social welfare is trumped by profit. This economic system spurred the development of our prison industrial complex, whereas another arrangement may have directed efforts toward increasing access to decent housing, health care, quality education, proper nutrition, and employment for those most in need. In short, capitalism is not conducive to collaborative and noncompetitive community building, rehabilitation, or other processes to provide humane living conditions and respect to all. Instead, a socialist system allocates the wealth of society to those who produce it—the workers— and is used in a planned and sustainable way for the benefit of all. In place of greed, domination, and exploitation, a socialist arrangement stands for solidarity, respect, and cooperation between all peoples.

Given that the prison system does not reduce crime or increase safety and is instead a structure of violence and social/racial control, abolishing prisons and creating an alternative system of accountability, such as restorative justice programs, is in order. These types of programs seek to provide direct healing to both the victim and the offender while also involving the community and the root cause of the conflict. No reform can make the prison industrial complex just or effective, and thus, many organizations across the country, including Critical Resistance and A New Way of Life Reentry Project, are working toward diminishing the prison system and fighting for more just social conditions and community-based ways to resolve problems.

Capitalism, racism, housing segregation, and the prison industrial complex have an enormous adverse impact on black and Latino students in urban schools as found in this study. Therefore, it is critical that larger structural changes are made so that all school environments can be places premised on humanity and self-development for all students regardless of race or class. Smaller changes should include repealing propositions that allow for school funding varying widely by neighborhood wealth. Schools should also operate under the input of parents, community members, and perhaps, most importantly, students. This could take the form of a community-based school board rather than those run by people with the most political power and resources. Furthermore, given their hostile and destructive presence on the lives of our most vulnerable youth, the pipeline, criminalization of black and brown youth, and zero tolerance policies must end. It would be irresponsible to allow for state-sanctioned violence and terrorism, under the guise of school safety, to continue to thrive in our schools.

Conclusion

These suggested actions, both big and small, support a radical change in schools at its *foundation.* Anything short of shining the spotlight directly on our use of segregation and the criminalization of black and brown skin will forever leave us ill equipped to achieve school equality. While it will be no easy feat to abolish white supremacy (in fact some even say it is impossible), we can at least acknowledge that it remains at the root of much suffering and inequality such as the school-to-prison pipeline and move forward from there. Talking about the school-to-prison pipeline without also talking about its connection to our legacy of slavery is like talking about surfing without mentioning water and waves; neither makes sense. Once we can openly agree to actively resist the black–white binary that was constructed during slavery, we have a fighting chance to not only dismantle the school-to-prison pipeline but also uproot the underlying causes of racial discrimination that perpetuate housing segregation and our unjust prison system. We know another world; a better more humane world is possible when enough people have the critical knowledge they need to spur collective and sustained efforts for social change. We sincerely hope that our chapter aids in this hopeful possibility.

Notes

1. Coates 2014.
2. Ibid.
3. Garcia and Yosso 2013, pp. 64–89.
4. Ibid.
5. Ibid.
6. https://www.aclu.org/racial-justice/what-school-prison-pipeline.
7. Skiba and Peterson 1999, pp. 372–382.
8. Domanick 2004.
9. Ibid.
10. "Monthly Report of Prison Population" 2007.
11. Ibid.
12. Ehlers, Schiraldi, and Lotke 2004.
13. Department of Justice, United States, 1975.
14. California Department of Education 2014.
15. Police in LAUSD Schools: The Need for Accountability and Alternatives, October 2010. http://www.dignityinschools.org/sites/default/files/Police%20in%20 LAUSD%20Schools.pdf.
16. "Ga. Police Handcuff, Arrest Kindergartner for Tantrum" 2012.
17. Clark 2004.

Bibliography

Alexander, Michelle. 2010. *The New Jim Crow: Mass Incarceration in the Age of Colorblindness.* New York: New Press.

California Department of Education. "Educational Demographics Unit." Accessed June 2014. http://www.education.ca.gov/.

Clark, Christine. 2004. "Diversity Initiatives in Higher Education: Multicultural Education as a Tool for Reclaiming Schools Organized as Breeding Grounds for Prisons." *Multicultural Education* 11 (3): 50–53.

Coates, Ta-Nehisi. 2014. "The Case for Reparations." *The Atlantic* (May 21). Accessed August 31, 2014. http://www.theatlantic.com/features/archive/2014/05/the-case-for-reparations/361631/.

Curtin, Mary Ellen. 2000. *Black Prisoners and Their World, Alabama, 1865–1900.* Charlottesville: University Press of Virginia.

Davis, Angela Y. 2003. *Are Prisons Obsolete?* New York: Seven Stories Press.

Department of Justice, United States. 1975. "Ad Hoc Committee on the Prevention and Management of Conflict and Crime in the Schools, Final Report." NCJ 078094, California Office of the Attorney General, 1515 K Street, Sacramento, CA, 41 pp.

Domanick, Joe. 2004. *Cruel Justice: Three Strikes and the Politics of Crime in America's Golden State.* Berkeley: University of California Press.

Ehlers, Scott, Vincent Schiraldi, and Eric Lotke. 2004. "Racial Divide: California's 3 Strikes Law." *Justice Policy Institute* (October 1).

Ehrlich, D. 2001. "Why Most Americans Think Politicians' 'Tough on Crime' Stance Has Gone Too Far." ACLU of Northern California. Accessed August 31, 2014. http://www.aclunc.org/news/opinions/why_most_americans_think_politi cians%27_tough_on_crime_stance_has_gone_too_far.shtml.

Fanon, Frantz. 1967. *Black Skin, White Masks.* New York: Grove Press.

Frankenberg, Erica. "Brown at 60: Great Progress, a Long Retreat and an Uncertain Future." Accessed May 19, 2014. http://civilrightsproject.ucla.edu/research/ k-12-education/integration-and-diversity/brown-at-60-great-progress-a-long-retreat-and-an-uncertain-future/Brown-at-60-051814.pdf.

"Ga. Police Handcuff, Arrest Kindergartner for Tantrum." CBSNews. April 17, 2012. Accessed September 1, 2014. http://www.cbsnews.com/news/ga-police-handcuff-arrest-kindergartner-for-tantrum.

Garcia, David G., and Tara J. Yosso. 2013. "'Strictly in the Capacity of Servant': The Interconnection between Residential and School Segregation in Oxnard, California, 1934–1954." *History of Education Quarterly* 53 (1): 64–89. doi:10.1111/hoeq.12003.

Gilmore, Ruth Wilson. 2007. *Golden Gulag: Prisons, Surplus, Crisis, and Opposition in Globalizing California.* Berkeley: University of California Press.

Greene, Judith, and Kevin Pranis. 2007. *Gang Wars: The Failure of Enforcement Tactics and the Need for Effective Public Safety Strategies.* Washington, DC: Justice Policy Institute.

Hofwegen, Van. 2009. "Unjust and Ineffective: A Critical Look at California's Step Act." *Southern California Interdisciplinary Law Journal* 18 (3): 679.

Lebowitz, Michael A. 2006. *Build It Now: Socialism for the Twenty-first Century.* New York: Monthly Review Press.

Males, Mike. 2000. "California's War on Drugs Targets Minorities." *Justice Policy Institute* 27 (October.

Meiners, Erica R. 2007. *Right to Be Hostile: Schools, Prisons, and the Making of Public Enemies.* New York: Routledge.

"Monthly Report of Prison Population." 2007. *California Department of Corrections and Rehabilitation.*

Omi, Michael, and Howard Winant. 1994. *Racial Formation in the United States: From the 1960s to the 1990s.* New York: Routledge.

Skiba, Russell J. 2000. *Zero Tolerance, Zero Evidence: A Critical Analysis of School Disciplinary Practice.* Bloomington: Indiana University Press.

Skiba, Russell, and Reece Peterson. 1999. "The Dark Side of Zero Tolerance: Can Punishment Lead to Safe Schools?" *Phi Delta Kappan* 80 (5): 372–382.

Sojoyner, Damien M. 2013. "Black Radicals Make for Bad Citizens: Undoing the Myth of the School to Prison Pipeline." *Berkeley Review of Education* 4 (2): 241–263.

Vitiello, Michael. 1997. "Can We Return to Rationality?" *The Journal of Criminal Law and Criminology* 87 (2): 395–481.

Chapter 7

Race-Based Stereotypes, Expectations, and Exclusion in American Education

*Tennisha Riley, Aysha Foster,
and Zewelanji Serpell*

Introduction

A long history exists in America of excluding students of color, particularly African American students, from schooling. In the early part of history, blacks were denied access to education altogether, with stringent laws in place to ensure compliance. Later, exclusion was more subtle and embedded in segregation—a system by which individuals were separated into different schools solely based on their race and one that relegated blacks to the most poorly resourced schools. After schools were integrated in the early 1950s, exclusion based on race arguably took on a more pernicious form—hidden racism—evidenced today by racial inequities in special education referral and placement, as well as racial disproportionality in disciplinary actions such as expulsion, suspension, and alternative placement.

While schooling is a universal right and legal requirement for all children, schools promote a particular and culturally defined way of being that systematically excludes many students of color from optimal educational experiences. In this chapter we argue that exclusion is driven by stereotyped appraisals and race-based expectations of classroom behavior and academic ability. Racial stereotypes are posited as being embedded in the minds of those tasked with educating as well as in the minds of students, but also built into the structure of schools and manifested in the form of faulty policy. Specific educational reform efforts and related school policies, such as "zero tolerance" and achievement standards based on race/ethnicity, are discussed as reinforcing racial stereotypes and enabling structural racism.

We conclude with a discussion about the importance of, and challenges associated with, developing solutions to deter raced-based exclusion and to facilitate racial equity in education.

Cultural Capital, Cultural Hegemony, and the "Right" Way to Be in School

While most teachers are not blatant racists, many probably are cultural hegemonists. They expect all students to behave according to the school's cultural standards of normality.[1]

In America, there is a "right way" to be in a classroom. This way is dictated by what Lisa Delpit calls "the culture of power,"[2] whose rules mirror the rules of the culture of those who have power in the society. In an American context, those with the greatest amount of power are middle class and white. The culture of power encompasses specific rules about how to "be" in one's self-presentation, interactions with others, and communication patterns. It also engenders how one should be physically and linguistically. Because the role of schools and schooling is to enculturate young people into the broader society, schools are essentially designed to support students who demonstrate the culture of power and negate or neglect those who do not. Several examples in the behavioral realm are relevant here. For example, compliance is a highly valued behavioral characteristic in the classroom setting and school context as a whole. Teachers are often evaluated on the basis of the "orderliness" of their students and/or their ability to resolve conflict in the classroom.[3] Therefore, teachers believe they must be in control, and the structure of the classroom should ensure that students above all obey them. The "machismo" or tough male behavioral repertoire often promoted by Hispanic and African American families as a means of socializing important cultural values of responsibility and family-centeredness can be easily misconstrued in a classroom context as noncompliance. This persona may be regarded as aggressive and resonate with negative stereotypes about minority males and precipitate conflict with the teacher. As such, when conflict arises between teachers and students, and control is lost, teachers frequently resort to removing the student from the classroom and referring them to the office. Another example of behavior related to compliance is direct eye contact. Direct eye contact is a value that is so much a part of the cultural ethos in school that it is not unusual to hear teachers demand—even during a reprimand—"look at me when I'm speaking to you!" This may be disconcerting and upsetting to children raised in cultural contexts in which direct eye contact is viewed as a challenge or sign of insubordination and, therefore, a behavior they will not typically exhibit toward their teachers. Instead, these students avoid direct eye contact with adults as a way of indicating appropriate deference and respect. However, teachers may infer the opposite message and instead regard the lack of eye contract as disrespect.

Delpit and others argue that the only way to mitigate the educational inequities that result from the types of cultural mismatch described earlier between students of color and their teachers is to make the rules of the culture of power explicit and to foster biculturalism, particularly among students of color from low socioeconomic backgrounds. Biculturalism entails the acquisition of "cultural capital." A term coined by Bourdieu and Passeron, "cultural capital" refers to a set of skills, habits, strategies, and behavioral repertoires that define the upper echelon of society and serve as the standard for performance evaluation in important environments such as schools.[4]

Effectively deployed, this cultural capital is like money in that it buys or enables access to a host of benefits that raise individuals' social status. The logic behind the biculturalism argument is therefore that "if certain behaviors are instrumental to success for sound (non-arbitrary) reasons, then schools should open up access to these cultural repertoires to students who lack them. This would transform what currently functions as a mechanism of social exclusion into a mechanism of social mobility."[5] The problem engendered in cultural capital is that by definition it reflects the culture of the dominant group, in this case middle-class white America. Hence, it is not clear if this capital is actually educationally valuable or if it is arbitrary and appears valuable only because it is reinforced and rewarded in school. There are some middle-class white American cultural values that do in fact promote success in school, for example, the strong emphasis on verbal skills. However, other cultural themes such as rugged individualism may be less essential for the learning process despite their currency in school.

Some researchers have argued that biculturalism may be effective but at a substantial psychological cost as students of color struggle to balance the challenge of being perceived as "acting white" while working to maintain their ethnic identity and social connections with same-race peers.[6] In addition, there are themes that arise from those of working-class backgrounds and nonwhite racial groups that confer distinct benefits that can support success in school. For example, Lareau contends that low-income families foster greater autonomy and this can result in high levels of initiative and respect for adults. Arguments that cultural ways of being that do not conform to the white middle-class ideal hamper effective learning have also been refuted by empirical studies, demonstrating that given the opportunity to learn in classrooms imbued with such themes as movement-expressiveness and communalism, African American students perform commensurate with or better than their Caucasian counterparts on a range of academic tasks, including mathematics, problem solving, reading comprehension, and story recall. As such, these researchers argue that the emphasis should be placed not on students of color lacking some critical cultural characteristic. Instead, we should focus on school reforms that capitalize on the cultural strengths children of color bring to school and make available a more diverse set of cultural themes from which all students can select and harness in their learning process.

The Macrosystem: Teacher Expectations in Broader Social Context

We cannot blame the schools alone. We live in a society that nurtures and maintains stereotypes: we are all bombarded daily, for instance, with the portrayal of the young black male as monster.[7]

Schooling entails growth in competence in several domains: cognitive, social, emotional, academic, and progressive incorporation into a specific society and its culture. Enculturation and growth occur through proximal processes. In Bronfenbrenner's ecological systems theory, proximal processes are regularly occurring reciprocal interactions between the person and the environment that vary systematically as a function of the unique characteristics of that person and his or her environment.[8] These processes occur within mutually influential systems, including the microsystem, such as the child's family or classroom; the mesosystem, representing interactions among different microsystems; and the macrosystem, representing societal norms and cultural values or mores.

For children of color in the United States, the macrosystem includes social stratification mechanisms in the form of racism, prejudice, discrimination, and oppression. These macrosystem variables operate within the proximal environment of schools and profoundly impact the child's development. For example, as a social stratification mechanism, racism functions as a system of oppression and accompanying ideology that is embedded in the structure of society and perpetuates racial inequality by denying opportunities to students whose physical features and culture differ from that of the white middle class. Racism manifests in teacher expectations and associated behaviors toward students of color and, regardless of the race of the teacher, is deeply embedded within their psyche and educational practice. A teacher's "views of a child may be influenced by aspects of the child's racial identity that become interwoven with historical stereotypes of low intelligence, stigmatized behaviors, poverty, or detrimental family circumstances."[9] Another example of racist ideology that may permeate the thought processes of teachers is a phenomenon Joyce King calls "dysconscious racism" or a tendency to uncritically accept white norms and privileges.[10]

While most research focuses on the micro-systemic interactions between individual children and their teachers, it is critical that the societal or macro-level context in which these interactions occur be considered as part and parcel of these interactions.[11] Societal racism is often detected and justified by racial stereotypes or overgeneralized accounts of the behavior of a particular racial group. Racial stereotypes have a profound impact on the schooling experiences of students of color. These stereotypes not only influence teachers' appraisal and response to the behavior of students of different races but also alter the climate in the classroom by establishing a basis for differential expectations and stereotype threat. Stereotype threat is situational—it is tension brought about by the knowledge of stereotypes associated with one's group and the possibility that one may be viewed through the lens of a negative stereotype, or the fear that one may do something that would inadvertently confirm the stereotype. In the case of African Americans, it is the fear of confirming stereotypes of low intelligence or poor academic ability. The irony about stereotype threat is that it inhibits performance, especially for students who typically perform well and care about performing well in the domain tested. As such, despite their ability, talented African American students underperform and bolster the negative stereotype of low academic ability in their racial group.

The Microsystem: Teacher Expectations and Student–Teacher Interactions

A teacher can make or break a child, favor or stigmatize him. Just as there are teachers who are inspiring, who can spark interest and turn students on to learning, there are teachers who can turn a student off, not only to school but to himself.[12]

The premise of much of the research on teacher expectations is that these expectations are based on stereotypes that differentiate racial, socioeconomic, and gender groups. Research results reveal that when applied to student motivation and achievement, stereotypes for particular racial groups are re- markably accurate, with effect sizes in the moderate to high range. Perhaps these results are not remarkable at all given the wealth of information teach- ers have about factors that influence students' academic outcomes and the fact that stereotypes likely reflect the social reality[13]—a substantial black– white achievement gap does in fact exist, and if teachers "expected" their African American students to do worse than their white students, they would likely be right.

The principal reason teacher expectations are posited as important in understanding the educational experience of students is the notion that a "self-fulfilling prophecy" operates, such that inaccurate expectations by teachers lead students to perform at levels consistent with these expecta- tions. By definition, self-fulfilling prophecies require that the initial judg- ment or expectation be false. Results of studies examining the veracity of this concept in education suggest that the evidence for self-fulfilling proph- ecies is mostly moderate to weak. However, the effects of self-fulfilling prophecies for African Americans are more substantial than they are for other groups, and in contexts where structural factors promote inequity, these effects may be significant and long lasting. For example, in a study by Hinnant, O'Brien, and Ghazarian, minority boys appear to suffer the consequences of low expectations, demonstrating their lowest performance when their abilities are underestimated, but also appear to reap the benefits of high expectations—exhibiting the greatest academic gains when their abilities were overestimated.[14]

Decontextualizing concepts like "teacher expectations" in the social sci- ence research may lead to the false conclusion that because teacher expec- tations are set by "accurate" group stereotypes, too much weight is being given to the role of expectations in determining achievement outcomes. We argue the contrary—that using stereotypes, albeit historically accurate ones, to set expectations for individual children can be profoundly detrimental for students of color. After all, a child comes to school to be transformed— to exceed expectations, and low expectations can get in the way of teachers working to actuate this transformation. Some examples follow. A teacher with presumably good intentions encourages an African American male to focus on developing his ability in a sport. A teacher may not contact par- ents when a student of color is exhibiting academic or behavioral difficul- ties because the teacher assumes these parents do not want to participate in school or have a low value of education. A teacher rationalizes to himself or herself that a student who does not show competency on a particular concept in a lesson is a "struggling learner" when in actuality the student has simply missed part of the lesson.

While there is little concrete evidence to substantiate the claim that teacher expectations *alone* determine the academic and social outcomes of their students, expectations are definitely related to the classroom behavior of both teachers and students. Low expectations and the transactional behaviors between students and teachers can profoundly impact the student–teacher relationship. Eccles and Roeser put it best in their statement that "there are risks associated with the complex interplay of policy, person characteristics of teachers and students that undermine proximal processes."[15] As such, it may be less that students will absorb teacher expectations, as the self-fulfilling prophecy work suggests, but rather that the expectations contribute to teachers' abdication of their teaching responsibilities. It is worthy of note that teacher expectations are particularly strong predictors of student outcomes in classrooms where students perceive high levels of differential treatment of students by the teacher.[16] Delpit states that it is not so much that teachers have expectations but rather that these expectations dictate how they think and behave toward students.[17] Several early studies reviewed by Brophy (1983) confirm that low teacher expectations are associated with differential student–teacher interactions and result in myriad teacher behaviors that compromise learning opportunities, including less praise and feedback for incorrect responses, and more criticism.[18] Low expectations based on stereotypes also compromise the establishment of meaningful student–teacher relationships. Students need to feel that their teachers know and understand them to establish trust and a sense of connectedness. Further, quality relationships between teachers and their students are extremely important—numerous studies demonstrate that high-quality relationships are associated with higher levels of academic motivation and social and academic success.

Teacher expectations often extend to the parents of the students in their classrooms. Racial biases and stereotyping or feeling culturally disconnected from parents may make teachers more reluctant to communicate with parents or engage them in a collaborative process to help resolve problems their child may be experiencing in the classroom. Previous negative experiences often limit teachers' willingness to engage parents and families in the schooling of their children. It is also the case that the quality of the relationship between parents and teachers can impact student outcomes, especially in early schooling, and that African Americans are particularly vulnerable to this influence.

Teacher Expectations and School Policies

Between-class ability grouping and curriculum differentiation provide examples of how school policy, teacher beliefs and instruction, and student characteristics can all conspire to create maladaptive transactions that perpetuate poor achievement and behavior.[19]

Preconceived beliefs about the abilities of students are heavily influenced by prejudicial views perpetuated in the wider society through media. However, school policies have also served as a mechanism for perpetuating racial stereotypes and contributing to existing teacher biases against students of color. The No Child Left Behind (NCLB) Act requires that states report their test data and many states elect to break the statistics down by race and ethnicity. In fact, several states (i.e., Washington, Florida, Alabama, Virginia) have adopted policies to report school success on achievement tests delineated by race and perceived ability. While this appears to be part of an effort to ensure schools are accountable for the failure or success of all students, reporting achievement data this way likely influences teachers' expectations and fuels self-fulfilling prophecies. The practice also appears to have little utility. For example, Hanushek and Raymond (2004) assessed accountability in the United States, after NCLB and the mandate to report achievement outcomes, and report that while accountability does seem to increase student achievement overall and for the various subgroups, the gains for African American students are small and therefore widen the white–black achievement gap.[20]

Shockingly, the reporting of achievement data by race has yielded new policies that set different pass rates, specifically for math and reading, for students according to their race. In Virginia, for example, the state legislation has developed academic math goals that specify expected passing rates as follows: 82 percent for Asian American students, 68 percent for white students, 52 percent for Hispanic students, and 45 percent for African American students. Such policies confirm many teachers' preconceived perceptions that students of color have little potential to achieve at the same level as their white counterparts. When queried in an interview for the *Pacific Standard* about these policy practices, Jeannie Oakes, presidential professor emeritus at UCLA, replied, "Once we put students in groups, we give them very different opportunities to learn—with strong patterns of inequality across teachers, experience, and competence . . . not only that minority and low-income children were likely to be placed in lower tracks but also that they were given the teachers who expected the least of them."[21]

Special Education Referral and Placement

The Harvard Civil Rights Project has documented persistent inequities in the referral process for African American children.[22] African American children have a higher likelihood of being referred and acquire a special education label that places them in the most impaired groups, specifically mentally retarded and seriously emotionally disturbed. In 1998, African Americans made up 11.4 percent of disabled students, with the number increasing to 12.2 percent within 10 years. Most alarming are the numbers reported for the identification of students as mentally retarded: the rates for white students between 6 and 21 years of age are less than half the rates for African American students.

Despite the stated goal of referral and labeling to enable students to access beneficial services, in actuality this process puts African American students at a further disadvantage. Not only are more African American students without disability falsely identified, if they actually do have a disability it is often misidentified. Misidentification typically translates into students not receiving appropriate services. Students of color suffer the burden of stigma and are far more likely than their Caucasian counterparts to be removed from regular education classes and educated separately in environments with the least qualified teachers, inappropriately large student/teacher ratios, and reduced access to needed mental health support. Statutes were added to the Individuals with Disabilities Education Improvement Act, Section 618 (d), in 2004, requiring states to evaluate racial disproportionalities and rectify inappropriate identifications, but substantial progress has not been documented these past 10 years.

Exclusion from quality educational experiences does not only come in the form of special education referrals but also in the form of low referrals of African American students to gifted and talented education (GATE) programs and Advanced Placement (AP) courses. The Department of Education's Office of Civil Rights' 2012 report indicates that African American elementary and middle school students make up only 10 percent of students enrolled in GATE programs, as compared to 62 percent of white students.[23] The underrepresentation of African American students in AP classes holds true for high school students as well. While the number of African American students taking an AP exam over the past decade showed a substantial increase, the numbers (108, 545) are still far less than that of white students (949, 986). African American students are also scoring at the bottom on AP exams with a mean grade of 1.91 and only 3.1 percent of them earning the highest marking of five.[24]

Behavioral Expectations and Zero Tolerance Policies

Zero tolerance policies in schools began as a response to school violence, drug-related occurrences, and concern about general school safety. Federal and state regulations regarding zero tolerance stipulated that any student bearing arms or drugs in school would face a mandatory one-year expulsion from school. In the early 1990s, zero tolerance policies were extended to relatively minor behaviors, such as smoking, classroom disruption, and insubordination. Correct implementation of zero tolerance policy in the school setting requires that minor and serious behavioral infractions or violations against school policies receive equivalent levels of discipline. "The policy assumption is that inflexibility is a deterrent because, no matter how or why the rule was broken, the fact that the rule was broken is the basis for the imposition of the penalty. This is intended as a behavior modification strategy: since those at risk know that it may operate unfairly, they may be induced to take even unreasonable steps to avoid breaking the rule."[25] Hence, school-wide discipline policies based on zero tolerance have allowed teachers to make strict and irreversible disciplinary decisions that have led to a disproportionate number of students of color being suspended and expelled and ultimately to a nontrivial amount of school dropout in this student population.

National reports indicate school suspensions and expulsions are being implemented as early as prekindergarten and disproportionately with children of color. For example, while African American children make up 18 percent of those enrolled in preschool programs within the United States, they make up nearly half (48 percent) of the number of preschoolers who have had more than one out-of-school suspension.[26] Children entering preschool are typically three to four years old and developmentally appropriate behaviors such as tantrum throwing and bathroom incidents are being met with developmentally inappropriate disciplinary action such as suspension. This poses several problems. First, children of preschool age do not possess the cognitive ability to understand school suspension as a punishment. Instead, they learn that any behavior deemed as "disruptive" results in removal or withdrawal from the system. The preschool setting is intended to help increase socialization skills and transition children into the educational setting and society, yet many African American children are excluded from this important learning process because teachers resort to removing the child from the classroom setting rather than working to understand and manage behavior they deem problematic.

At the middle and high school levels, Keleher (2000) reports a substantial increase in school suspensions and expulsions of African American students since the implementation of zero tolerance.[27] For example, when the policy was initiated in 1995, Chicago City schools saw a five-year increase from 23 expulsions per year to 657 expulsions per year, and the vast majority of students removed from school were African Americans. Tragically, many African American and Latino students were not suspended for serious infractions and were instead targeted for relatively minor and highly subjective behaviors such as disobedience and disrespect, and sometimes for poor school attendance.[28] Other studies indicate that in the high school context, students report receiving office referrals for even more minor behaviors such as loud verbal play, laughing, rough play, insults, and, at the most severe end, threatening behavior. Some behaviors may indeed be problematic in a classroom context, but the degree to which they are disruptive or warrant severe discipline is a matter of subjective opinion.

Caucasian students tend to be disciplined for more direct violations of school policy, including smoking, leaving without permission, vandalism, and obscene language. African American students receive harsh discipline for behavior that not only is subjective in nature but highlights the aforementioned interactional challenges bolstered by stereotypes. For example, teachers may experience fear or loss of control because broader societal images reinforce the perception of students with different cultural backgrounds as threatening and dangerous. Monroe (2005) describes media outlets as often depicting young black youth as violent and aggressive.[29] Repeated exposure to such images lends itself well to generalized stereotypes that nonwhite youth will display unexpected and aggressive behavior. Many studies suggest that teachers rate African American students higher on disruptive behavior rating scales than independent observers in the classroom.

Teacher perceptions and student behavior as they manifest in the context of zero tolerance policy implementation are complex. For teachers, general perceptions of minority students mixed with their expectations of "appropriate" school behavior create a context for exclusion. For students, perceptions of being unfairly targeted for disciplinary action can lead to the exhibition of behavior (indignation or anger) that puts them at greater risk for more severe action, such as school expulsion. The result of perceptions based on generalized stereotypes contributes to teachers making disciplinary decisions based on race rather than on individual personal experiences or a good understanding of individual differences in emotional expressiveness. Teachers may also deem exclusion as a necessary and appropriate disciplinary measure given wider societal messages that the best mechanism to curtail the perceived "aggression" of minority youth is to detain or exclude them from normal society. The disparate numbers for white and nonwhite students' exclusion from school appear to be consistent with disproportionality in wider societal rates of punishment (incarceration). African Americans make up a large proportion of inmates held in local jails and state prisons, and these numbers are mirrored in the school discipline literature, with African American students being two to five times more likely to be suspended than their white counterparts. It is not surprising then that school characteristics such as teacher attitudes and the structure of the administration explain a larger proportion of variance in school suspensions than do actual student behaviors.

Disciplinary policies like zero tolerance reinforce the notion that classroom compliance should come first, even at the cost of the student's well-being. Such policies also undermine the ability of teachers to "know" their troubled students and learn how to work with them to resolve challenging behavior. Teachers are also less inclined to exert the required effort to work toward conflict resolution. This is particularly evident among highly stressed teachers teaching in schools with students who are culturally different from them.

Disciplinary measures should be taken on the basis of objective judgments about whether the student actually poses a safety threat, not for a student who simply needs help. However, the fact that under zero tolerance minor and severe behavioral offenses are treated by the school administration as the same, means the vast majority of students referred to the office for minor offences are receiving overly punitive discipline. This practice jeopardizes students' ability to improve their behavior. Instead of promoting more adaptive, collaborative efforts to improve classroom behavior and academic achievement, such policies exacerbate student–teacher conflict and do not support cultural understanding and efforts toward interpersonal conflict resolution. Removal from the classroom also eliminates the possibility of addressing the problem in the context of its occurrence and removes the opportunity to help students regulate their behavior or break maladaptive patterns. Suspension and expulsion also put an undue burden on parents and often contribute to negative parental perceptions of the school.

There is little evidence that zero tolerance policies in schools are effective in deterring unwanted behavior and mounting skepticism about the effectiveness of these policies. Furthermore, the number of African American students being referred to the office for subjective behaviors such as excessive noise, threat, disrespect, and loitering is increasing. As such, many questions remain about the utility and fairness of these policies. The Obama administration is pushing to outlaw stringent disciplinary practices and in a recent statement Attorney General Eric Holder (2014) stated: "Too often, so-called 'zero-tolerance' policies—however well-intentioned—make students feel unwelcome in their own schools. They disrupt the learning process. And they can have significant and lasting negative effects on the long-term well-being of our young people—increasing their likelihood of future contact with juvenile and criminal justice systems." The U.S. Department of Education secretary and attorney general are developing new school discipline guidelines and state legislators are paying attention.[30] For example, the District of Columbia is creating new education policies that would reduce the number of students being excluded from the school process by way of disciplinary actions in both public and charter schools. The district is invested specifically in reducing the number of out-of-school suspensions for children under the age of five.[31] This effort is critical for improving equity in education, as removing students from the classroom denies them important learning opportunities and limits their capacity to develop self-regulatory behavior within the school context.

Conclusion and Recommendations

If we are to truly educate . . . we must learn who the children are, and not focus on what we assume them to be—at risk, learning disabled, behavior disordered, etc. This means developing relationships with our students, and understanding their political, cultural, and intellectual legacy.[32]

In this chapter, we have argued that the perceptions and expectations of teachers and school administrators play a large role in the exclusion of students of color from optimal educational experiences. Behavioral expectations and achievement-related expectations go hand in hand and frequently originate from and perpetuate racial stereotypes. Unlike findings regarding academic expectations that are mixed, research findings in the behavioral domain indicate true racial bias, in the sense that studies show that teachers make judgments about the behavioral repertoires of black students that do *not* reflect reality.

Exclusion sits at the intersection between teachers and students but is exacerbated by specific school policies and related reforms, particularly zero tolerance policies and achievement standards based on race/ethnicity. As such, we propose that efforts to mitigate the exclusion of students of color from schooling must focus on both micro- and macrosystem interventions. At the macro-systemic level, we must eliminate the overemphasis placed on compliance in schools, develop school policies that openly acknowledge individual differences, and recognize and harness students' cultural strengths. "A democratic curriculum and pedagogy must begin with recognition of the different social positionings and cultural repertoires in the classrooms, and the power relations between them."[33] As such, at the micro-systemic level we must transform teachers.

Teacher Training

If teachers are to function as the "gate keepers" of educational equity, we need to provide them the tools to serve this role well. High expectations are important to ensuring good academic outcomes for students who are perceived as underperforming, particularly low-income students of color, and a substantial body of literature on effective schools supports this perspective. It therefore seems worthwhile to consider interventions that target teacher expectations. TESA (Teachers Expectation and Student Achievement) is a behavior change program aimed at training and informing teachers on how to have high expectations for all students. Programs such as these are available for teachers to attend but are not required in all school systems or university curricula. Further, the most recent studies examining the impact of TESA on student achievement provide little, if any, support for the program's effectiveness. It is unclear if this intervention, despite yielding positive results in the 1970s when it was first implemented, continues to be effective.

Some have suggested more training modules focused on cultural and racial differences; however, these often reinforce existing group stereotypes and do not encourage teachers to attend to individual differences. Joyce King points out that teacher education programs must help dismantle the dysconscious racism that becomes embedded in the views of student-teachers who eventually become the teaching workforce. Exposing these teacher-students to information, albeit factual, about social inequalities is unlikely to yield a fundamental change in perspective about why inequities exist, nor foster a critical evaluation of their own self-identities, values, and ideologies. Teachers tend to feel deeply uncomfortable with talking about cultural differences, especially when the conversation arises in the context of discussions about race and education. There needs to be a fundamental restructuring of training that helps teachers dismantle racial stereotypes, confront their own personal biases, expose the influence of racism in the broader social context on their beliefs, and develop interpersonal skills that allow them to focus on students' individual differences, cultural orientations, and unique needs. Good teachers, of all races, attempt to socialize or teach children of color what it means to operate as members of the culture of power.[34] However, empowering teachers to do this requires that they recognize the cultural of power and buy-in to the notion that they can change their own cultural perceptions and that these changes will impact their students.

Stereotypes are also amenable to change. Contextual influences such as policy and social contact can fundamentally shift the perspective of teachers and school administrators. Research suggests that we can reduce stereotype threat by (1) attending to contextual factors that call attention to social identity or heighten threat and using threat reduction prompts (such as framing tasks so that students do not believe group differences exist); (2) providing opportunities for students to have their own culturally defined values affirmed in domains other than the one being evaluated (in this case values not associated with academic achievement); and (3) promoting a growth mind-set or a perspective that intelligence is not something one is born with, but rather a malleable characteristic that can be improved with hard work. Moreover, it seems that teaching teachers how to counter stereotype threat in students may be a viable mechanism for altering teacher expectations that are based on racial stereotypes. However, because academic stereotypes frequently represent a real phenomenon, the most powerful mechanism for enabling perspective shifts is to actually alter the reality. That is, teachers need an opportunity to observe students of color succeeding as the result of a teacher's high expectations and genuine effort to teach them.

We must proceed down the teacher-training path with care, and just as we do with students, assume that teachers are genuinely interested in learning and succeeding in their job. It is important that we find ways to maximize teachers' teaching potential and not to blame them for the academic failures of their students of color. It is critical that teachers understand and confront their personal biases, stereotypical views, and comfort with students who are culturally different from them. However, this is not something teachers can accomplish without explicit support from school administrators because it takes time and requires structural changes that dismantle hidden racism by restructuring policy. We know from previous research that discrepancies in priorities for teachers and administrators will likely interfere with efforts to effectively intervene in schools. We must ensure that administrators and teachers are in agreement and that there is building-level buy-in for making fundamental changes to referral, discipline, and placement practices.

Future policy efforts must also require teachers and administrators to work with students and their families to enable students to stay in classrooms in schools and work toward resolving problems in ways that are in the best interest of the student. This requires cultural sensitivity and respect for difference. Finding ways to connect, establish, and maintain communication and build trust with parents is critical for reducing exclusionary practices. Parents are an important source of information that might help divert away from exclusion and toward school-based social–emotional intervention. In addition, a plethora of studies suggest that engaging parents in their student's educational experiences increases the likelihood of academic success and helps reduce problem behavior.[35] Unfortunately, multiple barriers exist to engaging African American parents in school, especially parents of students who exhibit disruptive behavior in school. School personnel often form beliefs about family and parental function based on structural features such as single-parent status and family size. In addition, parents labeled as dysfunctional are seen as having little to offer and are either ignored or given menial tasks or roles in schools. Teacher training that provides specific guidance about how to effectively involve parents in the decision-making process related to disciplinary issues is critical. Teachers are frequently unprepared to make meaningful contact with parents, and research indicates that establishing a quality relationship built on trust and mutual respect is far more important for ensuring positive social outcomes for low-income African American students than is increasing the number of times a teacher contacts a parent.

In sum, education is a social justice issue, and as long as we pretend it is neutral, we will continue to observe vast inequities in opportunity and success among students of color. Improving teachers' understanding of developmentally appropriate behavior as well as cultural and contextual influences on behavior is essential to efforts to decrease the school exclusion of students of color. The cultural disconnect between the way students of color are expected to behave in the classroom and behavioral styles valued and reinforced at home may ultimately undermine the capacity of these students to succeed in school.[36] Perhaps then it is time that the cultural capital that students of color bring to the classroom be explicitly recognized and harnessed in the classroom. This incorporation may also foster respect and value for cultural diversity in the classroom as a whole.

Notes

1. Gay 2000.
2. Delpit 2006.
3. Sheets 1996, pp. 165–183.
4. Anderson 2012, pp. 105–129.
5. Ibid.
6. Ogbu 1990, pp. 45–57.
7. Delpit 2006.
8. Bronfenbrenner 1994.
9. Harry and Klingner 2014.
10. King 1991, pp. 133–146.
11. Diamond, Randolph, and Spillane 2004, pp. 75–98.
12. Collins and Tamarkin 1982.
13. Jussim and Harber 2005, pp. 131–155.
14. Hinnant, O'Brien, and Ghazarian 2009.
15. Eccles and Roeser 2009.
16. Jussim and Harber 2005, pp. 131–155.
17. Delpit 2003, pp. 14–21.
18. Brophy 1983.
19. Lamb and Bornstein 2011.
20. Hanushek and Raymond 2004, pp. 406–415.
21. Halpert 2012.
22. Losen and Orfield 2002.
23. U.S. Department of Education Office for Civil Rights 2011–2012.
24. Aud, Fox, and Ramani 2010.
25. Skiba and Knesting 2002.
26. U.S. Department of Education Office for Civil Rights 2011–2012.
27. Ibid.
28. Skiba et al. 2002, pp. 317–342.
29. Monroe 2005, pp. 45–50.
30. Brown 2014.
31. Ibid.
32. Delpit 2003, pp. 14–21.
33. Apple 1993, pp. 1–16.

34. Ladson-Billings 1995, pp. 465–491.
35. Palcic, Jurbergs, and Kelley 2009, pp. 117–133.
36. Boykin 1992.

Bibliography

Anderson, Elizabeth. 2012. "Race, Culture, and Educational Opportunity." *Theory and Research in Education* 10: 105–129.

Apple, Michael W. 1993. "The Politics of Official Knowledge: Does a National Curriculum Make Sense?" *Discourse* 14 (1): 1–16.

Aud, Susan, Mary Ann Fox, and Angelina Kewal Ramani. 2010. "Status and Trends in the Education of Racial and Ethnic Groups. NCES 2010–015." National Center for Education Statistics.

Boykin, A. Wade. 1992. Reformulating Educational Reform: Toward the Proactive Schooling of African American Children. ED 367 725.

Bronfenbrenner, Urie. 1994. "Ecological Models of Human Development." *International Encyclopedia of Education* 3 (2).

Brophy, Jere E. 1983. "Research on the Self-Fulfilling Prophecy and Teacher Expectations." *Journal of Educational Psychology* 75 (5): 631.

Brown, Emma. "D.C. Bill Would Ban School Suspensions for City's Pre-K Students." *The Washington Post.* Last modified July 13, 2014. http://www.washingtonpost.com/local/education/dc-bill-would-ban-school-suspensions-for-citys-pre-k-students/2014/07/13/3af8270c-07b6-11e4-8a6a-19355c7e870a_story.html.

Carter, Prudence L. 2003. "'Black' Cultural Capital, Status Positioning, and Schooling Conflicts for Low-Income African American Youth." *Social Problems* 50 (1): 136–155.

Civil Rights Data Collection, United States Department of Education Office for Civil Rights (2011–2012).

Coll, Cynthia Garcia, Keith Crnic, Gontran Lamberty, Barbara Hanna Wasik, Renee Jenkins, Heidie Vazquez Garcia, and Harriet Pipes McAdoo. 1996. "An Integrative Model for the Study of Developmental Competencies in Minority Children." *Child Development* 67 (5): 1891–1914.

Collins, Marva, and Civia Tamarkin. 1982. *Marva Collins' Way: Returning to Excellence in Education.* New York: Penguin Putnam Inc.

Delpit, Lisa. 2003. "Educators as "Seed People" Growing a New Future." *Educational Researcher* 32 (7): 14–21.

Delpit, Lisa. 2006. *Other People's Children: Cultural Conflict in the Classroom.* New York: New Press.

Diamond, John B., Antonia Randolph, and James P. Spillane. 2004. "Teachers' Expectations and Sense of Responsibility for Student Learning: The Importance of Race, Class, and Organizational Habitus." *Anthropology & Education Quarterly* 35 (1): 75–98.

Eccles, Jacquelynne S., and Robert W. Roeser. 2009. "Schools, Academic Motivation, and Stage-Environment Fit." In *Handbook of Adolescent Psychology*, eds. Richard M. Lerner and Laurence Steinberg (Vol. 1). New York: John Wiley & Sons.

Education Commission of the States (ECS). 2013. "School Attendance and Age Requirements." *Education Commission of the States (ECS)*. Denver, Colorado.

Fierros, Edward Garcia, and James W. Conroy. 2002. "Double Jeopardy: An Exploration of Restrictiveness and Race in Special Education." In *Racial Inequity in Special Education*, eds. D. J. Losen and G. Orfield (pp. 39–70). Cambridge, MA: Harvard Education Press.

Gay, Geneva. 2000. *Culturally Responsive Teaching: Theory, Research, and Practice.* New York: Teachers College Press.

Ghezzi, Patti. 2006. "Zero Tolerance for Zero Tolerance." *Atlanta Constitution* (March 20).

Glaze, Lauren E., and Erika Parks. 2011. "Correctional Populations in the United States, 2011." *Population* 6 (7): 8.

Gottfredson, Denise C., Elizabeth M. Marciniak, Ann T. Birdseye, and Gary D. Gottfredson. 1995. "Increasing Teacher Expectations for Student Achievement." *The Journal of Educational Research* 88 (3): 155–163.

Hamre, Brigett, and Pianta, Robert. 2003. "Early Teacher–Child Relationships and the Trajectory of Children's School Outcomes through Eighth Grade." *Child Development* 72: 625–638.

Hanushek, Eric A., and Margaret E. Raymond. 2004. "The Effect of School Accountability Systems on the Level and Distribution of Student Achievement." *Journal of the European Economic Association* 2 (2–3): 406–415.

Halpert, Julie. "Do We Still Segregate Students?" *Pacific Standard*, August 22, 2012. Accessed July 8, 2014. http://www.psmag.com/books-and-culture/do-we-still-segregate-students-45196.

Harry, Beth, and Janette K. Klingner. 2014. *Why Are So Many Minority Students in Special Education?: Understanding Race and Disability in Schools.* New York: Teachers College Press.

Harry, Beth, Janette K. Klingner, and Juliet Hart. 2005. "African American Families under Fire Ethnographic Views of Family Strengths." *Remedial and Special Education* 26 (2): 101–112.

Hinnant, J. Benjamin, Marion O'Brien, and Sharon R. Ghazarian. 2009. "The Longitudinal Relations of Teacher Expectations to Achievement in the Early School Years." *Journal of Educational Psychology* 101 (3): 662.

Jussim, Lee, and Kent D. Harber. 2005. "Teacher Expectations and Self-fulfilling Prophecies: Knowns and Unknowns, Resolved and Unresolved Controversies." *Personality and Social Psychology Review* 9 (2): 131–155.

Jussim, Lee, Kent D. Harber, Jarret T. Crawford, Thomas R. Cain, and Florette Cohen. 2005. "Social Reality Makes the Social Mind: Self-Fulfilling Prophecy, Stereotypes, Bias, and Accuracy." *Interaction Studies* 6 (1): 85–102.

Jussim, Lee, Thomas R. Cain, Jarret T. Crawford, Kent Harber, and Florette Cohen. 2009. "The Unbearable Accuracy of Stereotypes." *Handbook of Prejudice, Stereotyping, and Discrimination*: 199–227.

Keleher, Terry. 2000. "Racial Disparities Related to School Zero Tolerance Policies: Testimony to the US Commission on Civil Rights."

King, Joyce. 1991. "Dysconscious Racism: Ideology, Identity, and the Miseducation of Teachers." *The Journal of Negro Education* 60 (2): 133–146.

Ladson-Billings, Gloria. 1995. "Toward a Theory of Culturally Relevant Pedagogy." *American Educational Research Journal* 32 (3): 465–491.

Lamb, Michael E., and Marc H. Bornstein, eds. 2011. *Social and Personality Development: An Advanced Textbook*. New York: Taylor & Francis.

Losen, Daniel J., and Gary Orfield. 2002. *Racial Inequity in Special Education*. Cambridge, MA: Harvard Education Publishing Group.

Madon, S.J., L. Jussim, S. Keiper, J. Eccles, A. Smith, and P. Palumbo. 1998. "The Accuracy and Power of Sex, Social Class and Ethnic Stereotypes: Naturalistic Studies in Person Perception." *Personality and Social Psychology Bulletin* 24: 1304–1318.

Monroe, Carla R. 2005. "Why Are "Bad Boys" Always Black?: Causes of Disproportionality in School Discipline and Recommendations for Change." *The Clearing House: A Journal of Educational Strategies, Issues and Ideas* 79 (1): 45–50.

Neville, Helen A., and Alex L. Pieterse. 2009. "Racism, White Supremacy, and Resistance." In *Handbook of African American Psychology*, eds. Helen A. Neville, Brendesha M. Tynes, and Shawn O. Utsey. SAGE Publications.

Ogbu, John. 1990. "Minority Education in Comparative Perspective." *The Journal of Negro Education* 59 (1): 45–57.

Palcic, Jennette L., Nichole Jurbergs, and Mary Lou Kelley. 2009. "A Comparison of Teacher and Parent Delivered Consequences: Improving Classroom Behavior in Low-Income Children with ADHD." *Child & Family Behavior Therapy* 31 (2): 117–133.

Parrish, Thomas. 2002. "Racial Disparities in the Identification, Funding, and Provision of Special Education." In *Racial Inequity in Special Education*, eds. D. J. Losen and G. Orfield (pp. 15–37). Cambridge, MA: Harvard Education Press.

Patton, James M. 1998. "The Disproportionate Representation of African Americans in Special Education Looking behind the Curtain for Understanding and Solutions." *The Journal of Special Education* 32 (1): 25–31.

Serpell, Zewelanji N., and Andrew J. Mashburn. 2012. "Family–School Connectedness and Children's Early Social Development." *Social development* 21 (1): 21–46.

Serpell, Zewelanji N., Juanita Cole, and A. Wade Boykin. 2008. "Move to Learn: Enhancing Story Recall among Urban African American Children." *Journal of Urban Learning, Teaching and Research* 4: 73–85.

Sheets, Rosa Hernandez. 1996. "Urban Classroom Conflict: Student–Teacher Perception: Ethnic Integrity, Solidarity, and Resistance." *The Urban Review* 28 (2): 165–183.

Skiba, Russell J., and Kimberly Knesting. 2002. *Zero Tolerance, Zero Evidence: An Analysis of School Disciplinary Practice.* San Francisco, CA: Jossey-Bass.

Skiba, Russell J., Robert S. Michael, Abra Carroll Nardo, and Reece L. Peterson. 2002. "The Color of Discipline: Sources of Racial and Gender Disproportionality in School Punishment." *The Urban Review* 34 (4): 317–342.

Souto-Manning, Mariana, and Kevin J. Swick. 2006. "Teachers' Beliefs about Parent and Family Involvement: Rethinking Our Family Involvement Paradigm." *Early Childhood Education Journal* 34 (2): 187–193.

Steele, Claude M. 1997. "A Threat in the Air: How Stereotypes Shape Intellectual Identity and Performance." *American Psychologist* 52 (6): 613.

Steele, Claude M., and Joshua Aronson. 1995. "Stereotype Threat and the Intellectual Test Performance of African Americans." *Journal of Personality and Social Psychology* 69 (5): 797.

Taliaferro, Jocelyn DeVance, Jessica DeCuir-Gunby, and Kara Allen-Eckard. 2009. "'I Can See Parents being Reluctant': Perceptions of Parental Involvement using Child and Family Teams in Schools." *Child & Family Social Work* 14 (3): 278–288.

United States Department of Justice, "Attorney General Eric Holder Delivers Remarks at the Department of Justice and Department of Education School Discipline Guidance Rollout at Frederick Douglass High School" Justice News, January 8, 2014, accessed July 8, 2014, http://www.justice.gov/opa/speech/attorneygeneral-eric-holder-delivers-remarks-department-justice-and department-education.

Wu, Shi-Chang, William Pink, Robert Crain, and Oliver Moles. 1982. "Student Suspension: A Critical Reappraisal." *The Urban Review* 14 (4): 245–303.

Chapter 8

Disrupting the School-to-Prison Pipeline through Disability Critical Race Theory

Subini Ancy Annamma

Let me begin with a scenario that is all too common for children with emotional disabilities in schools.

> Shadin, a 15-year old African American female student, is handed a paper that has been photocopied in her Literature class. She looks at it and sees that the background is very dark which makes it hard to read. Shadin begins to feel frustrated. She skims it and sees several words she cannot pronounce. Her frustration rises. She hates reading in class and this is something the teacher requires that every student do, without exception.
>
> Shadin declares, "I can't do this, I'm not going to read."
>
> The Literature teacher responds, "Then I will have to write you up for not following directions."
>
> Shadin stands up and storms out of the room. The Literature teacher calls the School Security Officer to report that Shadin left without permission. The Security Officer catches up with Shadin in the hall and tells her to stop. She keeps walking. The Security Officer tells her to stop again but by this time Shadin is out the door. When Shadin returns to school the next day, she is told to go to the Principal's office. Waiting for her are the Principal and the Security Officer with two tickets, for disorderly conduct (for refusing to follow directions) and trespassing (for being in the halls without permission). Shadin swears at them and leaves again. When she returns to school, she will be given another ticket and a suspension.

In high schools across the country, versions of this scenario are taking place. Though this may seem extreme to those unfamiliar with large urban high schools, the preceding vignette is actually quite common; students are disciplined and ticketed for many small offenses in schools.[1] In my own experience as a special education teacher in an urban high school, I have had several students get ticketed for minor infractions like Shadin's, which is one entry point into the school-to-prison pipeline.

Race, Disability, and the School-to-Prison Pipeline

Too often, students from communities of color experience the school system as a funnel where they are routed from the schoolhouse doors to the doors of a prison; this phenomenon is known as the school-to-prison pipeline. At the heart of this exploration is how particular identity markers (e.g., race, disability) are related to education and incarceration. According to the American Civil Liberties Association, "The 'school-to-prison pipeline' refers to the policies and practices that push our nation's schoolchildren, especially our most at-risk children, out of classrooms and into the juvenile and criminal justice systems. This pipeline reflects the prioritization of incarceration over education."[2]

The school-to-prison pipeline disproportionately impacts students of color through excessive disciplinary actions and increased police presence in the schools. These students of color experienced being "racially criminalized—that is, hypercriminalized on the basis of one's race, or rather, the combined process(es) and/or predicament(s) of being simultaneously racialized and criminalized and the ongoing effects of simultaneous racialization and criminalization."[3] In this quote, Rabaka tied incarceration to race, as did Fredrick Douglas before him. In his speech *The Color Line in America,* Douglas (2000) condemned the American habit to "impute crime to color."[4] This historical connection between crime and color is linked to the present day as well and does not have an age restriction; juveniles of color are often associated with crime, similar to the adults in their communities.

W.E.B. DuBois was once caught and punished for stealing grapes with some white friends and was disturbed by the disproportionate sentencing he received. While the other white children were let off with a warning, the judge sentenced the young, black DuBois to a juvenile reform school. Had a white principal not stepped in to "provide supervision," DuBois's future could have easily become one of incarceration.[5] DuBois experienced the ways children of color were punished more severely than their white counterparts and how easily a child of color could be incarcerated.

Today, students of color are increasingly experiencing criminalization in urban schools. Through measures such as criminalizing small offenses, excessive disciplinary actions, harsh zero tolerance policies, increased police presence in schools, and "securing environments," using methods such as metal detectors, fencing, and even police dogs, large urban schools have created environments that reflect prisons. These actions have made it increasingly likely that the students housed within these schools will be funneled into the criminal justice system.

These connections between race, education, and crime have been essential to understanding how children of color become incarcerated. However, there are other points of social location in addition to race, which make it more likely that a student will be relegated to juvenile justice through additional school actions. In this chapter, I argue that perceptions of ability, disability, and labeling are directly related to young women's interactions with the pipeline. Though much has been written on the pipeline, the literature often leaves unexamined the intersections between special education status and other identity markers.[6] However, an average of 33 percent to 37 percent of students in juvenile systems have been identified with a disability, with some detention centers housing over 70 percent of juvenile inmates with a disability label.[7] In contrast, public schools have a national average of around 12 percent to 14 percent of students labeled with disabilities.[8] Moreover, being labeled with particular types of disabilities is correlated with being incarcerated; students with an emotional disability label make up almost 50 percent of the population of students with disabilities in juvenile justice, whereas they are less than 1 percent of the public school population.[9] Therefore, I argue that, along with disciplinary actions and policing in the schools, the school action of assigning particular students to special education is correlated with who is eventually incarcerated.

Disciplinary actions and over-policing in schools have been the focus of the majority of articles written on the pipeline. However, researchers have argued for the need to examine what it means to be assigned to special education for particular groups of students and how this relates to incarceration.[10] This chapter heeds that call and focuses on the assignment to special education and its relationship to the pipeline.

Educators, researchers, and the media often focus on the individual deficiencies that they claim lead to particular types of children becoming entangled in the pipeline. However, I believe these failures "are attributable not to the children themselves but rather to deficiencies in the institutions charged with caring for them."[11] These structural deficits are part of the educational debt we owe to children of color who have historically attended under-resourced schools. Instead of focusing on perceived deficiencies in individuals, I conduct the following analyses in this chapter: (1) explore the literature about students of color with disabilities; (2) reframe the pipeline via DisCrit and examine the affordances of this conceptual framework, and (3) examine potential solutions for dismantling the pipeline. Each of these steps is supplied to intervene in structures, to provide weapons to fight the structural violence that students of color and those with disabilities face.

The Literature

When connecting the often disparate research in disciplinary actions, special education, and law, there are several studies that lead to concern. Youth of color are more likely to be suspended and expelled for more subjective infractions, more likely to drop out, less likely to graduate, and more likely to be labeled with particular types of disabilities. Students in special education have traditionally been seen as a protected class in schools but, in fact, have rarely been protected from the deleterious effects of disproportionate disciplinary actions, poor teaching, and limited curriculum. In fact, students with a disability label are more likely to be referred for disciplinary actions and their chances of being suspended or expelled are more than double their general education peers, though students with disabilities were not more likely to cause injuries. Over 90 percent of the offenses for which students labeled with disabilities got suspended or expelled were acts such as altercations, disrespect, and disobedience—similar reasons as their non-disabled peers. Students of color with emotional disabilities are less likely than their white peers to attend schools with a comprehensive curriculum and are most likely to receive an education that neither prepares them for college nor provides vocational skills. This is most evident when viewing academic outcomes: African Americans with emotional disabilities graduate at a rate of 27.5 percent, whereas white youth with emotional disabilities graduate at a rate of 48 percent; 66 percent of African Americans labeled with emotional disabilities received failing grades versus only 38 percent of white students; 58 percent of African Americans with emotional disabilities dropped out of school, and 73 percent of all students with emotional disabilities who drop out are arrested within three to five years of leaving school, respectively. In other words, students with emotional disabilities are more likely to have lower grades, higher dropout rates, less educational and employment attainment, and increased criminal adjudication—and all of these characteristics are tied to lower literacy rates. Considering that students of color are overrepresented in the emotional disability category, we must assume that many have experienced these negative life outcomes associated with disability. Finally, a major factor in students of color becoming incarcerated was school failure in the form of disciplinary actions, grade retention, or special education assignment. Ultimately, this chapter ethically begins "with those who are facing the worst conditions, those who are most losing their lives, those people in prison."[12]

Reframing the Pipeline

The perspectives of critical race theory (CRT) scholars on the systemic inequities perpetuated through law, policies and practices, and the lines of research CRT have inspired major implications for theoretically informed avenues to address the pipeline. Though CRT is the central lens of this chapter, the intersectional focus required a discussion on ability and disability along with race in order to address the role of special education in the pipeline. Therefore, I incorporated CRT and disability critical race theory (DisCrit).[13] First, I review the origins of CRT and then DisCrit's origins and tenets. This is because CRT is an older and more mature branch of CRT than DisCrit, which is a younger, more recent offshoot. After the review, I combine common fundamental principles of CRT and DisCrit to examine the pipeline. Finally, I explore traditional theoretical stances of special education, school discipline, and juvenile justice research and differentiate my own.

Critical Race Theory's Origins

CRT was borne out of the Critical Legal Studies Movement (CLS) when scholars of color recognized that CLS was engaging in legal critiques based on class but ignoring racialized aspects of the law.[14] Derrick Bell (1979) questioned strategies of integration and converging interests as incomplete liberal solutions to racial inequities, while Mari Matsuda fought to center voices of nondominant communities in discussions. Along with Bell and Matsuda, other scholars of color such as Neil Gotanda and Kimberlé Crenshaw pushed CLS to include race in its analysis of ways the legal system perpetuates inequities. As CRT in the law grew, scholars in education took up CRT to challenge the racialization of schooling and focused on how CRT helped untangle the institutional and interpersonal racialized aspects of education and connect them. Scholars from across disciplines began to expand on CRT in ways that stretched the theory to encompass how racialized experiences were complicated by gender, immigration status, and language, to name a few; these branches of CRT later came to be known as FemCrit and LatCrit. Several other offshoots have since developed stretching the boundaries of CRT.

DisCrit's Origins and Tenets

DisCrit grew from the need to better understand how perceptions of ability and disability are racialized. Systems of education have a tendency to view individuals without context; that is, traditionally failure to achieve academically or behaviorally is often constructed as the responsibility of the individual student alone. However, critical scholars in special education argue that an individual cannot become labeled without considering context, culture, and history.[15] "The result of such inattention to sociocultural factors in shaping identification practices is that an inherently social process, the display and recognition of successful participation in classroom learning, has been largely portrayed as an objective means of identifying 'deficits' within individual learners."[16] However, historically critical perspectives in special education (e.g., Disability Studies, Inclusive Education paradigms) have often employed whiteness to ignore or superficially address ways that perceptions of race and ability were intertwined. CRT is a useful theory that can be used to directly question and expose the relation of marginalized identity markers to overrepresentation in the pipeline. CRT uncovered the way most special education, disciplinary inequity, and juvenile justice literature ignores race and theory and instead CRT encouraged keeping the history of attempts to prove racial inferiority at the front of our minds. However, CRT traditionally had not substantially addressed issues of perceptions of ability or special education.

DisCrit attempted to bridge these chasms by exploring the socially constructed and interrelated nature of both race and ability, and how perceptions of both are based on unmarked norms. In order to understand how students of color with disabilities embodiment and positioning reveal ways in which racism and ableism inform and rely on each other, DisCrit examined ways "race, racism, dis/ability and ableism are built into the interactions, procedures, discourses, and institutions of education, which affect students of color with dis/abilities qualitatively differently than White students with dis/abilities."[17]

DisCrit included seven tenets that were useful for examining the collusive nature of racism and ableism in larger society:

(1) DisCrit focuses on ways that the forces of racism and ableism circulate interdependently, often in neutralized and invisible ways, to uphold notions of normalcy.
(2) DisCrit values multidimensional identities and troubles singular notions of identity such as race *or* dis/ability *or* class *or* gender *or* sexuality.
(3) DisCrit emphasizes the social constructions of race and ability and yet recognizes the material and psychological impacts of being labeled as raced or dis/abled, which sets one outside of the Western cultural norms.
(4) DisCrit privileges voices of marginalized populations, traditionally not acknowledged within research.
(5) DisCrit considers legal and historical aspects of dis/ability and race and how both have been used separately and together to deny the rights of some citizens.
(6) DisCrit recognizes whiteness as property, and the intangible benefits of that property such as perceived ability, and gains for people labeled with dis/abilities have largely been made as the result of interest convergence with white, middle-class citizens.
(7) DisCrit requires activism and supports all forms of resistance.

Tenet 1 explores the concepts that racism and ableism are normal, not an aberration, and that they work in tandem. "Neither institutional racism alone nor institutional ableism on its own can explain why students of color are more likely to be labeled with dis/abilities and segregated than their white peers with and without dis/abilities."[18] Instead, through normalizing practices that are mutually constitutive, such as labeling a student "at-risk" for simply being a person of color, unmarked norms of whiteness are equated with ability and differences become viewed as biological deficits.

Tenet 2 troubles unidimensional views of identity because stigma and segregation are compounded by multiple identities. Being viewed as different from unmarked norms encourages educators to mark a child as disabled and to be a person of color with disability impacts the ways students experience education. Singular notions of identity miss the intersections of oppression. For example, a middle-class, white child who can afford the expensive diagnostic can be labeled with dyslexia and may benefit from her label (e.g., increased time on standardized tests, increased efforts at inclusion into the mainstream setting and curriculum, and additional time with a paraprofessional; each of which means more access to college), while a Latina with a more general learning disability label may endure a very different fate (e.g., segregated classrooms with less access to the general education curriculum, low expectations, and lack of services, all which make it more difficult to access college).

Tenet 3 exposes the social construction of race and disability as responses to differences from unmarked cultural normative standards. Those differences are then viewed as biological deficits. Once viewed as biological, these deficits are seen as something inherent in the child, something that can be accommodated for, but never shed. In other words, the label becomes reified and expectations for students are often lowered.

Tenet 4 focuses on counternarratives from the marginalized as essential to understanding any inequities that exist in education. These counter-stories must not stand alone but must be juxtaposed with the master-narrative. This moves us from a place of sympathy to instead focusing on what can be done to eradicate the master-narrative. It does not purport to give voice as oppressed people have a voice. Instead, this tenet demands we honor that voice by centering these stories.

Tenet 5 recognizes that historically, these labels of racially different and/ or disabled have been utilized to deny rights to particular people that the system has long since found unworthy of full citizenship. "Without racialized notions of ability, racial difference would simply be racial difference. Because racial difference has been explicitly linked with an intellectual hierarchy, however, racial differences take on additional weight."[19] Pseudo-sciences have been used historically to establish whiteness as superiority in both intellectual and moral realms. This racism then became normalized through laws, policies, and programs designed to codify white superiority by focusing on the inherent deficits of people of color and those with disabilities.

Tenet 6 examines ways that race and ability have become property and that those considered white and able experience economic benefits. In order to participate in those benefits, racialized and dis/abled communities have had to either work to pass as white and/or able, which reifies a binary of normal and abnormal, or leverage interest convergence. Interest convergence is when rights or economic benefits for oppressed citizens can occur only when they benefit the dominant group.

Finally, tenet 7 requires a commitment to activism. All activism forms are respected, from marching and protests to theorizing about inequities, and each is welcome. Each of the tenets put forth rejects "forces, practices, and institutions that attempt to construct dis/ability based on differences from normative cultural standards."[20]

Currently, students of color face classrooms that ignore their knowledge and cultural practices, promote deficit views of students, and assess them reductively by overreliance on standardized tests. Here, I provide a conceptual framework that recognizes both the sociocultural context and the larger structural inequities which impact disability labeling and education.

Conceptual Framework Tools

In order to understand how institutional and individual biases function, the conceptual framework I propose recognizes three affordances: First, racism and ableism are normal and ordinary in our society in the sense that normal is the unmarked white and able bodied; and bodies that are brown and black and perceived disabled are automatically considered abnormal and problematic. Institutional and interpersonal enforcement of these hegemonic norms happens in ways that create and strengthen inequities. Ignoring these realities undermines the fight for equity. These mutually constitutive processes are enacted through purportedly race and ability neutral practices and policies, which actually reinforce the unmarked norms of white and able. The unmarked norms contribute to the overrepresentation of students of color in disciplinary actions, often via punitive zero tolerance policies.

Zero tolerance policies, wherein students were automatically suspended or expelled for a range of behaviors, were largely adopted after the infamous Columbine shootings.[21] Though zero tolerance policies had originated during the War on Drugs, the incident at Columbine increased the hypervigilance of finding and excluding any child who could be considered a threat in order to prevent another tragedy like Columbine. However, these punitive disciplinary policies left much room for subjective applications, and school personnel used them to rid schools of unwanted children via removal and relegation to the juvenile justice system. The increase in suspensions and expulsions that has occurred partially due to zero tolerance policies has impacted particular students disproportionately, specifically students of color and those with disabilities.

Of great concern is that these ordinary and normalizing processes of ableism and racism lead to seeing differences from the unmarked norm as inherent deficits. Therefore, as overrepresentation of students of color in disciplinary actions began to garner attention, explanations such as increased behavioral disruptions by students of color or correlations between poverty and an inability to behave were immediately put forth. Neither reason, however, adequately explains disproportionality. Instead, African Americans in particular experienced more severe school punishments for less severe behavior. Students with a disability are often left out of research focused on discipline because they have particular rights afforded and their disciplinary rates are reported in ways that are rarely compatible with the rest of the general education population. However, when included in the research, students with disabilities have shown to be overrepresented and treated inequitably in disciplinary actions. Moreover, students labeled with an emotional disability were more likely to be referred and suspended than any other students in general or special education.

Second, these ordinary and normalizing processes that encourage seeing differences as deficits contributed to viewing race and disability as biological facts. Therefore, this conceptual framework problematizes these processes and recognizes the social construction of race and disability as society's response to differences from the norm. This response is enacted in the vast overrepresentation of students of color in special education, which has been identified as an issue since the inception of special education. There has been a consistent pattern of African American students being overrepresented in intellectual and emotional disabilities nationally and other students of color being overrepresented in particular judgment categories by state. Even after taking into account socioeconomic and demographic characteristics of school districts, gender and ethnicity continued to be a determining factor in being identified with a disability.

Third, "No person has a single, easily stated, unitary identity."[22] Historically, issues viewed through one lens, such as race, limit the understanding of ways gender and ability interacted with race. This conceptual framework emphasizes multidimensional identities and troubles singular notions of identity such as race or ability or gender. The affordances listed earlier stand in direct contradiction to traditional views of special education.

Traditional Views of Special Education

Traditionally, special education literature lacked "a coherent breakdown of the beliefs and values that undergird . . . education preferences."[23] In other words, research that traditionally examined ability and disability has been largely without explicitly stated theoretical commitments. However, much special education research is being driven by the medical model of disability, which searches for, diagnoses, and treats disabilities with remediation, or focuses on fixing the deficit within the student.[24] That is to say, the medical model treated disabilities as diseases that can be diagnosed objectively and assumed that the judgment of professionals is without bias. Once a disability has been "diagnosed" or "discovered," schools endorsed "treatment" with remediation of the student, which often focuses on teaching discreet skills in isolated contexts.[25] Furthermore, traditional research on disciplinary actions, special education, and juvenile justice often viewed learning and behavior issues as caused by a deficit within the student.[26] The focus on the individual ignored context and focused solely on the student. This traditional research was often ahistorical in that it ignored the ways perceptions of achievement, disability, behavior, and criminalization have been used as a tool to legitimize inequitable treatment of people and the intersections with other identity markers, especially race, to further marginalize particular populations.[27]

Conversely, critical theories argued that perceptions of ability must be understood within historical and current context of race, class, and gender.[28] Schools should not allow "a single person to bear the undue burden of being targeted, accused, labeled, explained, worried about, remediated, or even rehabilitated without an account of the conditions in which he or she lives."[29] Critical frameworks require us to ask the question, "What makes someone outside the range of typical in learning and behavior?"; they required an examination of conceptions of normal and what then falls outside the norm.[30] Critical theorists remind us, "In a stratified society, differences are never just differences; they are always understood, defined, and ranked according to dominant cultural norms, values, and practices."[31]

The literature related to the school-to-prison pipeline has focused mainly on overrepresentation of students of color in disciplinary actions and problematic zero tolerance policies. Rarely has the role of special education in the pipeline been addressed, a major gap in the literature; this conceptual framework allowed me to address another route into the pipeline. By embracing a critical conceptual framework centered in CRT and DisCrit, I reject deficit views of students. Furthermore, this CRT/DisCrit conceptual framework allowed me to question and expose the relationship of marginalized identity markers to the pipeline and widen the lens to understand the product of deeply entrenched racism embedded within educational and societal structures. By expanding the discussion surrounding this topic to include a rigorous analysis of ways the pipeline is perpetuated, I hoped to enhance the pipeline discussions.

Disrupting the Pipeline

DisCrit offers an opportunity to dis/able the pipeline. Traditionally, many young people of color with disabilities experience a cycle of labeling, surveillance, and punishment wherein once the lens of disability is used to diagnose and dissect their lives, their behavior is put under increased surveillance, labeled as problematic, and further punished. However, a cycle of criminalization does little to keep students in school and instead pushes them out. Simply stated, a cycle of criminalization is built on norms and standards that are unspoken yet strictly enforced. Alternatives must include recognizing that students of color with disability labels navigate the system with savvy and ingenuity. Disabling has traditionally been part of the cycle of criminalization, but can be reimagined as an act to disrupt the norms with unexpected bodies and minds. Dis/abling the system then means valuing students for what they bring to school.

However, the hegemony of traditional values often prohibits teachers and school administrators from honoring what students bring to the table, and conflicts arise that result in the enforcement of exclusionary discipline and zero tolerance practices. Restorative and transformative discipline can be effective alternatives. There will never be enough punitive consequences to "motivate" children into appropriate behavior. Positive relationships must be fostered in order for students to feel respected and cared for, which is the only way to make schools run effectively. Collaboratively recognizing the purpose and impact of behaviors, restorative discipline attempts to address the needs of both the harmed and the student who harmed by repairing harm in the community. Listening to students, particularly students who act out and become more marginalized, is a supposition of DisCrit. Furthermore, privileging the voices of all students involved resists the traditional practice to center adults as arbiters of punishment.

Beginning with a commitment from administration and school staff, all school personnel must be introduced to the philosophy and practice of "questioning the students around the impact (harm) of their behavior on others and relationship."[32] Shifting stances from equating discipline with punishment to discipline as synonymous with learning can provide an opportunity for children to grow and eventually regulate themselves;

moreover, it allows for a more individuated response to discipline aligning with the tenet of DisCrit which values multidimensional identities. Once focus moves to how to make things right, or repairing harm, teachers and students can work collaboratively to create solutions. Restorative discipline is not one set of practices and many do not agree on one definition; instead, it is an inclusive framework that guides groups to craft disciplinary solutions to their individual settings. Importantly, restorative approaches have shown initial promise at reducing racial disparities in discipline, one step in the pipeline.[33]

A major premise of this chapter is that individual behaviors are linked to systemic inequities; hence, restorative justice can be implemented poorly if it *solely* focuses on individual relationships.[34] Specifically, restorative approaches often leave out structural inequities, assuming there was justice previously when the reality is the majority of people being punished are victims of injustice. Considering the historical and social legacies of injustice, a tenant of DisCrit, means that we must integrate transformative justice as well. Transformative justice is defined as thinking deeply about and addressing the ways structural violence and institutional inequities impact individual behavior as well as the sociocultural context of school, neighborhoods, and communities.[35] In 2011 Zehr (2002) shared a series of questions that help to distinguish traditional forms of discipline, which perpetuate the cycle of criminalization, from restorative and transformative justice (see Figure 8.1).[36]

FIGURE 8.1   Questions Asked in Traditional, Restorative, and Transformative Justice

The questions Zehr asks shift the focus from traditional systems of punishment of an individual to repairing harm within a community by employing restorative and transformative discipline that will facilitate understanding social circumstances and structural inequities. Integrating both restorative and transformative discipline as responses to both individual behaviors and institutional inequities recognizes that racism and ableism are ordinary and that the social construction of ability and behavior are based on race, both essential premises of DisCrit.

Conclusion

Traditional systems of discipline and punishment in schools have fed the pipeline for far too long. "Effective alternatives involve both transformation of the techniques for addressing 'crime' and of the social and economic conditions that track so many children from poor communities, and especially communities of color, into the juvenile system and then on to prisons."[37] Restorative and transformative justice alone cannot solve the issues of poverty and racial disproportionality in discipline and special education; however, they can provide alternatives for addressing both. By recognizing both the individual impact on the community *and* the social inequities that contribute to disproportionality in labeling and discipline, we have the opportunity to disrupt the pipeline. By bringing a new conceptual framework to a pervasive issue, I was able to directly question and expose the relationship of marginalized identity markers, particularly special education status, to overrepresentation in the pipeline and widen the lens to understand the product of deeply entrenched racism and ableism embedded within educational and societal structures.

"If we continue to tell ourselves the popular myths about racial progress or, worse yet, if we say to ourselves that the problem of mass incarceration is just too big, too daunting for us to do anything about and that we should instead direct our energies to battles that might be more easily won, history will judge us harshly. A human rights nightmare is occurring on our watch."[38] Michelle Alexander's words, though focused on the mass incarceration of African American adults, also ring true for the ways our students are criminalized through the trapdoors of the school-to-prison pipeline. As a society, we must continue to ask ourselves why we have incarceration rates that are between 6 and 10 times that of other industrial countries and why that incarceration trend now begins in our schools and targets our most marginalized students. It is only by challenging ourselves that this human rights nightmare can begin to be addressed. It is my hope that this chapter can contribute to that aim.

Notes

1. Advancement Project, The, 2010.
2. American Civil Liberties Union 2008.
3. Rabaka 2010, p. 295.
4. Douglass 2000.
5. Du Bois 1968.
6. Kim, Losen, and Hewitt 2010.
7. Quinn et al. 2005, pp. 339–345.
8. Due to overrepresentation of students from nondominant communities in high-incidence disability categories, also known as judgment categories, in special education, I say "have been identified" or "labeled with a disability" since being identified does not guarantee the student actually has a disability. As Harry and Klingner (2006) note, "Many *have* questioned the accuracy of the professional judgments made in diagnosing" these disabilities. Overrepresentation of students with specific identity markers in high-incidence disability categories will be addressed later in the chapter (italics added).
9. Osher, Woodruff, and Sims 2002, pp. 93–116.
10. Meiners 2010.
11. Kim, Losen, and Hewitt 2010.
12. Meiners 2010.
13. Annamma 2013, pp. 1–31.
14. Crenshaw 1995.
15. Artiles et al. 2000, pp. 79–120.
16. Collins 2013, p. 2.
17. Annamma, Connor, and Ferri 2013b, p. 7.
18. Ibid., p. 11.
19. Ibid., p. 15.
20. Ibid., p. 17.
21. Wallace et al. 2008, p. 47.
22. Delgado and Stefancic 2012, p. 9.
23. Brantlinger 1997, p. 433.
24. Nocella 2008, pp. 77–94.
25. McDermott, Goldman, and Varenne 2006, pp. 12–17.
26. Erevelles 2000, pp. 25–47.
27. Connor 2008a.
28. Gutierrez and Stone 1997, pp. 123–131.
29. McDermott, Goldman, and Varenne 2006, p. 13.
30. Annamma 2013, pp. 1278–1294.

31. Gutiérrez Morales, and Martinez 2009, p. 218.
32. Thorsborne 2013.
33. Anyon et al. 2014.
34. Hereth 2012.
35. Lofton 2004, pp. 381–389.
36. Retrieved from http://emu.edu/now/restorative-justice/2011/03/10/restora tive-or-transformative-justice/.
37. Davis 2011, p. 21.
38. Alexander 2012, p. 15.

Bibliography

Advancement Project, The. 2010. *Test, Punish, and Push Out: How Zero Tolerance and High-Stakes Testing Funnel Youth into the School to Prison Pipeline.* Washington, DC: Author.

Alexander, Michelle. 2012. *The New Jim Crow: Mass Incarceration in the Age of Colorblindness.* New York: The New Press.

American Civil Liberties Union. 2008. "School to Prison Pipeline: Talking Points." Accessed June 14, 2011. http://www.aclu.org/racial-justice/school-prison-pipeline-talking-points.

Amstutz, Lorraine Stutzman, and Judy H. Mullet. 2005. *The Little Book of Restorative Discipline for Schools: Teaching Responsibility, Creating Caring Climates.* Intercourse, PA: Good Books, 2005.

Annamma, Subini (2014). "It Was Just like a Piece of Gum: Intersectionality and Criminalization of Young Women of Color with Disabilities in the School to Prison Pipeline." In *Practicing Disability Studies in Education, Acting toward Social Change,* eds. D.J. Connor, J.W. Valle, and C. Hale. New York: Teachers College Press.

Annamma, Subini. 2013. "Undocumented and Under Surveillance: A Case Study of an Undocumented Latina with a Disability in Juvenile Justice." *Association of Mexican American Educators Journal* 7 (3): 32–41. http://amaejournal.asu.edu/index.php/amae/article/view/144/122.

Annamma, Subini A., Amy L. Boelé, Brooke A. Moore, and Janette Klingner. 2013a. "Challenging the Ideology of Normal in Schools." *International Journal of Inclusive Education* 17 (12): 1278–1294.

Annamma, Subini Ancy, David Connor, and Beth Ferri. 2013b. "Dis/ability Critical Race Studies (DisCrit): Theorizing at the Intersections of Race and Dis/ability." *Race Ethnicity and Education* 16 (1): 1–31.

Anyon, Yolanda, Jeffrey Jenson, Inna Altschul, Jordan Farrar, Jeanette McQueen, Eldridge Greer, Barbara Downing, and John Simmons. 2014. "The Persistent Effect of Race and the Promise of Alternatives to Suspension in School Discipline Outcomes." *Children and Youth Services Review* 44: 379–386.

Aoki, Keith. 1997. "Critical Legal Studies, Asian Americans in US Law & (and) Culture, Neil Gotanda, and Me." *Asian Law Journal* 4: 19.

Artiles, Alfredo J. 1998. "The Dilemma of Difference Enriching the Disproportionality Discourse with Theory and Context." *The Journal of Special Education* 32 (1): 32–36.

Artiles, Alfredo J., Robert Rueda, Jesús José Salazar, and Ignacio Higareda. 2005. "Within-Group Diversity in Minority Disproportionate Representation: English Language Learners in Urban School Districts." *Exceptional Children* 71 (3): 283–300.

Artiles, A.J., S.C. Trent, P. Hoffman-Kipp, and L. López-Torres. 2000. "From Individual Acquisition to Cultural-Historical Practices in Multicultural Teacher Education." *Remedial and Special Education* 21 (2): 79–120.

Ashworth, J., S. Van Bockern, J. Ailts, J. Donnelly, K. Erickson, and J. Woltermann. 2008. "The Restorative Justice Center: An Alternative to School Detention." *Reclaiming Children and Youth* 17: 22–27.

Banner, Curtis, Laurent Bennett, Janet Connors, Sung-Joon Pai, Hillary Shanahan, and Anita Wadhwa. 2012. "How Can We Hold You? Restorative Justice in Boston Schools." In *Disrupting the School-to-Prison Pipeline,* eds. N. Cooc, R. Currie-Rubin, P. Kuttner, and M. Ng (pp. 76–89). Cambridge, MA: Harvard Educational Review.

Bell Jr., Derrick A. 1979 "Brown v. Board of Education and the Interest-Convergence Dilemma." *Harvard Law Review* 93: 518.

Berry, Theodorea Regina. 2010. "Engaged Pedagogy and Critical Race Feminism." *Educational Foundations* 24: 19–26.

Brantlinger, Ellen. 1997. "Using Ideology: Cases of Non-recognition of the Politics of Research and Practice in Special Education." *Review of Educational Research* 67 (4): 433.

Brayboy, Bryan McKinley Jones. 2005. "Toward a Tribal Critical Race Theory in Education." *The Urban Review* 37 (5): 425–446.

Browne, Judith A. 2005. "Education on Lockdown: The Schoolhouse to Jailhouse Track." *Advancement Project.*

Collins, Kathleen M., ed. 2013. *Ability Profiling and School Failure: One Child's Struggle to Be Seen as Competent.* New York: Routledge.

Connor, David J. 2008a. "Not So Strange Bedfellows: The Promise of Disability Studies and Critical Race Theory." *Disability and the Politics of Education: An International Reader,* 451–476.

Connor, David J. 2008b. *Urban Narratives: Portraits in Progress, Life at the Intersections of Learning Disability, Race, & Social Class.* Vol. 5. New York: Peter Lang.

Cooley, Sid. 1995. "Suspension/Expulsion of Regular and Special Education Students in Kansas: A Report to the Kansas State Board of Education." Topeka, KS: Kansas State Board of Education (ERIC Document Reproduction Service No. ED395403).

Crenshaw, Kimberlé. 1991. "Mapping the Margins: Intersectionality, Identity Politics, and Violence against Women of Color." *Stanford Law Review* 43 (6): 1241–1279.

Crenshaw, Kimberlé, ed. 1995. *Critical Race Theory: The Key Writings That Formed the Movement.* New York: The New Press.

Davis, Angela Y. 2011. *Are Prisons Obsolete?* New York: Seven Stories Press.

Delgado, Richard, and Jean Stefancic. 2012. *Critical Race Theory: An Introduction.* NYU Press.

Douglass, Frederick. 2000. *Frederick Douglass: Selected Speeches and Writings.* Chicago Review Press.

Drakeford, William, and Jeanine M. Staples. 2006. "Minority Confinement in the Juvenile Justice System." *Teaching Exceptional Children* 39 (1): 52–58.

DuBois, William Edward Burghardt. 1968. *The Autobiography of WEB Du Bois.* New York: International Publishers.

Dunn, Lloyd M. 1968. "Special Education for the Mildly Retarded: Is Much of It Justifiable?" *Exceptional Children* 35: 5–22.

Erevelles, Nirmala. 2000. "Educating Unruly Bodies: Critical Pedagogy, Disability Studies, and the Politics of Schooling." *Educational Theory* 50 (1): 25–47.

Erevelles, Nirmala. 2011. "'Coming Out Crip' in Inclusive Education." *Teachers College Record* 113 (10): 2155–2185.

Erevelles, Nirmala, and Andrea Minear. 2010. "Unspeakable Offenses: Untangling Race and Disability in Discourses of Intersectionality." *Journal of Literary & Cultural Disability Studies* 4 (2): 127–145.

Erevelles, Nirmala, Anne Kanga, and Renee Middleton. 2006. "How Does It Feel to Be a Problem? Race, Disability, and Exclusion in Educational Policy." In *Who Benefits from Special Education?: Remediating (Fixing) Other People's Children,* ed. E. Brantlinger (pp. 77–99). Mahwah, NJ: Erlbaum.

Ferri, Beth A. 2008. "Changing the Script: Race and Disability in Lynn Manning's Weights." *International Journal of Inclusive Education* 12 (5–6): 497–509.

Ferri, Beth A., and David J. Connor. 2010. "'I Was the Special Ed. Girl': Urban Working-Class Young Women of Colour." *Gender and Education* 22 (1): 105–121.

Gabbidon, Shaun L. 2012. *WEB Du Bois on Crime and Justice: Laying the Foundations of Sociological Criminology.* Aldershot, UK: Ashgate Publishing, Ltd.

Gregory, Anne, and Rhona S. Weinstein. 2008. "The Discipline Gap and African Americans: Defiance or Cooperation in the High School Classroom." *Journal of School Psychology* 46 (4): 455–475.

Gutiérrez, Kris D., P. Zitlali Morales, and Danny C. Martinez. 2009. "Re-mediating Literacy: Culture, Difference, and Learning for Students from Nondominant Communities." *Review of Research in Education* 33 (1): 218.

Gutiérrez, Kris D., and Barbara Rogoff. 2003. "Cultural Ways of Learning: Individual Traits or Repertoires of Practice." *Educational Researcher* 32 (5): 19–25.

Gutierrez, Kris D., and Lynda D. Stone. 1997. "A Cultural-Historical View of Learning and Learning Disabilities: Participating in a Community of Learners." *Learning Disabilities Research and Practice* 12 (2): 123–131.

Harry, Beth, and Janette K. Klingner. 2006. *Why Are So Many Minority Students in Special Education?: Understanding Race and Disability in Schools.* New York: Teachers College Press.

Hereth, Jane, Mariame Kaba, Erica Meiners, and Lewis Wallace. 2012. "Restorative Justice Is Not Enough: School-Based Interventions in the Carceral State." In *Disrupting the School-to-Prison Pipeline,* eds. S. Bahena, N. Cooc, R. Currie-Rubin, P. Kuttner, and M. Ng (pp. 240–264). Cambridge, MA: Harvard Educational Review.

Kim, Catherine Y., Daniel J. Losen, and Damon T. Hewitt. 2010. *The School-to-Prison Pipeline: Structuring Legal Reform.* NYU Press.

Ladson-Billings, Gloria. 2006. "From the Achievement Gap to the Education Debt: Understanding Achievement in US Schools." *Educational Researcher* 35 (7): 3–12.

Ladson-Billings, Gloria, and William F. Tate. 2006. "Toward a Critical Race Theory of Education." *Critical Race Theory in Education: All God's Children Got a Song*: 11–30.

Leonardo, Zeus, and Alicia Broderick. 2011. "Smartness as Property: A Critical Exploration of Intersections between Whiteness and Disability Studies." *Teachers College Record* 113 (10): 2206–2232.

Lofton, Bonnie Price. 2004. "Does Restorative Justice Challenge Systemic Injustices?" In *Critical Issues in Restorative Justice,* eds. H. Zehr and B. Toews (pp. 381–389). Monsey, NY: Criminal Justice Press.

Losen, Daniel. 2011. "Discipline Policies, Successful Schools, and Racial Justice." Boulder, CO: National Education Policy Center. http://nepc.colorado.edu/publication/disciplinepolicies.

Losen, Daniel J., and Gary Orfield. 2002. *Racial Inequity in Special Education.* Cambridge, MA: Harvard Education Publishing Group.

Losen, Daniel J., Gary Orfield, and Robert Balfanz. 2006. *Confronting the Graduation Rate Crisis in Texas.* Cambridge, MA: The Civil Rights Project, Harvard University.

Losen, Daniel J., and Russell J. Skiba. 2010. "Suspended Education: Urban Middle Schools in crisis." Los Angeles: The Civil Rights Project at UCLA. http://civilrightsproject.ucla.edu/research/k-12-education/school-discipline/suspendededucation-urban-middle-schools-in-crisis/Suspended-Education_FINAL-2.pdf.

Matsuda, Mari J. 1987. "Looking to the Bottom: Critical Legal Studies and Reparations." *Harvard Civil Rights-Civil Liberties Law Review* 22: 323.

McDermott, Ray, Shelley Goldman, and Hervé Varenne. 2006. "The Cultural Work of Learning Disabilities." *Educational Researcher* 35 (6): 12–17. McFadden,

Anna C., George E. Marsh II, Barrie Jo Price, and Yunhan Hwang. 1992. "A Study of Race and Gender Bias in the Punishment of Handicapped School Children." *The Urban Review* 24 (4): 239–251.

Meiners, Erica R. 2010. *Right to Be Hostile: Schools, Prisons, and the Making of Public Enemies.* New York: Routledge.

Morris, Ruth, ed. 2000. *Stories of Transformative Justice.* Toronto: Canadian Scholars' Press.

National Association of School Psychologists. 2007. *Truth in Labeling: Disproportionality in Special Education.* Washington, DC: National Education Association.

Nocella, A. 2008. "Emergence of Disability Pedagogy." *Journal for Critical Education Policy Studies* 6 (2): 77–94.

Osher, David, Darren Woodruff, and Anthony E. Sims. 2002. "Schools Make a Difference: The Overrepresentation of African American Youth in Special Education and the Juvenile Justice System." *Racial Inequity in Special Education,* 93–116.

Parrish, Thomas. 2002. "Racial Disparities in the Identification, Funding, and Provision of Special Education." In *Racial Inequity in Special Education,* eds. D. J. Losen and G. Orfield (pp. 15–37). Cambridge, MA: Harvard Education Publishing Group.

Patton, James M. 1998. "The Disproportionate Representation of African Americans in Special Education Looking behind the Curtain for Understanding and Solutions." *The Journal of Special Education* 32 (1): 25–31.

Payne, Allison Ann, and Kelly Welch. 2013. "Restorative Justice in Schools: The Influence of Race on Restorative Discipline." *Youth & Society*: 0044118X12473125.

Quinn, Mary Magee, David M. Osher, Jeffrey M. Poirier, Robert B. Rutherford, and Peter E. Leone. 2005. "Youth with Disabilities in Juvenile Corrections: A National Survey." *Exceptional Children* 71 (3): 339–345.

Rabaka, Reiland. 2007. *WEB Du Bois and the Problems of the Twenty-First Century: An Essay on Africana Critical Theory.* Lanham, MD: Lexington Books.

Rabaka, Reiland. 2010. *Against Epistemic Apartheid: WEB Du Bois and the Disciplinary Decadence of Sociology.* Lanham, MD: Lexington Books, p. 295.

Raffaele Mendez, Linda M., and Howard M. Knoff. 2003. "Who Gets Suspended from School and Why: A Demographic Analysis of Schools and Disciplinary Infractions in a Large School District." *Education & Treatment of Children* 26: 30–51.

Reid, D. Kim, and Michelle G. Knight. 2006. "Disability Justifies Exclusion of Minority Students: A Critical History Grounded in Disability Studies." *Educational Researcher* 35 (6): 18–23.

Reid, D. Kim, and Jan Weatherly Valle. 2004. "The Discursive Practice of Learning Disability Implications for Instruction and Parent—School Relations." *Journal of Learning Disabilities* 37 (6): 466–481.

Rios, Victor M. 2011. *Punished: Policing the Lives of Black and Latino Boys.* NYU Press.

Skiba, Russell J., Reece L. Peterson, and Tara Williams. 1997. "Office Referrals and Suspension: Disciplinary Intervention in Middle Schools." *Education & Treatment of Children* 20 (3): 295–315.

Skiba, Russell J., Robert S. Michael, Abra Carroll Nardo, and Reece L. Peterson. 2002. "The Color of Discipline: Sources of Racial and Gender Disproportionality in School Punishment." *The Urban Review* 34 (4): 317–342.

Solorzano, Daniel G., and Dolores Delgado Bernal. 2001. "Examining Transformational Resistance through a Critical Race and LatCrit Theory Framework Chicana and Chicano Students in an Urban Context." *Urban Education* 36 (3): 308–342.

Spade, Dean. 2012. "Trickle Up Social Justice." December 21, 2012. Accessed December 27, 2012. http://blip.tv/grittv/dean-spade-trickle-up-social-justice-part-2-of-2-6482084.

Suvall, Cara. 2009. "Restorative Justice in Schools: Learning from Jena High School." *Harvard Civil Rights-Civil Liberties Law Review* 44: 547.

Thorsborne, Margaret. 2013. "A Story of the Emergence of Restorative Practice in Schools in Australia and New Zealand: Reflect, Repair, Reconnect in van Wormer." In *Restorative Justice Today–Practical Applications,* eds. S. Katherine and Lorenn Walker (pp. 43–52). Los Angeles, CA: SAGE Publications, Inc.

Valencia, Richard R., ed. 2012. *The Evolution of Deficit Thinking: Educational Thought and Practice.* New York: Routledge.

Wald, Johanna, and Daniel J. Losen. 2003. "Defining and Redirecting a School-to-Prison Pipeline." *New Directions for Youth Development* 2003 (99): 9–15.

Wallace Jr., John M., Sara Goodkind, Cynthia M. Wallace, and Jerald G. Bachman. 2008. "Racial, Ethnic, and Gender Differences in School Discipline among US High School Students: 1991–2005." *The Negro Educational Review* 59 (1–2): 47.

Watts, Ivan Eugene, and Nirmala Erevelles. 2004. "These Deadly Times: Reconceptualizing School Violence by Using Critical Race Theory and Disability Studies." *American Educational Research Journal* 41 (2): 271–299.

Wing, Adrien Katherine, ed. 2000. *Global Critical Race Feminism: An International Reader.* NYU Press.

Zehr, Howard. 2002. *The Little Book of Restorative Justice.* Intercourse, PA: Good Books.

Part III

Race and Racialization in Schools and Curriculum

Chapter 9

The Race Problem: Its Perpetuation in the Next Generation of Science Standards

Eileen Carlton Parsons and
Dana N. Thompson Dorsey

"We hold these truths to be self-evident: that all men are created equal; that they are endowed by their Creator with certain unalienable Rights; that among these are life, liberty and the pursuit of happiness." This guiding principle and corresponding goals featured in the United States (U.S.) Declaration of Independence are as elusive today for some groups of U.S. citizens as they were in 1776 when the words were written. Within the United States, people are born into certain strata in society and most remain in them for the duration of their lives. In the instances in which a select few have moved from a lower stratum at birth to a higher stratum later in life, high-quality education, one vehicle for social mobility, has facilitated this movement.

Research links more quality education to greater earnings. For example, as stated in the *Next Generation Science Standards* (*NGSS*), the unemployment rate for high school graduates without a college degree and recent college graduates was 30 percent and 6 percent, respectively, and a holder of a bachelor degree is likely to earn a million dollars more over a lifetime.[1] Access to high-quality education and its benefits are becoming more difficult, especially along the lines of certain social identifiers like race and social class. The Organization for Economic Co-operation and Development observed that children born to less-educated parents in the United States struggled more than children in other developed countries to advance. Education and earnings, resources with racially skewed distributions, impact the ease at which and to the extent individuals attain life, liberty, and pursuit of happiness cited in the U.S. Declaration of Independence. Race, defined as "a concept which signifies and symbolizes social conflicts and interests by referring to different types of human bodies,"[2] with regards to science, technology, engineering, and mathematics (STEM) is the focus of this chapter.

The collapse of the U.S. economy and its slow recovery in tandem with the advances of STEM in other countries have reinvigorated the value of a STEM education. STEM jobs grew three times faster than non-STEM jobs in the past 10 years, and the STEM workforce, the impetus behind a vast majority of innovations on which U.S. prominence in the world economy is based, is projected to grow by 17 percent from 2008 to 2018, with other U.S. sectors experiencing on average a 10 percent growth.[3] In June 2013 alone, 3 million math- and science-related jobs remained vacant nationwide,[4] a figure greater than the projected 1 million shortfall of STEM professionals for 2022.[5]

The United States has previously relied on foreign-born STEM professionals to meet the STEM workforce demand. This option is becoming less sustainable as other countries invest in STEM, prepare and retain their own citizenry, and actively recruit their country's natives to return to their homelands after their training elsewhere. In order to meet the present and future workforce demand, the United States must prepare an additional 100,000 STEM professionals per year over its current rate of production.[6] The U.S. social group that overpopulates, historically and in contemporary times, STEM fields is European Americans. The participation of European Americans in STEM areas is on the decline, and it is projected that by 2050, they will be the numerical minority in the United States. In light of the demographic changes in the U.S. population and the decline of European Americans in STEM fields, STEM reform seems to seriously consider the educative experiences of people of color. The *NGSS* is one such effort.

This chapter examines *NGSS* with respect to race as it is filtered through the lens of critical race theory (CRT). *NGSS* appears to facilitate the development and advancement of all K-12 students, including students of color, in STEM. This chapter uses tenets of CRT to unpack and critique *NGSS* in order to examine if this STEM reform effort is what it appears to be. The chapter consists of four sections. The chapter begins with a discussion of CRT followed by an overview of *NGSS* and a CRT critique of it. The chapter concludes with suggestions on how educators can act to fulfill the promise of *NGSS*.

Critical Race Theory

CRT is a movement that consciously foregrounds race, racism, and power in the United States, and works to expose and eradicate white dominance in social, legal, political, and economic institutions. CRT began in the late 1970s and 1980s with the writings of several legal scholars who questioned the retrenchment of civil rights laws and advanced arguments regarding the ongoing oppression of racial and ethnic minorities in American law and society. Most of these like-minded scholars, who were primarily law professors of color, attended the 1987 Critical Legal Studies (CLS) Workshop on race, where they communicated their dismay over the direction of civil rights legislation and conveyed their clear disappointment over the focus and rhetoric of the CLS program. CLS was a liberal law school movement that challenged traditional doctrinal and policy analysis of legal scholarship in favor of a more social and cultural context perspective. However, a faction of activist scholars did not think the CLS program adequately represented the voices and struggles of racial and ethnic minorities in the fight for justice and equality. Thus, the ideological dissonance between members of the two groups—CLS and what is now CRT—launched the CRT movement with its first official meeting at the University of Wisconsin, Madison, in 1989.

The CRT founders believed "race and racism were fundamentally ingrained in American social structures and the historical consciousness of this country's ideology, legal systems, and fundamental conceptions of law, property, and privilege."[7] One of the initial purposes of CRT was to reinterpret "civil rights law with regard to its ineffectiveness in addressing racial injustices, particularly institutional racism and structural racism in the political economy."[8] Unlike traditional civil rights that embraces incremental progress, critical race theorists question "the very foundations of the liberal order, including equality theory, legal reasoning, enlightenment rationalism, and neutral principles of constitutional law."[9]

As CRT has gained attention and popularity, it has expanded into various disciplines, such as in education, sociology, psychology, cultural studies, political science, and philosophy. In addition, CRT has branched out into other equality movements acknowledging the voices, experiences, and challenges of various racial, ethnic, cultural, and marginalized groups around the world, namely Latinos (LatCrit), Asian Americans (AsianCrit), Native Americans (TribalCrit), critical race feminism (FemCrit), and the gay and lesbian communities (Queer-Crit). The splintering of CRT has drawn attention to other issues like immigration and nativism, sovereignty rights, class, language, gender identity, and sexual orientation discrimination. Despite the diverse interests and foci, CRT activists and scholars place their concerns in a common, broader perspective that includes economics, history, context, and group- and self-interest, as well as feelings and the unconscious. Accordingly, CRT follows six unifying themes that define the movement:

(1) CRT recognizes that racism is endemic to American life.
(2) CRT expresses skepticism toward dominant legal claims of neutrality, objectivity, color blindness, and meritocracy.
(3) CRT challenges ahistoricism and insists on a contextual/historical analysis of the law. CRT presumes that racism has contributed to all contemporary manifestations of group advantage and disadvantage.
(4) CRT insists on recognition of the experiential knowledge of people of color and their communities of origin in analyzing law and society.
(5) CRT is interdisciplinary.
(6) CRT works toward the end of eliminating racial oppression as part of the broader goal of ending all forms of oppression.[10]

Within these themes are concepts that have guided the CRT movement for the past two decades. The key concepts are as follows: (1) racism as ordinary, not aberrational; (2) interest convergence or material determinism; (3) narrative analysis and counter-storytelling; (4) intersectionality and antiessentialism; and (5) whiteness as property. Racism as ordinary, interest convergence, and counter-storytelling are of interest in this chapter and are briefly explained here.

Racism as Ordinary

CRT begins with the basic supposition that "racism is ordinary, not aberrational—'normal science,' the usual way society does business, the common, everyday experience of most people of color in this country."[11] On one hand, racism is systemic and is enacted through and perpetrated by institutions and formal and informal protocols and procedures. On the other hand, racism is idiosyncratic and is enacted by individuals through person-by-person interactions. The ordinariness of racism as described by critical race theorists means that it is difficult to alleviate or address. This primary element of CRT is based on the cycle of racial progress and retrenchment evident in U.S. history and contemporary times. "Retrenchment" refers to abrogation of progress when advances radically deviate from and threaten existent racial hierarchies. Throughout the racial history of the United States and in the present day, progress toward racial equality has been and continues to be followed by phases of resistance and retrenchment as social forces reassert white supremacy. Much of the racial progress in the United States has been attributed to liberalism. From a CRT perspective, liberalism simply maintains the racial status quo and, contrary to popular belief, does not lead to long-lasting racial advancement.

Since the abolition of slavery, racism has hidden behind the veil of liberalism or liberal theory. Liberalism and liberal theory focus on protecting the liberty of an autonomous human being, in which freedom, not equality, is treated as the highest political value. Liberalism and liberal theory assume the individual freedom to work hard allows all people in the United States to reach their highest potential, if they choose, so they may compete on an equal footing and level playing field with others. This assumption has produced the American myth of meritocracy, in which it appears all people are treated the same, have the same access to the same opportunities, and can achieve success through hard work. However, this myth of meritocracy ignores the social, political, and economic inequities that resulted from hundreds of years of systemic and systematic racism against groups of U.S. citizens, thereby dismissing the unequal footing and unleveled playing field according to race that exists in America. Intentionally or not, liberalism and meritocracy insulate racism from scrutiny and ultimately from remedy. This insulation is further supported by a color-blind philosophy.

In the 1896 infamous legal case of *Plessy v. Ferguson,* Justice Harlan proclaimed in his dissent: "Our Constitution is color-blind, and neither knows nor tolerates classes among citizens. In respect of civil rights, all citizens are equal before the law."[12] Justice Harlan's words in opposition to the Supreme Court's majority decision in *Plessy,* which legally sanctioned the separate-but-equal doctrine, supported the liberal idea that the U.S. Constitution contains neutral, objective principles equally applied to all. However, Gotanda argues, "A color-blind interpretation of the Constitution legitimates, and thereby maintains, the social, economic, and political advantages that whites hold over other Americans."[13] In this foundational CRT article, Gotanda continues to explain how interpreting the constitution as color-blind reinforces racial inequality and domination because color-blindness does not address less overt forms of racism or existing racial disparities. The color-blind approach for equality is expressed in rules that insist on treatment that is the same for all persons; these rules can remedy only the most blatant forms of discrimination rather than instances of covert racism. For instance, the color-blind approach does not address the disparate impact of school funding in low-income and high-minority neighborhoods, which results in dilapidated buildings, outdated textbooks, and limited and malfunctioning equipment, whereas the wealthy predominately white school district in an adjacent neighborhood that receives money from the same state government has the newest, state-of-the art resources.

The interconnected terms "color blindness," "neutrality," "objectivity," and "meritocracy" have controlled the legal and political narrative over the past several years, as well as have undergirded the notion that race is irrelevant in the United States, particularly with the election of President Barack Obama in 2008 and 2012.[14] Meritocracy denies "the influence of race and class in life success . . ., [which] allows the notion of race neutrality or colorblindness to be embraced,"[15] even though a wide racial achievement gap still exists in American public schools and employment and economic disparities persist between various racial and ethnic groups. Critical race theorists posit that there is a lack of understanding and revision of history, which allow the dominant group to ignore the fact that the gaps remain because different racial, ethnic, and socioeconomic groups did not and do not compete on neutral ground in employment, education, or in life. Furthermore, the once-liberal terms outlined earlier have been usurped to argue for the existence of a post-racial society where legislation and programs that have supported historically subjugated, underserved, and disadvantaged people in this country, such as the Civil Rights Act of 1964 and the Voters Rights Act of 1965, are no longer needed. Even though critical race theorists view racism as ordinary and ingrained in the fabric of life in the United States, they continue to battle it and bring attention to the historical and present context of racism and racial subordination in America.

Interest Convergence

Another key element of CRT is interest convergence or material determinism. One of CRT's founding fathers, Derrick Bell, proposed "interest convergence" to explain the so-called benefits that blacks and other racial and ethnic minorities on a whole have reaped, particularly since the *Brown v. Board of Education* decision in 1954. Bell defined the first rule of interest convergence as aligning the self-interests of whites and blacks temporarily. The notion of interest convergence sets forth the belief that racism benefits white elites materially (hence the term "material determinism") and working-class people psychically, which results in a society having no interest in eradicating racism. Litigation involving race-based issues and some government-supported programs that appear to protect the basic rights of racial and ethnic minorities are closely connected with the political and economic interests of white policy makers.

For instance, as previously interpreted and discussed by Thompson Dorsey, Derrick Bell claimed the U.S. Supreme Court's unanimous opinion in *Brown v. Board of Education* occurred

> at a time when a major distraction was needed from the United States' normal business of racial discrimination. The landmark civil rights decision intentionally coincided with the U.S. need to address the struggles with the Cold War, which entangled the loyalties of individuals in Third World countries who were Black, brown, and Asian, and could succumb to the power of Communism and threaten U.S. democracy. It was then, 1954, that the U.S. decided it could no longer politically afford to continue to carry stories of lynchings, racist law enforcement, murders, and blatant discrimination while battling communism.[16]

Chief Justice Warren deliberately composed a four-page opinion, so that it was short enough to be reprinted in newspapers around the world. As Derrick Bell explained, "Self-interest has been described . . . as the most basic and important force underlying white policy and action vis-à-vis blacks . . . [which] more often than not serves the interests of the actors or is accounted for by an incorrect perception of objective interest."[17] The basic civil rights conferred in the *Brown* case converged with the self-interests of U.S. foreign policy and elite white policy makers.

Unfortunately, the second rule of Bell's interest convergence states, "Even when the interest-convergence results in an effective racial remedy, that remedy will be abrogated at the point that policymakers fear the remedial policy is threatening the superior societal status of whites."[18] In other words, divergence is inevitable after converging interests no longer serve the white elites materially. School desegregation policies are an example of interest divergence. Federal oversight of school districts under desegregation orders and the demand for implementing desegregation policies in schools have greatly diminished since the 1990s; therefore, many schools around the country have resegregated. In fact, black and Latino students are more segregated today in the 21st century than they were in the late 1960s prior to the implementation of desegregation plans in school districts across the country.

Narrative Analysis and Counter-Storytelling

The third element of CRT of interest in this chapter is narrative analysis and counter-storytelling. This particular element may be the most liberating and empowering for persecuted individuals. Narrative analysis and counter-storytelling gives people, such as those who have been silenced by the oppressive and oftentimes ruling majority, a voice and opportunity to speak their truth. Delgado explains this CRT component as the out-group, those whose life experiences have been suppressed and marginalized by the dominant group, sharing their perspectives, histories, and realities in an effort to destabilize or minimize the power of the in-group's storytelling about members of the out-group. CRT elevates narratives that counter dominance and oppression, "stories that center the experiences of people of color and bring to light a reality that is often obfuscated in stories narrated by Whites."[19]

The Next Generation Science Standards (*NGSS*) and Its CRT Critique

The last set of widely adopted science education standards, *National Science Education Standards* and *Benchmarks for Science Literacy,* was drafted in the 1990s. *NGSS* was developed for the purpose of addressing the complexities and challenges of the 21st century. The problems that face the United States and the world are multifaceted. Creative and innovative solutions to these complex problems require a deep understanding and nimble application of content knowledge that transverses disciplinary boundaries.

NGSS Overview

NGSS seeks to address the 21st-century context by developing standards or goals for K-12 science education that includes engineering, which was omitted in earlier standards, and integrates three dimensions: science and engineering practices (SEPs), disciplinary core ideas (DCIs), and crosscutting concepts (CCs). The integration is concretized in performance expectations (PEs). The standards address each dimension for each grade.

SEPs were positioned as separate from content in previous standards but *NGSS* explicitly connects them. "Coupling practice with content gives the learning context, whereas practices alone are activities and content alone is memorization."[20] SEPs in *NGSS* resemble scientific inquiry highlighted in earlier standards, but *NGSS* articulates specific practices employed by scientists and engineers in response to the numerous interpretations of scientific inquiry that exist. In line with *NGSS,* K-12 students are expected to engage, at each grade level, the following eight practices:

(1) asking questions (for science) and defining problems (for engineering); (2) developing and using models; (3) planning and carrying out investigations; (4) analyzing and interpreting data; (5) using mathematics and computational thinking; (6) constructing explanations (for science) and designing solutions (for engineering); (7) engaging in argument from evidence; and (8) obtaining, evaluating, and communicating information.[21]

These practices both undergird and complement the content emphasized in *NGSS.*

Content in *NGSS* consists of DCI and CC. In order to illustrate learning as a developmental progression, *NGSS* revisits the same concepts at each grade level. *NGSS* is constructed to align with identified pathways for learning the selected scientific concepts with the culminating expectation that individuals would build throughout the K-12 spectrum understandings of natural phenomenon that correspond with the scientific canon. The DCIs and CCs increase in complexity and sophistication as learners proceed from grade K through 12.

To foster in-depth study of certain areas, developers of *NGSS* selected DCIs that are considered essential for the physical sciences, life sciences, and earth and space sciences with engineering embedded where appropriate. Four DCIs were identified for physical sciences, four for life sciences, and three for earth and space sciences; subideas accompany each of the DCIs. The core ideas for the scientific disciplines are connected, made more comprehensible for learners, and made more coherent by the crosscutting concepts.

NGSS features seven concepts common to the scientific disciplines featured in the standards. These CCs are implicitly addressed in previous standards. In order to accentuate their importance, *NGSS* highlights them as a major dimension of the standards and promotes explicit instructional support for them. The seven CCs are

(1) patterns, (2) cause and effect: mechanism and explanation, (3) scale, proportion, and quantity, (4) systems and system models, (5) energy and matter: flows, cycles, and conservation, (6) structure and function, and (7) stability and change.[22]

NGSS is organized to simultaneously emphasize the distinctiveness of and linkages among SEPs, DCIs, and CCs. The distinctiveness of each dimension that constitutes *NGSS* is illustrated in explicit descriptions that are demarcated from other text in the standards. The linkages are shown in the PEs that are described in the *NGSS* document as the intersections among SEPs, DCIs, and CCs. PEs state what learners should know and be able to do after instruction. The relationship of the PEs to SEPs, DCIs, and CCs is reiterated in the organization of *NGSS*: *NGSS* states the PEs, with supporting SEPs, DCIs, and CCs contained in boxes beneath them.

Even though the PEs and the three dimensions (SEPs, DCIs, and CCs) comprise the bulk of *NGSS, NGSS* also includes information to clarify the previously stated components and their connections. Descriptions of the development process, brief explanations and examples of content and practices, and supplementary information are among the clarifications.

A framework for K-12 science education: Practices, crosscutting concepts, and core ideas guided the construction of *NGSS*. An 18-member committee affiliated with the National Research Council engaged a two-year iterative process that involved writing, reviewing, and making review-driven decisions. Organizations, distinguished STEM professionals, science educators, and the general public reviewed the developing document "intended to provide the scientific consensus upon which to base K-12 science standards."[23] Once the framework was released, 26 states worked over a two-year period with 41 writers that included K-12 school and higher education personnel to translate the framework into *NGSS,* an effort directed by Achieve, Inc., and funded by several foundations and corporations (i.e., Carnegie, GE Foundation, Noyce, Boeing, Cisco, and Dupont). Large groups of expert reviewers at multiple times during the process, teams in the participating states, and the general public on two occasions examined drafts of the standards prior to their release in 2013.

The publicly released *NGSS* addressed the three dimensions previously described. In many cases, the standards include brief explanations and examples to further clarify the dimensions. Consider the third earth and space science PE for middle school that require students to design a method in line with scientific principles that both monitor and minimize a particular human impact on the environment. The clarification statement that accompanies this PE states, "Examples of the design process include examining human environmental impacts, assessing the kinds of solutions that are feasible, and designing and evaluating solutions that could reduce that impact. Examples of human impacts can include water usage (such as the withdrawal of water from streams and aquifers or the construction of dams and levees), land usage (such as urban development, agriculture, or the removal of wetlands), and pollution (such as of the air, water, or land)." The PE and clarification statements are followed by text that provides some details of the most relevant SEPs, DCIs, and CCs. The text also referred to supplementary information contained in the appendices.[24]

NGSS contains 13 appendices. The appendices describe in greater detail the development of NGSS and its three essential dimensions. The appendices also feature how NGSS connects with existent common core standards in mathematics and scientific literacy as well as offer suggestions on how to map NGSS onto middle school and high school courses. Student diversity is the explicit and primary focus of one of the appendices, Appendix D "All Standards, All Students: Making the Next Generation Science Standards Accessible to All Students." Students are classified into two general groups, dominant and nondominant. "Dominant" refers to groups of students who enjoy social and institutionalized privilege and who may or may not be a part of the U.S. numerical majority. Economically disadvantaged students, students from major racial or ethnic minority groups, students with disabilities, students with limited English proficiency, students in alternative education programs, and gifted and talented students comprised the nondominant groups addressed in Appendix D. The appendix discussed the learning opportunities and challenges proffered by NGSS for students of nondominant groups. The connections across school curricula, the inclusion of engineering as a way to redefine science such that it recognizes the historical contributions of other cultures and that it becomes relevant to students' everyday lives, and engagement in science by way of the SEPs were discussed as affordances of NGSS in making science accessible to nondominant and dominant groups. In addition, the NGSS appendix included a brief synthesis of the research on equitable learning opportunities. This synthesis featured three themes: valuing and respecting students' backgrounds by incorporating them into science teaching and learning; linking students' understandings that are developed over time in their homes and communities to scientific disciplinary knowledge; and allocating the level of material (e.g., equipment), human (e.g., well-prepared and experienced teachers), and social (e.g., highly influential and high-leverage relationships) resources necessary for high-quality educative experiences in science. The appendix concluded with a discussion of the context of U.S. public education and student diversity. This discussion described the changing demographics with respect to certain groups, the science achievement gaps among certain groups, and current educational policies that pertained to certain groups. The affordances, challenges, and context around diversity were illustrated in seven case studies posted on the *NGSS* website. One case titled "Case study 2: Students from racial and ethnic groups and the Next Generation Science Standards" was devoted to race and ethnicity. The contents of the second case study illustrated the changing demographics of the United States in the composition of the class, emphasized the affordances of *NGSS* for students from racially and ethnically nondominant groups, and described a teacher's use of instructional strategies that exemplified the three major themes of equity-focused research.

CRT Critique of *NGSS*

Student diversity was invisible in earlier documents like *National Science Education Standards,* one precursor to *NGSS*. Forms of student diversity are visible in *NGSS,* but this visibility is in the background. Student diversity is explicitly acknowledged and addressed in Appendix D and in the case studies posted on the *NGSS* website, venues that are somewhat separate from the core *NGSS* document and require initiative on the part of educators to access. The documents explicitly address some manifestations of student diversity more than others. Unsurprisingly, race and ethnicity are named in the demography cited in Appendix D and the case study but, as is the case in science education research, they are not distinguished from one another and ethnicity is implicated more often than race. Although student diversity is not integrated well into the standards per se, an effort to address student diversity, specifically race and ethnicity, is evident in *NGSS.* Proceeding from the front matter to the back matter of the *NGSS* documents, the three previously described elements of CRT—interest convergence, counter-storytelling, and racism as ordinary—are relevant to the document's treatment of race.

The front matter and the appendices of *NGSS* discussed why the new standards were developed and by whom. These discussions pivoted around what Secada called enlightened self-interest. The needs of the nation with regards to the innovative thinking and creativity necessary for the United States to be a world leader in the global community in juxtaposition to the projected demographic change of the United States from a numerical majority white nation-state to a nation-state of people of color dominated the justification for the new standards. Other justifications cited in the race and equity literature were not central in the *NGSS* document. For example, arguments to promote the American creed as indicated in its Constitution, to advance the highest moral social good, or to develop a more humane society were not prominent among the justifications. The enlightened self-interest arguments were further implicated by the funding sources for NGSS, which heavily represented the U.S. economic sector. The enlightened self-interest rationale for *NGSS* reflected the CRT element of interest convergence. As STEM becomes increasingly crucial to the global standing of nations and other countries make notable advances in STEM areas in concert with the projected changes in the U.S. demography, the material (economic in this case) interests of whites, the predominate decision makers in U.S. civic life, are threatened as the percentages of whites and the people of color pursuing STEM careers decline and remain stagnant, respectively. A less competitive United States in STEM translates into direct economic losses for whites, the U.S. racial group that enjoys the lion share of the nation's wealth, power, and prestige.

As one continues from the front matter to the text of the standards, the voices and perspectives of people of color as captured in the storytelling element of CRT are largely absent in the information provided to contextualize the disciplinary content. Clarification statements and examples provided in *NGSS* are more often than not generalizations that do not highlight the experiences of students of color. For example, the illustrations proffered for the third earth and space PE for middle school featured human impact on water and land usage and pollution but it did not impugn the oft racially skewed distribution of this impact (e.g., urban gentrification). However, Case Study 2 on the *NGSS* website demonstrated how educators could tailor the generalizations to reflect the concerns of the local community but the showcased issues were racially decontextualized. That is, the issues were racially neutral and the links among the issues and the racial groups significantly affected in their everyday lives remained hidden. Case Study 2 not only modeled the different instructional strategies educators could employ to make *NGSS* culturally relevant and culturally accessible but also modeled a color-blind approach, how to ignore and dismiss race and racism.

Racism as ordinary, the last previously explained element of CRT, surfaced in the exposition in Appendix D. The introduction of the appendix reiterated the increasing diversity of the U.S. population cited in previous sections of *NGSS*. Unlike the earlier discussion of the projected demographic changes in the United States found in *NGSS*, the text of Appendix D insinuated the mainstay of the racial hierarchy in its terminology of "dominant" and "nondominant" groups to reference student diversity. In Appendix D of *NGSS*, the dominant group referred to students who enjoyed social prestige and institutionalized privilege in the U.S. public domain and nondominant included those students excluded from such prestige and privilege. Although not stated explicitly, the text of Appendix D acknowledged the structural privileging of being white (e.g., "even where the dominant group(s) is the numerical minority, the privileging of its academic backgrounds persists"[25]) such that whites will retain power in civic life even though they will constitute in the future a numerical minority in the U.S. population. Appendix D advocates the negation of this privileging of "academic backgrounds" by valuing the knowledge, experiential and otherwise, that exists in nondominant groups and encouraging its articulation with the scientific canon and its incorporation into the teaching and learning of STEM. Racism as ordinary is also illustrated in the discussion of the material, human, and social resources for science instruction.

> School resources are likely to have a greater impact on the learning opportunities of non-dominant student groups. This is because the dominant group is more likely to have the benefits of other supports for their learning, such as better-equipped schools, more material resources at home, and highly educated parents. In contrast, the academic success of nondominant students depends more heavily on their school environment; yet, it is these students who are less likely to have access to high-quality learning environments. Thus, inequitable resources are a central concern.[26]

The text did not acknowledge the racial composition of these racially segregated environments in which high-minority enrollment schools receive less quality and fewer resources than their low-minority enrollment counterparts.

In contrast to earlier documents developed to reform science education, *NGSS* intentionally made diversity visible. The effort was compromised by positioning student diversity in the background (e.g., appendices and website external to published document) in lieu of integrating it throughout the document and by circumventing race and racism rather than including statistics, examples, and so on, to show skewed distributions for the topic under discussion (e.g., resource distribution by racial composition of largest U.S. school districts). Perhaps, educators can act to mitigate these shortcomings.

Fulfilling the Promise of *NGSS*: Moving beyond Color Blindness

As previously mentioned, *NGSS* seeks to address the 21st-century context by developing standards or goals for K-12 science education that includes engineering. In this attempt to guide the reform in science education, an effort to consider student diversity given the changing racial and ethnic demographics in the United States is evident in *NGSS*. In light of the changing demographics and disproportionate access to high-quality education for the growing U.S. populace of color, the country's future preeminence in STEM and the United States' basic ability to compete on a global scale make it necessary for *NGSS* to prominently focus on race and racism and how these issues factor into developing relevant, sustainable standards and goals. Although *NGSS* provided a blueprint for addressing student diversity, this blueprint offered a color-blind approach to race and racism. In the absence of explicit guidance, *NGSS* relies heavily on the expertise and professional judgment of educators to address race and racism in their implementation of the standards.

Under the current conditions, the expectation for educators to address race and racism in their implementation of *NGSS* is an expectation that has a small likelihood of being met. In general, educators lack the knowledge and the competencies to address race and racism in providing high-quality experiences in science education. Ongoing and intentional development of educators is needed. With respect to the three CRT elements racism as ordinary, interest convergence, and counter-storytelling, several aspects of professional development are essential.

First, it is crucial for professional development to elucidate racism in the normal, routine operations of science education writ large and in the educators' local communities. Generally, awareness is often limited to acts of blatant racism by individuals with very little, if any, comprehension of institutional racism, so professional development should be especially intentional in this domain. For example, educators could be given several small data sets that contain quality indicators for science education (e.g., college degrees and preparation of teachers) and prompted to engage in scaffolded inquiry activities in which they discern racial patterns in the distribution of material, human, and social resources. Perhaps, raising the awareness of educators who desire to remedy race-based disparities may encourage them to question the appropriateness of color blindness.

Color blindness is prevalent and embedded in the national script on race and racism, and a vast majority of educators consider it virtuous to "not see race and only individuals." In light of the horrid racial history in the United States, the desire to ignore and dismiss race and racism is understandable. The foundational commonsense premise of color blindness is that if there is no race then there is no racism. However, this logic and the pursuit of color blindness as the ideal perpetuate and exacerbate disparities across racial lines. In the absence of recognizing and acknowledging race, the effects of racism still exist; the present status of school desegregation with respect to resource allocation is an exemplar. In order for educators to fulfill the promise of *NGSS* and to relate *NGSS* to their local communities as encouraged in the *NGSS* document, they must first suspend the color-blind philosophy and view their localities from a race-conscious perspective. It would be helpful if policies would support this change in perspective but it is highly unlikely. Even in the midst of a system that is structured to maintain the racial status quo, educators must be courageous, see the race-related patterns that are overt and those that are covert, and use the science to articulate and to address them in order to fulfill the promise of *NGSS*. According to CRT, racism that operates at the level of institutions and individuals is ordinary but it can be disrupted. The success of *NGSS* for students of color is based on this disruption.

Second, professional development must help educators to understand the currency of STEM and the importance of diversifying STEM for the long-term prosperity of the United States. That is, professional development should help educators understand that STEM for a few is not in their best interest and the best interest of their loved ones and generations to come. For instance, professional development could include inquiry activities that require educators to develop cases in which they trace investments in developing human potential in children and the associated costs and benefits to society as these children become adults for different life trajectories—for example, preschool to prison or a STEM career. The goal of such professional development activities is to show that the development of "other people's children" in the United States eventually impacts the livelihood and prosperity of all.

Third, it is essential for the professional development to connect educators to the students of color in their care. Educators need to know the communities from whence their students come, understand the issues they face, and partner with students to improve their communities and their stations in life. In connecting with the communities of color, educators could begin to understand their students' stories, help students to articulate these stories in a way that facilitates change and action, use these perspectives to engage and connect the students to science, and nurture students' employment of the science they learn to change their communities. For example, educators and students could engage in efforts similar to those described by Tate. [27] Middle school students identified 25 problems that they believed plagued their communities. The cluster of 13 liquor stores within a 1,000-foot radius of their school was among them. The students used their mathematical and scientific knowledge to document the negative influences of the cluster in their communities and researched the financial backing of the franchises and championed change.

Coda

On one hand, as indicated in this CRT critique *NGSS* is far from perfect. It makes diversity visible but it advocates an approach to race and racism that perpetuates the racial status quo. On the other hand, *NGSS* broaches, though timidly, racism; outlines an enlightened self-interest rationale for making high-quality science experiences accessible to students of color that aligns with the tide of the times; and alludes to the fact that the experiences and perspectives of students of colors differ from the white majority. Like many education documents with the potential to influence public policy, *NGSS* provides the package that is left at the doorstep for educators to unwrap. How educators unwrap the package for the students of color will indelibly affect the degree to which the next generation is able to realize the following: "We hold these truths to be self-evident: that all men are created equal; that they are endowed by their Creator with certain unalienable Rights; that among these are life, liberty and the pursuit of happiness."[28]

Notes

1. Shierholz, Sabadish, and Wething 2012.
2. Omi and Winant 1994, p. 55.
3. Langdon et al. 2011.
4. Basken 2013.
5. Carnevale, Smith, and Strohl 2010.

6. President's Council of Advisors on Science and Technology 2012.
7. Bell 1980b; Crenshaw et al. 1995.
8. Lynn and Adams 2007, citing Parker and Lynn 2002, p. 9.
9. Delgado and Stefancic 2001, p. 3.
10. Matsuda et al. 1993, p. 6.
11. Delgado and Stefancic 2001, pp. 6–7.
12. *Plessy v. Ferguson,* p. 559.
13. Gotando 1991, p. 1.
14. Delgado and Stefancic 2014.
15. DeCuir-Gunby 2007, p. 28.
16. Thompson Dorsey and Chambers 2014.
17. Bell 1980a p. 40.
18. Bell 2004, p. 69.
19. Parsons, Rhodes, and Brown 2011, p. 953.
20. *NGSS,* vol. 1 2013, p. xiv.
21. Ibid. vol. 2, 2013, p. 48.
22. Ibid., p. 79.
23. *NGSS,* vol. 1, 2013, p. v.
24. Ibid., p. 93.
25. *NGSS,* vol. 2, 2013, p. 25.
26. NGSS 2013, pp. 33–34.
27. Tate, W.F., IV (2008). "Geography of opportunity": Poverty, place, and educational outcomes. Educational Researcher, 37(7), 397–411.
28. U.S. National Archives & Records Administration.

Bibliography

Basken, Paul. 2013. "Crusader for Better Science Teaching Finds Colleges Slow to Change." *The Chronicle of Higher Education* (June 17).
Bell, Derrick A. 1976. "Serving Two Masters: Integration Ideals and Client Interests in School Segregation Litigation." *The Yale Law Journal* 85 (4): 470–516.
Bell, Derrick A. 1980a. "Brown v. Board of Education and the Interest-Convergence Dilemma." *Harvard Law Review* 93 (3): 518–533.
Bell, Derrick A. 1980b. *Race, Racism and American Law.* Boston, MA: Little, Brown and Co.
Bell, Derrick A. 1987. *And We Are Not Saved: The Elusive Quest for Racial Justice.* New York: Basic Books.
Bell, Derrick A. 1995. "Brown v. Board of Education and the Interest Convergence Dilemma." In *Critical Race Theory: The Key Writings That Formed the Movement,* eds. Kimberlé Crenshaw, Neil Gotanda, Gary Peller, and Kendell Thomas (pp. 20–29). New York: The New Press.
Bell, Derrick A. 2004. *Race, Racism and American Law* (5th ed.). New York: Aspen Publishers.

Brown, Kevin, and Darrell Jackson. 2014. "The History and Conceptual Elements of Critical Race Theory." In *Handbook of Critical Race Theory in Education*, eds. Marvin Lynn and Adrienne D. Dixson (pp. 9–22). New York: Routledge.

Carnevale, Anthony P., Nicole Smith, and Jeff Strohl. 2010. *Help Wanted: Projections of Jobs and Education Requirements through 2018.* Washington, DC: Georgetown University Center on Education and the Workforce.

Crenshaw, Kimberlé W. 2011. "Twenty Years of Critical Race Theory: Looking Back to Move Forward." *Connecticut Law Review* 43 (5): 1253–1352.

Crenshaw, Kimberlé W., Neil Gotanda, Gary Peller, and Kendall Thomas, eds. 1995. *Critical Race Theory: The Key Writings That Formed the Movement.* New York: The New Press.

Dalton, Harlon L. 1987. "The Clouded Prism." *Harvard Civil Rights-Civil Liberties Law Review* 22: 435–447.

DeCuir-Gunby, Jessica T. 2007. "Negotiating Identity in a Bubble: A Critical Race Analysis of African American High School Students' Experiences in an Elite, Independent School." *Equity & Excellence in Education* 40 (1): 26–35.

Delgado, Richard. 1984. "The Imperial Scholar: Reflections on a Review of Civil Rights Literature." *University of Pennsylvania Law Review* 132 (3): 561–578.

Delgado, Richard. 1987. "The Ethereal Scholar: Does Critical Legal Studies Have What Minorities Want?" *Harvard Civil Rights-Civil Liberties Law Review* 22: 301–322.

Delgado, Richard. 1989. "Storytelling for Oppositionists and Others: A Plea for Narrative." *Michigan Law Review* 87 (8): 2411–2441.

Delgado, Richard, and Jean Stefancic. 2001. *Critical Race Theory: An Introduction.* New York: New York University Press.

Delgado, Richard, and Jean Stefancic. 2014. "Discerning Critical Moments." In *Handbook of Critical Race Theory in Education,* eds. Marvin Lynn and Adrienne D. Dixson (pp. 23–33). New York: Routledge.

Dixson, Adrienne D., and Celia K. Rousseau. 2005. "And We Are Still Not Saved: Critical Race Theory in Education Ten Years Later." *Race, Ethnicity, and Education* 8 (1): 7–27.

Freeman, Alan D. 1978. "Legitimizing Racial Discrimination through Antidiscrimination Law: A Critical Review of Supreme Court Doctrine." *Minnesota Law Review* 62: 1049.

Gotanda, Neil. 1991. "A Critique of 'Our Constitution Is Color-Blind.'" *Stanford Law Review* 44: 1–68.

Kluger, Richard. 2004. *Simple Justice: The History of Brown v. Board of Education and Black America's Struggle for Equality.* 2nd ed. New York: Knopf.

Langdon, D., G. McKittrick, D. Beede, B. Khan, and M. Doms. "STEM: Good Jobs Now and for the Future." Department of Commerce, Economics, and Statistics Administration. July 2011. http://www.esa.doc.gov/Reports/stem-good-jobs-now-and-future.

Lawrence III, Charles R. 1987. "The Id, the Ego, and Equal Protection: Reckoning with Unconscious Racism." *Stanford Law Review* 39 (2): 317–388.

Lawrence III, Charles R. 2001. "Two Views of the River: A Critique of the Liberal Defense of Affirmative Action." *Columbia Law Review* 101 (4): 928–976.

Lopez, Ian F. H. 2006. "Colorblind to the Reality of Race in America." *The Chronicle of Higher Education* (November 3).

Lynn, Marvin, and Maurianne Adams. 2002. "Introductory Overview to the Special Issue Critical Race Theory and Education: Recent Developments in the Field." *Equity & Excellence in Education* 35 (2): 87–92.

Matsuda, Mari. 1987. "Looking to the Bottom: Critical Legal Studies and Reparations." *Harvard Civil Rights-Civil Liberties Review* 22: 323.

Matsuda, Mari J., Charles Lawrence, Richard Delgado, and Kimberlé Crenshaw, eds. 1993. *Words That Wound: Critical Race Theory, Assaultive Speech and the First Amendment.* Boulder, CO: Westview Press.

Mitchell, Kara. 2013. "Race, Difference, Meritocracy, and English: Majoritarian Stories in the Education of Secondary Multilingual." *Race, Ethnicity and Education* 16 (3): 339–364.

National Academy of Sciences. 2007. *Rising above the Gathering Storm: Energizing and Employing America for a Brighter Economic Future.* Washington, DC: National Academies Press.

National Academy of Sciences. 2011. *Expanding Underrepresented Minority Participation: America's Science and Technology Talent at the Crossroads.* Washington, DC: National Academies Press.

National Science Board. 2012. *Science and Engineering Indicators 2012.* Arlington, VA: National Science Foundation (NSB 12-01).

NGSS Lead States. 2013. *Next Generation Science Standards: For States, by States.* Washington, DC: The National Academies Press.

Omi, Michael, and Howard Winant. 1994. *Racial Formation in the United States: From the 1960s to 1990s.* 2nd ed. New York: Routledge.

Organization for Economic Co-operation and Development (OECD). "Education at a Glance: 2012." OECD Publishing. http://dx.doi.org/10.1787/eag-2012-en.

Parker, Laurence, and Marvin Lynn. 2002. "What's Race Got to Do with It? Critical Race Theory's Conflicts with and Connections to Qualitative Research Methodology and Epistemology." *Qualitative Inquiry* 8 (1): 7–22.

Parsons, Eileen C. 2014. "Chapter 9: Unpacking and Critically Synthesizing the Literature on Race and Ethnicity in Science Education." In *The Handbook on Research in Science Education*, eds. Norman Lederman and Sandra Abell (posthumously) (2nd ed.) (pp. 167–186). New York: Routledge.

Parsons, Eileen C., Billye Rhodes, and Corliss Brown. 2011. "Unpacking CRT in Negotiating White Science." *Cultural Studies of Science Education* 6: 951–960.

Plessy v. Ferguson, 163 U.S. 527 (1896).

President's Council of Advisors on Science and Technology. 2012. *Engage to Excel: Producing One Million Additional College Graduates with Degrees in Science, Technology, Engineering, and Mathematics.* Washington, DC: Executive Office of the President, President's Council of Advisors on Science and Technology.

Rodriguez, Alberto. 1997. "The Dangerous Discourse of Invisibility: A Critique of the National Research Council's National Science Education Standards." *Journal of Research in Science Teaching* 34 (1): 19–37.

Secada, Walter G. 1989. "Enlightened Self-Interest and Equity in Mathematics Education." *Peabody Journal of Education* 66 (2): 22–56.

Shierholz, H., N. Sabadish, and H. Wething. 2012. "The Class of 2012: Labor Market for Young Graduates Remains Grim." Economic Policy Institute. http://www.epi.org/publication/bp340-labor-market-young-graduates.

Tate IV, William F. 2008. "'Geography of Opportunity': Poverty, Place, and Educational Outcomes." *Educational Researcher* 37 7: 397–411.

Thompson Dorsey, Dana N. 2013. "Segregation 2.0: The New Generation of Segregation in the 21st Century." *Education and Urban Society* 45 (5): 533–547.

Thompson Dorsey, D.N., and T.L. Venzant Chambers 2014. "Growing C-D-R (Cedar): Working the Intersections of Interest Convergence and Whiteness as Property in the Affirmative Action Legal Debate." *Race, Ethnicity and Education* 17 (1): 56–87.

Ullucci, Kerri, and Dan Battey. 2011. "Exposing Colorblindness/Grounding Color Consciousness: Challenges for Teacher Education." *Urban Education* 46 (6): 1195–1225.

U.S. Census Bureau. "Population Estimates," 2011. http://www.census.gov/popest/national/asrh/%202008-nat-detail.html.

U.S. National Archives & Records Administration. "Declaration of Independence." *The Charters of Freedom: A New World Is at Hand.* http://www.archives.gov/exhibits/charters/declaration_transcript.html.

Chapter 10

The Racialization of Mathematics Education

Joi A. Spencer and Victoria M. Hand

This chapter examines the racialization of mathematics education within the context of U.S. K-12 education. While it is widely acknowledged that mathematics education houses chronic disparities between groups of students from more- versus less-dominant racial, ethnic, and linguistic groups, fewer stories are told about the role of mathematics education in creating and fueling these disparities.[1] The grand narrative of black failure and white success is told without regard to the realities of racism, which shape the experiences of both black and white (and all students) in U.S. society. We argue that the same way in which whiteness affords those identified as white with "material and nonmaterial" benefits,[2] the experiences of those identified as black are shaped by entrenched notions of racial hierarchy and inferiority.[3] As a result, mathematics education is a profoundly racialized experience in students' lives.[4] Increasingly, the processes and structures that play a role in students' racialized experiences have been under investigation in the field of mathematics.[5] The argument we develop in this chapter is developed from this work and our experiences as mathematics education researchers. Here, we set out to illustrate how the process of racialization gets constructed from the ground up—in moments of classroom life, within the schools in which those classrooms are situated, and within the structures and systems which constitute those schools.

As other chapters in this book have detailed, racism is a reality of American education. In the case of the American public school, it is both its inheritance and its living wage. The historical realities of racism, which allowed whites but denied blacks the right to acquire property, receive inheritances, work for a wage, and to have legal protection of these (property, inheritance, and wages), help to explain the expansive differences in wealth that we see in the United States today. Those benefits did not simply accrue to whites in a tiny snapshot of time. Rather the arrangement ensued for centuries both during and after African American enslavement. As professors of mathematics education, we argue that mathematics education has played a crucial role in the perpetuation of economic benefits to whites and of deficit perspectives of African American and other racial/ethnic communities.

Racism's wages are not only material. They are reconstituted in the stories that are told. These narratives work to reinforce and even justify those material advantages, rendering them normal and natural. Mathematics unlike any of the other school subjects is uniquely poised to reinforce the story that racism tells. Racism tells a story that human beings are divided into groups based on phenotypic features and that these groupings are hierarchically arranged. Racism both posits that there are biological differences and then assigns differing value to those differences. Both lies are reified through an intricate, and largely sanctioned, system of stories and practices.

One such story relates to intelligence. Mathematical thought has come to be seen as the apex of that intelligence. Western man has been constituted through powerful stories about the nature of knowledge. Western knowing is logical versus intuitive, methodological (scientific) versus episodic, and universal versus local. The very idea of intelligence is tied to these notions of Western knowing. Standardized examinations of intelligence (modern IQ tests) serve to reinforce them. Mathematics and the practices of mathematics fit nicely to support these notions of Western man. Mathematics is a systematic science designed for generalizability. As we will describe, the idea of Western man, intellectual superiority, and mathematics converge. Children who perform well in mathematics, then, are defined as intellectually superior and mathematical and are often white and male. As educational resources are doled out unevenly, those with greater access to (quality) mathematics instruction and opportunities (beliefs about their inherent intellectual gifts) produce higher mathematical test scores—reinforcing the story of racism.

Through the tireless efforts of researchers like Danny Martin, the role of the system of mathematics education in heightening experiences of racialization among groups of children is becoming widely accepted in the field of mathematics education.[6] A primary reason for this is the recognition that mathematics carried out in school is a particular type of cultural activity that was produced within cultural communities and that mathematics classrooms themselves function as cultural communities. In other words, the field is beginning to recognize that mathematics teaching and learning *necessarily* involve issues of race, culture, and power and that the stories perpetuated by mathematics education about the intelligence of whites on one end versus African Americans on the opposite end were (and continue to be) cultural constructions.

We examine the relation of mathematics education to issues of race, culture, and power and describe how features of what we call *school mathematical practices* are related to the perpetuation of racism in society. This work is the result of conversations, research, and imaginings with colleagues as members of the Diversity in Mathematics Education Center for Learning and Teaching. We note that while we use the term "we" throughout the chapter, as individuals we have different experience with and perspectives on mathematics education. Spencer comes from an urban, low-income, working-class African American family. As a public school student, she saw firsthand the highly racialized system of mathematics-course tracking. These experiences shaped her work as a middle school mathematics teacher and her current work as a mathematics teacher educator. Hand is a white female from an upper-middle-class family. She has studied children's mathematics learning in both formal and informal environments, including in middle and high school classrooms. The litmus test for the validity of this chapter is the felt experiences of African American students and communities, as well as our experiences as mathematics education researchers and teacher educators.[7]

Equity, Accumulated Advantages, and Invisible Racism

Before we move forward, it is important to define some terminology. Equity is an important concept for educators. It is most often juxtaposed with the term "equality." While equality is concerned with sameness, equity is concerned with fairness. If a tornados strike two towns, leveling one and causing minor damage in the other, equality would give both towns the same amount of help. However, equity would provide more resources to the town that was leveled, recognizing that it needed more help to be restored. Extending the analogy, if in one town residential areas were hit hardest, while in the other town infrastructure such as highways were hardest hit, equality would provide both towns with the exact same kind of aid. It would ignore the different needs. On the other hand, aid workers operating from an equity frame would provide the towns with the specific kinds of support they needed to regain their normalcy.

While the preceding town analogies are a good way to begin our understanding of equity, we must caution that they are merely analogies. They do not relay the complexities involved with achieving equity in social systems. In the case of schools, for example, differences/disadvantages/damages are not always material. In the case of two students where one comes from a household where multiple generations have advanced graduate degrees and the other will be the first in his or her family to complete high school, we cannot simply hand the latter student a bag of "generations of college attendance." Such a bag would need to contain the decades of formal and informal networks, the social positions, and the power, as well as the wealth resulting from the degrees obtained over multiple generations of the former student's family.

Racism, then, can most easily be understood as those *accumulated advantages*.[8] Being able to own property, operate a business, accumulate wealth from one's labor, and have one's rights and wealth legally protected are all historic advantages that whites had in the United States. We can add to this list the psychological advantages that racism bestowed on whites, such as an assurance of safety and personhood, individual fulfillment via being able to pursue one's curiosities and passions, and living in a society where one's cultural practices, physical features, and ways of being were seen as normal (and even superior) to others. Those historic benefits of being white have not disappeared. While it is no longer legal to deny blacks the right to own property, the accumulated wealth that whites have garnered by their historic acquisitions remains. In the context of education, this wealth matters greatly and manifests itself in the kinds of schools white children have access to, the salaries teachers in those communities can expect to receive, and the learning opportunities afforded to those students.

Perhaps equal to if not greater than these material advantages are the nonmaterial ones. For example, a high school district serving a majority of white students automatically offers very few low-level mathematics courses. White students learn mathematics from teachers (the majority of whom are white) who see their cultural practices, language, and communities as normal. The mathematics examples used in classrooms draw on the lives and experiences of whites. White students get to experience built-in mathematics role models in the form of their mathematics teachers. White students get to learn mathematics from teachers who assume that they are intelligent and come from an educated and concerned family. One can imagine a vastly different scenario. A high school district serving mostly African American students offers mostly low-level mathematics courses and only a few high-level ones. Black students learn mathematics from teachers who see their cultural practices, language, and communities as deficient. The mathematics examples used in classrooms do not draw on the lives or experiences of African Americans. With very few black mathematics teachers, African American students do not experience built-in mathematics role modeling. Black students may or may not learn from teachers who assume that they are intelligent and that they come from an educated and concerned family. These advantages and disadvantages—this racism—operate in virtual invisibility in mathematics classrooms, in schools, and in U.S. society. In his now classic 1947 work Ralph Ellison wrote, "I am an invisible man. No I am not a spook like those who haunted Edgar Allan Poe; nor am one of your Hollywood ectoplasms. I am a man of substance, of flesh and bone, fiber and liquids-and I might even be said to possess a mind. I am invisible, understand, simply because people refuse to see me."9

The invisible racism of which Ellison and others have spoken helps to explain why despite the dismantling of legalized discrimination, deep patterns of racial inequity persist. Invisible racism is a super and subconscious reality in U.S. society and persists despite the average citizen's belief that he or she is not racist. Examining this notion, the vast majority of U.S. teachers, principals, and school personnel would never use the N-word toward a student, sit all of their black students at the back of their classroom, or implement a policy where black students received only the most outdated textbooks. Each one of these acts would be considered racist. However, thousands of teachers and principals operate in schools where black students receive inadequate academic preparation, receive mathematics lessons with low cognitive demand, are overlooked for gifted testing, and are rarely enrolled in honors or Advanced Placement mathematics courses. These practices continue virtually uncontested. This is because racism is etched into our norms, ideations, and projections. It helps to explain both what we do and, as Ellison declares, what we *refuse* to see.

Here, we examine how invisible racism functions through a particular aspect of the system of mathematics education to afford disproportionate access to material and psychological resources for educational success.

Invisible Racism Operating through School Mathematical Practices

Invisible racism is perpetuated through the system of mathematics education in large part due to a lack of recognition of the relation between current practices and broader cultural and historical processes. In this section we illustrate how the characteristics of what we call *school mathematical practices* are shaped by (and shape) sociohistorical processes and have implications for the experiences of racialization of students, their families, and society writ large.

School mathematical practices are particular types of cultural practices that involve learning mathematics in school. Cultural practices such as this are orchestrated by individuals in their moment-to-moment social activity as individuals embody particular roles, expectations, and values in pursuing personal and collective goals.[10] In the mathematics classroom, this involves the teacher and students engaging in activities that they take to be learning mathematics. This moment-to-moment activity is necessarily shaped by cultural expectations, norms, structures, and systems of meanings functioning at broader scales, which are ultimately linked to those of particular ethnic and racial communities.[11] For example, there is often an assumption that students' achievement in school is a direct result of their level of effort. This story of motivation and achievement functions in classrooms to provide categories for students ("motivated," "lazy"), and is also an aspect of white privilege, in which the accumulated (dis)advantages of nonwhite communities are not made explicit. Individuals respond to expectations and meanings at these broader scales as they engage in local cultural practices that have become routine and transparent over time.[12] This means that as individuals go about their daily lives, they are involved in producing and re-producing culture, privilege, marginalization, and racism. We are not generally aware, however, of the minute and mundane ways that we perpetuate racism, since cultural practices are highly interconnected and interwoven into the fabric of our everyday lives.

This perspective on racism—as remade in daily life through cultural practices, instead of contained in specific acts and structures—is central to the racialization of mathematics education. Forms of mathematical knowing and reasoning that are common in school are embedded in cultural practices, and these practices can be traced to particular racial and ethnic communities. In the sections that follow, we outline four features of school mathematical practices that distinguish them from other forms of mathematical activity and that perpetuate systemic inequality for white and black students.

Feature 1: School Mathematics Practices Were Produced Largely within White Communities

Historically, school mathematical practices have been tied to social and cultural communities comprised of mathematicians, scientists, and mathematics teachers. Statistically, these communities comprise individuals from white, middle to upper-class backgrounds. Mathematics that has been developed for centuries by communities around the world is largely missing from school mathematics curricula. Instead, the cultural practices of school mathematics (which includes use of tools such as textbooks) have been modeled after ways of communicating and reasoning mathematically, and of organizing social relations in ways that reflect the practices of whites in Western nations who have had the opportunity to attend college and were largely successful in mathematics. These practices reflect a set of value hierarchies organized in these communities about what is powerful, perceptive, legitimate, and virtuous activity in the world.

Since school mathematical practices are tied to middle- and upper-class white communities, children from these communities have greater access to preschool and informal familial and communal practices that prepare them for elementary school mathematics. This is not to say that these children possess a greater *understanding* of mathematical concepts, rather that they have learned mathematical procedures and ways of reasoning that are privileged in school. These accumulated advantages with respect to school mathematical practices make the playing field unequal at a very young age. While this is true for most school subjects, the features described in the subsequent sections serve to exacerbate these early disparities in mathematics education.

Feature 2: School Mathematical Practices Draw from Stereotypical Views of Mathematical Activity and Are Treated as Isolated from Other Cultural and Social Activities

When asked to draw a picture of someone who does science or mathematics, children often sketch a white man working alone with lab equipment or on complex mathematical formulas and laws.[13] This image of mathematicians as white, male, and isolated forms as early as elementary school among children of all different racial backgrounds and undergirds the assumption that mathematics is a part of white communities. This image also reinforces the idea that in comparison to most school subjects, which involve perspective, judgment, and interpretation, mathematics is cut and dry. The mathematics that students learn in school is "beyond debate," since it was discovered or invented by mathematicians long ago and can be repeatedly proved through logical thinking processes. As a result, mathematical concepts, principles, procedures, and solutions are taken to be self-evident, meaning that they can be arrived at through processes that do not depend on cultural perspectives or values. Children who demonstrate prowess in mathematics are viewed as having a genetic predisposition for logical-mathematical reasoning. The relation of children's natural giftedness in logical reasoning to their membership in white communities is unmarked.

While mathematical reasoning draws heavily on logical deduction and the manipulation of symbolic notation, mathematics is also an applied, creative, and intuitive activity that involves actively mathematizing the world.[14] Numerous professional communities develop and produce mathematics in the process of carrying out tasks and solving problems (e.g., engineers, artists, economists). More important, human beings engage in creative mathematical activity in their routines of everyday life.[15] This mathematical activity is shaped by the context that we find ourselves in (e.g., a grocery store versus basketball practice), the tools available to us for carrying out mathematical process, and our goals. We don't even recognize that we are doing mathematics because it simply becomes a tool in service of a broader goal. Thus, mathematical activity is first and foremost social and cultural activity, and many of the mathematical concepts addressed from kindergarten through high school become familiar to us first outside of school.

To treat mathematicians as independent from a professional community is also unwarranted and assigns them a position of privilege in society. Even when working alone, mathematicians are continually building off of each other's ideas and communicating their findings to a broader community. The community of mathematicians functions like any other community, in that it develops, engages in, and is constantly changing a set of practices and norms for carrying out its activities. These norms and practices reflect certain values and perspectives about the world, which are derived in cultural and racial communities. While all professional communities have ties to racial and cultural communities, as mentioned earlier, the community of mathematicians has largely remained white and male. Thus, these links remain strong. To situate judgments about the validity of mathematical practices solely with this elite community, then, without interrogating the relation of the practices valued by this community to those of particular cultural and ethnic communities is problematic.

These narrow images of mathematics, who can do it, and what does and does not count as legitimate mathematical activity support a perspective of *mathematics learning* as a straightforward and individual process, in which a select group of students can reason deductively until arriving at a correct solution. Stories of mathematical ability as based in genetics (of white communities) and of mathematical activity as an individual process based solely on logical thinking processes have made mathematics education an ideal candidate for the functioning of invisible racism.

Feature 3: Learning Mathematics in School Is Equated with the Memorization of Abstract Mathematical Procedures

Following from the perspectives of mathematics described earlier, school mathematical practices tend to be organized around individual seatwork, in which students commit to memory a set of procedures and apply them to large problem sets. This is in contrast to the preponderance of research that indicates that productive mathematics learning involves actively making sense of mathematical concepts and procedures and the connections between them.[16] Engaging students in rich conversations around multifaceted mathematics problems in which they are asked to explain, justify, and critique mathematical ideas with each other not only promotes deeper learning but also enables a greater range of students to perceive themselves as capable of doing mathematics.[17] The recently adopted Common Core Standards for K-12 mathematics builds on this research through standards for mathematical content and classroom practices.[18] Yet school mathematical practices have remained largely stagnant over the past 20 years, despite the efforts of mathematics teachers, mathematics teacher educators, and administrators to initiate this and other reforms. This situation holds true particularly for African American students in low-income schools that do not have the accumulated advantages required to support reform efforts like the Common Core.

Feature 4: School Mathematical Practices Afford the Use of Measurable and Quantifiable Test Questions

The fact that mathematics is viewed as primarily dependent on logical processes and that mathematics classrooms tend to be organized around the memorization and recall of mathematics facts and procedures has made mathematics a prime subject for the application of standardized assessments. Generally, students are taught to solve mathematics problems using the specific procedures authorized (by the teacher or textbook) for the problems. Thus, if a child reaches a correct answer on a test, it can be assumed that the child has applied a proper procedure to solve the problem. This means that it is unnecessary to evaluate the student's reasoning process: the solution stands on its own. Situations like this, in which a child's response to a multiple-choice question is assumed to directly and accurately measure the skill or understanding being assessed, lends itself to the use of standardized assessments. Unlike in other subjects, in which there is accommodation for misinterpretations of a question or problem, or for different forms of reasoning, school mathematical practices support a perspective of mathematical solutions as unequivocal. Since the solutions are decisive, and the scores are treated as an accurate representation of mathematical ability, they can be used to compare children's capacity for logical thinking processes.

We have shown, however, that to a certain degree what is being measured by standardized tests is a child's ability to participate in the practices of school mathematics. As described earlier, the practices of school mathematics are linked to a particular vision of mathematics, to the community of mathematicians, and, ultimately, to white communities. Given this scenario, it makes sense for there to be a significant gap in the scores on standardized tests of achievement between white and black students. Black, Latino and students from other less-dominant racial and ethnic backgrounds are being compared to their white peers based on a system that privileges whites. By definition, then, mathematics education is a system of white privilege.

It is important to emphasize the word "system" in our argument. The features of school mathematical practices are interrelated and mutually dependent. Because of this, we do not lay blame for the racialization of mathematics education with a particular community, practice, or idea. For many years, mathematicians have attempted to diversify their community to invite more women and groups from less-dominant ethnic and racial backgrounds. These efforts have largely failed, we argue, in part due the invisible racism that pervades K-12 mathematics education. As mathematics education researchers, we also understand the importance of disciplinary research informing practice and policy. However, taking a sociocultural perspective on education means that we cannot separate disciplinary ideas from how they play out in classrooms and educational contexts. We view the recent turn in educational research toward a model of practice–research partnerships, in which researchers work alongside practitioners, policy makers, and community leaders to address our children's educational experiences to be a step in the right direction.[19] Research–practice partnerships in mathematics education, in particular, must attend to the role of broader contexts, historical structures, and current practices in shaping opportunities to learn mathematics for different groups of students.

Implications of the Invisible Racism of School Mathematics

The implications of school mathematical practices for the perpetuation of privilege and oppression in society are numerous. Here, we focus primarily on ramifications for the views of intelligence, the practice of tracking, and identities of white and black children as capable human beings.

First, the stories of mathematical ability as based in genetics and of mathematical activity as the definitive act of rational thinking have made mathematics a proxy for the measurement of general intelligence. The shape of the curve generated by scores of standardized exams of mathematics can be mapped onto a bell curve of intelligence, whereby the individuals in the lower quartiles (black and brown) are perceived to be less naturally gifted than individuals in the upper quartiles (white and Asian).[20] The dual mappings play into societal stereotypes about which racial and ethnic groups are more intelligent than others. This mapping is also reinforced by a view of intelligence as a singular, fixed trait (versus malleable and multifaceted components of a complex system), which again can be easily correlated with another heritable trait: skin color. When viewed as proxies for intelligence, scores on high-stakes mathematics assessments can also serve as objective and indirect assessments of students' potential in and beyond college. This is a primary means through which learning mathematics in school becomes a racialized experience for students. As white and Asian children continually receive higher scores on the tests than their African American, Latino, and Native American peers, and these scores are treated as indicators of ability and college readiness, mathematics education fuels societal privilege and oppression along racial lines.

Students' scores on math tests are also a key means of sorting and differentiating students into different academic groupings in school. We are referring here to the practice of tracking, in which students are distributed across different levels of a subject area based on educational achievement and "promise." There has been a tendency for schools to use mathematics scores (and fluency in the English language) as the primary mechanism for tracking their students. Formal tracking begins around middle school, when students are placed into pre-algebra or algebra around eighth grade. (Note that as Western nations push through standards for all students to take algebra while in middle school, formal tracking occurs before eighth grade.)

The informal practice of tracking starts much earlier, when students are placed into ability groups in their elementary school classrooms. On the face of it, teachers employ tracking to differentiate the curriculum for their learners. Research indicates, however, that students are often "stuck" in tracks that preclude college preparatory courses, and that tracking tends to fall along ethnic and racial lines.[21] The result of early tracking is that black students have less access than whites to mathematical understandings that are critical to algebra learning in middle school and, as a result, are not able to take the math courses required for college entrance.[22] In other words, tracking inhibits the opportunities to learn of black and brown students.

In addition, because mathematical intelligence is viewed as a reasonable measure of intelligence, success and opportunities in school mathematics are guarded vigorously. Researchers have documented situations in which upper-middle-class parents fight for their children to be placed in the highest mathematics tracks as early as elementary school and will attempt to dismantle efforts to detrack mathematics courses. Jeannie Oakes and colleagues have documented the struggles of schools and districts to detrack their courses and provide the same high-level curriculum across all student groups.[23] Time and again these efforts are thwarted when more privileged parents insist that their students (based on test scores or other measures) should receive additional services and opportunities. Studies also show that holding grades and test scores constant, white students were still more likely to be placed in higher-tracked mathematics courses.[24] Many of these placements were based on informal means—such as a parent's request or teachers' judgments about students' behavior.

Tracking and surveillance of school mathematical practices, together with the perception of mathematical capacity as a measure of general intelligence, has had profound implications for the perspectives of black students and communities about their capacity as humans. Not only do students' identities as mathematics learners shape their achievement and persistence in school mathematics, and vice versa, but mathematics achievement shapes students' perspectives of themselves as mathematics learners (and tacitly, we argue, intelligent human beings).[25] Reconciling one's racial identity with an identity as a mathematical learner can have deeply negative connotations for black students.[26] The negative perceptions and hidden stereotypes that follow from participating in school mathematical practices and the achievement gap based on race and ethnicity wreak havoc with the identities that black and brown students are developing on a daily basis in mathematics classrooms. Again, the relation of school mathematical practices to particular social and cultural communities remains hidden, leading groups of students to attribute their success or failure to (in)ability, (lack of) effort, and membership in a particular racial group.

Not only do these narratives and discourses shape how black and brown students see themselves, but they also shape how they are seen by those in charge of educating them: their mathematics teachers. Na'ilah Nasir and Niral Shah's 2011 research with African American male mathematics students demonstrated the following: (1) These students were aware of the narrative that cast black students as bad in math and Asian students as good in math; (2) acknowledging this stereotype, black students routinely pushed against it—providing counter-stances and narratives; and (3) these students had to contend against the narratives that teachers held about them as young black males (i.e., juvenile delinquent and class clown).[27] Nasir and Shah conclude that their data "suggest that African American students do not typically have a choice to simply ignore these issues, as their awareness of the narratives means that the narratives are salient artifacts within the classroom space that may be deployed against them in some way, usually to position them in ways detrimental to learning. . . . The young men and boys that we interviewed were, thus, not simply aware of racialized narratives about school and math performance; they found themselves regularly needing to respond to these narratives. . . . As educators, and as a society, we cannot underestimate the burden such negotiation places on student."[28]

In the sections that follow, we explore how school mathematical practices play out in the activities of teachers and students in the mathematics classroom. Likewise, we examine how classroom mathematical activity serves to reinforce broader structures and policies through which school mathematical practices flourish.

School Mathematical Practices within the Mathematics Classroom

Mathematics classrooms tend to be places where students become easily sorted and categorized into competent and incompetent members and in which students have little opportunity to contest this system of meaning. Categorization occurs along the lines of students who are "smart" and "motivated," versus "lazy" and "slow."[29] Why is categorization a prominent feature of math classrooms versus other classrooms? It stems from the perspective of mathematics as a straightforward process of achieving the correct answer in as little time as possible. In this way, either you "get" the answer (and over time, mathematics) or you don't, and the time it takes you to do so correlates directly with your natural talent. The "mathematically intelligent" students quickly stand out, since they respond to the teacher's questions quickly and accurately and receive high marks on their tests. As a result, mathematics classrooms tend to have fixed and highly visible hierarchies of intelligence, or what have been called *classroom status hierarchies*.[30] Status hierarchies in mathematics classrooms generally follow racial and ethnic lines, reifying the perspective of intelligence as differentially distributed along the racial lines of students. Why are the classroom and societal hierarchies aligned? The reasons partially reside in the confluence of characteristics of mathematics described in the previous section. The early socialization in ways of reasoning about and communicating about the world (and mathematics) that takes place before and during preschool means that white children enter elementary school with forms of participation that are aligned with those valued in school. These school discourse practices favored white and Asian students in all school subjects. However, a very strict version of these discourse practices (focused on logical and abstract reasoning versus telling interesting stories or making sense of phenomenon in the world) is the only one valued and counted in mathematics classrooms and rehearsed by white students at a very early age. Thus, groups of children quickly become stratified into these hierarchies and generally remain there.

Another factor is the heavy emphasis on classroom management, which follows from a perception of doing mathematics as largely dependent on logical thinking skills. This means that all other forms of activity are treated as detrimental to students' learning, and it is easy to distinguish the off-task activities from pure logical thought. This misreading of mathematics learning means that African American children who are expected to become socialized into the practices of white communities and who are pushing against this socialization and negative stereotypes about their communities can appear distracted, off-task, and/or oppositional.[31] This early labeling feeds into tracking systems, through which children who have behavior issues are sorted into lower-track math classes and are eventually taken off of the college track. Being placed in a low track early in a student's educational career also has a negative impact on the student's self-efficacy and confidence in schooling broadly.

We have described how features of school mathematical practices perpetuate invisible racism and how they are cultivated in and through classroom mathematical activity. As mathematics educators, we are not arguing that the development of school mathematical practices in this way was intentional. Rather, we are arguing that mathematics as a domain and as embedded in the cultural practices of schools easily lends itself to the racialization of mathematics education. This focus on school mathematics learning as a cultural practice demonstrates that our system is not "neutral" or "natural." It is incumbent upon us, then, to expose this hidden system of racism and to challenge the stories and perspectives that fuel it.

"First 15" Mathematics in Under-resourced, Hyper-segregated Schools

We have spent considerable time in mathematics classrooms that serve African American and Latino students from poor, low-income, and working-class families. Many of the students are the children of immigrants. Others live in foster care, have parents who are incarcerated, and experience at least some degree of uncertainty related to meals and shelter. It is not our intention to present a deficit view of these communities. Like all other places in America, these communities want the best for their kids.

We have noticed that there are certain beliefs (and stances), however, that teachers and school administrations often take toward children and families in these communities. This stance is clear when one visits the front office, and it is often clear when one visits mathematics classrooms. The mathematics presented in these classrooms is often of an inferior caliber—both in content (what gets taught) and in pedagogy (how students are engaged in what gets taught). Joi Spencer has characterized the mathematics problems that students in these classrooms work on as "first 15" problems.[32] Those who have worked from a typical mathematics textbook will recall that the first 15 or so problems at the end of a chapter or unit are designed to give students practice on the most basic ideas in that unit or chapter. These basic problems can be completed without much struggle. When you venture beyond these initial tasks, however, you are challenged to demonstrate a much greater depth of mathematical knowledge and skill. Tasks beyond the first 15 are more likely to be aligned with the Common Core and other reforms, in that they push students to work with multiple concepts simultaneously, to demonstrate knowledge of mathematical rules as well as cases when those rules operate differently, to justify their solutions, and to consider the mathematical dilemmas of scientists, engineers, economists, and mathematicians. In hyper-segregated, under-resourced classrooms, students very rarely have an opportunity to work on these latter problems. Undoubtedly one of the reasons that African American and Latino students fare worse on standardized mathematics exams than white and Asian students is the kind of mathematics problems they are (and are not) presented with in their classrooms. As such, first 15 problems serve to underprepare and underdevelop these students in mathematics.

First 15 problems diminish student interest in mathematics. Because mathematics is presented in such anemic ways—as mere steps to follow, these students do not see the richness or purposefulness of the subject. Teachers might believe that giving students complex mathematics tasks (such as those found after number 15) will scare them away. On the converse, not allowing them to see the richness of mathematics, students become disengaged, lowering their participation in the subject. As students participate less and less, they actually learn less mathematics. As they learn less and achieve less, their opportunities to engage in rich mathematics get cut off through an insidious system of tracking. In predominantly black and Latino schools, tracking manifests itself in a preponderance of low-level mathematics course offerings. In predominantly white and Asian schools (where black, Latino, and Native American students are in the minority), mathematical course enrollments fall along racial lines. In both scenarios, low-tracked, low-level mathematics courses are almost impossible to emerge from—setting up students for few to no future mathematics and STEM opportunities.

First 15 problems also impact the relationship that students develop toward mathematics. Researcher Jane Margolis and colleagues compared technology courses in schools serving a majority of low-income students of color to those in middle-class white schools. Their findings revealed much of what we see in the mathematics education world.[33] Students in the former schools were offered courses in typing and word processing, while students in the latter were offered computer science courses. The authors demonstrated how schools' course offerings positioned students differently to technology. The students of color were positioned as consumers and users of technology, while the white and Asian students were positioned as its creators. Mathematics classrooms often re-create this same dynamic. They do not question mathematics, engage with it, banter with their teachers about, or even consider its purpose in the world. They simply follow its steps and obey its rules. The kind of instruction that these students receive, then, assures them that (1) mathematics cannot be questioned, and (2) were it ever to be questioned, it would be done so by someone other than himself or herself. This positioning matters, because doing well in school is as much about how one performs as how one sees oneself in relation to the subject being learned. The powerful messaging embedded in our current system of mathematics education conveys to many white and Asian students that they are the thinkers, explorers, and conquerors—that mathematics belongs to them.

Low-quality instruction, with few opportunities to develop mathematical skill, think deeply about mathematics, engage with others in sense making, and to acquire a sense of ownership, does not engender successful, resilient, and competitive students. This kind of instruction is normative and invisible in schools serving students of color. Few question it, and many do not even recognize that it is present. This instruction is maintained through discourses (these kinds of students are not capable of doing such rigorous mathematical work) and practices (we do not offer AP calculus here because there has never been much interest in it).

In an effort to close the gap between the mathematics achievement of its black and Latino students on the one hand and white and Asian students on the other, The Rockville Centre School District in Long Island, New York, took definitive steps against watered-down first 15-type mathematics education.[34] Beginning with their middle schools, all mathematics courses were detracked and infused with an accelerated curriculum. Unlike in previous years where only the highest-achieving students were allowed to take accelerated mathematics courses, all middle schoolers in the district took the same mathematics courses and all courses included the accelerated curriculum. The results of this new arrangement astounded the district. In previous years, merely 23 percent of regular education African American and Latino students passed the algebra-based regents exam in mathematics. After the new program, 75 percent of these students passed the exam. This program benefited white and Asian regular education students as well, helping to raise their passing rate from 54 percent to 95 percent. By the time that the first cohort of detracked and accelerated students graduated from senior high school, 82 percent of all African American or Hispanic and 97 percent of all white or Asian students earned the regents diploma.

Providing a high-quality, engaging, and rigorous mathematics education to all children is possible. Such a provision can open up new identities as well as opportunities for students of color. Reform mathematics alone, though, will not do away with the inequities that we see in mathematics education. Just as the high hopes accompanying the *Brown v. Board of Education* decision were diminished through institutionalized, invisible racism, inequity must be addressed on numerous fronts. While studies like the one mentioned have shown that changes to mathematics instruction and tracking practices can narrow the gap, the long history of disenfranchisement among African American, Latino, and other less-dominant racial and ethnic groups in mathematics education cannot be erased. Further research is needed to understand how this invisible system operates and can be dismantled at all levels of the mathematics education system.

Conclusion

The importance of mathematics education is rarely up for debate. The United States continually emphasizes this importance, the need for more mathematics teachers, and a greater focus on math and science education. Initiatives like Race to the Top, for example, center around STEM education[35] and politicians from both the left and right promote its centrality to the nation's overall success. It is difficult to untangle mathematics education out of current STEM fervor. However, as mathematics educators we feel it is critical to challenge its preeminence in society and to lay bare its function in diminishing and dehumanizing black and brown communities. Because mathematics is currently the measure of intelligence, communities of people that hold mathematics knowledge have an unwarranted position of authority over those communities that do not.

Moving the entire nation toward greater mathematics achievement will be a function of truth telling in relation to why so few students of color currently achieve in mathematics. To begin with, the racism that exists in society, schools, and classrooms must be brought out of its shadows. Mathematics achievement is rarely won on a level playing field. Notions of a racial hierarchy in relation to intelligence in general and mathematics intelligence specifically shape which groups of students receive the opportunity to learn mathematics, get positioned as smart, and which ones succeed. It does not take a mathematician to realize such inequities and to find them unacceptable.

Notes

1. Martin 2013.
2. Tatum 1997.
3. Martin 2009b.
4. Ladson-Billings 1997; Martin 2009b, 2003; Nasir 2011.

5. D'Ambrosio et al. 2013; DiME 2007; Gutiérrez 2013; Martin 2009a; Nasir 2011; Secada, Fennema, and Byrd Adajian 1995; Tate 1994; Stinson 2006.

6. D'Ambrosio et al. 2013; DiME 2007; Martin 2009b.

7. Our focus on African American students is intentional. Historically blacks and whites have been cast as racial binaries, with whites possessing positive and blacks negative attributes. Blacks in U.S. society experience persistently high rates of incarceration, unemployment, and overall low school success, which we identify as evidence of their racial positioning in U.S. society. The positioning of peoples based on skin color is not unique to the United States as peoples with deep skin tones almost worldwide experience societal marginalization. Our decision to focus on African Americans, then, is intended to help the reader consider the case of students of color in general. It is in no way meant to discount the experiences of Native, Mexican American, Puerto Rican, Chinese, Japanese, and countless other groups who have and/or currently do suffer from the impact of racism in schools.

8. Brown et al. 2003; Tatum 2003.

9. Ellison 1952, prologue, p. 3.

10. Lave 1988; Vygotsky 1978; Wertsch 1998.

11. Gutiérrez and Rogoff 2003.

12. Hand, Penuel, and Gutiérrez 2012.

13. Chambers 1983; de Abreu 1995; de Abreu and Cline 2003.

14. Freudenthal 1973.

15. Rogoff and Lave 1984.

16. Boaler 1997; Bransford, Brown, and Cocking 1999; National Council for Teachers of Mathematics (NCTM) 2000.

17. Boaler and Staples 2008.

18. The Common Core State Standards Initiative, http://whttp://www.corestan dards.orgwww.corestandards.org.

19. Gutiérrez and Penuel 2014.

20. Artiles 2011.

21. Muller et al. 2010; Oakes 1990.

22. Venezia and Kirst 2005.

23. Oakes and Lipton 2002; Wells and Oakes 1996.

24. Oakes 1990.

25. Martin 2007.

26. Martin 2006.

27. Nasir and Shah 2011.

28. Ibid., pp. 41–42.

29. Horn 2007.

30. Cohen and Lotan 1997.

31. Hand 2010.

32. Spencer 2006.

33. Margolis et al. 2008.

34. Burris and Welner 2005.

35. www.ed.gov/news/press-releases/200-million-now-available-race-top-round-three.

Bibliography

Artiles, Alfredo J. 2011. "Toward an Interdisciplinary Understanding of Educational Equity and Difference the Case of the Racialization of Ability." *Educational Researcher* 40 (9): 431–445.

Boaler, Jo. 1997. *Experiencing School Mathematics: Teaching Styles, Sex, and Setting.* Philadelphia: Open University Press.

Boaler, Jo, and Megan Staples. 2008. "Creating Mathematical Futures through an Equitable Teaching Approach: The Case of Railside School." *Teachers College Record* 110 (3): 608–645.

Bransford, John, Ann L. Brown, and Rodney R. Cocking. 1999. *How People Learn: Brain, Mind, Experience, and School.* Washington, DC: National Academy Press.

Brown, Michael K, Martin Carnoy, Troy Duster, and David B Oppenheimer. 2003. *Whitewashing Race: The Myth of a Color-Blind Society.* Oakland, CA: University of California Press.

Burris, Carol Corbett, and Kevin G. Welner. 2005. "Closing the Achievement Gap by Detracking." *Phi Delta Kappan*, 594–598.

Chambers, D.W. 1983. "Stereotypic Images of the Scientists: The Draw-a-Scientist Test." *Science Education* 67 (2): 255–265.

Cohen, Elizabeth G., and Rachel A. Lotan. 1997. *Working for Equity in Heterogeneous Classrooms.* New York: Teachers College Press.

D'Ambrosio, B., Marilyn Frankenstein, Rochelle Gutiérrez, Signe Kastberg, Danny Martin, Judit Moschkovich, Edd V. Taylor, and David Barnes. 2013. "Addressing Racism." *Journal for Research in Mathematics Education* 44 (1): 23–36. doi:10.5951/jresematheduc.44.1.0023.

de Abreu, G. 1995. "Understanding How Children Experience the Relationship between Home and School Mathematics." *Mind, Culture, and Activity* 2 (2): 119–142.

de Abreu, G., and T. Cline. 2003. "Schooled Mathematics and Cultural Knowledge." *Pedagogy, Culture and Society* 1 (1): 11–30.

DiME. 2007. "Culture, Race, Power, and Mathematics Education." In *Handbook of Research on Mathematics Teaching and Learning*, ed. Frank Lester (pp. 405–434). Reston, VA: NCTM.

Ellison, R. 1952. *Invisible Man.* New York: Modern Library.

Freudenthal, Hans. 1973. *Mathematics as an Educational Task.* New York: Springer.

Gutiérrez, K., and Barbara Rogoff. 2003. "Cultural Ways of Learning: Individual Traits or Repertoires of Practice." *Educational Researcher* 32 (5): 19–25.

Gutiérrez, Kris D., and William R. Penuel. 2014. "Relevance to Practice as a Criterion for Rigor." *Educational Researcher* 43 (1): 19–23.

Gutiérrez, Rochelle. 2013. "The Sociopolitical Turn in Mathematics Education." *Journal for Research in Mathematics Education* 44 (1): 37–68.

Hand, Victoria. 2010. "The Co-construction of Opposition within a Low-Track Mathematics Classroom." *American Educational Research Journal* 47 (1): 97–132.

Hand, Victoria, William Penuel, and K. Gutiérrez. 2012. "(Re)Framing Educational Possibility: Attending to Power and Equity in Shaping Access to and within Learning Opportunities." *Human Development* 55: 250–268.

Horn, Ilana S. 2007. "Fast Kids, Slow Kids, Lazy Kids: Modeling the Mismatch Problem in Math Teachers' Conversations." *Journal of Learning Sciences* 16 (1): 37–79.

Ladson-Billings, Gloria. 1997. "It Doesn't Add Up: African American Students' Mathematics Achievement." *Journal for Research in Mathematics Education* 28 (6): 697–708.

Lave, Jean. 1988. *Cognitive in Practice: Mind, Mathematics, and Culture in Everyday Life.* Cambridge: Cambridge University Press.

Margolis, Jane, Rachel Estrella, Joanna Goode, Jennifer Jellison Holme, and Kimberly Nao. 2008. *Stuck in the Shallow End.* Cambridge MA: MIT Press.

Martin, Danny. 2003. "Hidden Assumptions and Unaddressed Questions in Mathematics for All Rhetoric." *The Mathematics Educator* 13 (2): 7–21.

Martin, Danny. 2006. "Mathematics Learning and Participation as Racialized Forms of Experience: African American Parents Speak on the Struggle for Mathematics Literacy." *Mathematical Thinking and Learning* 8: 197–229.

Martin, Danny. 2007. "Mathematics Learning and Participation in African American Context: The Co-construction of Identity in Two Intersecting Realms of Experience." In *Diversity, Equity, and Access to Mathematical Ideas*, eds. N. Nasir and Paul Cobb (pp. 146–158). New York: Teachers College Press.

Martin, Danny. 2009a. *Mathematics Teaching, Learning, and Liberation in the Lives of Black Children.* New York: Routledge.

Martin, Danny. 2009b. "Researching Race in Mathematics Education." *Teachers College Record* 111 (2): 295–338.

Martin, Danny. 2013. Race, Racial Projects, and Mathematics Education. *Journal for Research in Mathematics Education* 44 (1): 316–333.

Muller, Chandra, C. Riegle-Crumb, K.S. Schiller, L. Wilkinson, and K.A. Frank. 2010. "Race and Academic Achievement in Racially Diverse High Schools: Opportunity and Stratification." *Teachers College Record* 112: 4.

Nasir, Na'ilah Suad. 2011. *Racialized Identities: Race and Achievement among African American Youth.* Stanford, CA: Stanford University Press.

Nasir, Na'ilah Suad, and Niral Shah. 2011. "On Defense: African American Males Making Sense of Racialized Narratives in Mathematics Education." *Journal of African American Males in Education* 2 (1): 24–45.

National Council for Teachers of Mathematics (NCTM). 2000. *Principles and Standards for School Mathematics.* Reston, VA: Author.

Oakes, J. 1990. *Multiplying Inequities: The Effect of Race, Social Class, and Tracking on Opportunities to Learn Math and Science.* Santa Monica, CA: RAND.

Oakes, Jeannie, and Martin Lipton. 2002. "Struggling for Educational Equity in Diverse Communities: School Reform as Social Movement." *Journal of Educational Change* 3 (3–4): 383–406.

Rogoff, Barbara, and Jean Lave, eds. 1984. *Everyday Cognition: Its Development in Social Context.* Cambridge: Harvard University Press.

Secada, Walter G., Elizabeth Fennema, and Lisa Byrd Adajian. 1995. *New Directions for Equity in Mathematics Education.* Cambridge: Cambridge University Press.

Spencer, Joi. 2006. "Balancing the Equations: African American Students' Opportunity to Learn Mathematics with Understanding in Two Central City Schools." Unpublished doctoral dissertation, University of California at Los Angeles.

Stinson, David W. 2006. "African American Male Adolescents, Schooling (and Mathematics): Deficiency, Rejection, and Achievement." *Review of Research in Education* 76 (4): 447–506.

Tate, William F.I.V. 1994. "Race, Retrenchment, and the Reform of School Mathematics." *Phi Delta Kappan* 75: 447–485.

Tatum, Beverly Daniel. 1997. *"Why Are All of the Black Kids Sitting together in the Cafeteria?" and Other Conversations about Race.* New York: Basic Books.

Tatum, Beverly Daniel. 2003. *"Why Are All the Black Kids Sitting Together in the Cafeteria?": And Other Conversations about Race.* New York: Basic Books.

Venezia, Andera, and Michael W. Kirst. 2005. "Inequitable Opportunities: How Current Education Systems and Policies Undermine the Chances for Student Persistence and Success in College." *Educational Policy* 19 (2): 283–307.

Vygotsky, Lev Semenovich. 1978. *Mind in Society: The Development of Higher Psychological Processes.* Cambridge: Harvard University Press.

Wells, Amy Stuart, and Jeannie Oakes. 1996. "Potential Pitfalls of Systemic Reform: Early Lessons from Research on Detracking." *Sociology of Education*: 135–143.

Wertsch, James V. 1998. *Mind as Action.* New York: Oxford University.

Chapter 11

Bridging the Gap and Diversifying Teaching Education

Donald Easton-Brooks

Introduction

Historical data indicates that the schools and schooling systems have not responded effectively to the academic success of students of color. There have been a number of approaches, policies, and research on strategies designed to help students of color become more academically successful. Of these approaches, research has been clear that a greater connection or continuity between the home culture and school culture of students of color will yield greater academic success.[1] Over the past couple of decades, many preservice teachers and classroom teachers have engaged in multicultural education and culturally responsive training as a way to learn how to connect with students from various cultures. However, the issue of increasing success among students of color is still minimal. Recent research findings show that the academic success of students of color is more than connecting teachers with the home culture of students with school culture. Studies have found that when teachers of color are a part of the students' academic lives, students of color tend to perform academically better than when they are not engaged with a teacher of color.[2] However, of concern is that there is a disproportion of teachers of color to students of color in U.S. public schools. In addition, many states and public districts are becoming more and more diverse, as some districts have seen their population of color make up more than 50 percent of their total school population.

This suggestion here is not to eliminate white teachers because it cannot be assumed that having only teachers of color will magically correct the issue. However, as researchers argue, diversifying the teacher education profession can open up opportunities to discuss the challenges of connecting diverse home cultures with school cultures, as well as assisting in effective policies for promoting better school environments and academic outcomes for students of color.[3] For instance, research shows schools and teachers account for less than 10 percent of the changes in the academic outcomes of students.[4] However, Easton-Brooks et al. (2010) has also shown that if students of color have at least one experience with a teacher of color, the teacher accounts for or explains up to 17 percent of the difference in the academic performance of students of color.

In this chapter, I will first show the demographic changes facing the United States and U.S. public schools. Second I will point out the need for increasing the retention of teachers of color and present the impact of teachers of color on the academic outcomes of students of color. Next, I will show findings validating the impact of teachers of color on students of color. Then, I will address the impact of the diversity gap between teachers and students on the academic achievement of students of color. Finally, I will conclude with a summary of suggestive strategies designed to aid in diversifying U.S. public schools.

Demographic Trends in the United States

In 1980, whites made up 80 percent of the U.S. population.[5] In 2010, whites made up 64 percent of the U.S. population.[6] During this time, the African American population continues to make of 13 percent of the U.S. population, with the shift in the demographics occurring between whites, Latinos, and Asians. Further, as seen in Table 11.1, over a two-decade span, the percentage of non-white U.S. population has grown at a considerably faster rate than the white U.S. population. The largest population growth has been in the Asian/Pacific Islanders, followed by the U.S. Latino population. While

TABLE 11.1   Percentage of Change in U.S. Demographics

Population	Percentage of Increase
African American students	39
Asian/Pacific Islanders	260
Latinos	192
Native Americans	68
White	10

Source: U.S. Census 2006.

there has also been noticeable growth in the Native Americans, there has been moderate growth in the African American and white population. The U.S. Census Bureau predicts that by 2020, the U.S. ethnic minority population will increase by 32 percent, meaning that people of color will make up nearly 40 percent of the total U.S. population.

U.S. Census (2011) report concluded that between 2010 and 2050 the growing trend among people of color would continue (see Table 11.2). The report shows that the percentage of whites in the United States is expected to decrease by roughly 18 percent. It is predicted that Latinos will nearly double by 16 percent to 30 percent and the Asian population will increase by 3 percent. The report predicts only a slight increase in African Americans over the next 40 years. Likewise, the census data shows that between 1990 and 2011, there has been a noticeable increase in the birth of Latinos and Asian American populations and a decrease in the whites, African American, and Native American populations (see Table 11.3). These findings suggest that along with the ethnic shift in the U.S. population, it can be anticipated more people and students will be living in the United States and attending our schools for whom English is a second language.

TABLE 11.2   U.S. Census Population Projections (2010–2050)

Demographics	2010 (%)	2050 (%)
Non-Hispanic whites	64.7	46.3
Hispanics/Latinos (of any race)	16.0	30.2
African Americans	12.9	13.0
Asian Americans	4.6	7.8

Source: U.S. Census 2011.

TABLE 11.3   Birth Rates (1990–2011)

Ethnic Groups	1990	2011	Change (%)
White non-Hispanic	2,626,500	2,150,926	−18
African American	661,701	583,079	−12
Hispanic/Latino	595,073	912,290	+65
Asian American	141,635	253,864	+56
	39,051	46,536	−16

Source: U.S. Census 2011.

These demographic changes also have impacts on U.S. public schools. During a 10-year span between 1993 and 2003, the student of color population increased 7 percent, with Latino and Asian students representing the largest increase in history. In 2004, students of color made up 42 percent of U.S. public school enrollments; with 4 out of 10 students in U.S. schools being students of color.[7] In addition, Ingersoll and May (2011) found that between 1988 and 2008 the number of students of color in public schools increased 73 percent while white students decreased by 2 percent. It is predicted that by 2026, students of color will represent 70 percent of the public school population.

Trends in Public School Teachers' Population

While there is a need to increase the percentage of teachers of color in public schools, research shows that there has actually being an increase in the percentage of people of color going into teacher education. Research shows that students of color make up 41 percent of the elementary public population and 31 percent of the secondary schools population, with only 16 percent of public schools being staffed by teachers of color.[8] However, the nationally representative data from the Schools and Staffing Survey and the Teacher Follow-Up Survey showed that while the gap between the percentage of students of color and teachers of color exists, since the late 1980s, the number of white teachers has decreased while the number of teachers of color has increased.[9] Ingersoll and May (2011) found that while the percentage of white teachers increased 41 percent, the percentage of teachers of color increased 96 percent. These findings show that the growth in the percentage of teachers of color has more than doubled the growth in white teachers. This increase can be attributed to programs such as Teach for America, the New Teacher Project-Fellowship Program, the Urban Teacher Enhancement Program, the North Carolina Teaching Fellows Scholarship Program, and Teacher Tomorrow in Oakland. Findings found that more than a quarter of African American and Latino teachers come through alternative licensure programs, compared to 11 percent of white teachers.[10]

Ingersoll and May (2011) also show that since the 1980s, the percentage growth in teachers of color has been greater than the growth of students of color. While these findings show that there is a notable increase in the percentage of teachers of color over the two decades, teachers of color are only 16 percent of the public school teaching population. Therefore, the gap between students and teachers of color is still considerably large. These findings do also vary by ethnic groups. For instance, prior to 1978, African American teachers represented 12 percent of the field. In 2011, African American teachers made up 7 percent of the teacher education population.[11]

As teachers of color engage in the field, research shows that these teachers respond to education somewhat different than their white counterparts. Studies show that teachers of color are primarily employed in public schools serving high-poverty, high student of color, and urban student populations.[12] Further, teachers of color are nearly three times more likely than white teachers to work in schools with students from families and communities with high stress factors. In turn, white teachers are more likely to leave schools with a higher percentage of students of color when these schools have high poverty or are in urban communities. These findings show that teachers of color are more willing to engage with those students of color from communities in which there might be a higher percentage of students who are not performing well academically.

However, while teachers of color are entering the field of education at a higher rate that white teachers, Ingersoll and May (2011) found that over the past 20 years, teachers of color transferred from school to school or left the profession at statistically significant higher rate than their white counterparts. The gap in the turnover rate has grown over a 20-year span. For instance, in 1988, there was a 0.7 percent difference in the turnover rate between teachers of color and white teachers. In three academic years (1994–1995, 2004–2005, and 2008–2009), there was a 3 percent to 4 percent difference in the turnover rate between teachers of color and white teachers. Salary could be one of the contributing factors to transfers and turnover, as Boser (2011) found that more than 50 percent of African American (63%) and Latino (54%) teachers were not satisfied with their pay, while less than 50 percent white (48%) teachers were not satisfied with their pay.

Given that teachers of color are often more employed in high-needs schools, factors such as classroom resources and professional development opportunities had little to do with these teachers leaving the classroom. While Ingersoll and May (2011) found that 35 percent of the teachers of color who left the profession return, they found that these teachers' feelings on their ability to make decision and the degree to which these teachers felt they were in control of their instruction were the most influential factors for why teachers of color leave the field. These findings suggest that when inputs of teachers of color are valued, these teachers tend to stay in the classroom. The pressing point of these findings is that teachers of color are teaching in schools with higher populations of students of color in high-challenging schools. This desire to teach in these schools may come from their desire to impact the change in the lives of students of color.[13] However, what these teachers may be finding is that standardized test outweighs the need for connecting with students on a more cultural and civil level. Given their engagement with high-needs schools, teachers of color are less satisfied with the way their school was run in comparison to white teachers.[14]

The findings presented in this section show that despite the gap between teachers and students of color, the effort to graduate and recruit teachers of color is greater than that in previous decades. However, it seems that keeping or retaining teachers of color has become a new challenge. With this challenge, studies have shown that there is a tremendous need for keeping teachers of color in the field. Research findings has shown that when elementary-age students of color are engaged with at least one teacher of color, they perform higher on academic achievement tests than those students of color who have never engaged with a teacher of color.[15]

The Impact of Teachers of Color on Students of Color

Over the years researchers have shown that there is a strong association between culture and knowledge in relationship to teachers of color when linked to the teaching and instructional practice geared toward students of color.[16] The rationale here is that it is critical to understand and link instructional practices with the home culture of students and school culture.[17] Also given the similarities in culture or their relational teachers' understanding of the culture of students of color, these teachers are better able to bridge the gap between home and school cultures of these students.[18] Studies have even found that the teachers tend to evaluate the academic performance of students of their own ethnicity more favorably than students of other ethnic groups.[19] Given the disproportion of white teachers to students of color, the practice of evaluating students based on ethnic bias puts students of color at a great disadvantage.

The trend of teachers evaluating students of their own ethnicity differently can been seen in Dee's (2004) study, which shows that when a student was in the classroom with a teacher of his or her same ethnicity and gender, the student was less likely to be perceived as disruptive by the teacher. Rimm-Kaufman and Pianta (2000) found that when describing students, white teachers tend to describe students of color as having a hard time following directions, being immature, and coming from disorganized homes. Meier, Stewart, and England (1989) further described that students of color were suspended, expelled, or placed in special education classes less when they attended schools with a larger proportion of teachers of color than when they attended schools with a smaller proportion of teachers of color. The findings suggest that the perception and experience of students of color when interacting with a teacher of color are notably different than the perception and experience of students of color when interacting with white teachers. Students of color have a more positive academic experience when given the opportunity to interact with a more diverse teacher population.

Again, these findings are not meant to suggest that if schools simply hire teachers of color to work directly with students of color, then the problem with academic performance among students of color will be resolved. Rather, the findings presented here show that there is a significant connection between teachers and students of color, which can result in great academic experience for these students. As Milner (2006) proposed, researchers and educators should strive to identify the attributes held by successful teachers of color and train all teachers on how to employ those strategies when working with students of color.

Impacts of Teachers of Color on Measurable Outcomes

The findings discussed earlier present evidence that teachers of color positively impact the academic lives of students of color because of their positive perception and evaluation of these students. In turn, these students have a must richer learning experience. However, when trying to ascertain the value teachers of color have on student outcomes, policy makers typically consider only quantitative, measurable outcomes, such as standardized test scores. Over the past 10 years, research assessing the impact of teachers of color on measureable outcomes on students of color has increased and shown positive statistically significant findings. Dee's (2004) study on teachers, race, and student achievement examined the impact of black teachers on black students, and between white teachers on white students in Tennessee. Dee used longitudinal data from Tennessee's Project STAR. The data was collected on students entering kindergarten in 1985 and follow-up data was collected over the following three years. Dee examined the effects of teachers of students of their same race based on students' scores on the Stanford Achievement Tests in math and reading. The findings indicated that test scores among black and white students were higher when assigned to a teacher of their own ethnicity. The findings also showed that smaller class size, being female, and free lunch eligibility also made a difference in achievement scores of students in a classroom with a teacher of their same ethnicity.

Dee also found a statistically significant association between student/teacher of the same race and small class size, and free/reduced lunch eligibility on test scores, with scores in mathematics increasing 2.3 and reading increasing 3.1 percentile points higher when students of color are in the same classroom with teachers of their same race. Similar cross-sectional studies showed that the reading skills[20] and the mathematics achievement[21] of black students increased when a black teacher was teaching these students.

Further research by Dee suggested that black students were significantly less likely to have a teacher of their own ethnicity, which correlates with national data on the disposition of white teachers to students of color ratio. Students eligible for free/reduced lunch were also significantly less likely to have a teacher of their own ethnicity. More notably, the study found that students assigned to a teacher of their own ethnicity were associated with higher achievement scores in both mathematics and reading. Kindergarten students with a teacher of their own ethnicity scored 3.6 percentile points higher in mathematics.

In a similar study, Clewell et al. (2005) noted an increase in the reading and mathematic scores of black and Latino elementary students in fourth and sixth grades when taught by a teacher of their same ethnicity. When Latino students were taught by a Latino teacher, their mathematics scores at fourth and sixth grades were higher than those Latino students who were not taught by a teacher of their same ethnicity. The reading scores of Latino students when taught by a Latino teacher were also higher than Latino students who were not taught by a Latino teacher.

Given that the studies of Dee (2004) and Clewell et al. (2005) did not use data from a national representative sample, policy makers are more reluctant to suggest that the findings are not relevant on a national scale and cannot be generalized to the entire U.S. population. However, these studies present foundational findings on the impact of teachers of color on academic test scores of students of color. Subsequent studies focus more on the long-term effects of teachers of color on the academic achievement scores of students of color. These studies examined the long-term effects and academic growth of students of color who were taught by a teacher of color.

In one longitudinal study using a national representative sample, Easton-Brooks et al. (2010) examined the long-term effect and reading score growth of black students, when having at least one black teacher between entering kindergarten and ending fifth grade. They used a two-level hierarchal linear model, which allowed them to examine the effects black teachers had on the reading test scores and reading test score growth of black students between kindergarten and fifth grade.[22] Easton-Brooks et al. reported that black students who had at least one black teacher between kindergarten and fifth grade scored 1.50 points higher in reading than those students who did not have at least one black teacher during this same time. The researchers also found that for black students who had at least one black teacher between kindergarten and fifth grade, reading scores increased 1.75 points per year higher than black students who did not have a black teacher. In addition, those students with at least one black teacher scored at least seven points higher in reading than black students who did not have a black teacher by the time these students completed fifth grade. Other findings show that having some exposure to a black teacher had a significant effect on gender, with black females scoring 2.31 points higher at kindergarten than males.

While the study by Easton-Brooks et al. (2010) focused on the effects of black teachers on the reading achievement scores of black students, Eddy and Easton-Brooks (2011) suggested that the relationship between the teachers' and students' language/ethnic dialect may have influence on reading achievement scores and the relationship between black teachers and students. The belief is that positive interactions between black teachers and students can be increased more likely by familiarity associated with cultural engagement and cultural language. Their research supports the earlier work of Delpit (1995), who found that the usage of language and language styles (grammar and syntax, discourse style and interaction patterns, and behavioral norms) encourages the interaction between teachers and students of the same ethnicity. This familiarity can serve as a tool for helping teachers connect with the students in their classrooms. Eddy and Easton-Brooks (2011) further concluded that parents/guardians tend to focus more on the reading development of their children than on mathematics development. Therefore, schoolteachers tend to teach most of the mathematics skills to students in early grades. Unlike reading, where cultural language can be used to provide meaning of words in context, the interpretation of mathematics constructs from a cultural framework can propose instructional difficulties. In order to learn more about the impact of race and cultural awareness on student learning in mathematics. Eddy and Easton-Brooks (2011) replicated the study by Easton-Brooks et al. (2010). They investigated whether the effects of black teachers in a nonlanguage-related subject matter such as mathematics would show a significant long-term effect on the mathematic scores of black students.

Easton-Brooks et al. (2010) concluded that black students with at least one black teacher did perform higher on mathematics achievement test than black students who did not have a black teacher between kindergarten and fifth grade. The data showed that students who were exposed to at least one black teacher scored significantly (1.44 points) higher on the mathematics achievement test at the end of kindergarten than students who did not have at least one black teacher between kindergarten and fifth grade. In addition, by the end of fifth grade, the growth in the mathematics scores of these students was at least 0.64 points higher than those students who did not have at least one black teacher between kindergarten and fifth grade. Different from the study by Easton-Brooks et al. (2010), this study found that the percentage of students of color in the school had a significant effect on mathematics scores. For instance, those black students in schools with a lower percentage of students of color and who had at least one black teacher scored a significant 3.01 points higher than black students in schools with a lower percentage of students of color and who had at least one black teacher. In addition, the gap in the scores of these students increased significantly 0.63 points per year. In other words, the data suggested that having at least one black teacher significant impacted the mathematics achievement of black students who attended predominantly white schools.

Historically, research is clear that students of color do not perform well on standardized tests. However, the findings in this section show that teachers of color have a statistically significant impact on the academic test scores of students of color on standardized tests. Teachers influence student scores more than instructional practice. Findings suggest further that the attributes teachers of color bring to the table effect a positive change in the achievement scores of students of color on standardized tests.

States Response to Diversifying Teacher Education

Some initiatives, such as Pathways2teaching, Oregon Teacher Pathways, and Call Me Mister, have made efforts to increase the number of teachers of color in the field of education. However, on the state level, many states have not yet invested in diversifying its teacher population and reducing the gap between the percentage of teachers of color and students of color. Boser (2011) has shown that there are some strong spots and weak spots in reducing this gap. With this, Boser developed a teacher diversity gap index, which ranks states on the percentage point difference between teachers of color and students of color (see Table 11.4).[23] The index scores represent the difference in the percentage. Boser found that more than 20 states had a gap between teachers of color and students of color 25 percent or greater.

To make better sense of this index, Easton-Brooks (2013) ran a correlation analysis between the state rankings as measured by Boser's TDI achievement test score gap from the National Assessment of Educational

TABLE 11.4   Boser Teacher Diversity Index (TDI) Ranking

State	TDI	State	TDI
ME	4	PA	23
VT	4	MS	24
WV	4	OR	24
NH	6	TN	24
KY	11	WA	25
MT	12	NC	26
WY	12	SC	26
ID	13	CO	27
ND	13	FL	27
SD	13	OK	27
IA	14	RI	27
AL	15	VA	27
MO	17	CT	28
HI	18	GA	29
OH	18	LA	29
UT	18	NM	29
IN	19	DE	30
WI	19	NJ	31
KS	21	AK	32
MD	21	TX	32
MN	21	NY	33
AR	22	AZ	34
MA	22	IL	35
MI	22	NV	41
NE	22	CA	43

Source: Compiled by the author from Bose (2011).

Progress dataset, by state, between Latino and white students and black and white students. A Pearson correlation analysis was used to determine if there was a correlation between the TDI and the achievement gap for each group in reading and mathematics at eighth grade. The results showed that there was a significant correlation on all measures ranging between $r = .46$ to .77. These findings suggest that as the gap in the percentage of teachers of color and student of color increases, the state Latino/white and black/white achievement score gap increases significantly.

What was noticed in the Boser index was that there were four states (Vermont 4%, Maine 4%, West Virginia 4%, and New Hampshire 6%) with a less than 10 percent gap between students and teachers of color. However, these states (Vermont 6%, Maine 6%, West Virginia 7%, and New Hampshire 8%) have the lowest people of color population in the country. To further understand the impact of the findings from the TDI, a State and School Teacher Diversity Index (SSTDI) was created for this chapter (see Table 11.5). The SSTDI assessed the difference between the TDI and the percentage of people of color in the state to determine if the gap in the teacher/student

TABLE 11.5   State and School Teacher Diversity Index (SSTDI) Ranking

State	Percentage People of Color	TDI	SSTDI	State	Percentage People of Color	TDI	SSTDI
MN	17	21	−4	KY	14	11	3
NE	18	22	−4	ID	16	13	3
IA	11	14	−3	WA	28	25	3
PA	21	23	−3	CO	30	27	3
OR	22	24	−3	AR	26	22	4
RI	24	27	−3	OK	31	27	4
ND	11	13	−2	AK	36	32	4
WI	17	19	−2	DE	35	30	5
IN	19	19	−1	NV	46	41	5
MT	12	12	0	VA	35	27	8
TN	24	24	0	AZ	42	34	8
OH	19	18	1	NC	35	26	9
KS	22	21	1	NY	42	33	9
MI	23	22	1	SC	36	26	10
CT	29	28	1	NJ	41	31	10
IL	36	35	1	LA	40	29	11
ME	6	4	2	FL	42	27	15
VT	6	4	2	GA	44	29	15
NH	8	6	2	CA	60	43	17
WY	14	12	2	AL	33	15	18
SD	15	13	2	MS	42	24	18
MO	19	17	2	TX	55	32	23
UT	20	18	2	MD	45	21	24
MA	24	22	2	NM	60	29	31
WV	7	4	3	HI	77	18	59

Source: Compiled by the author.

population is responsive to the overall people of color population in the state. The calculation is basically the sum equal to (the percentage of people of color in the state)—(TDI [percentage of teachers of color is the state—percentage of students of color in the state]). A Pearson correlation between the TDI and the SSTDI showed a significantly strong positive correlation ($r = .73, p = .01$). These findings show that the greater the percentage of people of color population in a state, the higher the gap between students and teachers of color. For instance, in California, the people of color make up 60 percent of the population and the gap in their student/teacher population is 43 percent. Therefore, the gap between TDI and SSTDI is 17 percent. These findings suggest that the gap in the student/teacher population of California is greater than 17 percent of the overall state population. Further, the SSTDI for Minnesota is –4 percent. These findings suggest that the gap is –4 percent of the population and student/teacher of color gap, or in other words, there are not enough people/adults of color in Minnesota to cover the 21 percent student/teacher of color gap in their public schools.

Other findings in Table 11.5 show that of those states with less than a 25 percent people of color population, the SSTDI for that state is between –4 and 3. These findings suggest that states like Maine, Vermont, and Iowa do not have enough of a people/adult of color population to cover the gap between their teachers and students of color. Of those states with an SSTDI of 26 percent to 40 percent, the SSTDI is between 3 and 9. Of those states with an SSTDI between 41 and higher, the SSTDI for the state is between 10 and 59. Again, as the findings show, those states with a higher population of color have a significantly higher gap in their student/teacher population.

These findings indicate that states with a larger student/teacher gap in the school population of color are experiencing these gaps between the school and their connection with their populations of color. As population shifts across the country and many schools' population continues to shift, these states will need to develop strategies to better engage their diverse populations. As the findings in the chapter show, one of the critical factors in increasing the academic success of students of color is by engaging these students with more teachers of color.

Conclusion

This chapter demonstrates that as the U.S. population shifts, the challenge for public schools is to create a more diverse teacher workforce. Teachers of color have increased at a rate that is double that of white teachers over the past two decades. However, schools have not done enough to recruit and retain these teachers. The impact of not creating a more diverse workforce has had a negative influence on students of color. Current research clearly indicates that teachers of color have a favorable impact on the students of color both in expectations[24] and in academic outcomes.[25] Studies have shown that when interacting with teachers of color, students' academic performance is higher; students tend to be treated more respectfully, and students' long-term educational experience is positively affected.

The need to diversify the teaching workforce remains. More and more people of color are making an effort to pursue the field of education or are seeking careers in education. However, school systems and state governments have to engage at the same level in hiring and retaining a more diverse teacher workforce. More research is needed to better understand the impact of teachers of color on all students as well as on the overall environment of the school setting. For instance, limitation to this line of inquiry is the effects of quality-certified teachers on the academic performance of students of color at the elementary, middle, and high school level. In addition, the influence of male teachers of color on the academic outcomes of students of color is another under-researched area.[26]

Indeed, diversifying the teacher workforce is key to increasing student achievement. The task, however, is not an easy one. There are many challenges to diversifying teacher education. One challenge stems from the fact that there is a dearth of students of color, and students in general, pursuing careers in the field of education. In fact, less than 10 percent of college students choose education as their major. Most of these students go into fields such as business and social science.[27] Most students go into fields such as business and social science.[28] Milner (2006) proposed that the field of education should identify the attributes of successful teachers of color and train all teachers to employ those strategies with students of color. In short, evidence suggests that successful strategies used by successful teachers of color benefit all students, not just students of color.[29] Further, the desire to diversify teacher education is on the minds of other fields. Researchers are finding that having a more diverse field is beneficial to their field. Studies have shown that having a more diverse workplace reduces tension in work environments.[30] Studies have also shown that in higher education, having more diversity among the mentoring relationship between faculty and students increases the grade point average, number of units completed, and retention rate by the end of students' first year in college.[31] The findings also show that these students stay on campus to pursue graduate studies and complete teaching credentials at a higher rate than those not mentored by same race mentors. Further, research in the counseling and therapeutic field has also found that having a more diverse workforce produces desirable outcomes.[32]

It is a common argument that many of the reasons that people of color are not going into teacher education are low teacher salaries, rigorous testing standards in schools and more demanding certification and licensing requirements, and social perception of the teaching profession. However, the number of people of color going into teacher education has doubled over the past two decades in comparison to whites. One of the points that must be raised is whether these professionals are getting jobs with public schools and whether public schools are doing enough to keep these professionals. Teachers of color are nearly three times more likely than white teaches to leave the field of education. Boser (2011) proposes the following solutions to many of these problems. He suggests increasing federal oversight of and increased accountability for teacher preparation programs and creating statewide initiatives to fund teacher preparation programs aimed at ethnic minority teachers. In addition, efforts should be made by policy makers to increase salaries and/or incentives to entice qualified teachers of color.

I recommend further that school district human resources officers, school administrators (principals), and teacher education programs increase efforts to recruit and retain ethnic minority teachers.[33] To improve the academic achievement of students of color, it is critical that human resources officials at the school district level further examine data and findings on the impact teachers of color make on the lives of students of color and utilize the findings to improve current school practices. While Ingersoll and May (2011) demonstrated the increase in teachers of color over the past two decades, it is important that human resources departments continue their efforts in recruiting more teachers of color and develop strategies for improving the retention of these teachers. Human resources departments must intentionally aim to diversify their teacher workforce. Recruiters should make every effort to attend job fairs at Historically Black Colleges and Universities, which produce the largest percentage of African American teachers,[34] and Hispanic Serving Institutions. These institutions offer an excellent pool of diverse educators seeking employment. Relationships need to be formed with these colleges and universities to recruit high-quality students, especially in high-needs areas such as mathematics, science, and special education in urban schools. More directly, principals can play a key role in reaching out to teachers of color. Principals, particularly those looking for teachers in high-needs areas, should work closely with school district hiring officials to diversify, recruit, hire, and retain qualified ethnic minority teachers. In most situations, the principal is the final decision-making authority on what teachers will be hired at the local school site.

On the state level, educational policy makers need to take more of an initiative to fund opportunities and programs designed to increase their teacher of color population. An example of this can be seen in the state of Oregon. The state supports six initiatives at the public school and university levels designed to create pipelines for people of color to engage in the field of education starting from 11th grade through college. One program funded by the state is the Oregon Teacher Pathway program at Eastern Oregon University, which mirrors the Pathways2teaching program at the University of Colorado at Denver. These programs have shown to have great impacts on the lives of students of color even if they do not go into teacher education, on promoting social justice in the community, and in increasing awareness of the need to diversify the field of education.

In conclusion, this chapter presents evidence that the teachers of color had a strong and significant impact on the academic lives of students of color and increasing this population is an effective strategy for increasing the academic outcomes among students of color. In addition, as more teachers of color enter the field of education, more research on this topic is needed, especially related to populations in which languages other than English is a significant part of a student's culture. As the U.S, demographics continues to change, it is critical that the U.S. education system continue to change to meet the needs of these populations.

Notes

1. Banks 1996; Easton-Brooks, Lewis, and Zhang 2010; Foster 1990, 1997; Gay 2000; Holmes 1990; Irvine and Irvine 1983; Ladson-Billings 1994; Ledlow 1992; Lewis 2006; Lynn 2006; Milner 2006; Reed-Danahay 2000; St. Germaine 1995.

2. Clewell, Puma, and McKay 2005; Dee 2004; Easton-Brooks 2013; Easton-Brooks, Lewis, and Zhang 2010; Eddy and Easton-Brooks 2011; Hanushek 1992.

3. Banks 1996; Easton-Brooks, Lewis, and Zhang 2010; Foster 1990 1997; Gay 2000; Holmes 1990; Irvine and Irvine 1983; Ladson-Billings 1994; Lewis 2006; Lynn 2006; Milner 2006; Ogbu 2003; Shipp 1999.

4. Easton-Brooks and Davis 2009; Hanushek, Kain, and Rivkin 2002.

5. Gibson and Jung 2002.

6. U.S. Census Bureau 2011.

7. U.S. Department of Education 2006.

8. Ingersoll and May 2011.

9. Bireda and Chait 2011; Boser 2011; Ingersoll and May 2011.

10. Bireda and Chait 2011; Boser 2011.

11. Feistritzer 2011.

12. Bireda and Chait 2011; Boser 2011; Ingersoll and May 2011.

13. Miller 2006.

14. Boser 2011.

15. Dee 2004; Easton-Brooks, Lewis, and Zhang 2010; Eddy and Easton-Brooks 2011.

16. Foster 1994, 1995, 1997; Henry 1998; Ladson-Billings 1994; Lewis 2006; Milner 2006; Milner and Howard 2004; Ogbu 2003; Shipp 1999.

17. Banks 1996; Gay 2000; Milner 2007; Nieto 2000.

18. Foster 1990, 1997; Holmes 1990; Irvine and Irvine 1983; Ladson-Billings 1994; Lewis 2006; Lynn 2006; Milner 2006; Ogbu 2003; Shipp 1999.

19. Casteel 1998; Ehrenberg, Goldhaber, and Brewer 1995; Ferguson 1998; Zimmerman et al. 1995.

20. Hanushek 1992.

21. Clewell, Puma, and McKay 2005.

22. Easton-Brooks, Lewis, and Zhang 2010.

23. Boser 2011, p. 2.

24. Casteel 1998; Ehrenberg, Goldhaber, and Brewer 1995; Ferguson 1998; Zimmerman et al. 1995.

25. Clewell, Puma, and McKay 2005; Easton-Brooks, Lewis, and Zhang 2010; Eddy and Easton-Brooks 2011.

26. Lynn 1999, 2002 2006; Milner 2007.

27. Dickson 2010; Porter and Umbach 2006.

28. Ibid.

29. Easton-Brooks, Lewis, and Zhang 2010; Milner 2006.

30. Elliott and Smith 2001; Field and Caetano 2010; Flicker et al. 2008.

31. Campbell and Campbell 2007.

32. Cabral and Smith 2011; Shin et al. 2005.

33. Easton-Brooks, Lewis, and Zhang 2010.

34. Lewis 2006.

Bibliography

Ainsworth-Darnell, James A., and Douglas Downey. 1998. "Assessing the Oppositional Culture Explanation for Racial/Ethnic Differences in School Performance." *American Sociological Review* 63: 536–553.

Bireda, Saba, and Robin Chait. 2011. *Increasing Teacher Diversity: Strategies to Improve the Teacher Workforce.* Washington, DC: Center for American Progress. ERIC, ED 535654.

Banks, James A. 1996. *Multicultural Education, Transformative Knowledge, and Action: Historical and Contemporary Perspectives.* New York: Teachers College Press.

Boser, Ulrich. 2011. *Teacher Diversity Matters: A State-by-State Analysis of Teachers of Color.* Washington, DC: Center for American Progress. ERIC, ED 535665.

Cabral, Raquel R., and Timothy B. Smith. 2011. "Racial/Ethnic Matching of Clients and Therapists in Mental Health Services: A Meta-analytic Review of Preferences, Perceptions, and Outcomes." *Journal of Counseling Psychology* 58 (4): 537–554.

Callender, Jamie. 2004. "Value-Added Assessment." *Journal of Educational and Behavioral Statistics* 29 (1): 5.

Campbell, Toni Ann, and David E. Campbell. 2007. "Outcomes of Mentoring At-Risk College Students: Gender and Ethnic Matching Effects." *Mentoring & Tutoring: Partnership in Learning* 15 (2): 135–148.

Casteel, Clifton A. 1998. "Teacher–Student Interactions and Race in Integrated Classrooms." *Journal of Educational Research* 92: 115–120.

Clewell, Beatriz. C., Michael J. Puma, and Shannon A. McKay. "Does It Matter If My Teacher Looks Like Me? The Impact of Teacher Race and Ethnicity on Student Academic Achievement." Paper presented at the Annual Meeting of the American Educational Research Association, Montreal, Canada, April 2005.

Darling-Hammond, Linda. 2000. "Teacher Quality and Student Achievement: A Review of State Policy Evidence." *Educational Policy Analysis Archives* 8 (1). http://epaa.asu.edu/ojs/article/view/392.

Dee, Thomas S. 2004. "Teachers, Race, and Student Achievement in a Randomized Experiment." *Review of Economics and Statistics* 86 (1): 195–210.

Delpit, Lisa. 1995. *Other People's Children: Cultural Conflict in the Classroom.* New York: New Press.

Dickson, Lisa M. 2010. "Race and Gender Differences in College Major Choice." *The Annals of the American Academy of Political and Social Science* 627 (1): 108–124.

Easton-Brooks, Donald. 2013. "Ethnic-Matching in Urban Education." In *The Handbook on Urban Education,* eds. Rich Milner and Kofi Lomotey (pp. 97–113). London: Routledge.

Easton-Brooks Donald, and Alan Davis. 2009. "Teacher Qualification and the Achievement Gap in Early Primary Grades." *Education Policy Analysis Archives* 17 (5): 1–19.

Easton-Brooks, Donald, Chance Lewis, and Yubo Zhang. 2010. "Ethnic-Matching: The Influence of African American Teachers on the Reading Scores of African American Students." *National Journal of Urban Education & Practice* 3: 230–243.

Eddy, Colleen, and Donald Easton-Brooks. 2011. "Ethnic Matching, School Placement, and Mathematics Achievement of African American Students from Kindergarten through Fifth Grade." *Urban Education* 46 (6): 1280–1299.

Ehrenberg, Ronald G., Daniel Goldhaber, and Dominic Brewer. 1995. "Do Teachers' Race, Gender, and Ethnicity Matter? Evidence from the National Educational

Longitudinal Study of 1998." *Industrial and Labor Relations Review* 48 (3): 547–561.

Elliott, J.R., and R.A. Smith. 2001, May 1. "Ethnic Matching of Supervisors to Subordinate Work Groups: Findings on 'Bottom-Up' Ascription and Social Closure." *Social Problems* 48 (2): 258–276.

Ferguson, Ronald F. 1998. "Teachers' Perceptions and Expectations and the African American-White Test Score Gap." In *The Black-White Test Score Gap*, eds. Christopher Jencks and Meredith Phillips (pp. 273–317). Washington, DC: Brookings Institution Press.

Field, Craig, and Raul Caetano. 2010. "The Role of Ethnic Matching between Patient and Provider on the Effectiveness of Brief Alcohol Interventions with Hispanics." *Alcoholism: Clinical and Experimental Research* 34: 262–271.

Flicker, Sharon M., Holly Barrett Waldron, Charles W. Turner, Janet L. Brody, and Hyman Hops. 2008. "Ethnic Matching and Treatment Outcome with Hispanic and Anglo Substance-Abusing Adolescents in Family Therapy." *Journal of Family Psychology* 22 (3): 439–447.

Foster, Michele. 1990. "The Politics of Race: Through the Eyes of African-American Teachers." *Journal of Education* 172: 123–141.

Foster, Michele. 1994. "Effective Black Teachers: A Literature Review." In *Teaching Diverse Populations: Formulating a Knowledge Base,* eds. Etta R. Hollins, Joyce E. King, and Warren C. Hayman. Albany: State University of New York Press.

Foster, Michele. 1995. "African American Teachers and Culturally Relevant Pedagogy." In *Handbook of Research on Multicultural Education,* eds. James A. Banks and Cherry A. McGee Banks. New York: Macmillan.

Foster, Michele. 1997. *Black Teachers on Teaching.* New York: New Press.

Gay, Genvia. 2000. *Culturally, Responsive Teaching: Theory, Research and Practice.* New York: Teachers College Press.

Hanushek, Eric A. 1992. "The Trade-Off between Child Quantity and Quality." *Journal of Political Economy* 100 (1): 84–117.

Hanushek, Eric A., John F. Kain, and Steven G. Rivkin. 2002. "Inferring Program Effects for Specialized Populations: Does Special Education Raise Achievement for Students with Disabilities?" *Review of Economics and Statistics* 84 (4): 584–599.

Henry, Annette. 1998. *Taking Back Control: African Canadian Women Teachers' Lives and Practice.* Albany: State University of New York Press.

Holmes, Barbara J. 1990. "New Strategies Are Needed to Produce Minority Teachers." In *Recruiting and Retaining Minority Teachers* (Guest Commentary), ed. Arthur Dorman. Oak Brook, IL: North Central Regional Educational Laboratory.

Ingersoll, Richard, and May, Henry. 2011. *Recruitment, Retention, and the Minority Teacher Shortage.* Philadelphia, PA: Consortium for Policy Research in

Education, University of Pennsylvania and Center for Educational Research in the Interest of Underserved Students, University of California, Santa Cruz.

Irvin, Jacqueline J. 1990. *Black Students and School Failure: Policies, Practices, and Prescriptions.* Westport, CT: Greenwood Press.

Irvine, Russell W., and Jacqueline J. Irvine. 1983. "The Impact of the Desegregation Process on the Education of Black Students: Key Variables." *The Journal of Negro Education* 52 (4): 410–422.

Ladson-Billings, Gloria. 1994. *The Dreamkeepers: Successful Teachers of African American Children.* San Francisco, CA: Jossey-Bass.

Ledlow, Susan. 1992. "Is Cultural Discontinuity an Adequate Explanation for Dropping Out?" *Journal of American Indian Education* 31 (3): 21–36.

Lewis, Chance W. 2006. "African American Male Teachers in Public Schools: An Examination of Three Urban School Districts." *Teacher College Record* 108 (2): 224–245.

Lynn, Marvin. 1999. "Toward a critical Race Pedagogy: A Research Note." *Urban Education* 33: 606–626.

Lynn, Marvin. 2002. "Critical Race Theory and the Perspectives of Black Men Teachers in the Los Angeles Public Schools." *Equity & Excellence in Education* 35: 87–92.

Lynn, Marvin. 2006. "Education for the Community: Exploring the Culturally Relevant Practices of Black Male Teachers." *Teacher College Record* 108: 2497–2522.

McCaffrey, Daniel F., J. R. Lockwood, Daniel Koretz, Thomas A. Louis, and Laura S. Hamilton. 2004. "Models for Value-Added Modeling for Teacher Effects." *Journal of Educational and Behavioral Statistics* 29 (1): 67–101.

Meier, Kenneth J., Joseph Stewart, and Robert E. England. 1989. *Race, Class, and Education: The Politics of Second Generation Discrimination.* Madison: University of Wisconsin Press.

Milner, H. Rich. 2006. "The Promise of Black Teachers' Success with Black Students." *Educational Foundations* 20 (3–4): 89–104.

Milner, H. Rich. 2007. "African American Males in Urban Schools: No Excuses Teach and Empower." *Theory into Practice* 46 (3): 239–246.

Milner, H. Rich, and Tyron Howard. 2004. "Black Teachers, Black Students, Black Communities and Brown: Perspectives and Insights from Experts." *Journal of Negro Education* 73 (3): 285–297.

Nieto, Sonia. 2000. *Affirming Diversity: The Sociopolitical Context of Multicultural Education.* 3rd ed. New York: Longman.

Ogbu, John. 2003. *Black American Students in an Affluent Suburb: A Study of Academic Disengagement.* Mahwah, NJ: Lawrence Erlbaum Associates.

Porter, Stephen R., and Paul D. Umbach. 2000. College Major Choice: An Analysis of Person-Environment Fit. *Research in Higher Education* 47 (4): 429–449.

Reed-Danahay, Deborah. 2000. "Habitus and Cultural Identity: Home/School Relationships." In *Rural France in Schooling the Symbolic Animal,* eds. Bradley A. U. Levinson, Kathryn M. Borman, Margret Eisenhart, Michele Foster, and Amy E. Fox. Lanham, MD: Rowman & Littlefield.

Rimm-Kaufman, Sara E., and Robert C. Pianta. 2000. "An Ecological Perspective on the Transition to Kindergarten: A Theoretical Framework to Guide Empirical Research." *Journal of Applied Developmental Psychology* 21: 491–511.

Rowan, Brian, Richard Correnti, and Robert J. Miller. 2002. "What Large-Scale, Survey Research Tells Us about Teacher Effects on Student Achievement: Insights from the Prospects Study of Elementary Schools." *Teachers College Record* 104 (8): 1525–1567.

Rubin, Donald B., Elizabeth A. Struart, and Elaine L. Zanutto. 2004. "A Potential Outcomes View of Value-Added Assessment in Education." *Journal of Educational and Behavioral Statistics* 29: 103–116.

Sanders, William L., Arnold M. Saxton, and Sandra P. Horn. 1997. "The Tennessee Value-Added Assessment System: A Quantitative, Outcomes-Based Approach to Educational Assessment." In *Grading Teachers, Grading Schools: Is Student Achievement a Valid Measure?,* ed. Jason Millman (pp. 337–350). Thousand Oaks, CA: Corwin Press.

Shin, Sung-Man, Clifton Chow, Teresita Camacho-Gonsalves, Rachel J. Levy, Elaine Allen, Stephen Leff. 2005. "A Meta-analytic Review of Racial-Ethnic Matching for African American and Caucasian American Clients and Clinicians." *Journal of Counseling Psychology* 52 (1): 45–56.

Shipp, Veronica H. 1999. "Factors Influencing the Career Choices of African American Collegians: Implications for Minority Teacher Recruitment." *Journal of Negro Education* 68 (3): 343–351.

St. Germaine, Richard. 1995. "BIA Schools Complete First Step of Reform Effort." *Journal of American Indian Education* 35 (1): 30–38.

U.S. Census Bureau, 2011. Overview of Race and Hispanic Origin: 2010 by Karen Humes, Nicholas Jones, and Roberto Ramirez. C2010BR-02, March.

U.S. Census Bureau. 2006. *Statistical Abstract of the United States: 2006.* 126th ed. Washington, DC: U.S. Government Printing Office.

U.S. Census Bureau. 2002. *Historical Census Statistics on Population Totals by Race, 1790 To 1990, and by Hispanic Origin, 1970 to 1990, for the United States, Regions, Divisions, and States* by Campbell Gibson and Kay Jung. WPS: 562002, September.

U.S. Department of Education, National Center for Education Statistics. 2006. *The Condition of Education 2006* by Patrick Rooney, Susan Choy, Gillian Hampden-Thompson, Stephen Provasnik, and Mary Ann Fox. NCES 2006-071, June.

National Center for Education Information. *Profiles of Teachers in the U.S. 2011* by C. Emily Feistritzer. ISBN 1-928665-18-7, July 2011.

Webster, William J., and Robert L. Mendro 1997. "The Dallas Value-Added Accountability System." In *Grading Teachers, Grading Schools: Is Student Achievement a Valid Measure?*, ed. Jason Millman. Thousand Oaks, CA: Corwin Press.

Zhang, Yubo. 2007. "Effects of Teacher-Student Ethnic Matching on Kindergarteners' Academic Achievement and on Teachers' Ratings of Kindergarteners' Academic Performance." Doctoral dissertation, University of Virginia.

Zimmerman, Rick S., Elizabeth L. Khoury, William A. Vega, Andrea G. Gil, and George J. Warheit. 1995. "Teacher and Parent Perceptions of Behavior Problems among a Sample of African American, Hispanic, and Non-Hispanic White Students." *American Journal of Community Psychology* 23 (2): 181–198.

Part IV

Race and "Cost" Debate in School Reform

Chapter 12

The Opportunity for Equity: School Improvement Grants

Theresa Saunders

The goal of public education with public funds is to develop the capacity of the individual for the common good of the society. In order for this to happen there must be access and engagement by the individual and the society as partners in the construction, implementation, and assessment of the educational process. When this does not happen it is the result of structural inequalities that eventually erode the aspirations and potential of the larger community resulting in various forms of disconnectedness and loss.

This chapter begins with an overview of a federal grant program, the School Improvement Grant (SIG), and discusses its purpose, operational structures, and implementation results for the two initial cohorts of schools nationally and in an individual state. It is followed by the presentation of a perspective on the structure of education that includes the rights of children, the development of human capital, and a structure for equitable funding. The conclusion contains a summary and recommendations for effectual change in the design and implementation of federally funded grant programs.

Expanding Title 1

The federal government first authorized the SIG in 2001 under Title 1 section 1003(g) of the Elementary and Secondary Education Act of 1965. At that time over 13,000 schools were in some form of improvement status under the No Child Left Behind legislation. An additional 4,900 schools were in some form of restructuring, and more schools were entering restructuring annually than were exiting. This was in spite of the fact that the schools could select their reform model, and funding was provided to states that awarded the funds, via a competitive process, to districts to use in their lowest-performing schools. Unfortunately, failing schools selected the least rigorous and disruptive option of intervention for implementation. Consequently, not much was heard or done by the schools receiving this funding. However, when there was a recession in 2008 almost $100 billion of federal economic-stimulus aid was appropriated for education as a one-time provision. This funding was designed as an effort to stimulate the economy, invest in public services, such as education, and help ensure the economic health of the United States Also provided was an additional $10 billion to Title 1, Part A, funds called the American Recovery and Reinvestment Act (ARRA) of 2009. The funds were to be spent quickly in order to save and create jobs so that employment layoffs could be averted. They were also to be spent with a long-term view to improving student achievement, school improvement, and reform. They provided grants to state educational agencies (SEAs) "to use to make competitive sub grants to local educational agencies (LEAs) that demonstrate the greatest need for the funds and the strongest commitment to use the funds to provide adequate resources in order to raise substantially the achievement of student in their lowest-performing schools."[1]

This type of funding was unprecedented and it caused states to make structural changes in the education aid and services provided to students with disabilities. With these changes also came concern about the long-term effects of short-term funding, and the concerns were justified as researchers found that the additional funds did not improve conditions for the students; rather, it perpetuated already existing inequities. These included states increasing the poverty threshold to make more students eligible without concern for what was to happen when the ARRA funds no longer existed and hiring staff that provided no direct service to students who were most in need in order to provide for adult employment.

The long-term view for ARRA funds required progress on four reforms to help close the achievement gap. These were as follows:

1) make progress toward rigorous college- and career- ready standards and high-quality, valid and reliable assessments for all students; 2) establishing pre-K-to-college-and-career data systems that would track the progress of students: 3) make improvements in teacher effectiveness and in the equitable distribution of qualified teachers for all students, especially those who are

most in need; and 4) provide intensive support and effective interventions in the lowest-performing schools.[2]

The Conditions for Funding SIG Schools

In order to receive ARRA School Improvement Grant Funding (SIG) each state had to develop different tiers and compare the tiers as part of a process that included a top to bottom (TTB) rating for each school. By May 2010 Michigan had developed and implemented its TTB list and there were 224 schools that were identified and eligible to participate in the statewide competition for ARRA SIG funding.

Applying for the funding required that a local school district select one of four reform models to implement during the three-year length of the grant. The models were the following:

- Turnaround model: Replace the principal and rehire no more than 50 percent of the staff and grant the principal sufficient operational flexibility (including in staffing, calendars/time, and budgeting) to implement fully a comprehensive approach to substantially improve student outcomes.
- Restart model: Convert a school or close and reopen it under a charter school operator, a charter management organization, or an education management organization that has been selected through a rigorous review process.
- School closure: Close a school and enroll the students who attended that school in other schools in the LEA that are higher achieving.
- Transformation model: Implement each of the following strategies: (1) replace the principal and take steps to increase teacher and school leader effectiveness; (2) institute comprehensive instructional reforms; (3) increase learning time and create community-oriented schools; and (4) provide operational flexibility and sustained support.[3]

These four models served as individual structures on which all other ideas to reform the schools depended. They were also the support for the purpose of the program, which had changed significantly from the 2009 announcement. This new purpose was to "ensure that all children have a fair, equal, and significant opportunity to obtain a high quality education and reach, at a minimum, proficiency on challenging State academic achievement standards and state academic assessments."[4]

The change in purpose established 12 items to be accomplished, one of which was "distributing and targeting resources sufficiently to make a difference to local educational agencies and school where needs are greatest."[5]

At the time the maximum amount given to a school was $500,000. However, to accomplish this new purpose, it was changed to $2 million per school by October 2010.

The SIG Process as a Model of Structural Justice

Florida, as one of the states responding to and funded by the SIG grant application process, selected several schools for implementation of the grant. One of these schools was Miami Central Senior High. The school was underperforming academically (below a C state level rating) and was predominantly children of color living in an unincorporated area of northern Miami-Dade County. President Barack Obama, in presenting the SIG program nationally, visited and addressed Miami Central High School, where he highlighted the work being done to improve the school and thereby the educational options for students. From his perspective the SIG schools were opportunities to "prove the naysayers wrong"[6] because they were making progress in turning themselves around. He went on to talk about the skills and work of the principal and teachers, the program offerings, and the engagement of parents and community members. Most important, though, he shared the fact that 40 of the 50 states were participating in the SIG program as evidenced by their adoption of increased standards for teaching and learning. From his perspective the change was structural, that is, a bottom-up approach, for unified collaboration, work, and achievement. He believed that Congress should follow this model regarding current education law and enable improved responsibility, reform, and results. These results would ensure that America has the "highest proportion of college graduates in the world so it out-educates other countries and wins the future for the United States of America."[7]

Two things are evident as part of the president's remarks, First, there had been some monitoring of the work being done at Miami Central High School. This monitoring had included conversations and personal visits with the principal, staff, students, and parents about the reform at the school and its relationship to the national conversation and concepts of education "responsibility, reform and results."[8] The school had taken the necessary steps to persuade monitors that they were an example of this paradigm of progress that could be presented as a model to motivate other struggling educational systems.

The second issue was the focus on structures of equity. That is, the president established the fact that the nation was in a new position requiring a new structure of interactive equity. This structure provided families (employees) and businesses (employers) what they most needed for short-term success. This, from his perspective, was a new structure. A pivotal turning point. He makes it clear that what we had been doing and how it had been done had changed. The prototypical example of this change was the steps taken by the government to accelerate recovery, spur hiring, and economic growth by admittedly providing tax cuts and business investment write-offs. His conversation lets us know that the nation had previously been in a different place in which there was an established set of operational protocols based on previously determined criteria for structural equity, that is, how business in the nation was conducted. However, a difficult recession had changed the effectiveness of this paradigm. Something different was required in order to get through the challenges being faced by the nation. These challenges required, even if short term, a new position on reform, responsibility, and results.

With any new position, whether job, space, location, interaction, relationship, and so on, comes the need to adjust. That is, our previous position had established protocols for operation that enabled our success in that position. When a changed position is required, the entire system has to adjust. A new structure for equity must be established, and this can be difficult depending on the degree of change required. The president makes the connection between what the school had done and what the nation had done. But he takes it further than the current scenario of success. He takes the analogy into the future. That is, he established the fact that the school, in order to survive, had to make substantive structural equity changes and the nation, in order to do the same, will have to use the same process.

President Barack Obama understood that the pre-SIG educational structures in Miami Central High School lacked the type and expanse of equity needed for substantive change or reform. The school staff, in attempting to address the conditions set forth by the government regarding the SIG application process, put themselves in a pivotal position and created what he deemed to be a more equitable process. This happened because the structure came from the people doing the work—administrators, staff, teachers, students, and parents. Their collaboration had created movement toward their goal, causing a structural shift of significance. By suggesting that this process be used as a vehicle for changing current education law, the president declared that the existing structure of "law making" was less equitable than one that would engage all constituents. But participatory engagement was not all that was being required. The real engagement was to make things focus on responsibility, reform, and results. This, though veiled, was a direct description of what the president saw as a structural inequity of Congress. That is, it lacked the system necessary for changed structural equity. There wasn't full engagement of the legislators in the design, implementation, and accountability of successful governmental social structures. Rather, they refused to come together regarding the structures and thereby increased the inequity of the existing structures and rendered the system immobile, deadlocked, without momentum, and failing. They had become what the school no longer was and the school had become what they could be.

Monitoring the SIG Program

The monitoring process of the US Department of Education (ED) regarding the SIG program is the regular and systematic examination of a State's administration and implementation of a Federal education grant. . . . (It) is necessary to ensure that all children have a fair, equal, and significant opportunity to obtain a high-quality education . . . (and) assesses the extent to which States provide leadership and guidance for LEAs and schools in implementing policies and procedures that comply with the statutes and regulations of Title 1, section 1003(g).[9]

Monitoring establishes the structure of relationship between the ED and the states with an emphasis on (1) accountability for the wise use of resources to educate and prepare the students of the nation, (2) data collection regarding state and local needs, and (3) data use to design initiative and national leadership activities via technical assistance.[10] This requires that the ED be an advisor and partner with the states regarding their ability to implement the requirements of the SIG. It also requires that the ED monitor its own achievement concerning the performance on objectives, performance measures, and targets in an effort to achieve measurable results for students. In essence, the monitoring process is a structure of equity designed to check responsibility, reform, and results. By virtue of it being a "partnership" it calls into question the issue of equity. That is, does a partnership mean that there is equity in the relationship? The obvious answer is "no." The ED is a partner only in the sense that it has provided the context for the receipt and use of funds that the states have agreed to accept and perform. The rest of the relationship is as a necessary advisor. This implies that there is an expectation that the states ultimately will not do the right thing(s) and require nonnegotiable direction.

There are six areas of the SIG monitoring process. Each area is composed of a series of questions requiring a response from different constituents of the school community. The monitoring process itself can be conducted as a desk process via tele- or videoconferencing or as an onsite visit. In either case there are specific protocols for the composition of each answering group and a set of questions designed specifically for them to address. The six areas of monitoring and respondents are as follows: (1) Application Process answered by the SEA and LEA; (2) Implementation answered by the SEA, LEA, School Leadership Team, Teacher Group, Parents, and Students; (3) Fiscal answered by the SEA and LEA; (4) Technical Assistance answered by the SEA, LEA, and School Leadership Team; (5) Monitoring answered by the SEA, LEA, and School Leadership Team; and (6) Data Collection answered by the SEA, LEA, and School Leadership Team.[11] This process is a structure that both determines and explains the relationship between the federal government and the SEA, LEA, School Leadership Team, Teacher Group, Parents, and Students. That is, the federal government has created a hierarchy where the SEA is responsible for them; the LEA is responsible for the SEA, the School Leadership Team for the LEA, the Teacher Group for the Teacher Leadership Team, the Parents for the Teacher Group, and the students for their parents. It is enabled by the limits on questions to all school community members. Parents and students are asked only one type of question. Why? It is not an expectation that they be exposed to the answers to some of the areas of questions. In fact the process is designed so that they will not know about some of the issues concerning SIG operations. This scenario requires some thoughtful response, but it makes clear the structural inequity of the SIG program.

This is not a change from what currently exists in traditional school settings. Rather, it is a reinforcement of the existing traditional hierarchy of social and operational paradigms in schooling. It is as if the federal government is demanding, via supportive funding, the solidification of the existing operational paradigm while verbally supporting change from that paradigm to something much more collaborative. Apparently, paradigm shifting collaboration is easier said than can be identified through a monitoring process. This is because the structure established by the SIG process wasn't designed to be a change from the existing structure. It was, by default, designed to collect information from all constituents yet limiting the expectation of information to some groups and giving unlimited information to others. Knowledge is power and the control of it determines the breadth and depth of equity in any system, but especially a system such as education that is built and operates via knowledge.

The clear example of this position is seen in the fact that the only two groups that are permitted to answer all of the questions posed in the monitoring process are the SEA and the LEA. In a truly collaborative process every group should be able to answer the questions posed to any group because each group has had a voice in the process in every area. To do less is to acknowledge that there is a hierarchy, a space, and a place where some voices are heard and others are not. In this space only the elite enter and exit. What is evident is that structures can remain as they are while engaging more participation from people in their limited space and given limitations to their voice. Consequently, that is what happened to the structural opportunity of the SIG. The federal government extended its reach into state operations and the state extended its reach into local operations while everything else stayed as it was, structurally. This process, though, is not all bad. It's just that it doesn't allow for real change, the kind that requires new structural designs and spaces of equity that engender new kinds and levels of success.

This lack of change from continuing structural sameness is evident in the findings of the SIG program at both the national and local, in this case Michigan, positions. That is, the voices of Teacher Groups, Parents, and Students are not heard as part of the general conversation of the reported findings. They are, though, found within the fiscal documentation addressing the allocation and expenditures of the SIG funds at the district/school levels. This occurs because the funding provided to the schools was based on student voices, that is, student academic achievement data; and in most schools the only acceptable voice of students is their work—homework, tests, quizzes, assignments, athletics, performances, attendance, and proficiency scores. The voice of the staff is heard via what is done with and for them as they respond to the many and varied voices of students as learners and in community.

Findings

The research on the SIG program began during the first year of implementation and has continued annually. Consequently, there are two cohorts that have completed their three-year program cycle. In the 2010–2011 baseline report, the goal was to determine the SIG-related policies and practices states were going to implement and the characteristics of the eligible and awarded schools. Key policy findings regarding Cohort 1 were that (1) 27 states were using three years of data to identify their lowest-performing school, (2) 50 states were using the turnaround, transformation, and closure models, (3) 37 states were going to use some formal instrument to determine LEA capacity, (4) 39 states planned to monitor through site visits, and (5) 26 states planned to provide support to the SIG schools. Michigan used three years of assessment and graduation rate data to determine eligible schools, approved the use of all four reform models, used the LEA application as a self-report of LEA capacity, developed a monthly site visit monitoring model and supported the schools through technical assistance that consisted of a designated liaison, an approved external provider list, and quarterly network meetings to improve LEA and school capacity.[12]

Researchers from the Institute of Education Sciences (IES), gathering data on the first cohort of SIG-funded schools, found that 16 percent (15,277) of all schools nationwide were eligible to participate in the SIG program. However, the preponderance of awards went to high-poverty, high-minority, urban high schools to implement the transformation model. The awarded amount of funding on average was $2.54 million for Tier 1 and Tier 2 schools and $520,000 for Tier 3 schools. Consequently, the average three-year award varied by state. The average total SIG award was $2.60 million for Tier 1, $2.47 million for Tier 2, and $0.52 million for Tier 3, with an average annual per-pupil award of $1,490.00, $1,130.00, and $330.00 for Tiers 1, 2, and 3, respectively.[13]

In Michigan the selection process resulted in 228 schools or 5 percent of all schools in Michigan being eligible. Ten of these or 4.4 percent were Tier 1, 98 or 43 percent were Tier 2, and 120 or 52.6 percent were Tier 3. Twenty-eight schools were selected—3 from Tier 1 and 25 from Tier 2. This is significant because Michigan received the seventh largest amount of funding—$135.9 million. The average award per school in the state was $2.96 million with an average annual per-pupil award of $1,420.00.[14]

Moreover, most of the schools receiving the award in Michigan had poverty rates between 35 percent and 100 percent and were more than 25 percent minority. These schools were also generally urban high schools with over 600 students per building, and all but four of the buildings were regular education centers that selected the Transformation Model.[15]

The review of Cohort 2 of the SIG program had three of the same key findings as identified in Cohort 1. They are as follows: (1) most of the states created new lists of SIG-eligible school for Cohort 2, (2) many states modified the process for determining district capacity with new criteria, and (3) most of the states changed how they were supporting the SIG-funded schools to include areas of state restructuring, designated support staff, quality control for external providers, professional development, improved tools, and creating networks.[16] Michigan adopted new criteria for the identification for Cohort 2 schools to include the fact that the highest-quality SIG applications in combination with lowest achievement were given priority and retained all other program components established for Cohort 1.[17]

IES researchers also found that fewer schools were eligible for Cohort 2 (12,445 schools or 14 percent) of all public schools in the nation, with 81 percent having been previously eligible for Cohort 1. Ultimately, 600 of the schools were awarded grants. Like Cohort 1 most of the schools selected the Transformation or Turnaround models and were generally high schools in urban settings with high poverty and high minority populations. The schools also varied significantly in the amounts awarded. Cohort 2 had 315 schools from Tier 1, 174 from Tier 2, and 11 from Tier 3.[18] Likewise, Michigan had a decrease in the number of schools SIG-—eligible (198) and selected fewer schools (24).[19]

The average total award and per-pupil amounts were larger in Cohort 2 than in Cohort 1. Specifically, Tiers 1 and 2 schools received total average awards of $2.63 million or $1,690 annually per pupil and $3.17 million or $1,480 per pupil. Tier 3, Cohort 2, schools received, on average, $0.81 million or $870.00 annually per pupil.[20] Michigan SIG-awarded schools received, on average, $4.30 million per school with an annual per-pupil amount of $1,960, which was $540.00 more per pupil than was received for SIG-awarded Cohort 1 schools (Tables 12.1–12.5).[21]

Based on the data provided by the federal government, the SIG program was a very important and substantive design in function and operations for public education in the United States. It required states to look critically at the schools within their jurisdiction and make data-informed decisions about their effectiveness as educational programs. It also required that schools—administrators, teachers, parents, and students—have conversations about their school and its effectiveness for the students attending it in terms of current and future educational and economic aspirations. The process brought focused individual and collective accountability to a system fraught with unbridled individualism at every functional level. Moreover, it gave resources to support ideas and opportunities to design change in potentially, really effective ways.

TABLE 12.1 Baseline Data of SIG Program—Cohorts 1 and 2: Michigan and United States

Characteristics of SIG Awarded Schools by Tier, Poverty Level, and Minority Level

Metric	Michigan	United States
Number of schools awarded		
• Cohort 1	28	1,228
• Cohort 2	24	600
Tier 1		
• Cohort 1	3	514
• Cohort 2	0	315
Tier 2		
• Cohort 1	25	312
• Cohort 2	24	174
Tier 3		
• Cohort 1	0	402
• Cohort 2	0	111
Poverty level low (0 to <35%)		
• Cohort 1	2	76
• Cohort 2	0	43
Poverty level medium (35% to <75%)		
• Cohort 1	11	533
• Cohort 2	14	185
Poverty level high (75% to 100%)		
• Cohort 1	15	607
• Cohort 2	10	327
Minority level low (0 to <25%)		
• Cohort 1	4	224
• Cohort 2	0	62
Minority level medium (25% to <75%)		
• Cohort 1	9	264
• Cohort 2	7	121
Minority level high (75% to 100%)		
• Cohort 1	15	736
• Cohort 2	17	398

Source: Compiled from Steven Hurlburt et al., *Baseline Analyses,* p. c-1; Steven Hurlburt, Susan B. Therriault, and Kerstin C. Le Floch, *School Improvement Grant,* p. c-1.

TABLE 12.2 Baseline Data of SIG Program—Cohorts 1 and 2: Michigan and United States

Characteristics of SIG Awarded Schools by Urbanicity, School Level, and School Size

Metric	Michigan	United States
Urban		
• Cohort 1	17	641
• Cohort 2	16	304
Suburban		
• Cohort 1	6	297
• Cohort 2	8	168
Rural		
• Cohort 1	3	284
• Cohort 2	0	111
School level elementary		
• Cohort 1	4	394
• Cohort 2	5	221
School level middle		
• Cohort 1	7	241
• Cohort 2	8	125
School level high		
• Cohort 1	16	495
• Cohort 2	11	207
School size under 200 students		
• Cohort 1	1	155
• Cohort 2	0	87
School size 201 to 400 students		
• Cohort 1	1	292
• Cohort 2	2	118
School size 401 to 600 students		
• Cohort 1	6	283
• Cohort 2	8	146
School size over 600 students		
• Cohort 1	7	494
• Cohort 2	14	230

Source: Compiled from Steven Hurlburt et al., *Baseline Analyses,* p. c-3; Steven Hurlburt, Susan B. Therriault, and Kerstin C. Le Floch, *School Improvement Grant,* p. c-3.

TABLE 12.3 Baseline Data of SIG Program—Cohorts 1 and 2: Michigan and United States

Characteristics of SIG-Awarded Schools by School Type

Data Area	Michigan	United States
Regular school		
• Cohort 1	25	1,130
• Cohort 2	24	546
Special education center		
• Cohort 1	2	11
• Cohort 2	0	11
Vocational school		
• Cohort 1	0	9
• Cohort 2	0	3
Alternative/other school		
• Cohort 1	1	74
• Cohort 2	0	23
Charter school		
• Cohort 1	1	67
• Cohort 2	0	41

Source: Compiled from Steven Hurlburt et al., *Baseline Analyses,* p. c-5; Steven Hurlburt, Susan B. Therriault, and Kerstin C. Le Floch, *School Improvement Grant,* p. c-5.

TABLE 12.4 Baseline Data of SIG Program—Cohorts 1 and 2: Michigan and United States

Characteristics of SIG-Awarded Schools by Intervention Model

Data Area	Michigan	United States
Turnaround model		
• Cohort 1	9	168
• Cohort 2	7	91
Restart model		
• Cohort 1	0	33
• Cohort 2	0	29
School closure model		
• Cohort 1	0	16
• Cohort 2	0	2
Transformation model		
• Cohort 1	19	603
• Cohort 2	17	367

Source: Compiled from Steven Hurlburt et al., *Baseline Analyses,* p. c-7; Steven Hurlburt, Susan B. Therriault, and Kerstin C. Le Floch, *School Improvement Grant,* p. c-7.

TABLE 12.5   Baseline Data of SIG Program—Cohorts 1 and 2 Characteristics of SIG-Awarded Schools by Percent Free/Reduced Lunch Status, Race/Ethnicity, Urbanicity, and School Level

Metric	Cohort 1	Cohort 2
Free/reduced lunch status	72.5	68.2
Race/ethnicity school average percent of students		
White	26.4	20.2
African American	41.1	40.6
Hispanic	27.2	33.4
Native American	2	2.2
Asian	2.9	3.4
Urbanicity		
• Large/midsized city	52.4	52.1
• Urban fringe/large town	24.1	28.8
• Small town/rural area	23.6	19
School level		
• Elementary	32.4	37.9
• Middle	22	21.4
• High	39.8	35.5
• Nonstandard	5.8	5.1

Source: Compiled from Steven Hurlburt, Susan B. Therriault, and Kerstin C. Le Floch, *School Improvement Grant*, p. 26.

Interestingly, the schools in the program made improvements. Among the highlights were the fact that on average, proficiency rates of students increased in both math and reading. Also, the reform model, school level, and/or locality of the school didn't seem to have significant negative impact on learning by students as proficiency rates improved in all of these conditions.[22]

All of this activity and the successes paint a picture that suggests there have been structural changes in education that have yielded these results from a more equitable space. Specifically, the sheer volume of the process—SEA and LEA agreement to nonnegotiable conditions, robust competition of participants, additional fiscal resources, and frequent monitoring and support—would result in greater equity for participants—school staff, parents, and students. It would appear that all of the constituents were pulling together to attain the goal of improved academic performance by students. However, this was not true. In spite of all the focus, planning, work, and engagement, the fundamental structure of education in the United States did not change. It was just reinforced, in law at the mandate of the federal government and in compliance with the state government. Specifically, the federal government established that there is a hierarchical and legal structure in public education that must be acknowledged and used if federal educational funds are to be used.

The Structure of Education

In the United States, education from early childhood through 12th grade is a decentralized system based on the Constitution of the nation. It enables and reserves power over education to each state and local authorities as well as to individual schools. Therefore, there are a variety of laws at the federal, state, and local levels that define and govern aspects of the system. Currently, the system has four major components—performance data, curriculum, teachers, and students. These four components interact with each other based on a variety of conditions and influences—social, economic, and political. However, the core of the system is the relationship between teachers and students, which has been and generally remains hierarchical. McMullin, writing on Inequality in the Encyclopedia of Aging, suggests that each person has status or a "position in society"[23] that is either ascribed or achieved. If it is ascribed, then the characteristics of individuals are the determining factors. Generally, in this case the person has no control over his or her characteristics and thus the status afforded him or her. Such areas include sex, age, race, and ethnicity. Achieved status, though, refers to the attainment of some accomplishment via education or occupation. In both cases, the status provided is related to issues of power.

Power is the ability of a group or individual "to impose their will on others regardless of resistance"[24] and inclusive of economic and political structures that determine resource allocations and opportunities. Children, including teenagers in states, are provided legal authority for driving, drinking, and employment based on age. In this sense they have less status and power than those considered to be adults in the society. They are also vulnerable because they may lack the levels and kinds of education required in various settings. Again, they would have less status and power than those who are older with significantly more education and lived experiences. Consequently, children and youth must be integrated into the larger society in ways that are inclusive individually and socially so they are not relegated to lives of marginality due to persistent structural inequalities that fail to deliver jobs, services, or other opportunities with which to realize capabilities. This process requires that individual students develop personal efficacy and voice so as not to become victims of injustice.

Dorling states that there are five tenets or beliefs that support injustice. They are as follows: "Elitism is efficient, exclusion is necessary, prejudice is natural, greed is good and despair is inevitable."[25] Each of these beliefs creates a distinct set of victims—the delinquents, the debarred, the discarded, the debtors, and the depressed. Of special interest are the delinquents, that is, children found to be "simple or limited at learning when tested."[26] It is estimated that 9 percent of the national student public school enrollment are African American boys. However, in some special education categories, such as mental retardation (cognitive impairment), emotional disturbance, and learning disability, their enrollment percentage is 20 percent, 21 percent, and 12 percent, respectively.[27]

Through the Michigan Department of Education researchers found that African American students made up 17 percent of student enrollment in the state, but in school they were underrepresented with only 7 percent in math and 7 percent in reading in the top 30 percent of students. However, they were overrepresented in the bottom 30 percent, being 31 percent in math and 29 percent in reading. Furthermore, 75 percent of African American students scored below the state average, meaning that more than 50 percent of the African Americans who attended a school for a full academic year tested in the 2012–2013 year scored in the bottom 30 percent of students statewide.[28] This is important because it is these schools and ones like them that are struggling with underperformance and overrepresentation of African American students and apply for SIG funds. They are eligible for funding because they rank in the bottom 5 percent of schools in their state, and in Michigan they contain the majority (72%) of African American students in the State.

What is also interesting is that these schools receive funding based on student need as manifest through student work compiled as data from test scores, attendance records, behavior reports, and grades, and yet their voices are silenced by low expectations in the continuing existence of a structure that, while promoting injustice, makes them victims. They, lacking the necessary academic acumen, social skills, political access, and voice, become statistics in a school-to-prison pipeline that includes physical, social, economic, and mental incarceration.

The Rights of Children and Youth

On April 20, 1964, in Pretoria, South Africa, Nelson Mandela, on trial for sabotage, told the Supreme Court that he had an ideal for which he was prepared to die. This ideal included the right to an education of and with equality for Africans in South Africa. Specifically, he said,

> The complaint of Africans, however, is not only that they are poor and the whites are rich, but that the laws which are made by the whites are designed to preserve this situation. There are two ways to break out of poverty. The first is by formal education, and the second is by the worker acquiring a greater skill at his work and thus higher wages. As far as Africans are concerned, both these avenues of advancement are deliberately curtailed by legislation.
>
> The government has always sought to hamper Africans in their search for education. There is compulsory education for all white children at virtually no cost to their parents, be they rich or poor. African children, however, generally have to pay more for their schooling than whites.
>
> Approximately 40% of African children in the age group seven to 14 do not attend school. For those who do, the standards are vastly different from those afforded to white children. Only 5,660 African children in the whole of South Africa passed their junior certificate in 1962, and only 362 passed matric.
>
> This is presumably consistent with the policy of Bantu education about which the present prime minister said: "When I have control of native education I will reform it so that natives will be taught from childhood to realise that equality with Europeans is not for them. People who believe in equality are not desirable teachers for natives. When my department controls native education it will know for what class of higher education a native is fitted, and whether he will have a chance in life to use his knowledge."[29]

During this time Dorling records that "the South African government spent 12 times as much on educating each European child as on each African child."[30] In comparison by 1990 inner-city children in America were having half as much spent on their secondary education as children in affluent suburbs. During 2003 inner cities were 90 percent children of color—black or Hispanic, and "inequalities in State school spending in America had risen four-fold."[31] Indeed, a "(g)ood, fair, just education is not provided in societies where the accepted belief is that different children have different capacities, where it is presumed that most people are always destined to struggle, and that each has a low limit to what they can be expected to achieve."[32] But such is the case in the United States today. How we fund a project is a reflection of the value we give to it and those who participate in it.

Human and Social Capital

The Inclusive Wealth Report 2012 was published by the United Nations (UN) on 20 nations in an effort to address the question, what is wealth and what can be done to both increase and sustain it? The UN researchers, led by Sir Partha Dasgupta, determined that it is the "social worth"[33] of a nation's assets manifest in seven forms—reproducible capital, human capital, knowledge, natural capital, population, institutions, and time. In the report they focused on three of the forms—physical capital, such as machinery and buildings; human capital or the population's education and skills; and natural capital like land, fossil fuels, and minerals. There were also issues that had no specific dollar amount that could be attached to them, and prices had to be estimated. An example of this is beekeeping, which enables the creation of honey (an item that can be packaged and sold) as well as provides pollination of trees, a service that cannot be purchased or priced.

A major finding of the research was that sustainable development was required as a focus now and for future generations. In order for this to happen, governments needed to encourage education, increase public infrastructure, and decrease the extraction of their natural resources. The report goes on to say that human capital is the primary form of capital that has offset the decline in natural capital in most nations, and it has increased in every country. Its significance relates to a newly developing concept—social capital.[34]

Social capital was initially used in sociology to discuss human relationships and their value. Over the years this area of study has become increasingly important as it has expanded to define relationships and networks of trust, in individuals and institutions. Aiding this growth has been technology through social networking. Such agencies as "Angie's List" that are based on local business and professional interactions for services have come to dominate the field with online ratings, data analysis, and recommendations for an ever-increasing range of local services using an international platform. These resources enable access and information, as well as opportunity, sustainability, service, an increased well-being of citizens who participate through online and real time connections, interactions, work, economic and personal development, and personal voice. Like beekeeping, the development of social capital is a commodity that is service with a price though it is priceless. The structure created to enable and support this paradigm is flexible due to a variety of contexts in which it must operate. Everyone can participate to the degree that he or she desires in a manner that is consistent within the specific relationship; and every voice is heard because each voice has impact on the structure.

This design is also the domain of what the current status of public education is. Technology now enables everyone, including students and teachers, to learn whatever he or she wants, when he or she wants, and how he or she wants to learn. Fundamentally, the structure of the system has changed. However, the funding stream that supports education has not changed. It is the same hierarchical design that has always existed because there is a predominant view that limits the voice of those for whom the system has low expectations, generally, underperforming students and their families. Royce states that "(t)he allocation of public funds for education is a matter of political power, not individual choice. . . . It is precisely their . . .— economic marginalization, their lack of political power, their social and residential segregation—that limits . . . access to education and training."[35] He believes that education is only a key to success and this requires not only for the individual to have an appropriate education, but also the requisite social capital. The success or failure of a person in life is not, in his opinion, dependent on education, training, or job experience. It is directly a result of social capital—who you are, who you know, where you work, and the jobs that are available. This is true for students and staff in underperforming schools. Consequently, it is difficult for many of these schools to find, hire, and retain highly qualified and effective teachers. The social capital they participate in, via the schools, is not significant enough to outweigh other options without substantive natural capital, working conditions, and compensation, physical capital. Unfortunately, what is true for teachers and other staff is also true for students and their parents.

The difference, however, is that the parents and students are dependent on the available social systems to provide some significant amounts of the additional natural capital via their work in the community. An example of this is field trips through class or school curricula. This collaborative engagement enriches everyone and is critically important to personal and community development.

The issue is that underperforming schools have untapped and thus low levels of realized wealth and perceived well-being. This is established by the fact that in the first year of SIG implementation the two areas with the most evident change were the climate and culture of the school and teacher collaboration.

Trujillo and Renee establish this position by stating,

> While the program channels grants to participating schools . . . it does not maintain funding beyond three years, nor does it alter the basic, inadequate funding structures for public education. . . . Generations of research show that the SIG reforms are based on faulty evidence, unwarranted claims and they ignore contradictory evidence. The most prominent error is the claim that these corporate-based models can yield transformative results. The second most prominent error is the assumption that the drastic recon-stitution of school staff will prove beneficial. Neither claim is supported by research. . . . Fundamentally, the SIG policy is . . . the NCLB market-based approach to education, not a change in direction. The policy assumes that schools behave . . . as private corporations . . . behave when it relies on com-petition, monitoring, and rigid accountability.[36]

It is this policy that differs from a democratic process of public educa-tion that treats schools as a public good. In such a structure opportunities are created for public deliberation (voice) and self-governance. The goal of such a system would be to provide all students with equitable opportuni-ties for learning, to participate in the larger society, and to improve social change. This is the nature of education for both human and social capital development.

Equitable Funding in SIG Schools

Although there were specific metrics schools had to address as part of the SIG monitoring process, many of the budget decisions were designed for the applying school to develop. In some cases the School Leadership Team drafted them and in others they were drafted by central office staff. But in all cases the actual recordkeeping, that is, requisitions, invoices, and formal contract approval by school boards, was facilitated and kept by the district office. In Michigan the Final Expenditure Reports (FERs) for each school year were filed with the Michigan Department of Education by the district offices. In order to have as complete a file on expenditures as possible, due to closures, consolidations, and so on, a review was made of the 2012–2013 academic year. This was the final year of funding for SIG Cohort 1 schools and the second year of SIG Cohort 2 schools. The data reviewed was the 2012–2013 FERs for each LEA district. Amounts in each of the funded areas were totaled and averaged in order to give an overall picture of how funds were spent (Table 12.6).

TABLE 12.6 Michigan School Improvement Grant: Summary of District Final Expenditure Reports for 2012–2013

Expenditure Areas, Number of District Responses, and Percent of Total Expenditure by Area

Expenditure Areas	Salaries	Benefits	Purchased Services	Supplies and Materials	Capital Outlay	Other
Number of district responses	28	28	28	26	4	3
Percentage of total expenditures	23.68	10.64	29.63	35.52	0.5	0.04

Source: Compiled from LEAs Reporting Final Expenditures in Michigan Electronic Grants System.

There were six areas of expenditures that a school could choose to use to pay for program implementation. These were salaries of hired staff and the benefits that are required; purchased services, such as consultants; professional learning opportunity, improvement facilitators, safety and security staff from a vendor, and so on; supplies and materials such as books, equipment, technology, and consumable items for use in a specific student-based program; capital outlay such as technology carts or tables; and other items such as food and materials for parent meetings.

The data in Table 12.6 indicates that over 34 percent of SIG funding went directly into staff compensation. This increases to more than 63 percent when combined with purchased services. Thus, almost two-thirds of the SIG funding went to purchase human capital services for adults. This is significant because none of the questions in the SIG monitoring document ask students or their parents about SIG funding and the use of fiscal resources. Clearly, there was no intention of them knowing about or being engaged in the budget development process for SIG so they had no voice in the allocation plan. However, the SEA and LEA had full knowledge of the funds and the discretion to engage whoever they wanted in the decision making regarding the funds. Therefore, some constituents were included and some were not. The end result is that, from all indications, those who had information regarding the fiscal components of SIG used it to their collective benefit. What does this mean, potentially, for school funding with federal, state, or local resources?

Summary and Implications

Interestingly, in 2011 the U.S. secretary of education commissioned an Equity and Excellence Commission to "collect information, analyze issues, and obtain broad public input regarding how the Federal government could increase educational opportunity by improving school funding equity."[37] After over a year of study, this group of men and women sent a report to the Secretary of Education entitled, "For Each and Every Child."[38] Their first conclusion was that "(o)ur system does not distribute opportunity equitably. Our leaders decry but tolerate disparities in student outcomes that are not only unfair, but socially and economically dangerous."[39] Thus, the commission recommended that "the federal government must take more seriously its profoundly important responsibility to assist and encourage states and districts . . . within the general framework of a partnership."[40] One has to ask, "Really?" Given the commission's current work in the partnership arena with the SEAs and LEAs regarding SIG funding, this prospect does not hold much hope for change that will enable less inequity in the nation. So what should be done?

Ainscow et al. argue that the real question is not who gets what, but contrarily, "what is it that resources enable people to do"[41] regarding their capabilities? Addressing this question brings to light the larger issue of what the capabilities of individuals are and how they are identified in ways that are tangible enough to be pursued via educational options. The significance of this paradigm cannot be overestimated. Most of the people in the world are people of color, and the sheer numbers and percentages are growing in the United States. The idea of assisting these young people and their families understand the larger context of life possibilities would substantively change our nation and the world. Therefore, the best place to start in answering these questions is with laws because they give us prevailing and expected structures that we can accept or refuse to use.

One such law is The Convention on the Rights of Children established as an international requirement in 1989 by the United Nations General Assembly. It consists of 54 articles on the basic human rights that should be afforded all children. It is founded, per the preamble, on the ideas that they should be afforded the necessary protection and assistance so they can fully assume their responsibilities within the community, and require full and harmonious development of their personality in order to be fully prepared to live an individual life in society in the spirit of peace, dignity, tolerance, freedom, equality, and solidarity.[42] This is a place to start.

Taken as a paradigm with the ideas of Ainscow et al., it suggests that the first step is to establish an "ideal for which we are prepared to die" regarding the importance of developing the capabilities of children, specifically, children of color, in Michigan and the nation. It would progress via honest conversations with all constituents in a transparent informational environment. This would include options regarding all available resources—human (social and educational), natural (time), and physical (financial, technological, vocational), for their lives. It would be followed by collaboratively creating, implementing, and assessing best practices in the authentic engagement of children, their parents, and business owners, as well as school, LEA and SEA staff. And then? Doing the hard work of making it happen. This process can occur in any setting at any time, and now is as good as tomorrow or next week. Its impact would certainly shift the structures of existing power in all areas and move more people of color into the manifestation of their capabilities resulting in a human capital system with greater equitability.

Notes

1. United States Department of Education 2014.

2. United States Department of Education. "American Recovery and Reinvestment Act of 2009: Title I, Part A Funds for Grants to Local Education Agencies." April 1, 2009.

3. United States Department of Education. "Applications Now Available for $3.5 Billion in Title I School Improvement Grants to turn Around Nation's Lowest Achieving Public Schools." 2009.

4. Ibid.

5. United States Department of Education. "Title I—Improving the Academic Achievement of the Disadvantaged."

6. The White House 2011, p. 3.

7. Ibid., p. 4.

8. Ibid.

9. United States Department of Education 2013, p. 3.

10. Ibid.

11. Ibid., pp. 4–52.

12. Hurlburt et al. 2011, pp. 7–18.

13. Ibid., pp. 21, 34.

14. Ibid., pp. 23, 25, 35.

15. Ibid., pp. C3, C-5, C-7.

16. Hurlburt et al. 2012, p. 5.

17. Ibid., p. 9.

18. Ibid., p. 17.
19. Ibid., pp. 20–21.
20. Ibid., p. 29.
21. Ibid., p. 31.
22. United States Department of Education 2014.
23. McMullin 2002, pp. 707–708.
24. Ibid.
25. Dorling 2010, p. 1.
26. Ibid., p. 3.
27. Adkison-Bradley et al. 2006.
28. Flores 2010.
29. Mandela 1964. "An Ideal for Which I Am Prepared to Die."
30. Dorling 2010, p. 62.
31. Ibid., p. 64.
32. Ibid., p. 83.
33. Dasgupta et al. 2012.
34. Ibid., pp. 272, 278.
35. Royce 2009, pp. 74–75.
36. Trujillo and Renee 2012.
37. "Archived Information: The Equity and Excellence Commission: A Report to the Secretary." http://www2.ed.gov/about/bdscomm/list/eec/equity-excellence-commission-report.pdf.
38. "Archived Information: The Equity and Excellence Commission: A Report to the Secretary." http://www2.ed.gov/about/bdscomm/list/eec/equity-excellence-commission-report.pdf, p.3.
39. "Archived Information: The Equity and Excellence Commission: A Report to the Secretary." http://www2.ed.gov/about/bdscomm/list/eec/equity-excellence-commission-report.pdf, p.9.
40. Ainscow et al. 2012, p. 7.
41. United Nations Human Rights. "Convention on the Rights of the Child" 1989.
42. United Nations Human Rights. "Convention on the Rights of the Child" 1989.

Bibliography

Adkison-Bradley, Carla, Philip D. Johnson, Glinda Rawls, and Darryl Plunkett. 2006. "Overrepresentation of African American Males in Special Education Programs: Implications and Advocacy Strategies for School Counselors." http://files.eric.ed.gov/fulltext/EJ901152.pdf.

Ainscow, Mel, Alan Dyson, Sue Goldrick, and Mel West. 2012. *Developing Equitable Education Systems*. New York: Routledge.

Alexander, Michelle. 2010. *The New Jim Crow: Mass Incarceration in the Age of Colorblindness*. New York: The New Press. http://www.kropfpolisci.com/racial.justice.alexander.pdf.

Angie's List. "How It Works." http://www.angieslist.com/how-it-works.htm.

The Annie E. Casey Foundation. *Race for Results: Building a Path to Opportunity for All Children.* Baltimore, MD: The Annie Casey Foundation. Accessed April 17, 2014. http://www.kidscount.org.

Bangura, Yusef. 2010. *Combatting Poverty and Inequality: Structural Change, Social Policy and Politics.* Geneva: United Nations Research Institute for Social Development.

Dasgupta, Partha, Anantha Duraiappah, Pablo Munoz, Elorm Darkey, Kirsten Oleson, Leonie Pearson, Kevin J. Mumford, Giles Atkinson, Matthew Agarwala, Charles Perrings, Edward B. Barbier, Heather Tallis, Stephen Polasky, Juan S. Lozano, Stacie Wolny, Chris Perry, Paul Ekins, and Pablo Fuentenebro. 2012. *Inclusive Wealth Report 2012.* New York: Cambridge University Press. http://www.unep.org/pdf/IWR_2012.pdf.

Dorling, Daniel. 2010. *Injustice: Why Social Inequality Persists.* Bristol, UK: Policy Press.

Flores, Shannon S. 2014. "'Quantifying the Achievement Gap' Baseline Characteristics of African-American Student Achievement in Michigan." PowerPoint presented at the Michigan Department of Education Achievement Gap meeting, Lansing, Michigan, June.

Gorard, Stephen, and Emma Smith. 2010. *Equity in Education: An International Comparison of Pupil Perspectives.* New York: Palgrave MacMillan.

Hurlburt, Steven, Kerstin C. Le Floch, Susan B. Therriault, and Susan Cole. *Baseline Analyses of SIG Applications and SIG-Eligible and SIG-Awarded Schools* (NCEE 2011–4019). Washington, DC: National Center for Education Evaluation and Regional Assistance, Institute of Education Sciences, U.S. Department of Education, 2011. http://ies.ed.gov/ncee.

Hurlburt, Steven, Susan B. Therriault, and Kerstin C. Le Floch. 2012. *School Improvement Grants: Analyses of State Applications and Eligible and Awarded Schools* (NCEE 2012–4060). Washington, DC: National Center for Education Evaluation and Regional Assistance, Institute of Education Sciences, U.S. Department of Education. http://ies.ed.gov/ncee.

Hurst, Charles E. 2001. *Social Inequality: Forms, Causes, and Consequences.* Boston, MA: Allyn & Bacon.

Klein, Alyson. 2010. "Education Budget Plan Wielded as Policy Lever." *Education Week* 29.

Klein, Alyson. 2010. "Taking Aim at AYP Called Timely, Risky." *Education Week* 29.

Korukonda, Appa R., and Chenchu R. T. Bathala. 2004. "Ethics, Equity, and Social Justice in The New Economic Order: Using Financial Information for Keeping Social Score." *Journal of Business Ethics* 54: 1–15.

Le Floch, Kerstin C., Beatrice Birman, Jennifer O'Day, Steven Hurlburt, Diana Mercado-Garcis, Rose Goff, Karen Manship, Seth Brown, Susan B. Therriault, Linda Rosenberf, Megan H. Angus, and Lara Hulsey. 2014. *Case Studies of Schools Receiving School Improvement Grants: Findings after the First Year of Implementation* (NCEE 2014–4015). Washington, DC: National Center for Education Evaluation and Regional Assistance, Institute of Education Sciences, U.S. Department of Education. http://ies.ed.gov/ncee.

McMullin, Julie. 2002. "Inequality." In *Encyclopedia of Aging*, eds. David J. Ekerdt, Robert A. Applebaum, Karen C. Holden, Stephen G. Post, Kenneth Rockwood, Richard Schultz, Richard L. Sprott, and Peter Uhlenberg. (vol. 2, pp. 706–711). New York: Macmillan Reference USA.

McNeil, Michele. 2010. "Red Flags Raised over Inequities as Consequence of Stimulus Aid." *Education Week* (February 24).

Michigan Department of Education. "ARRA School Improvement Grant Business Rules Leading to Eligibility for the School Improvement Grant." May 17, 2010. http://michigan.gov/documents/mde/04a_-_SIG_Business_Rules_324480_7 .pdf.

Michigan Department of Education. "Quantifying the Achievement Gap Baseline Characteristics of African-American Student Achievement in Michigan." June 2014.

Michigan Department of Education. "School Improvement Grant (SIG) School Ranking Business Rules Full Narrative Version." http://www.michigan.gov/ documents/mde/06_-_SIG_Rules_Full_Narrative_324483_7.pdf.

Ramirez, Al. 2002. "The Shifting Sands of School Finance." *Educational Leadership* 60: 54–57.

Royce, Edward. 2009. *Poverty and Power: The Problem of Structural Inequality.* Lanham: Rowman & Littlefield.

Sleeter, Christine. 2003. "Reform and Control: An Analysis of SB 2042." *Teacher Education Quarterly* Winter: 19–30.

Trujillo, Tina, and Renee, Michelle. 2012. *Democratic School Turnarounds: Pursuing Equity and Learning from Evidence.* Boulder, CO: National Education Policy Center. http://nepc.colorado.edu/publication/democratic-school-turnarounds.

Turner, Ani. "The Business Case for Racial Equity." PowerPoint presented at the Health Equity Workgroup Webcast, April 17, 2014.

United Nations Human Rights. "Convention on the Rights of the Child." November 20, 1989. http://www.ohchr.org/EN/ProfessionalInterest/Pages/CRC.aspx.

United States. "Federal Registry." October 28, 2010. https://www.federalregister .gov/articles/search?conditions%5Bagency_ids%5D=126&conditions%5Bpub lication_date%5D%5Bis%5D=10%2F28%2F2010&conditions%5Btype%5D= NOTICE.

United States Department of Education. "American Recovery and Reinvestment Act of 2009: Title I, Part A Funds for Grants to Local Education Agencies." April 1, 2009. http://www2.ed.gov/policy/gen/leg/recovery/factsheet/title-i .html.

United States Department of Education. "Applications Now Available for $3.5 Billion in Title I School Improvement Grants to Turn Around Nation's Lowest Achieving Public Schools." December 3, 2009. http://www2.ed.gov/news/pressreleases/2009/12/12032009a.html.

United States Department of Education. "Archived: About—Equity and Excellence Commission." 2012. http://www2.ed.gov/about/bdscomm/list/eec/about/html.

United States Department of Education. "Archived: Members—Equity and Excellence Commission." 2012. http://www2.ed.gov/about/bdscomm/list/eec/members/html.

United States Department of Education. "Archived: Equity and Excellence Commission." 2012. http://www2.ed.gov/about/bdscomm/list/eec/index/html.

United States Department of Education. "Archived Information: Equity and Excellence Commission Charter." 2012. http://www2.ed.gov/about/bdscomm/list/eec/documents.html.

United States Department of Education. "Archived Information: The Equity and Excellence Commission: A Report to the Secretary." 2012. http://www2.ed.gov/about/bdscomm/list/eec/equity-excellence-commission-report.pdf.

United States Department of Education. "Baseline Analyses of SIG Applications and SIG-Eligible and SIG-Awarded Schools." 2011.

United States Department of Education. "Office of School Turnaround (OST) Monitoring Plan for School Improvement Grant (SIG) October 1, 2013 to September 30, 2014." October 1, 2013. http://www2.ed.gov/programs/sif/sigmonitoringplan2012-2013.pdf.

United States Department of Education. "Recovery Act." Accessed September 30, 2010. http://www.ed.gov/recovery.

United States Department of Education. "School Improvement Grant (SIG) National Assessment Results Summary: Cohorts 1 and 2." February 14, 2014. http://www2.ed.gov/programs/sif/assessment-results-cohort-1-2-sig-schools.pdf.

United States Department of Education. "School Improvement Grants." 2014. www2.ed/gov/programs/sif/index.html.

United States Department of Education. "School Improvement Grant State Summaries Cohort 1 Schools." June 25, 2013. http://www2.ed.gov/programs/sif/sig_state_data_summary_sy10-11.pdf.

United States Department of Education. "Title I—Improving the Academic Achievement of the Disadvantaged." September 15, 2004. http://www2.ed.gov/policy/elsec/leg/esea02/pg1.html.

United States Department of Education. "USNEI General Information Resources about Education in the United States." 2008. http://www.ed.gov/about/offices/list/ous/international/usnei/edite-index.html.

United States Department of Education. "USNEI Organization of U.S. Education." 2008. http://www2.ed.gov/about/offices/list/ous/international/usnei/edite-index.html.

Walsemann, Katrina M., Gilbert C. Gee, and Annie Ro. "Educational Attainment in the Context of Social Inequality: New Directions for Research on Education and Health." *American Behavioral Scientist* 57: 1082–1104. doi:10.1177/000276 4213487346. September 15, 2004. http://www2.ed.gov/policy/elsec/leg/esea02/pg1.html.

The White House. "Remarks by the President at Miami Central High School in Miami, Florida." March 4, 2011. http://www.whitehouse.gov/the-press-office/2011/03/04/remarks-president-miami-central-high-school-miami-florida.

Chapter 13

What Do Students "Deserve"? Narratives of Merit and Worth in Public Discussions of Educational Controversies

Sabrina Zirkel

Questions of merit and worth saturate the educational world. As educators, we find ourselves deeply embedded in an endeavor in which individuals are persistently subjected to assessments of their relative value, merit, and—indeed—worth. We grade students' work, rank students at graduation, and offer (or deny) admission, honors, scholarships, and awards. In all of this work, we engage in judgments about who deserves what and why. The educational enterprise was, in large part, designed for this purpose—to sort and rank students according to culturally bound ideas of intellectual merit. Merit, in these characterizations, is seen as a fixed or unchanging, knowable, and objectively defined construct.[1] It is conceived to be both easily defined and easily recognized. Conversations about controversies of race and ethnicity in education are often centered in questions about who has merit, who is "deserving" or "worthy," and when and how we define these constructs. In this chapter, I explore how concepts of merit, deservingness, and worth are often "raced" in our public conversations about educational controversies. Through the lens of critical race theory (CRT), I argue that a wide range of cultural narratives are employed in these conversations that implicitly identify all things "white" as good and all things "of color" as bad. I explore three areas of controversy in public education: resource allocation in schools, student discipline in urban public schools, and competitive college admissions. In each, I document the ways that race and ethnicity shift the criteria that a (largely white) public uses to discuss who deserves what in education, and how members of the public report the criteria they use for making these judgments.

I use three distinct cases to frame my discussion of these controversies. The cases are taken from my work on public discussions of race and ethnicity in education and are used to highlight how public conversations about controversial issues in education often quickly morph into debates and judgments about "merit" and "worth." The first case concerns a school board decision to cut expensive before- and after-school science labs in order to address a wide racial achievement gap in a local high school by investing that money in programs for struggling students. Public discussion followed on who "deserved" those funds. In the second case, a self-described very "tough" middle school principal is accused of abusing students and families (of color), and public conversations discuss whether these actions were perhaps "justified." The third case examines controversies regarding the admissions processes and outcomes of two elite, highly competitive universities, and public discussion focuses on the criteria that ought to drive admissions in such situations. These three cases explore very different issues in education, yet all consider controversies that ultimately focus on issues of race and ethnicity in schools and what is "fair" and "just." Implicitly, each is also about who is seen as having merit or is worthy of different kinds of educational resources.

In each case, the news story about the events elicited a large number of public comments about the issues in question. Much of the public discussion about these events focused extensive attention on issues of merit and worth—who deserves what, when, and why? In every case, these controversies became public and were covered in newspapers and other media. People engaged in extensive online debate in comment boards, blogs and other medium. I use these comments to explore questions about how students in each case are viewed. My focus is on uncovering how notions of merit and worth—particularly the merit and worth of students and families of color—are socially constructed in different contexts. Most important, I am interested in how questions of merit and worth are raced—that is, how the race of students and/or parents shifts the criteria by which a student is defined as worthy of humane treatment, extra resources, or admission to an elite university by a largely white public when considering a variety of educational policy questions.

Social Construction of Merit and Worth

A central concept informing this chapter concerns the social construction of merit and worth.[2] Ideas about merit and worth are sometimes discussed as though these judgments are "natural" based on objective, universally understood information. The assumption is that merit and worth are objective attributes qualified by inherently "obvious" or "transparent" notions of what is good, worthy, and deserving. For example, when we talk about college admissions, much reference is made to the quality of different applicants based on their high school grades and SAT or ACT scores. In reality, there is no such thing as an objective, perfect measure of students' capacities, nor do we even agree on which capacities are most important or meaningful. The slipperiness with which we move from socially constructed notions of who is "meritorious" to assumptions that these are natural categories that are easily defined and measured is a central concern of this chapter.

Social constructions of merit and worth about students and families in the discussions that follow mirror, in many ways, discussions of public conceptualizations of the deserving and "undeserving" poor that go back nearly 40 years.[3] Conceptualizations of "deservingness" in conversations about "the poor" follow certain neoliberal ideals about individual responsibility for one's own outcomes in life. Theorists who have focused on the role of conceptions of deservingness with regard to people living in poverty note that poor individuals are often viewed in unequal terms. In much public discourse, there are distinctions made between the deserving poor— who fit with popular narratives that allow them to be "excused" for their economic status. Conversely, the "undeserving poor," for whom broad sections of the public hold little sympathy, are widely regarded in popular discourse as being "responsible" for their own poverty because of a presumed lack of qualities that fit certain neoliberal ideals about individual determination for one's life outcomes. Such individuals are therefore deemed unworthy of a social safety net. In public discussions about merit and worth in schools, popular narratives also drive judgments of who is deserving—and also who is not.

Critical Race Theory and Educational Controversies

CRT contains at least three critical assumptions that are helpful here: (1) much of American life is inherently raced, particularly whenever questions about access to resources are at stake; (2) property rights trump human rights in our thinking about most issues;[4] and (3) the central role of narrative in our understanding of events, including the use of stories and counterstories to illuminate and reveal the racialized nature of events that might otherwise remain hidden.[5] The controversies discussed here invoke questions about who is worthy and deserving of a variety of different resources and they raise questions that are inherently subjective. Socially constructed narratives and ideas about race and ethnicity are embedded within public discussion of how to resolve these controversies. Indeed, many of our most deeply held and implicit beliefs about race and ethnicity are revealed in conversations about relative worth. The conceptions of merit and worth revealed in these conversations are often raced and strategic, as CRT would predict. Put bluntly, definitions of merit and worth change and shift in ways that support white access to resources.

In the first case, the controversy surrounds the allocation of actual educational dollars: Who should be the recipient of special tax dollars allocated to a racially, ethnically, and economically diverse high school? The second controversy concerns a far less tangible resource—who deserves harsh treatment in schools? Who deserves to be treated with kindness and respect? In the final case, the controversy is centered on admissions criteria to elite universities: What are and ought to be the criteria for discerning which students to admit? In each instance, the positions taken in online public discussions about controversial issues consistently privilege white students. In these public debates—engaged in by what appears to be a predominantly white set of people—the students who are perceived as having the greatest merit and being the most deserving of the available resources are, not surprisingly, white students. By examining the three cases together, we can more easily observe the ways that standards shift and conceptions of merit and worth change with the race of the students being discussed.

Case One: Who Deserves "Special" School Dollars?

Berkeley High School is a highly racially, ethnically, and economically diverse high school in a semi-urban, liberal, university town setting. Despite a great deal of rhetoric and interest in creating a school that serves all students equally well, the high school has a very large and long-standing racial achievement gap[6,7] in student performance and persistence. Extra tax dollars have been committed to the district by local taxpayers, yet how best to use these funds is a subject of some debate. For many years, a portion of these funds was used to pay for before- and after-school laboratory science classes to supplement lecture courses during the regular school day. After much internal discussion, the school district decided to divert these funds for other purposes. School authorities determined that the before- and after-school science labs exacerbated, rather than attenuated, the large racial achievement gap at the school. High-achieving students from affluent families, who could afford private tutors, were able to utilize these labs to add a large number of Advanced Placement science classes to their academic records. In contrast, poorer students, typically of color, were regularly failing the labs and, consequently, science, which impeded their ability to graduate from high school. Additional details on the curricular and pedagogical issues and the rationale for the change can be found elsewhere.[8]

The proposed change prompted a lot of debate locally and even nationally and internationally about science education and how to address issues of equity and racial justice in schools. Several newspaper articles were written about it, and national radio talk shows also raised the question, using it to prompt conversations about how best to spend educational dollars. Several disturbing themes emerged in these conversations.[9] The theme most pertinent to this discussion was the debate that emerged around who deserves access to these additional school funds and which students and educational endeavors are worthy of investment.

The overwhelming majority of comments from local parents and community members as well as national commentators and members of the general public converged on one core belief: students who perform well are more deserving of educational resources and investment than students who perform poorly. This argument was made most succinctly by a local newspaper commenter whose online moniker was "Tickyul": "The top 10 percent in this school are the ones who will make great advances for this country. . . . The biggest dollars should be poured into the brightest students, not the dummies or even the average students. Take money away from the smartest and waste it on dumbells, not a good idea."[10] Public sentiment supported this idea and promoted the following rationale: investments of scarce resources should be given to the highest achieving because they have the most to give back, rather than to those who are struggling because struggling students were presumed to have little or no potential. Precisely why some students were doing well and others were not was never questioned, nor was there any effort to move away from the supposition that those who were doing poorly had little or no potential to improve.

The narratives implicit or explicit in public comments about why some students do well and others do not were often focused on what was assumed to be some kind of "raw" natural intelligence or were based on a presumption that some students, parents, and families "care" about education and some "do not." In either case, the prevalent narrative suggested that the achievement differences between students were immutable and further asserted that certain students were deserving and worthy of educational resources while others were not. Often, the comments were quite blunt and even harsh. For example, another commenter, Seanx, stated: "It is time to just let the worst students go. With state and local budgets destroyed, it is time to save those worth saving. Regardless of race. Hurting the good students is obscene. And very possibly criminal fraud."[11]

The argument that members of the public are making here—rather explicitly—is that worthiness and merit are defined solely by how well students are doing in school. Those who are doing well are presumed to be working hard and "talented" and, consequently, they are deserving of resources and opportunities. Times are tough, so the argument goes, but given our limited resources, we need to invest in the most deserving, the most worthy: those who are doing well. But, I question: Is this always how we see "worthiness"? Are worth and merit always defined in terms of who is performing well? In the case described earlier, those who were performing well were overwhelmingly white and middle class or affluent. What happens when nonwhite students are the ones who are "doing well"? What if nonwhite students are doing better than their white peers? What then? Who is most deserving in that instance? The next two cases I describe involve situations in which students of color are performing well.

Case Two: Who Deserves Care and Respect in School?

This next case involves a public charter middle school in an urban community, the student body of which is nearly 100 percent students of color (1 out of nearly 200 students identified as white). The school received a great deal of positive attention and press because of students' high levels of performance on standardized tests.[12] The school was named a "Blue Ribbon School," a national recognition afforded to fewer than 300 schools across the nation. My students and I visited the school to learn more about it and witnessed a number of troubling actions.[13] For example, during our visit, the principal of the school shouted racial epithets at one of our African American male graduate students and chased him out of the building for arriving late. He sexually harassed another student in our presence and regaled us with many stories of similarly disturbing actions he and his teachers had taken with students, such as making them sit on the floor if they forgot their homework, refusing to allow students to eat lunch if they forget to bring lunch from home, and shaving a boy's head as punishment for a school infraction.

We filed formal complaints about the school with the Office of Civil Rights, and our letters were leaked to the press. This leak led to a series of stories in the local newspapers about the principal and the school. Public conversation and some investigative reporting revealed many prior complaints from teachers and parents that outlined similarly outrageous acts as well as serious allegations of cheating, embezzling, and other misconduct.[14] The newspaper stories about the school documented several allegations about the school principal (including an allegation that he pushed a teacher down a flight of stairs and another allegation that he publicly and repeatedly called one mother a "whore"). This ignited a public conversation about the school, the students' tremendous academic success, and the principal. The conversation centered, sometimes explicitly, on the juxtaposition of the principal's behavior and the students' academic performance. For example, the *Oakland Tribune* ran a story about this principal entitled "Madman, Genius, or Both?"[15]

The overarching question discussed by the public in newspapers and radio talk shows about this principal and the actions and events described at this school boiled down to a central question: Did the students' academic performance somehow justify or excuse the principal's actions? The overwhelming majority of public comments suggest that the principal's actions were entirely justified *because* of the stellar academic performance of the students in this school. In other words, rather than protecting the students and seeing them as worthy and deserving victims of unwarranted harsh treatment, the students' success performed the opposite function. As "urban" students of color, their success somehow made comments see them as the kind of students who "need" and "deserve" this harsh treatment.

Opinions expressed in public discussion suggested that these children deserved, even needed, harsh and arguably illegal punishment for small infractions, such as sitting on the floor all day for forgetting their homework or not eating if they forgot their lunch. People felt these high-performing students deserved being subjected to racial epithets or sexually harassing comments and that their parents and teachers deserved similar treatment. Why? People believed that high-performing children of poverty and color required harsh treatment in order to achieve and maintain success. Some acknowledged that the way the principal treated students was extreme but felt that the students were deserving of it anyway. For example, one person commented about a San Francisco Chronicle article: "[This principal] wouldn't work in most schools, but the fact is that his style works with certain students (emphasis added). Look at our current system! It fails children! [This principal] took the kids left behind in Oakland and made fine products out of them."[16]

This sentiment was not uncommon. Several people agreed that this is how "certain" (e.g., poor, black, and brown) students need to be treated to succeed. Another person stated: "It's true his approach is 'unconventional' . . . I didn't believe in his method at first, but there is a *demographic of students* which needs [this] approach to education [emphasis added]."[17]

Some respondents took a slightly different perspective. Even though they were surprised by the principal's behavior, they did not question it. Another person wrote: "Though I would not ascribe to exactly the same measures as [the principal] . . . I like his school's results. This is proof enough to me that he knows what is working with *inner city kids* (emphasis added)."[18] Someone commented: "I'm sure some of the children were handled roughly by [the principal]. Perhaps even harmed to a small degree. But let's compare that small harm with the superior education they received."[19] The overwhelming presumption appeared to be that the students' success emerged as a result of the harsh treatment rather than in spite of it.

Despite doing well, these high-achieving middle school students were not seen as deserving of even basic human kindness and protection. People advanced the narrative that without strict discipline, children of poverty and color would not succeed. I posit that what is at issue here is a different kind of educational resource. The resource is not money, equipment, or even qualified teachers. It is a much more basic resources: care and respect in school. At issue here are disparities in how members of the public talk about who deserves even this most basic resource.

Case Three: Who Deserves Admission to Elite Universities?

In this third and final case, I turn attention to the issue of admission to elite colleges and universities. Issues of race and ethnicity have been central to many public discussions of higher education admissions over the years, with debates about affirmative action playing an important part in those discussions. Central to all these discussions are differing conceptions of who deserves to be admitted to elite colleges and universities and how merit is assessed in such competitive situations. An essential dilemma confronting elite universities is admission criteria. Admission to elite universities is extremely competitive, and getting only more so, meaning that, inevitably, these colleges and universities are *choosing between* highly qualified students rather than *seeking and locating* highly qualified students. In fall 2014, Stanford accepted only 5.09 percent of its applicants and Harvard, Yale, and Princeton 5.9 percent, 6.72 percent, and 7.28 percent, respectively.

Admission to elite public universities revealed a similar pattern of increasing competitiveness.[20] Such tight admissions procedures heighten the anxiety of those seeking such admission and lead to inevitable disappointment for many. This disappointment and frustration over admission to highly competitive colleges and universities inevitably lead to numerous controversies and debates about university admissions processes and decisions. What acceptance criteria should a university use? What is fair? What is appropriate? What kinds of questions do/can/should factor into these decisions? In this case, I review two such conversations about competitive university admissions to explore how the nature of the discussion changes depending on "who" is being discussed. In these conversations, we see a disturbing level of shifting criteria for admission proposed depending on the race of the applicants involved.

The first of these conversations took place on the website Inside Higher Education (IHE). IHE ran a story prompted by a widely viewed YouTube video posted by Sy Stokes, a male African American student at UCLA. The video calls attention to how few African American males are currently enrolled at UCLA and the high percentage of African American male students at UCLA who are there on athletic scholarships. Stokes asks the university and the public to question this pattern. The video was widely viewed (at the time of this writing, over 2 million people had viewed the video on YouTube) and generated a great deal of discussion on IHE as well as within the academic community more broadly.

I focus on the IHE discussion because IHE is primarily read by university faculty. I believed that faculty might be well-poised to offer critical insights into the college admissions process and might be more reflective about the dilemmas of college admissions at elite institutions. In particular, they might be in a position to critique a heavy reliance on grades and test scores to the exclusion of all else. Instead, I found that although opinions expressed about the story on the IHE website included a range of different perspectives, there were remarkably few voices questioning the basic contours of the admissions process. Only a small percentage of commenters questioned how we know who "deserves" admission or interrogated conventional ideas about how we defined a "qualified" applicant. Roger Clegg, a conservative academic who writes regularly for conservative outlets about issues of race and ethnicity, expressed a popular sentiment in the conversation:

> UCLA should be try [sic] to find and admit the best qualified students, regardless of skin color or national origin. It should not be trying to achieve

a particular, politically correct racial and ethnic mix. It should not give preferential treatment on the basis of race and ethnicity. And it should not be intimidated by illogical, inaccurate, dishonest, self-pitying videos.[21]

This comment received 46 "likes" on the IHE website, more than any other comment in the discussion.

Others shared this opinion and voiced their presumption that the reason so few male African Americans were enrolled at UCLA was that there were very few academically qualified African American male students. For example, "Catorenasci" wrote:

> The University of California system has been trying to find more *academically qualified* black students since the late 1960's, at the very least. . . . The biggest problem early on was that there simply weren't very many prospective black students who were *academically qualified* under the standard criteria. . . . There are still very few academically qualified black applicants to UC, even under the easier criteria today.[22]

Few questioned their own assumptions that admissions decisions are based on purely quantitative information and that this is the best measurer of "quality" in college applications (I have no direct knowledge of how UCLA makes its admissions decisions). Moreover, few commenters questioned the assumption that the low numbers of African American male students at UCLA must be because there are few academically qualified applications. In fact, this assumption is not accurate.

Recent surveys of admitted applicants revealed that many highly qualified African American students are admitted to the two most competitive University of California campuses (Berkeley and UCLA), but a high proportion choose to go elsewhere. Sixty percent of African American students admitted to UC Berkeley opted to attend another college, and surveys of admitted students who choose a different college reveal that many African American students choose not to matriculate at UCLA or Berkeley for two primary reasons: (1) a strong perception within the African American community that these campuses are unfriendly to African Americans[23] and (2) prospective African American students often received better financial aid packages from other universities.[24] Thus, there are many, complex, and important reasons why so few African Americans matriculate at UC Berkeley and UCLA, but these are discounted or overlooked entirely in favor of tired narratives about the lack of "qualified" African American applicants.[25]

As a contrast, I focus on public conversations about Jian Li, a young man who filed a formal complaint with the Office of Civil Rights in 2006, claiming that Princeton had denied his application for admission on the basis of race.[26] Jian Li is a Chinese-born, U.S. permanent resident student. At the time of his application to college, his application included perfect SAT 1 scores as well as an extremely high grade point average (GPA) that placed him in the top 1 percent of his high school class. His applications to Princeton, Harvard, Stanford, The University of Pennsylvania, and MIT were rejected, though he was admitted to Yale University.[27] This case is explored in greater depth elsewhere[28]—here, I offer some of the key arguments made in public, online conversations about the case.

Jian Li's complaint to the Office of Civil Rights noted that Asian Americans have relatively low rates of admission at Ivy League universities (never more than 20%), and he alleged that the GPAs and test scores needed for admission were far higher for Asian Americans than other racial or ethnic groups at these colleges.[29] A story about his lawsuit ran in the Princeton student newspaper, the *Daily Princetonian*,[30] and this was soon followed by an editorial run in the *Daily Princetonian*'s annual joke issue. The joke editorial mocked the lawsuit and Asian American students:

> I the super smart Asian. Princeton the super dumb college, not accept me. I get angry and file a federal civil rights complaint against Princeton for rejecting my application for admission. What is wrong with you no color people? Yellow people make the world go round. We cook greasy food, wash your clothes, and let you copy our homework. . . . Princeton University is racist against me, I mean, non-European Americans.[31]

After the editorial was printed, a public conversation ensued, about both the racist nature of the editorial and why the *Princetonian* decided to publish it, but also about the questions that the lawsuit raised about admission to Princeton and other highly competitive universities. What was happening? Why were Asian American numbers generally in the range of 15 percent of the student body across the Ivy League, and what should it be? Were Asian American student numbers artificially suppressed in the admissions process? How do universities make admissions decisions, and how should they? In this conversation, among Princeton students and alumni—an inherently elite group—suddenly, a different set of arguments emerged about how to identify the "most qualified" applicants. A number of white people argued that it would, in fact, be ridiculous for a major, elite university to rely solely on grades and test scores in admissions. For example, "Exasperated Student" contended: "He (Jian Li) may be successful in terms of 'numbers,' but that does not mean that he has the personality or drive to warrant admission to Princeton."[32] Nor was "Exacerbated student" is not alone in this assessment. Repeatedly, comments spoke to the limitations of test scores and grades to fully inform an admissions committee about their applicants, and argued further that attention should be paid to more "personal" factors. Moreover, a disturbing number of commenters *presumed* that Asian American must be lacking on some personal dimension. For example, Julia <3 wrote: "If someone has devoted their entire life to such incredibly boring and time consuming activities they shouldn't get into a college because most likely it means their social intelligence isn't worth a nickel and sometimes social intelligence can be as important as talent or intellectual intelligence."[33]

In this conversation, where members of the predominantly white, *Daily Princetonian* readership weighed in on the merit and deservingness of Asian American applicants who often outperformed white American applicants on grades and test scores, the debate shifted about the criterion that should be used to determine who is worthy of admissions and how we should compare applicants. Suddenly, grades were no longer the primary measure of "quality" or predictive of school success, and commenters argued that grades and test scores alone could not tell the whole story. In order to explain the rejection of Asian students who sometimes had superior academic records, a different measure of worthiness emerged. In this context, commenters in online public discussions argued that universities needed to learn about "the whole person," when determining who were the "most qualified" applicants.

Shifting Standards of Deservingness and Worth

Public conversations about race and ethnicity in education often operate as though the issues involved are simple rather than complex. In each of three controversies, judgments about merit and worth emerged—when the controversy itself centered on other issues. Moreover, race and ethnicity played a significant role in commenters' determination of deservingness, merit, and worth. People argued passionately about "what should be done" and "what is fair and good," but in each case, public outcry favored keeping resources (money, opportunities, and even care) for white students while denying those same resources to students of color. Deservingness or worthiness was defined as "white." Nonwhite students, more often than not, were deemed "unworthy" and undeserving.

In the controversy surrounding the funding of science labs at Berkeley High, students of color who were not doing well were misconstrued as undeserving and unworthy of educational resources. The broad, though not universal, agreement among online comments about the controversy was that "smart" and "successful" kids were entitled to more financial resources at the school because they were a better investment. This seemed fair to commenters because they held an underlying assumption that whether people do well or not is more or less solely the result of their own efforts, and contempt was levied against "those" families and "those" students who are not performing well academically in school. They were described as "lazy," "unmotivated," and "unconcerned about education." The narrative that emerges from this first case is that students who wish to succeed do well, and therefore students who succeed deserve whatever extra resources we can give them.

The next two controversies, however, revealed the limits of that perspective—namely, that successful students can also be seen as undeserving when those successful students are students of color. In the controversy surrounding the harshly punitive and abusive middle school principal at an urban charter middle school, conceptualizations of what highly academically successful urban youth and their families (of color) deserve differed markedly from what successful white students were thought to deserve in the first case. Despite their academic success, successful students (and their families) of color were described as not deserving of respect, kindness, consideration, or autonomy. Rather than being celebrated as worthy of all kinds of investment because of their tremendous level of success, these students and families were described as "needing" to be treated with contempt and abuse. Whereas in the Berkeley High controversy, successful children (who were predominantly white) were seen as implicitly hard-working, dedicated, and deserving, the highly successful students of color were seen as somehow deserving abuse and harsh punishments for routine infractions, and to have their families treated with contempt. These judgments are classed as well as raced, and issues of poverty undoubtedly played a role in public assumptions about the children in this school.[34]

In the controversies surrounding admission to elite universities, the comments of members of the public—predominantly white public in these contexts—revealed shifting standards and perspectives regarding how to define "qualified applicants." By comparing the two conversations next to each other, we can see how these shifting notions of "quality" and merit benefited white applicants in each context. Standardized test scores and high school grades were discussed as the "best" measure of quality when the belief was white students would outperform on those measures, but those same measures were denigrated as "superficial" and not "revealing the whole person" in a context in which white applicants might underperform relative to applicants from another group.

Derrick Bell[35] reminds us that the nature of racism is that it is permanent because it is slippery. Improvements in one area can easily be undone in another area. As overt racism becomes less and less acceptable, we see concomitant increases in what has variously been called "dysconscious,"[36] "modern,"[37] or "color-blind"[38] racism. The narratives we see employed in the public controversies reported here are—intentionally or not—strategic devices through which resources are funneled away from students of color and toward white students. They function to divert attention away from the moral and human rights of students of color and their families and instead focus attention on what are seen as the very "real" property rights of white Americans. These property rights extend from disproportionate financial resources in public schools to places in elite universities. These narratives define and redefine who is worthy and how merit is measured in ways that serve white interests, all while the speaker may be unaware that is what he or she is doing. The nature of narratives is that they frame a plausible argument about the way the world works, and in doing so they paint what appears to be a rationale argument that protects and serves the interests of one racial group over all others.

Narratives inform our understanding of the racialized patterns of academic performance that we see—making these outcomes seem "normal" and natural, and as a result they serve to reinforce existing, inequitable patterns of educational outcomes. These racialized narratives shape our conceptions of deservingness and create shifting notions of merit and worth in education. In the cases examined in this chapter, white students were seen as more deserving—no matter the resource in question (financial, psychological, or opportunity offered). In each context, public conceptions of merit and worth followed from what white students did in each context. White students performing well academically? The conclusion is: "Give them more money." Students of color doing well academically? The conclusion is: "Make sure they are harshly disciplined to 'keep them in line.'" White students presumed to have higher SAT scores and/or GPA's? The conclusion is: "Base admissions decisions solely on scores because scores are how best to measure 'quality.'" White students presumed to have lower SAT scores and/or GPA's? The conclusion is: "Admissions decisions must be based on assessment of the 'whole person' because scores are not an ideal way to measure quality." No matter what students of color did or faced, no matter what their academic profile, in the narratives explored here, their actions were deemed less deserving of educational dollars, kindness, respect, and opportunity. My hope is that we can begin to have more honest conversations about the ways that racialized thinking and racialized narratives are deeply embedded—indeed, "baked into" our thinking about and defining of merit and worth in education.

Acknowledgments

The author wishes to thank Terry M. Pollack and Priya Shimpi for their assistance in this work. She would also like to thank Mills College for sabbatical support during work on this manuscript.

Notes

1. Zirkel and Pollack 2014.
2. Baez 2006.
3. Bullock 2008; Katz 1989; Lott and Bullock 2007.
4. Gillborn 2008.
5. Ibid.; Gillborn 2014; Ladson-Billings 2014.
6. Berkeley Unified School District 2013.
7. Noguera and Wing 2006.
8. Pollack and Zirkel 2013.
9. Zirkel and Pollack 2014.
10. Gammon, 2007.
11. Ibid.
12. Rawh 2006.
13. Zirkel et al. 2012.
14. Johnson 2004.
15. Murphy 2007.
16. Asimov, 2007.
17. Ibid.
18. Gammon, 2007.
19. Murphy, 2007.
20. Anderson 2014.

21. Jaschik 2013.
22. Ibid.
23. Allen-Taylor 2013.
24. Ibid.
25. Ibid.
26. Carroll 2006.
27. Ibid.; Shea 2006.
28. Shimpi and Zirkel 2013.
29. Shea 2006.
30. Carroll 2006.
31. Editorial 2007.
32. Editorial, Daily Princetonian, 2007.
33. Ibid.
34. Leonardo and Hunter 2007.
35. Bell 1993.
36. King 1991.
37. Dovidio and Gaertner 2004.
38. Bonilla-Silva 2006.

Bibliography

Allen-Taylor, J. Douglas. 2013. "Why Black Students Are Avoiding UC Berkeley." *East Bay Express* (November 6).

Anderson, Nick. 2014. "College Admissions for the Class of 2018: An Imperfect but Closely Watched Metric." *Washington Post* (April 3).

Asimov, N. 2007. "Breaking the Rules Is Nothing New to Uprep Principal: Arrests, Fights, and Bare-Knuckles Politics among Hallmarks of Isaac Haqq's History." *San Francisco Chronicle* (July 8).

Baez, Benjamin. 2006. "Merit and Difference." *Teachers College Record* 108: 996–1016.

Bell, Derrick. 1993. *Faces at the Bottom of the Well: The Permanence of Racism.* New York: Basic Books.

Berkeley Unified School District. *Berkeley High School 2011–12 School Accountability Report Card.* Berkeley, CA, 2013.

Bonilla-Silva, Eduardo. 2006. *Racism without Racists: Color-Blind Racism and the Persistence of Racial Inequality in the United States.* Rowman & Littlefield.

Bullock, Heather E. 2008. "Justifying Inequality: A Social Psychological Analysis of Beliefs about the Poor." In *The Colors of Poverty: Why Racial and Ethnic Disparities Persist,* eds. Ann Chih Lin and David R. Harris. New York: Russell Sage Foundation.

Carroll, Kate. 2006. "Rejected Applicant Alleges bias against Asians." *The Daily Princetonian* (November 13).

Dovidio, John F., and Samuel L. Gaertner. 1986. *Prejudice, Discrimination, and Racism: Historical Trends and Contemporary Approaches.* Orlando, FL: Academic Press.

Dovidio, John F., and Samuel L. Gaertner. 2004. "Aversive racism." In *Advances in Experimental Social Psychology,* ed. M. P. Zanna (pp. 1–52). San Diego, CA: Academic Press.

Editorial. 2007. "Princeton University Is Racist against Me, I Mean, Non-European Americans." *The Daily Princetonian* (January 17).

Gammon, Robert, 2007. "Too Hot for School? Tough-Love Principal [Name] Says It's Okay for Him to Use Racial Taunts Because He's a Minority and His Tactics Work." *East Bay Express* (May 9)

Gillborn, David. 2008. *Racism and Education: Coincidence or Conspiracy?* London: Routledge.

Gillborn, David. 2014. "Racism as Policy: A Critical Race Analysis of Education Reforms in the United States and England." *The Educational Forum* 78 (1), Taylor & Francis Group.

Jaschik, Scott. 2013. "To Be a Black Man at UCLA." *Inside Higher Education* (November 11).

Johnson, Charles. 2004. "A Charter on Success in Oakland." *San Francisco Chronicle* (August 23).

Katz, Michael B. 1989. *The Undeserving Poor: From the War on Poverty to the War on Welfare.* New York: Pantheon Books.

King, Joyce E. 1991. "Dysconscious Racism: Ideology, Identity, and the Miseducation of Teachers." *Journal of Negro Education* 60: 133–146.

Klein, Eric. 2009. "Berkeley High May Cut Out Science Labs." *East Bay Express* (December 28).

Ladson-Billings, Gloria. 2014. "Foreword: They're Trying to Wash Us Away: The Adolescence of Critical Race Theory in Education." In *Critical Race Theory in Education: All God's Children Got a Song*, eds. A. D. Dixon and C. K. Rousseau (pp. v–xiii). NY: Routledge.

Leonardo, Zeus, and Margaret Hunter. 2007. "Imagining the Urban: The Politics of Race, Class, and Schooling." In *International Handbook of Urban Education,* eds. W. T. Pink and G. W. Noblit (pp. 779–801). The Netherlands: Springer.

Lott, Bernice, and Heather E. Bullock. 2007. *Psychology and Economic Injustice: Personal, Professional, and Political Intersections.* Washington, DC: American Psychological Association.

Murphy, Katy. 2007. "Madman, Genius, or Both?" *Oakland Tribune* (June 15).

Noguera, Pedro, and Jean Yonemura Wing. 2006. *Unfinished Business: Closing the Racial Achievement Gap in Our Schools.* San Francisco, CA: Jossey-Bass.

Pollack, Terry M., and Sabrina Zirkel. 2013. "Negotiating the Contested Terrain of Equity-Focused Change Efforts in Schools: Critical Race Theory as a Leadership Framework for Creating More Equitable Schools." *The Urban Review* 45 (3): 290–310.

Rawh, Grace. 2006. "Oakland First: Charter Wins Blue Ribbon." *Oakland Tribune* (September 26).

Shea, Christopher. 2006. "Victim of Success? Are Asian American Students Discriminated against in College Admissions?" *Boston Globe* (November 26).

Shimpi, Priya M., and Sabrina Zirkel. 2013. "One Hundred and Fifty Years of 'The Chinese Question': An Intergroup Relations Perspective on Globalization and Immigration." *Journal of Social Issues* 68: 534–558.

Zirkel, Sabrina. 2014. "Slippery Concepts of Merit and Worth in Conversations about Admission to Elite Universities." Unpublished manuscript, Mills College.

Zirkel, Sabrina, and Terry M. Pollack, "'Just Let the Worst Students Go': A Case Analysis of Public Discourses about Race, Merit and Worth." Manuscript submitted for publication, 2014.

Zirkel, Sabrina et al. 2012. "Isn't That What 'Those Kids' Need? Urban Schools and the Master Narrative of the 'Tough' Urban Principal." *Race, Ethnicity, and Education* 13: 137–158.

Chapter 14

A Racial Opportunity Cost Analysis of Charter Schools and Parental Involvement

Ramon M. Griffin, Elizabeth Gil, Stefanie Marshall, Gregory J. White, James Wright, Muhammad Khalifa, and Terah T. Venzant Chambers

Introduction

In 1954, the United States Supreme Court ruled unconstitutional the racial segregation permeating America's schools. The landmark *Brown v. Board of Education* decision initiated the domino effect that would strike down a variety of discriminatory legislation, but despite the Court's decision to desegregate, implementing the decision was difficult.[1] The Court's decision was too broad, resulting in gaping loopholes that savvy whites, intent on preserving their way of life, exploited. The *Brown* decision specifically targeted school segregation, and while this was a significant step toward equity, structures such as racial residential segregation, employment discrimination, school resource disparities, and a host of other interconnected concerns went unaddressed. Some argue that not sufficiently addressing these issues impeded the desegregation process. As a result of our inability to fully address these educational issues "millions of black children [have not experienced] the decision's promise of equal educational opportunity."[2] Today, the evidence of this oversight remains visible, and black and brown students unequivocally experience subpar education in publicly funded schools—the very essence of what the *Brown* Court sought to address.

Sixty years after the *Brown* ruling, we examine the current situation for students of color in public schools and offer a contemporary analysis of the challenges they face. We utilize a racial opportunity cost (ROC) frame (defined later) to examine the relationship between students of color and their school environment—and the costs to students of color and their families as a result of navigating this landscape. Specifically, we use this framework to examine two timely educational issues: school choice and parental involvement. We begin with a brief overview of the theoretical framework used in our analysis, ROC. We then offer separate analyses of school choice and parental involvement research using this framework. Finally, drawing from the arguments presented in this chapter, we provide implications for future research, policy, and practice.

Racial Opportunity Cost (ROC)

Opportunity cost is a traditional economic term used to reflect inherent trade-offs in the decision-making process where making one decision (e.g., having cake) necessarily precludes another (e.g., eating the cake). Venzant Chambers and her colleagues used the term "racial opportunity cost" as a way to understand the relationship between the school environment and students of color and their ability to attain academic success.[3] As a theoretical framework, ROC can be used to examine the impact on students of color resulting from navigating the racialized school norms permeating their school culture. Figure 14.1 depicts this relationship between the school, at the institutional level, and the individual student.

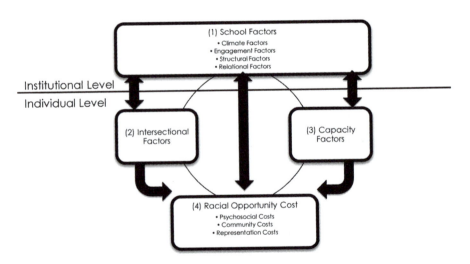

FIGURE 14.1   Racial Opportunity Cost[4]

The cycle begins at the top of Figure 14.1 with School Factors, at the Institutional Level. School Factors encompass all aspects of a school's culture. Specific School Factors that emerged from previous research include, Climate Factors (e.g., the norms and culture governing of the school), Engagement Factors (e.g., the sense of belonging and community), Structural Factors (e.g., within-school stratification), and Relational Factors (e.g., personnel engaging in open dialogue concerning issues of race). The arrows are meaningful in that they show the direction of the various influences. Thus, School Factors directly impact individual students. And individual students and the ROC they experience can have an influence on overall school culture. In addition, there are other aspects of an individual student's identity that may also play a role in their ROC. These additional factors include Intersectional Factors, which account for factors outside of race that contribute to the experiences of students in school (e.g., gender, ethnicity, socioeconomic status). The other component included is Capacity Factors, which account for an individual student's resilience in a situation.[5]

This ROC framework is built from interdisciplinary research that separates the *objective* measures of academic success, such as grades or test score performance, from the *subjective* markers with which they may be conflated, including dressing, speaking, or behaving in a particular manner. These expectations begin at the earliest stages of schooling, as Beth Hatt discussed in her work in an ethnographic study of a kindergarten classroom, where she found that "smartness signified not only a cultural practice of social control but a process of ascribing social power defined along lines of class and race."[6] Thus, while this construction of academic success in racialized school environments has been taken up in previous research, ROC acts as a vessel to collate this work and then also to understand the impact on students of color as a result of pursuing academic success in this context.

Racial Opportunity Cost and School Choice

A current alternative to the challenging plight of traditional public school systems is to allow families to "choose" where their child attends school. The effectiveness of school choice as a remedy to the ills and inequalities of public education, however, is questionable. The term "school choice" encompasses many different arrangements, including inter-district choice, intra-district choice, magnet schools, and voucher programs. However, the most popular form of school choice in use in public schools today is the charter school. The premise of school choice is that families are extended more freedom and flexibility to choose the best educational opportunities for their children beyond their assigned neighborhood school and that this competition will also result in an increase in the quality of traditional public schools.

Contrary to what many initially predicted, most of the students who attend charter schools are also students of color. Given that this population has been historically underserved in U.S. schools, how they fare in charter schools is of particular concern. In fact, in 2012, the Center for Education Reform found that 50 percent of all charter school students are "at risk" and over 60 percent qualify for free and reduced lunch.[7] However, although the population of the schools has increased in diversity, charter schools, particularly those that serve significant numbers of these predominantly minority, high-poverty schools, have not necessarily addressed the underlying institutional-level concerns that often result in high ROC for students of color.

Racial Opportunity Cost and Charter Schools

Charter schools commenced with two schools in 1991 and have dramatically risen to over 6,400 today.[8] Today, most charter schools share three common characteristics: (1) They are free, public, and accountable to the public (at least theoretically); (2) they do not impose residential requirements; and (3) they are privately managed by an organization that has a charter or contract with an authorizer.[9] From there, however, the similarities end. The laws that govern the structure and operation of charter schools vary greatly from state to state. For example, charters can range from new start-ups and conversions to campus program charters and college or university charters.

This flexibility is a feature of charter schools, which are given the autonomy to implement policies and create structures that seemingly maximize academic achievement and student motivation without interference from a local board of education. However, some argue that this flexibility comes with a significant downside in that this unrestricted freedom allows some charters to fly under the accountability radar and claim academic gains that may not exist. For example, a 2009 CREDO study of nearly three-quarters of U.S. public schools examined students' reading and math scores, finding that more than a third of these students would have fared better academically had they remained in their local public school. Less than 20 percent of the sample schools posted student math scores that surpassed the local traditional public school—for nearly half of the schools, any gains were negligible.[10] These statistics are both alarming and concerning, especially considering that families of color choose to attend charter schools because they think charters have higher academic expectations and will provide a more rigorous and student-centered curriculum than would their local neighborhood school.

Charters have not lived up to expectations in other respects, as well. Many scholars have argued that charter schools have not actually provided more options with respect to educational options for families of color. Discussing this issue in greater detail, Kristen Buras also questioned the merits of school choice when referring to the Tomorrow School Reforms that were instituted in New Zealand in the early 1990s. Buras noted that because "schools had more applications than spaces, they drafted an 'enrollment scheme' to spell out the criteria [they] would use for selecting students."[11] Hence, in these types of situations, "choice" is an illusion.

On the other hand, more prestigious charter schools with large proportions of more affluent, white students were given the opportunity to choose which students they accepted. Many charter schools in the United States employ similar enrollment practices and have drawn criticism from parents, activists, and public school advocates nationwide. Although parents in the United States do have the choice to send their child to allegedly advantaged charter schools, there is growing evidence that black students still confront discrimination and cultural domination in those spaces.

The authors argue in *Between a "ROC" and a School Place* that people of color may feel tension between societal expectations and their own racial community norms and that this tension mirrors the "double consciousness" idea DuBois addressed over a century ago.[12] DuBois defined double consciousness as the "sense of always looking at one's self through the eyes of others, of measuring one's soul by the tape of a world that looks on in amused contempt and pity."[13]

The phenomenon of double consciousness is useful in examining a popular practice in a New Orleans charter school. Educational historian and researcher Diane Ravitch described a rather disturbing practice in one predominantly Black New Orleans charter school. In an article on an educational blog entitled "Charters In New Orleans Explain Why Students Must 'Walk the Line,'" Ravitch described how "many charters in New Orleans tape a line in their hallways and insist that students must walk on the correct side of the line and failure to do so would result in unnecessarily harsh punishments."[14] She went on to say that critics of the policy believe that it prepared students for prison, not college. In one case, a student's disability made it difficult to walk, but even he was not exempt from following suit. Supporters of this policy claimed that it "save[d] time and [taught] automatic obedience to small rules, which later translate[d] into unquestioning obedience to rules and authority, preparing students to succeed in life."[15]

Critics charge that the proponents of such policies in charter schools assume that children of color have not been taught discipline and are prone to challenge authority. These assumptions and the resultant polices are not only riddled with deficit thinking but also support the idea that schools are complicit in coagulating and reviving the existing social and economic norms of society.[16] Policies like these can have a devastating psychological effect on students of color and their ability to perform academically. The ROCs that students pay in these environments is significant.

Another source of concern in charter schools is the curriculum. Parents and students frequently have little input in the curriculum, student and family handbooks, cultural blueprints, discipline policies, and uniform policies. The experiences and values of students and parents are essentially ignored. Yet, as mentioned earlier, students must still abide by the rules or face "unnecessarily harsh penalties."[17] The ROCs for students of color tend to be both punitive and cumulative, because they are punished for not conforming to normative rules of the larger white society, while their culture and heritage is denied or devalued.

The lived experiences, ways of knowing, learning, and thinking, may have to be recalibrated in charter schools in order for greater numbers of students of color to be academically successful in these schools. Given the current educational policy era, a thorough investigation of the ROC framework and the price that students of color pay every day throughout their educational journey is warranted.

Racial Opportunity Cost and Parental Involvement

Just as ROC offers us a way to see how educational environments impact the academic success of students of color, the concept can also be applied to how educational environments foster or discourage parental involvement for families of color. Studies have found that *parental involvement,* defined as active participation in children's education, greatly impacts children's academic achievement, with parental expectations serving as a predictor of academic attainment. When the school engages parents, parents can become viable partners in their child's education. If they are included, informed, and welcomed by the school, parents are more likely to participate, thereby reducing the distance between school and home that results in a higher ROC of academic success. However, schools have not traditionally welcomed all parents equally.

Race, class, culture, and language shape parental participation in public schools, individually and collectively. Parental involvement, however, is not viewed in the same way across racial, cultural, and economic lines. The involvement and concerns of affluent parents, for example, are often seen as an asset, while input and priorities of low-income parents are viewed as a liability and often marginalized. Low-income parents are frequently seen as the cause of their children's low achievement. To make matters worse, many low-income parents experience a culture–school divide. Several factors account for this divide. All too often schools do not value the cultural background of poor families. Language barriers, unequal opportunities to participate meaningfully, past negative school experiences, and prohibitive work schedules that are not accommodated in the way schools have structured their parent involvement programs all contribute to a disconnect between parents and schools. Further, treating all parents as the same "obfuscates the importance of tackling the nature and consequences of structural racism"[18] and a failure to recognize ethnic diversity may increase involvement gaps between parents who are involved and those who are not.

Researchers on Latino parental involvement in schools, for example, have found that traditional methods of parental involvement are generally not adequate for engaging Latino parents with specific cultural and linguistic needs. Gerardo López, Jay Scribner, and Kanya Mahitivanichcha observed that most approaches to parental involvement rely on a cultural deficit approach that emphasizes traditional forms of parental involvement without considering the ways in which the nature of parental involvement may vary across groups. Further, parents who are marginalized in schools because of racial, class, and cultural differences may, in turn, be perceived as not caring about their children's education.

Racial Opportunity Cost and Families of Color

Establishing environments that open avenues to meaningful participation of parents of students of color has the potential to reduce ROC. Settings that foster a sense of belonging for parents, and those that recognize the importance of school agents nurturing trust, have the potential to increase parental engagement and therefore improve students' educational experiences as well. When community needs are recognized and met by schools, students are more likely to experience a reduction in the "conflict both internally and externally when their pursuit of academic success means moving further from the norms and values of their racial community."[19]

However, as schools often view parental involvement as something that happens within school walls, they may undervalue the steps that parents take outside of the school building to foster their children's engagement in school. Latino scholars have addressed this narrow view of parental involvement. Angela Valenzuela found that for Latino families, the concept of "education" includes parents' role of instilling in their children "a sense of moral, social, and personal responsibility [that] serves as the foundation for all other learning."[20] Furthermore, parents value real-world lessons for their children, *consejos* in Latino families that contribute "to their children's education based on their community cultural norms and expectations."[21] If parents turned their educational efforts with their children only toward the norms promoted by schools, their children would miss out on learning from their families' cultural perspectives and aspects, including language and a sense of collectivism.[22]

Parents' expanded notions of education may not manifest themselves as a physical presence in a school building and may be misread by school agents who then may develop negative assumptions regarding whether parents are involved in their children's education at all. When school agents hold negative assumptions of their students' families, it is likely that barriers between home and school will form.

A Sense of Belonging

A sense of belonging and acceptance fosters success. Parents' feel a sense of belonging when their needs and concerns are addressed. Sometimes it is necessary to have candid conversations about race or racial issues because parents' specific needs are often related to their cultural and racial identities. López, Scribner, and Mahitivanichcha found that successfully involving migrant parents requires recognizing their cultural and educational strengths, as well as the economic and structural barriers facing their families. Schools that hold themselves accountable for and aim to meet parental needs above all other involvement considerations are successful in engaging migrant families.

Yvonne DeGaetano's study on parental participation in an English-language learner program documented how a school was able to lower ROC by promoting belonging and acceptance of its students' families. The program emphasized language strategies to increase bilingualism, and it used "culture as a mediator for learning"[23] as parents grew in knowledge as well as in confidence regarding their understanding of U.S. school functioning and expectations.

DeGaetano found that "for Latino parents . . . emphasis on language and culture was a critical factor in their becoming involved in schools and in schooling" and identified the presence of Latinos working on a parental involvement project who could speak Spanish as a factor in the parental involvement program's success.[24] She further noted that the team facilitating the program worked from the premise that parents had much to offer and came with their own sets of knowledge. As they learned more about how they could engage in their children's formal learning, they became "active as allies in their children's schooling."[25]

In studying local household knowledge and its potential applications to children's schooling, Norma González, Luis C. Moll, Martha Floyd-Tenery, Anna Rivera, Patricia Rendón, Raquel Gonzales, and Cathy Amanti found that when parents' "funds of knowledge" and their "lived experiences [were] . . . validated as a source of knowledge,"[26] social networks in the private sphere were transferred to public arenas, including their children's schools. Furthermore, just as "build[ing] on the language and cultural experience of students"[27] opens learning opportunities, building on parental knowledge increases engagement with families through a sense of community and trust. As in the case of the parental English-language learner program, a respect for family members' knowledge from lived experiences reduced ROC and increased a sense of belonging in a community.

Studies on engagement of families of color, then, offer insight into how school agents may help to positively shape the school experiences of students of color and their families, thereby reducing ROC. Researchers preparing a series of college planning workshops for middle school parents found that for Latino immigrant parents, welcoming aspects, including Spanish-language materials, native language workshop delivery, and the presenter's demeanor, created an environment of trust. As parents became exposed to resources about college in these tailored workshops, they shared the information with their children, their extended families, and their community, and they began planning toward their children's postsecondary opportunities. The series of workshops was successful because, aside from addressing the general informational needs of parents, workshop organizers also addressed specific concerns expressed by Latino parents.

Muhammad Khalifa, furthermore, states that "for some communities, school leaders must earn credibility, trust, and establish rapport."[28] This suggests that schools with populations of parents who have been marginalized by traditional school structures of parental involvement need leaders of the schools their children attend to view their roles as transcending the walls of the school. The study found that a principal who was highly visible in the community and took on a role as a community leader fostered trust and increased rapport between the school and community, in turn changing parents' relationships with the school and improving children's academic outcomes. Research has shown that when families who have been traditionally marginalized in schools experience interactions that recognize and respect their cultures and languages, parental engagement increases. When students witness improved relationships between home and school, ROC is reduced through a decreased home–school divide.

Implications

The ROCs that black and brown families regularly weather in order to find "success" are often unexplored because the institutionalized expectations, norms, and practices in educational spaces are based on white, middle-class standards. "At issue is not whether a student is actually smart or academically capable, but rather whether their presentation of 'smart' and 'capable' is judged to be correct."[29] The perception of being "smart" can also be linked to the "involved" parent. Cultural experiences, language, and family norms and values shape their involvement with schools.[30]

Norms and Values: Expectations in Charter Schools

This research illuminates the distinct gap between the norms and values of school and those of the families of color they serve. The level of success that students are able to achieve is directly related to their ability to negotiate the challenging terrain within a white normed society. Black and brown students who are viewed as successful within the charter school settings learn to navigate this system and to conform, albeit not without incurring ROC. Alternatively, students who are unwilling to conform are in jeopardy of being viewed as low-achieving, a disciplinary problem, or in need of special learning accommodations. The consequence of labeling students in this way in turn perpetuates structures of stratification that may be the result of a system that does not necessarily reflect academic achievement but rather the lack of conformity to racialized academic standards.

To rectify this situation, schools must be willing to respect and better understand the community in which they serve, and to allow that understanding to shape expectations and norms. Norms and values within a school must be flexible in order to support the norms and values of the home environment and acknowledge the value of parental involvement. When this does not happen, marginalized populations are ostracized, potentially causing them to withdraw from actively participating in their children's education. This a common experience for students of color. Consequently, some parents and students of color decide that the ROCs are too great and opt out of success as defined by the school.

Parental Involvement

Rather than assuming that there is a lack of parental involvement, we should question whether school expectations align with those of parents of color and whether or not the lines of communication are open. Attention should be given to understanding the cultural needs and expectations of families. In order to understand the needs of the African American and Latino communities, schools must hold themselves accountable for understanding the diverse communities that they serve. This may require establishing coalitions and space for discussions on race and culture. Issues that may be of concern to parents include race, limited English experience, and different understandings of parental responsibilities than traditionally expected within the U.S. context. Addressing such issues and concerns head-on can promote a level of communication that will possibly reconcile some of the ROCs. However, not addressing these matters will result in a continued communication gap between school agents and the community, resulting in negative impacts on student achievement. There should also be specific outreach for communities of color based on their expressed needs in order to foster a sense of belonging.

Schools must be deliberate in how they engage with parents and specifically focus on instituting practices that promote a sense of belonging among parents to the school community. As previously stated, parental involvement plays a key role in the academic experiences of children. In order to promote belonging, neutral opportunities for discussion must be better prioritized in order to understand the needs of parents.

Schools should also consider ways in which they can support empowering parents as educational allies. This could be in the form of parent organizations, focus groups, staff members who can communicate with parents in their native language, and sessions engaging with parents on the U.S. educational system, all in hopes of supporting parental belonging. Another way is to utilize spaces within the community in order to be visible and to show that the school is interested in the community as a whole.

Conclusion

We started this chapter with a reminder about the landmark *Brown v. Board of Education* decision, legislated to address inherent inequities within the public school system. The Jim Crow legislation imposed on American blacks was deeply felt within public schools and was the catalyst that brought forth the monumental court case. Sixty years after *Brown* the problems affecting black youth are exacerbated as the urban public school system is in a state of crisis. From this crisis emerged discourses around redressing public education with privatization and school choice models as leading alternatives. What is not addressed in these discourses of privatization and choice is the impact of the ROC that black and Latina/Latino families and students must consider. At the same time, parents of color are similarly affected by school environments that may not value their ways of being involved in their children's education. In both of the educational issues discussed here in this chapter, school choice and parental involvement, it is clear that understanding the nuances of the school environment in order to lower the ROC incurred by students and families of color is an important first step.

Notes

1. Baugh 2011.
2. Ibid.
3. Venzant Chambers et al. 2014.
4. Venzant Chambers and Huggins 2014.
5. Ibid.
6. Hatt 2012.
7. Center for Education Reform 2014.
8. Ibid.
9. National Conference of State Legislatures 2014.
10. Miners 2014.
11. Buras and Apple 2005.

12. Venzant Chambers and Huggins 2014.
13. DuBois 1994.
14. Ravitch 2014.
15. Ibid.
16. Nolan 2011.
17. Venzant Chambers and Huggins 2014.
18. Crozier 2001.
19. De Gaetano 2007.
20. Venzant Chambers, Locke, and Medina in press.
21. Ibid., p. 10.
22. Ibid.
23. De Gaetano 2007, p. 147.
24. Ibid.
25. Ibid., p. 160.
26. González, Moll, and Amanti 2005.
27. Ibid.
28. Khalifa 2012.
29. Venzant Chambers and Huggins 2014.
30. Baugh 2011.

Bibliography

Anderson, James. *A Tale of Two Browns: Constitutional Equality and Unequal Education.* Urban Education Speaker Series presented at the Lecture Conducted from Michigan State University. East Lansing, MI, 2014. Announces the Schools Contributing the Most Graduates to Its 2012 Teaching Corps. Teach For America (2012-09-05). Accessed August 24, 2013.

Baugh, Joyce A. 2011. *The Detroit School Busing Case: Milliken v. Bradley and the Controversy over Desegregation.* Landmark Law Cases and American Society. Lawrence: University Press of Kansas.

Bell, Derrick. 2009. *Brown v. Board of Education and the Interest Convergence Dilemma.* Edited by Edward Taylor, David Gillborn, and Gloria Ladson-Billings.

Bourdieu, Pierre, and Jean-Claude Passeron. 1977. *Reproduction in Education, Society and Culture.* London: Sage Publications.

Brayboy, Bryan, and Emma Maughan. 2009. "Indigenous Knowledges and the Story of the Bean." *Harvard Educational Review* (Spring) 79 (1): 1–23.

Buenavista, Tracy Lachica, Uma M. Jayakumar, and Kimberly Misa-Escalante. 2009. "Contextualizing Asian American Education through Critical Race Theory: An Example of U.S. Pilipino College Student Experiences." *New Directions for Institutional Research* 142: 69–81.

Buras, Kristen L., and Michael W. Apple. 2005. "School Choice, Neoliberal Promises, and Unpromising Evidence." *Journal of Educational Policy* 19: 550–564.

Carter, Prudence L. 2006. "Straddling Boundaries: Identity, Culture, and School." *Sociology of Education* 79: 304–328.

Carter Andrews, Dorinda J. 2009. "The Construction of Black High-Achiever Identities in a Predominantly White High School." *Anthropology & Education Quarterly* 40 (3): 297–317.

Center for Education Reform. 2014. http://en.wikipedia.org/wiki/Center_for_Education_Reform.

Center on Reinventing Public Education. "Charter Schools and Public School Choice." Last modified 2014. Accessed August 30, 2014. http://www.crpe.org/research/charter-schools-and-public-school-choice.

Clark, John M. 1919. "Economic Theory in an Era of Social Readjustment." *The American Economic Review* 9 (1): 280–290.

Crozier, Gill. 2001. "Excluded Parents: The Deracialisation of Parental Involvement." *Race Ethnicity and Education* 4 (4): 329–341.

De Gaetano, Yvonne. 2007. "The Role of Culture in Engaging Latino Parents' Involvement in School." *Urban Education* 42 (2): 145–162.

Delgado, Richard. 2012. *Critical Race Theory: An Introduction.* 2nd ed. New York: New York University Press.

Delgado, R., and Jean Stefancic. 2001. *Critical Race Theory: An Introduction.* 1st ed. New York: New York University Press.

Dreilinger, Danielle. "Video Explains Why New Orleans Collegiate Academies Charter Students 'Walk the Line.'" NOLA.com. June 9, 2014. Accessed August 30, 2014.

DuBois, William Edward Burghardt. 1994. *The Souls of Black Folk. Dover Thrift Editions.* New York: Dover.

Dudziak, Mary. 1988. "Desegregation as a Cold War Imperative." *Stanford Law Review* 61.

Emdin, Christopher. 2010. *Urban Science Education for the Hip-Hop Generation.* Rotterdam: Sense Publishers.

Fann, Amy, Karen McClafferty Jarsky, and Patricia M. McDonough. 2009. "Parent Involvement in the College Planning Process: A Case Study of P-20 Collaboration." *Journal of Hispanic Higher Education* 8 (4): 374–393.

Fordham, Signithia. 2008. "Beyond Capital High: On Dual Citizenship and the Strange Career of 'Acting White.'" *Anthropology & Education Quarterly* 39: 227–246.

Fordham, Signithia, and John Ogbu. 1986. "Black Students' School Success: Coping with the Burden of 'Acting White.'" *The Urban Review* 18: 176–206.

Frazier, E. Franklin. 1997. *Black Bourgeoisie.* 1st ed. New York: Free Press Paperbacks.

González, Norma, Luis C. Moll, and Cathy Amanti. 2005. *Funds of Knowledge: Theorizing Practice in Households, Communities, and Classrooms.* Mahwah, NJ: L. Erlbaum Associates.

Griffin, Ramon M. "Colonizing the Black Natives: Reflections from a Former NOLA Charter School Dean of Students." Cloaking Inequity. March 24, 2014. Accessed August 30, 2014. http://cloakinginequity.com/2014/03/24/coloniz ing-the-black-natives-reflections-from-a-former-nola-charter-school-dean-of-students/.

Hanushek, Eric. 2001. "Efficiency and Equity in Education." NBER Reporter.

Hatt, Beth. 2012. "Smartness as a Cultural Practice in Schools." *American Educational Research Journal* 49 (3): 438–460. doi: 10.3102/0002831211415661.

Irizarry, Jason G., and John Raible. 2011. "Beginning with El Barrio: Learning from Exemplary Teachers of Latino Students." *Journal of Latinos and Education* 10 (3): 186–203.

Khalifa, Muhammad. 2012. "A Re-NEW-ed Paradigm in Successful Urban School Leadership: Principal as Community Leader." *Educational Administration Quarterly* 48 (3): 424–467.

Kolderie, Ted. "Ray Budde and the Origins of the Charter Concept." Education Evolving (July 1, 2005).

Kozol, Jonathan. 2012. *Savage Inequalities: Children in America's Schools*. New York: Broadway Paperbacks.

Ladson-Billings, Gloria. 2009. "Just What Is Critical Race Theory and What's It Doing in a Nice Field Like Education?" In *Race Is . . . Race Isn't: Critical Race Theory and Qualitative Studies in Education*, eds. Edward Taylor, David Gillborn, and Gloria Ladson-Billings (pp. 7–30). Boulder, CO: Westview Press.

Leonardo, Zeus. 2009. *Race, Whiteness, and Education. The Critical Social Thought Series*. New York: Routledge.

López, Gerardo R., Jay D. Scribner, and Kanya Mahitivanichcha. 2001. "Redefining Parental Involvement: Lessons from High-Performing Migrant-Impacted Schools." *American Educational Research Journal* 38 (2): 253–288.

Louisiana Association of Public Charter Schools. Last modified 2014. Accessed August 30, 2014. http://lacharterschools.org/charter-schools.

Mathis, William J. 2013. "Research-Based Options for Education Policymaking: English Language Learners and Parental Involvement." http://nepc.colorado .edu/files/pb-options-7-ellparents.pdf.

Mignolo, Walter D. 2012. *Local Histories/Global Designs: Coloniality, Subaltern Knowledges, and Border Thinking*. Princeton Studies in Culture/Power/History. Princeton, NJ: Princeton University Press.

Mincer, Jacob. 1958. "Investment in Human Capital and Personal Income Distribution," *The Journal of Political Economy* 66 (4): 281–302.

Miners, Zach. "Charter Schools Might Not Be Better." U.S. News. June 17, 2009. Accessed August 30, 2014.

Moll, Luis, Cathy Amanti, Deborah Neff, and Norma Gonzalez. 1992. "Funds of Knowledge for Teaching: Using a Qualitative Approach to Connect Homes to Classrooms." *Theory into Practice* 31: 132–141.

National Alliance for Public Charter Schools. "Estimated Number of Public Charter Schools and Students, 2013–2014." February 2014. Accessed February 2014.

National Conference of State Legislatures. "Charter Schools." Accessed August 30, 2014. http://www.ncsl.org/research/education/charter-schools-overview.aspx.

Ndimande, Bekisizwe S. 2005. "Altering Common Sense: An Analysis of Black parents' School Choice and Perceptions of South African Desegregated Public Schools." Unpublished doctoral dissertation, University of Wisconsin-Madison.

Nolan, Kathleen. 2011. *Police in the Hallways: Discipline in an Urban High School.* Minneapolis: University of Minnesota Press.

Oakes, Jeannie. 2005. *Keeping Track: How Schools Structure Inequality.* New Haven, CT: Yale University Press.

Omi, Michael. 1994. *Racial Formation in the United States: From the 1960s to the 1990s.* 2nd ed. New York: Routledge.

Orr, Marion, and John Rogers. 2010. "Unequal Schools, Unequal Voice: The Need for Public Engagement for Public Education." In *Public Engagement for Public Education: Joining Forces to Revitalize Democracy and Equalize Schools,* eds. Marion Orr and John Rogers (pp. 1–24). Palo Alto, CA: Stanford University Press.

Ravitch, Diane. "Charters-in-New-Orleans-Explain-Why-Students-Must-Walk-the-Line/." *Diane Ravitch's blog A site to discuss better education for all* (blog), June 12, 2014. Accessed August 30, 2014. http://dianeravitch.net/2014/06/12/charters-in-new-orleans-explain-why-students-must-walk-the-line/.

Renzulli, Linda, and Vincent Roscigno. 2007. "Charter Schools and the Public Good in Contexts." *American Sociological Review* 6 (1): 31–36.

Reynolds, Arthur J., Nancy A. Mavrogenes, Mavis Hagemann, and Nikolaus Bezruczko. 1993. Schools, Families, and Children: Sixth Year Results from the Longitudinal Study of Children at Risk.

"Schools Criticized for Bans on Dreadlocks, Afros." *USA Today* (September 26, 2013). Accessed August 31, 2014.

Scott, Janelle. 2012. "Educational Movements, Not Market Moments." *Dissent* 59 (1): 72–75.

Solorzano, Daniel, and Tara Yosso. 2002. "Critical Race Methodology: Counterstorytelling as an Analytic Framework for Educational Research." *Qualitative Inquiry* 8 (1): 23–44.

Sugrue, Thomas J. 2005. *The Origins of the Urban Crisis: Race and Inequality in Postwar Detroit.* 1st ed. Princeton Studies in American Politics. Princeton: Princeton University Press.

Taylor, Ed, David Gillborn, and Gloria Ladson-Billings. 2009. *Foundations of Critical Race Theory in Education.* New York: Routledge.

Texas Education Agency. Last modified August 25, 2014. Accessed August 30, 2014. http://www.tea.state.tx.us/index2.aspx?id=392.

"TFA: The International Brotherhood of Corporate Interests." *EduShyster.com Keeping an eye on the corporate education agenda* (blog), January 6, 2014. Accessed August 30, 2014. http://edushyster.com/?p=3954.

Tuitt, Franklin, and Dorinda Carter. 2008. "Negotiating Atmospheric Threats and Racial Assaults in Predominantly White Educational Institutions." *Journal of Public Management & Social Policy* 14 (2): 51–68.

Vasquez Heilig, Julian, Muhammad Khalifa, and Linda C. Tillman. 2013. *Why Have NCLB and High-Stakes Reforms Failed?: Reframing the Discourse with a Post-Colonial Lens.* In *Handbook of Urban Education,* eds. K. Lomotey and R. Milner. New York: Routledge.

Venzant Chambers, Terah. 2009. "'The Receivement Gap': School Tracking Policies and the Fallacy of the 'Achievement Gap.'" *The Journal of Negro Education* 78 (4): 417–431.

Venzant Chambers, Terah T., Kristin S. Huggins, Leslie A. Locke, and Rhonda M. Fowler. 2014. "Between a 'ROC' and a School Place: The Role of Racial Opportunity Cost in the Educational Experiences of Academically Successful Students of Color." *Educational Studies* 50 (5): 464–497. doi:10.1080/001319 46.2014.943891

Venzant Chambers, Terah T., Leslie A. Locke, and Annel D. Medina. In press. "That Fuego, That Fire in Their Stomach": Academically-Successful Latinas/os and *Racial Opportunity Cost. International Journal of Qualitative Studies in Education.*

Venzant Chambers, Terah T., and Kristin Shawn Huggins. 2014. "The Influence of School Factors on Racial Opportunity Cost for High-Achieving Students of Color." *Journal of School Leadership* 24: 189.

von Wieser, Friedrich. 1967. "Social Economics (1914)." A. Ford Hindrichs, trans. (New York, 1927): 128.

von Wieser, Friedrich. 1891. "The Austrian School and the Theory of Value." *The Economic Journal* 1: 1108–1121.

What Is a Charter School. n.d. http://www.calcharters.org/understanding/what-are-charter-schools.html.

Woodson, Carter Godwin. 1933/2013. *The Mis-education of the Negro.* New York: Tribeca Books.

Part V

Beyond High School

Chapter 15

Affirmative Action in Higher Education

Julie A. Helling

Race matters for reasons that really are only skin deep, that cannot be discussed any other way, and that cannot be wished away. Race matters to a young man's view of society when he spends his teenage years watching others tense up as he passes, no matter the neighborhood where he grew up. Race matters to a young woman's sense of self when she states her hometown and then is pressed, "No, where are you really from?", regardless of how many generations her family has been in the country. Race matters to a young person addressed by a stranger in a foreign language, which he does not understand because only English was spoken at home. Race matters because of the slights, the snickers, the silent judgments that reinforce that most crippling of thoughts: "I do not belong here."
—Justice Sonia Sotomayor (dissenting), Schuette v. Coalition to Defend Affirmative Action, Integration and Immigrant Rights and Fight for Equality by Any Means Necessary (BAMN), *572 U.S. ___ (2014)*

Introduction

When I was in law school, a fellow student that I considered a friend of mine noted, "We can never *really* be friends because I'm black and you're white."[1] It was said calmly as a statement of fact, announced with such certainty that I was taken aback.

"If that's true, it makes me very sad," I offered meekly. I had just spent two years in the Peace Corps in Niger, West Africa, and had to admit that I did not at times feel the possibility of genuinely connecting with the local people there because our life experiences and worldviews were so different. It had not occurred to me that I might face a similar experience on returning home.

He shrugged. "You can never understand what things are really like because the world works differently for you."

Over 20 years later, I am lucky enough that I still get family Christmas newsletters from this gentleman. We continued to hang out during law school to the extent that his female partner jokingly said it was a good thing that she knew I was a lesbian or she would start to wonder about things. I have a favorite memory of getting to introduce him to parts of my world, things he had not seen before, such as a lesbian nightclub, even as I got to know things about him. Today I would call him a friend I knew from law school but hold the caveat he set, that I must understand that the world works differently for me as a white person because I have white privilege and am not subject to the societal racism that he endures as a person of color.

On the other end of the spectrum I have a friend from law school who emigrated from East Africa when he was about three years old.[2] He, too, identifies as black. He is one of the best friends I made in law school and today we speak regularly on the phone. Despite the difference in our races, our ability to probe important issues and often—but not always—come to similar conclusions through spirited conversation is important to both of us.

Identity is complex, and our good friendship could be in spite of race or even because of it, as we share a strong interest in social justice and the effects of race. Or the bond between us could exist because, though we did not know each other at the time, we both were raised in the same neighborhood until fourth grade and our fathers were both professors at the same university.

Though we are given physical characteristics at birth that are often construed by society through the socially constructed concept of race, none of us are endowed with essentialist racial natures. We may quickly embrace cultures we are exposed to or identify with, which may deeply inform our own conceptions of self. So can a person of color and a white person ever truly be friends? I definitely believe that it is possible, but it seems to depend on the particular people involved, and it is important to honor the position of the person subject to oppression.

Ultimately, all three of us graduated from the University of Michigan Law School in 1993, and a decade later the U.S. Supreme Court decided two of the most important cases on affirmative action in higher education admissions, both of which involved our alma mater: *Gratz v. Bollinger* (2003) (involving undergraduate admissions to the University of Michigan)[3] and *Grutter v. Bollinger* (2003) (involving admissions to the University of

Michigan Law School).[4] These cases need close examination, and in doing so I am lucky enough to have that personal experience with the university sued.

In addition, I currently have the privilege of being a professor in the Law, Diversity and Justice curriculum in a small interdisciplinary college (around 400 students) set in the middle of a medium-sized public university (about 15,000 students).[5] This situation means that, despite being part of a large institution, I have the delight of instructing small 10–18 student seminars where I can often connect with students in meaningful ways.

One of the classes I teach regularly is American Legal Systems, where I focus on the theme of "Race and Education," and cover the leading affirmative action admissions cases in higher education. Students learn how to read legal cases and struggle with the issues involved in appraising programs that try to increase the number of students of color (among other communities) at various educational institutions. Discussions on these issues often reveal deeply held beliefs about race, diversity, and equity.

This past spring 2014 was a particularly charged section of American Legal Systems, as the national media picked up remarks made by President Bruce Shepard[6] of Western Washington University (WWU) (where I teach) in his blog. The blog noted our duty to increase enrollment of students of color to reflect state demographics and included the line "If we are as white in ten years as we are today, Western will have failed as a university."[7] President Shepard has said the exact thing at convocations for six years, but this year it was picked up by the national media, to a subsequent flurry of attention from unkind quarters. For example, a small group of white supremacists came to the WWU campus one day and unfurled a large banner that read: "Diversity" = White Genocide.[8] WWU students responded to the controversy with a Diversity Rally on campus that drew about 700 participants.[9]

Given this backdrop of past and present experiences with higher education, it has been a good time to reflect on the effects of race in higher education, on the efforts to increase the number of students of color in universities, and how to improve the experience of students of color currently enrolled. In this chapter, I advance the following claims:

(1) That the term "affirmative action" encompasses so many different approaches that it is almost absurd to say one is "for affirmative action" or "against affirmative action," and therefore, each approach used must be evaluated closely on its own merits;

(2) That the U.S. Supreme Court—and therefore the universities trying to employ race in admissions—has used the idea of an enhanced educational experience for students in the support of pursuing diversity in the classroom. Because white students (and white faculty) are actually the ones who currently benefit the most from allowing the use of race in admissions decisions under an enhanced educational experience rationale, I argue that the stronger justification for allowing the use of race in admissions decisions is to remedy past and current societal discrimination; and

(3) That the current Supreme Court is moving toward prohibiting colleges and universities from taking race into account at all in admissions decisions.

Use of the Term "Affirmative Action"

The term "affirmative action" comes from President John F. Kennedy's 1961 Executive Order 11114, which declared that it was "the policy of the United States to encourage by affirmative action the elimination of discrimination" in employment.[10] While this intention is surely admirable, it is critical to know exactly which "action" is being discussed before coming to any conclusions about its merit.

To make a judgment about affirmative action that addresses its efficacy, legal and ethical implications, one must look closely at the specific mechanism employed. In the context of higher education, for example, affirmative action might mean simply making extra efforts to encourage students of color to apply. Or it might mean that a set number of points are added to the admission files of students of color. Or is there a holistic review of the admissions files of all students where race is but one factor? Should retaining teachers of color who were hired more recently during a layoff over white teachers with more seniority to keep a more diverse classroom experience for all students be a prohibited approach? In these situations, context matters, and it is important to unearth all the factors involved. One might easily be "for" one mechanism of affirmative action and "against" another. A knee-jerk reaction of pro or con is unhelpful.

My own position is that conceptually I am in favor of the idea of affirmative action in employment (and many other areas, including in education and the criminal justice system) but that particular methods of pursuing the goal may be objectionable. In short, reasonable minds operating in good faith can still differ on the proper role of affirmative action.

The complexity of race-conscious mechanisms can be seen in a situation that arose while I was in law school. One of my best friends from law school (the friend who came from Africa at age three and is black) got accepted to the highly competitive Michigan Law Review staff at the end of our first year. He had made a point in his application of not identifying his race, and his application was otherwise anonymous. The other students of color who had made it onto the staff of the Law Review had checked the box indicating their race in the application process (an action they had shared publicly at one point). I make no judgment about their choosing to disclose their race, or my friend choosing not to disclose. My purpose is merely how the situation played out.

Students were generally expected to complete the work of writing a Note (a student-written law review article) in their second year as part of being selected to advance to the Editorial Board of the Law Review for the third (and final) year of law school. As someone who finished the requisite staff work during our second year, my friend was the only person of color who then advanced to a coveted position on the Editorial Board.

One of the concerns with affirmative action mechanisms is the belief that it paints a stigma on all members of the racial group targeted, that the assumption is that all members of that group only reached a particular level because of affirmative action, not because of their own achievements. My friend felt that stigma as employers interviewing white Michigan law students would inquire if there was an affirmative action policy for the Law Review (which there was, hence the box to check about race on the application to join the Law Review).

Once on the Editorial Board, my friend attempted to raise the issue of reconsidering having an affirmative action policy for the Law Review. This attempt was controversial and initially blocked by procedural maneuvering by other members of the board. My friend then sent a six-page memo to the Editorial Board, outlining his concerns with having an affirmative action policy where the grade point average (GPA) cutoff for admission to the Law Review staff was lower for students of color (and the writing criteria was also less).

The memo led to a six-hour emergency meeting by the Editorial Board. Two issues were raised initially: (1) should there be a GPA cutoff for anyone? and (2) should there be a lower GPA cutoff for students of color?[11] My friend's argument touched only briefly on the potential unfairness of different standards for white students, but really focused on how the affirmative policy was unfair to black students. He wrote that while having Law Review service on a white student's resume was a mark of great distinction, minority Law Review students have only a "dubious credential in the struggle for competitive employment. While interviewing with law firms and judges,

'Law Review' on a minority student's resume signifies merely that one did not both write a competition piece worthy of a zero *and* fall below a minimum grade point average of an unknown level, hardly a distinction in the competitive process of job hunting."[12]

In the memo he made the point strongly, "Personally, I'm tired of having my achievements doubted. When my wife told her workmates I was accepted by U of M law school, one person muttered, 'it's no wonder, he's black and blind.' Finally, with the Law Review, I thought I could attain recognition for my merit rather than my color. Unfortunately, my membership is tainted by last year's policy. I only hoped we could spare this year's minority students."[13] At that emergency meeting the Editorial Board voted to retain the affirmative action policy for racial minorities at that time. (I do not know the current state of the policy, if any, for the Michigan Law Review.)

For me, the Law Review affirmative action controversy raises a number of concerns that are in conflict with each other. First, I questioned if I was entitled to an opinion on the matter at all given that I was not on the Law Review and I was not a student of color. I ultimately decided that unlike some controversies that revolved around decision making by primarily communities of color, this issue depended on a lot of decision making by white people as well (historically the Michigan Law Review's Editorial Board was almost entirely white). I try to recognize issues where I should defer to the communities involved, but this issue was one about which I was willing to make my own judgment.

Second, although I support the idea of a holistic review using race as one factor during higher education admissions, I have a hard time with the idea of a Law Review affirmative action policy. A race-conscious admissions process makes sense to me because the law school does not control the experience of students prior to coming to the school and thus such a process may be necessary to remedy the "persistent racial inequality in society."[14]

In contrast, the law school does have—or should have—relative control over the first-year experience of law school.[15] All students should receive the same educational opportunity, and if they do not, the fundamental problem should be unearthed and addressed rather than considering race in a few cases in the second and third years on the Law Review.

Therefore, while I support race-conscious admissions, I am leery of race-conscious affirmative action mechanisms for the Law Review once students are at the law school. The more effective approach would be to make sure that enough students of color are admitted initially so individual students do not feel isolated and to ensure that sufficient support services for all students to succeed are in place.

But I admit I could be wrong in my assessment. Affirmative action is complex and my thoughts on individual mechanisms can shift as I weigh new information and viewpoints. The tension of what is equitable in the context of our racist history is a demanding one. Our legal history demonstrates this tension and it is to the legal history that we must now turn.

A Short Legal History of Affirmative Action in Higher Education Admissions

It is important to understand the legal history of affirmative action in higher education admissions to understand how courts have approached the idea of affirmative action in this context and to understand what affirmative action mechanisms are constitutionally permissible. In 1954, the U.S. Supreme Court gave a rousing description of the benefits that flow from public education:

> Today, education is perhaps the most important function of state and local governments. Compulsory school attendance laws and the great expenditures for education both demonstrate our recognition of the importance of education to our democratic society. It is required in the performance of our most basic responsibilities, even service in the armed forces. It is the very foundation of good citizenship. Today it is a principal instrument in awakening the child to cultural values, in preparing him for later professional training, and in helping him to adjust normally to his environment. In these days, it is doubtful that any child may reasonably be expected to succeed in life if he is denied the opportunity of an education. Such an opportunity, where the state has undertaken to provide it, is a right which must be made available to all on equal terms.
>
> —*Chief Justice Earl Warren,* Brown v. Board of Education, 73 S. Ct. 686, 691 (1954)

Brown v. Board of Education was a seminal case in constitutional litigation involving public education. It was the end of the state-imposed "separate but equal" doctrine, but though the Court declared the value of public education, it was clear from the beginning that education was not a right guaranteed by the federal constitution because equality in education was necessary only "where the state has undertaken to provide" education,[16] meaning, of course, that the state may choose to not offer any education at all.

If the government does undertake to provide public education, this education must comport with the Fourteenth Amendment of the U.S. Constitution, which requires that

> No State shall make or enforce any law which shall abridge the privileges or immunities of citizens of the United States; nor shall any State deprive any person of life, liberty, or property, without due process of law; *nor deny to any person within its jurisdiction the equal protection of the laws.* (italics added)

The reach of "equal protection" in higher education admissions was put to the test in 1978 in the U.S. Supreme Court decision *Regents of the University of California v. Bakke.*[17] This case involved a white male named Allen Bakke who sued the University of California because the state medical school reserved 16 out of 100 seats for "disadvantaged" minority students. Bakke had not been accepted to the medical school and blamed the affirmative action mechanism in place for this rejection.

Justice Lewis Powell, as the crucial vote in this case, delivered the opinion of the deeply divided nine-member Court. The test required by the Equal Protection Clause of the Fourteenth Amendment when the government uses race as a factor in any decision is called "strict scrutiny."[18] As the name implies, a court must turn the highest degree of scrutiny on the decision by the state to use race as a factor. Such a use of race is constitutionally acceptable only if the state's interest is "compelling" and the use of race is "narrowly tailored" to achieve that interest.[19]

Ultimately, because of Powell's deciding vote, the Court held that strict numerical quotas were unconstitutional, but that it was permissible to have an admissions plan where "race or ethnic background is simply one element— to be weighed fairly against other elements—in the selection process." Thus, university personnel may seek the "attainment of a diverse student body" using race as one factor as long as they stay within the constitutionally permissible boundaries set by the *Bakke* case.[20]

Bakke and the strict scrutiny test were front and center again in the twin lawsuits brought against the University of Michigan in 1997 involving the undergraduate admissions plan (the *Gratz* case) and the law school admissions plan (the *Grutter* case), both plans that attempted to take race into account as a factor in determining who got admitted. The resulting opinions by the Supreme Court in 2003 had a Court that involved a new set of justices with two exceptions—William Rehnquist, a justice on the *Bakke* case, was now the chief justice presiding on the Michigan cases. In addition, Justice John Paul Stevens was on the *Bakke* Court as well as *Grutter* and *Gratz.*

Jennifer Gratz, a white woman, brought a lawsuit because she believed that the automatic 20 points added to the university's admissions index for an applicant who was considered to be from an underrepresented racial or ethnic group—which Michigan considered "African Americans, Hispanics, and Native Americans"—was the reason she did not get into University of Michigan's College of Literature, Science and the Arts. Membership in an underrepresented racial or ethnic community was only one factor considered in admissions decisions. Other factors used included the quality of an applicant's high school, the strength of an applicant's high school curriculum, an applicant's unusual circumstances, an applicant's geographical residence, and an applicant's alumni relationships.[21]

The Court reviewed Michigan's use of an automatic 20-point bonus for underrepresented racial or ethnic minorities in light of the *Bakke* case. Chief Justice Rehnquist ultimately held for the Court in *Gratz* that "because the University's use of race in its current freshman admissions policy is not narrowly tailored to achieve respondents' asserted compelling interest in diversity, the admissions policy violates the Equal Protection Clause of the Fourteenth Amendment." Thus, in *Gratz* as in *Bakke,* the Court prohibited the use of a fixed numerical approach to affirmative action in higher education admissions.

Decided by the Court the same day as the *Gratz* case, the *Grutter* case involved a white woman named Barbara Grutter who sued the University of Michigan Law School over its admissions policy because she did not get in. She claimed her rejection was because the law school used a policy drafted in 1992 where race was considered as one factor "to ensure that a critical mass of underrepresented minority students would be reached so as to realize the educational benefits of a diverse student body."[22] According to the law school, the term "critical mass" did not indicate a specific number but was meant to be an amount "that encourages underrepresented minority students to participate in the classroom and not feel isolated."[23] In addition, Michigan argued, when a critical mass is present, "racial stereotypes lose their force because nonminority students learn there is no 'minority viewpoint' but rather a variety of viewpoints among minority students."[24]

Underlying this discussion is the disturbing fact that without recognition of race in admissions decisions, African Americans, Hispanics, and Native

Americans "might not be represented in meaningful numbers" at the law school.[25] For reasons that are complex and beyond the scope of this chapter, Law School Admission Test score and undergraduate grade point totals alone do not result in sufficient enrollment of these underrepresented communities. For example, in 2000, 14.5 percent of the entering law school class in 2000 was composed of underrepresented minority students under a race-conscious admissions policy. It was predicted that if race had not been considered, this group would have been only 4 percent of the entering class.[26]

It is important to recognize that this phenomenon is predominantly an issue at elite educational institutions, where competition is the most fierce (Michigan Law School typically receives more than 3,500 applications for a class of around 350 students).[27] Not surprisingly, many students want to attend elite schools because employment and leadership opportunities are usually greater there (e.g., Michigan Law Review editors are sometimes chosen to serve as Supreme Court law clerks).

Justice Sandra Day O'Connor—who had agreed with the Court's decision in *Gratz*—delivered the opinion of the Court in *Grutter*. She wrote that in *Bakke* Justice Powell had rejected several interests as compelling enough to justify the use of race as a factor. First, reducing the deficit of "traditionally disfavored minorities" in a profession was not sufficient.[28] Second, "remedying societal discrimination" was also rejected because "such measures would risk placing unnecessary burdens on innocent third parties."[29] Third, increasing the number of doctors likely to practice in underserved communities was insufficient as well. In the end, according to Justice Powell, only one interest of the state was sufficiently compelling as to allow the use of race as a factor: the "attainment of a diverse student body."[30]

Justice O'Connor echoed this conclusion that the one interest sufficed in *Grutter*: "Today we endorse Justice Powell's view that student body diversity is a compelling state interest that can justify the use of race in university admissions."[31] While she included language that the possibility of remedying past racial discrimination as a compelling interest was discussed in other Supreme Court cases, the law school advanced its argument only on the strength of obtaining "the educational benefits that flow from a diverse student body,"[32] and Justice O'Connor used only one paragraph in her decision to allude to remedying past discrimination.[33] Clearly, the interest that received affirmation was the principle of student body diversity.

The law school sought this diversity by seeking to "enroll a 'critical mass' of minority students."[34] Justice O'Connor stated that the benefits of this approach are "substantial,"[35] emphasizing that "the Law School's admissions policy promotes 'cross-racial understanding,' helps to break down racial stereotypes, and 'enables [students] to better understand persons of different races' [citations omitted]. . . . These benefits are 'important and laudable,' because 'classroom discussion is livelier, more spirited, and simply more enlightening and interesting' when the students have the 'greatest possible variety of background.'"[36]

Justice O'Connor also pronounced a time limit on any efforts using race as a factor under this interest. She wrote, "We expect that 25 years from now, the use of racial preferences will no longer be necessary to further the interest approved today."[37]

Ultimately, Justice O'Connor voted for the applicant in *Gratz* (where the automatic 20 points for disadvantaged minority students was ruled unconstitutional). She ruled for the university in *Grutter* (upholding a holistic review of the admissions file where race is but one factor), demonstrating once again that it is possible to dismiss one mechanism of affirmative action but support another.

This short legal history gives a basic introduction to the rationale promoted by the Court for allowing the use of race as a factor in higher education admissions. The next section will consider who are primarily benefited—underrepresented people of color or white students—by employing this rationale.

Classroom Diversity Rationale Really Benefits White Students Most

Members of communities of color in the United States are (currently) in the minority and the dominant U.S. culture is a Judeo-Christian, heterosexual, white male-centered culture. To advance in most academic and business realms, people must conform to its norms as these are usually the standards applied to performance in these areas. This phenomenon means that most people of color must understand the dominant culture to get ahead in this country in terms of wealth and status. That is, people of color must understand the standards imposed by the dominant White culture, and then make a decision as to whether they can accept and/or wish to follow those standards (within parameters that range from what is literally safe to do in a racist society, to what is genuinely a value they hold). Virtually everyone has access to the basic tenets of the dominant U.S. culture (i.e., the use, even if unknowing, of white privilege, and the lingering premise of white supremacy), as this information is replicated repeatedly in school systems, television and movies, and the media. In short, most people of color in the United States know a fair amount about White culture, while most white people have a much more limited awareness of cultures based in communities of color.

Most people of color who have succeeded in reaching college or graduate school are particularly likely to know a lot about the White culture because they have had to understand it (or at least suffered through it) to be considered "successful" in their academic performance by mostly white evaluators in mostly white systems. On the other hand, most white people in the United States can generally have little knowledge of history, beliefs, or practices in communities of color without many (or even any) repercussions.

So if most people of color already know a fair amount about the dominant culture because they have to interact with it just about every day, but white people do not often know much about people of color, who truly benefits from admitting a few more students of color to institutions of higher education? In general, it is the white students (and white faculty) who do, because they are potentially gaining access to increased knowledge of different perspectives held by members of communities of color. At the most cynical reading of the justification of educational benefits of classroom diversity, the justification is accepted because the white elite may want to understand communities of color better so they (white people) are able to function more effectively in leadership roles, as white people will likely continue to dominate those positions in this country as long as white privilege still plays a part.

Recall that remedying past discrimination was an interest viewed with suspicion by the Court. While Justice Powell acknowledged that "no one denies the regrettable fact that there has been societal discrimination in this country against various racial and ethnic groups,"[38] he worried that such a rationale would "would risk placing unnecessary burdens on innocent third parties"[39] (read mostly innocent white students) and the *Grutter* decision followed this precedent. However, the rationale of a classroom diversity interest that benefited cross-racial understanding was considered palatable. It is palatable because it offered a great benefit to white students who often needed the exposure to people of color to be effective in the workplace, the armed services and other important societal institutions where some strides have been made in increasing representation of people of color.

I am not denying that a classroom composed of a wide range of backgrounds—racial, ethnic, and life experiences—enlivens the discussion for all students. Certainly, students of color also need exposure to people of all races—including white people and the various communities within their own race. But the reality is that among college students in the United States, a substantial majority are still white, and there is a dearth of students of color in higher education. Ultimately, the benefit of classroom diversity as it currently functions adheres more to the white students and faculty than to the students of color.

I am in favor of cross-racial understanding and am deeply grateful for what I have learned from students and colleagues of color. One treasured example of my own increased understanding from a diverse classroom stems from my time in the University of Michigan Law School when I had the opportunity to co-teach the undergraduate class Women and the Law with two other law students. It was a wonderful display of varied viewpoints exchanged between H. (a straight Latina woman), C. (a straight African American woman), and me (a white lesbian woman). At one point H. and I were teasing C. about her upcoming wedding and what we were joking about was its "traditional" nature even though the three of us were informed and empowered Women's Studies instructors.[40]

"You're probably even going to take his last name," we teased.

"Of course," C. replied. She explained that her last name was related to the experience of slavery and questioned why she should feel any need to hang on to it. Not surprisingly, that shut us up.

I am grateful for that semester of co-teaching with those two amazing, dynamic people and sometimes think of it as the high point of teaching in a way that truly informed our students—and me—of the wonderful complexity of the world, of the difficult and divisive issues that must be confronted. In this section I am not disparaging the goal of classroom diversity, and I believe that diversity does enhance everyone's educational experience. But there are costs to using the predominant rationale of obtaining classroom diversity (acceptable to many white people) instead of the stronger justification of remedying past discrimination (thought to imperil and blame innocent white people), costs that must be acknowledged. The next section will illuminate the toll that the Supreme Court's approach takes on students of color.

"Students of Color Are Not Your Textbook"

In teaching regularly on race and education at WWU, I often learn more about the various barriers that students of color face in higher education.

This past spring 2014, because of WWU president Shepard's blog post calling for an increased representation of students of color to help match changing state demographics, a small group of white supremacists stood in the center of the WWU campus and unfurled a long banner that read: "Diversity" = White Genocide. Angry parents wrote that they would never send their children to such an "antiwhite" university. And there were threats of violence against President Shepard that required security precautions. WWU students responded admirably with a Diversity Rally, which included speakers from various racial and ethnic backgrounds. The primary theme of the rally was one of campus unity.

During the Diversity Rally several students of color held signs, one of which read "Students of Color Are Not Your Textbooks." I heard that there was some frustration on the part of the rally organizers over the signs because it seemed a counter to the projection of overall unity and positivity in the face of hatred that was desired. It was not my rally, nor is it my place to judge whether there is a "better" approach for such a rally given that I am not experiencing racism nor being viewed as a walking textbook.[41] But whatever one might think of the sign at that particular rally, it raises the important issue of the *experience* of students of color in the higher education setting.

Built into the Supreme Court's rationale of classroom diversity and the quest for a "critical mass" of students of color is the very real pressure placed on students of color to enhance cross-racial understanding by contributing to the classroom discussion. Inherent in the Court's approach to classroom diversity is an implication that students of color are present to educate others on their viewpoints and communities. While the Court may not have originated the pressure on students of color to educate white people, the rationale of educational diversity strengthens its legitimacy. Using a rationale of remedying discrimination instead would help legitimize the fact that racism is still a problem in our country and that students of color deserve to be in the classroom whether or not they can spend the energy to educate white students (and white faculty) on communities of color. Thus, if the rationale for taking race into account as a factor for admissions were to make up for past (and current) racial discrimination instead of for classroom diversity, the inherent pressure to educate white people might be lessened.

Sadly, while Justice O'Connor in *Grutter* briefly alluded to the possibility of using past racial discrimination as a rationale for using race as a factor in admissions, the Court has recently held in the case *Fisher v. University of Texas at Austin* (2013) that *Bakke* did not allow the rationale of "[r]edressing past discrimination" to serve as a compelling interest sufficient for using race in cases of higher education admissions.[42] Justice Anthony M. Kennedy, writing for the Court, explained that a university cannot replicate the processes of "judicial, legislative, or administrative findings of constitutional or statutory violations" that determine the government has, in fact, violated the law through racial discrimination.[43] What was missing, according to Justice Kennedy, were findings that would demonstrate the existence of discrimination on the basis of race (e.g., segregated public schools) and that the state discrimination required the continued intervention of the state on the basis of race to remedy the situation (desegregating all public schools), usually for a specified term.

According to the *Fisher* Court, a university's mission is an educational one, and it is not equipped with the processes or the authority to determine the existence of racial discrimination in a legal sense or to determine the permissible remedies for such discrimination. This means that public universities can use only one interest—the enhanced educational experience from a diverse classroom—to meet the strict scrutiny standard of having a compelling state interest. In fact, Justice Kennedy made a point in his conclusion that benefits of student body diversity are "the only interest that this Court has approved in this context [higher education admissions]."[44]

Thus, we are now locked into the dominant rationale for the use of race as one factor in higher education admissions decisions as the educational interest, not the interest of remedying racial discrimination that should be used.

Fisher shows that the legal ground of affirmative action has been shifting even as I write this chapter. It is, therefore, to the most recent affirmative action in higher education cases that we must now turn.

Current Legal Status of Affirmative Action in Higher Education Admissions

The U.S. Supreme Court has discretion over which appeals it will accept, so it could have chosen not to hear the *Fisher* case in the first place. The Court did not need to take the 2013 *Fisher* case on appeal and in doing so betrayed a willingness to reconsider the underlying principles of *Grutter*.

The facts of *Fisher* are remarkably similar to the facts of the *Grutter* case. Abigail Fisher, a white woman, sued the University of Texas at Austin (UT) because she believed that UT's use of race as one factor in undergraduate admissions decisions was the reason she was rejected for the class entering in Fall 2008.[45] Fisher charged that the Texas admissions policy violated the Equal Protection Clause.

Texas has been one of the states struggling with—and divided over—the idea of employing affirmative action in its higher education admissions policies. When a decision by the Court of Appeals for the Fifth Circuit in *Hopwood v. University of Texas* "struck down the use of race-based criteria in admissions decisions at UT's law school,"[46] Texas stopped any use of race as a factor in university admissions. *Hopwood* was decided in 1996, after *Bakke* and before *Grutter.* Because it was the Fifth Circuit Court of Appeals—but not the Supreme Court—that decided *Hopwood,* the decision controlled only those states that like Texas lay inside the Fifth Circuit.

In 1997, the Texas legislature enacted the Top Ten Percent Law,[47] which required that "Texas high school seniors in the top ten percent of their class be automatically admitted to any Texas state university."[48] This law was passed as an attempt to increase minority enrollment.[49] However, its success was built on a perverse basis: "While the Top Ten Percent Plan boosts minority enrollment by skimming from the tops of Texas high schools, it does so against this backdrop of increasing resegregation in Texas public schools, where over half of Hispanic students and 40% of black students attend a school with 90%–100% minority enrollment."[50]

When the Supreme Court decided *Grutter* in 2003, it allowed the University of Texas to again consider race and ethnicity in admissions in a holistic review of factors, while the Top Ten Percent Law continued in force. Abigail Fisher's argument was that the combination of the two mechanisms made her case different from the facts in *Grutter* so that the courts needed to look at her claim. She asserted that the Top Ten Percent Law was race-neutral and sufficient and that the numbers of disadvantaged minority students at Texas had surpassed "critical mass," so that there was no compelling interest to justify the UT policy. Thus, according to Fisher, race could not be a factor in Texas' undergraduate admissions policy without violating the Equal Protection Clause.

When hearing a case, trial courts have an option of granting summary judgment to one of the sides. Summary judgment is granted when the court determines that there is no "genuine issue of material fact" and that the law is clear who will win based on the facts.[51] Drawing on *Grutter,* the United States District Court for the Western District of Texas granted summary judgment to the University of Texas when presented with the *Fisher* case.[52]

When the Court of Appeals for the Fifth Circuit (the intermediate appellate level of federal courts) ruled on the *Fisher* case in 2011, the Fifth Circuit panel concluded that "the Top Ten Percent Law alone does not perform well in pursuit of the diversity that *Grutter* endorsed and is in many ways at war with it."[53] The Court of Appeals panel that reached this opinion noted that under the Top Ten Percent Law, "minority students remain clustered in certain programs, limiting the beneficial effects of educational diversity."[54] The court reasoned that "if UT is to have diverse interactions, it needs more minority students who are interested in and meet the requirements for a greater variety of colleges, not more students disproportionately enrolled in certain programs. The holistic review [using race as a factor] endorsed by *Grutter* gives UT that discretion, but the Top Ten Percent Law, which accounts for nearly 90% of all Texas resident admissions, does not."[55] Ultimately, the Court of Appeals for the Fifth Circuit panel agreed with the lower court and held in favor of the university.

The Court of Appeals also noted a time limit on its judicial approval, much like the admonishment Justice O'Connor gave in *Grutter* that she expected race-conscious admissions mechanisms to last only for the next 25 years. For the Fifth Circuit panel, it noted that it expected the university to keep monitoring the process and that the court approved the policy only until the next census count.[56]

After losing in the Western District Court and Court of Appeals for the Fifth Circuit, Fisher appealed to the U.S. Supreme Court. The Court, though it did not have to take the case (which would have left the University's victory intact), chose to hear the appeal. By taking a case so similar to *Grutter,* the Court demonstrated a willingness to reconsider whether race should be used at all.

Justice Kennedy wrote the opinion for the 7–1 majority (Justice Elena Kagan did not participate). Justice Kennedy relied on *Bakke* and *Grutter* in concluding that the *Fisher* case needed to be remanded (sent back down) to the Fifth Circuit because the appellate court had not applied a level of scrutiny to the university's decision that was strict enough. The Fifth Circuit was ordered to review the case again and this time was not to show the level of deference it had to the university's assertion that the school's admissions policy was based on a compelling interest and narrowly tailored to achieve that interest.

Thus, the Supreme Court did not, at this time, overturn *Grutter*'s possibility of a constitutionally permissible holistic review of a higher education admissions policy that used race as one factor. However, two justices—Justice Antonin Scalia and Justice Clarence Thomas—wrote concurrences stating their view that *Grutter* was wrongly decided and that race as a factor in government decision making should never be a factor. Justice Scalia noted his dissent in *Grutter* but also stated that Fisher had not explicitly asked the Court to overturn *Grutter* so he joined the majority's opinion in full.[57] Justice Thomas wrote directly, "I would overrule *Grutter*."[58]

Justice Ruth Bader Ginsburg, the sole dissenter, wrote that the Top Ten Percent Plan was, in fact, race-conscious, not race-neutral, because it relied on the reality that public high schools in Texas "are still predominantly composed of people from a single racial or ethnic group," a fact she referred to as "segregation."[59] She even stated that the government should be able to consider the "overtly discriminatory past," suggesting she understood past racial discrimination as a compelling interest.[60] Justice Ginsburg argued that among "constitutionally permissible options, I remain convinced, 'those that candidly disclose their consideration of race [are] preferable to those that conceal it."[61] While she agreed with the Court keeping the equal protection framework established in *Grutter*, she did not agree that the case had to be sent back down to a lower court for further review. She was, however, sadly alone in her viewpoint on the Court, and the case was sent back to the Court of Appeals for the Fifth Circuit to review it under a stricter form of scrutiny.

As recently as July 15, 2014 (while I was writing this chapter), the Fifth Circuit panel released its new opinion, still upholding the judgment in favor of the University of Texas even after applying the stricter level of scrutiny.[62] In being asked to consider mechanisms that looked solely at socioeconomic status rather than race, the Court of Appeals for the Fifth Circuit observed:

> At bottom, the argument is that minority students are disadvantaged by class, not race; the socioeconomic inquiry is a neutral proxy for race. *Bakke* accepts that skin color matters—it disadvantages and ought not be relevant but it is. We are ill-equipped to sort out race, class, and socioeconomic structures, and *Bakke* did not undertake to do so. To the point, we are ill-equipped to disentangle them and conclude that skin color is no longer an index of prejudice; that we would will it does not make it so.[63]
> —*Circuit Judge Patrick E. Higgenbotham,*
> Fisher v. Texas (5th Cir. 2014)

Abigail Fisher, who has appealed all unfavorable court decisions thus far, will likely appeal this latest ruling from the Fifth Circuit. As the U.S. Supreme Court has discretion over whether to hear cases, it is possible that the Court will take up the *Fisher* case once again if it suspects the Court of Appeals for the Fifth Circuit still did not apply the correct level of scrutiny. Thus, the affirmative action terrain in higher education continues to shift.

Also of importance is the fact that though a state *may* use race as one factor in higher education admissions, states are not *required* to use race in any way according to the recent case of *Schuette v. BAMN* (decided on April 22, 2014). In it, the U.S. Supreme Court upheld the right of states to use their legislative process to prohibit what was termed "discrimination" or "preferential treatment" in public university admissions decisions.[64] This means that state voters "may choose to prohibit the consideration of racial preferences in governmental decisions, in particular with respect to school admissions."[65]

Justice Sotomayor's dissenting opinion, which was longer than the other four opinions combined, argued that the democratic process cannot always protect minority groups and that is why affirmative action and policies like it are so important. As she wrote, "We are fortunate to live in a democratic society. But without checks, democratically approved legislation can oppress minority groups. For that reason, our Constitution places limits on what a majority of the people may do."[66] Her argument did not persuade the majority of the Court (only Justice Ginsburg joined her dissent), and so the Court held in favor of allowing Michigan voters to prohibit race as a factor in higher education admissions.

As the Supreme Court upholds state votes against the use of race-conscious admissions plans and the Court seems poised to hear more on the *Fisher* case, hanging on to the promise of *Grutter*'s holistic race-conscious review of college and university admissions files appears more and more difficult. At the moment, *Grutter*'s holding making it constitutionally permissible to consider race as one factor is still good law. It is not clear, however, what the future will bring.

Conclusion

This chapter explored the status of affirmative action in higher education admissions processes. Justice Powell in *Bakke* summarized the key arguments against the use of race as a factor in higher education admissions, terming such a mechanism a "preference." He wrote:

> Moreover, there are serious problems of justice connected with the idea of preference itself. First, it may not always be clear that a so-called preference is

in fact benign. Courts may be asked to validate burdens imposed upon individual members of a particular group in order to advance the group's general interest. . . . Nothing in the Constitution supports the notion that individuals may be asked to suffer otherwise impermissible burdens in order to embrace the societal standing of their ethnic groups. Second, preferential programs may only reinforce common stereotypes holding that certain groups are unable to achieve success without special protection based on a factor having no relationship to individual worth. . . . Third, there is a measure of inequity in forcing innocent persons in [Bakke's] position to bear the burdens of redressing grievances not of their making. (citations omitted)[67]

On the other end of the spectrum, the Court of Appeals for the Fifth Circuit in its most recent *Fisher* opinion (2014) made arguments in support of race-conscious admissions, drawing on the enhanced educational experience of a diverse classroom rationale and following Justice O'Connor's opinion in *Grutter*. The Court of Appeals for the Fifth Circuit defined the virtues of diverse perspectives in classroom as falling into three categories: (1) more varied perspectives (including livelier classroom discussion); (2) professionalism (students are better prepared for a diverse workforce); and (3) civic engagement (fosters participation by members of all racial and ethnic groups in the leadership and civic engagement of the nation).[68]

The place to start sorting out the complex issue of racial discrimination is stated eloquently by Justice Sotomayor in her powerful *Schuette* dissent: "The way to stop discrimination on the basis of race is to speak openly and candidly on the subject of race, and to apply the constitution with eyes open to the unfortunate effects of centuries of racial discrimination." As she argues, "Race matters." Skin color should not lead to discrimination, but it has, and it does, and it will continue to matter in American culture for the foreseeable future (Justice O'Connor's wish for an end to the need to consider race within 25 years notwithstanding).

Justice Sotomayor in *Schuette* shares, "I have faith that our citizenry will continue to learn from this Nation's regrettable history; that it will strive to move beyond those injustices towards a future of equality." But even with this optimism, Justice Sotomayor stresses, "For much of its history, our Nation has denied to many of its citizens the right to participate meaningfully and equally in politics. This is a history we strive to put behind us. But it is a history that still informs the society we live in, and so it is one we must address with candor."[69]

In the end, while I am fully in favor of using a race-sensitive[70] mechanism in a holistic review of higher education admissions files, these measures alone are not nearly enough. We should not fool ourselves that taking race into account in a few cases toward the end of the educational process will solve the problem of communities of color being underrepresented on campus (and in professions such as the law). Providing scholarships to first-generation college students, having active recruitment in communities whose first language is not English, and providing adequate support services for racial and ethnic identities, academic assistance, and counseling services once students of color are on campus are just a few of the many necessary methods to increase representation of communities of color at universities. These activities may be money and labor intensive, but they are crucial if we are serious about improving the number—and experiences—of successful students of color on campus.

There is much work to be done to make the United States—and higher education—truly equitable. As Justice Sotomayor tells us, race and racial discrimination must be discussed with candor and an understanding of our history. We must start having this discussion long before college by teaching the complete, multifaceted history of the United States in K-12 so that every student knows the true heritage of the United States, the good, the bad, and the complex. If we accept that reasonable minds can differ on the subject of what to do about racial discrimination, perhaps we can start and maintain the necessary conversation.

This chapter started with a story about whether a white person can ever reach true friendship with a person of color. The obstacles of white privilege (often leading to unintentional but harmful ignorance) and racism stand in the way. Ultimately, identity is a complex, often shifting concept, and the only way to find out if these obstacles can be bridged is to try holding the ideas of individual identity, community identity, and lived experience close at hand. The experience of being told by a black law student that we could not really be friends because I was white was another example that, at least for the present, race still matters even in the world of higher education. Race matters for all of us, not just people of color. It matters at a personal level and at an institutional level, and it must be addressed at all levels.

The United States has much to make up for its terms of its racist history.[71] I embrace Justice Sotomayor's choice of cautious optimism and believe that we will strive as a nation to move forward to a "future of equality,"[72] as long we undertake the journey with candor, courage, and honesty.

Notes

1. I use "Black" when I refer to Black culture, but lowercase for black and white when I am referring to the socially constructed—but deeply potent—concept of race. I thank Professor Kim Forde-Mazrui for his thoughtful remarks on this subject. Kim Forde-Mazrui 2013, 987, 989 fn. 4.

2. This student was born in Uganda but was actually a Kenyan citizen until after law school (when he became a U.S. citizen). He has lived in the United States since he was three years old. His father is black and originally from Kenya, while his mother is white and originally from Britain.

3. *Gratz v. Bollinger,* 539 U.S. 244 (2003).

4. *Grutter v. Bollinger,* 539 U.S. 306 (2003).

5. Fairhaven College of Interdisciplinary Studies, Western Washington University (WWU). The college began in 1967 with a social justice mission and has always prided itself on trying to address social issues. The college is known for not providing letter grades but instead having the students write a self-evaluation, which the instructor responds to with a narrative assessment. (The other colleges at Western Washington University all use traditional letter grades rather than the narrative assessments.)

6. For those who believe that race unfortunately matters in understanding context (as I do), I note that Western Washington University president Bruce Shepard is a white male.

7. Bruce Shepard 2014. http://www.wwu.edu/president/blog/posts/24.shtml.

8. To see a chilling photo of beaming white supremacists with the banner in front of one of WWU's academic buildings, see http://whitegenocideproject.com/washington-anti-white-university-gets-its-come-uppings/. Goode 2014.

9. Stone 2014. http://www.westernfrontonline.net/news/article_6b805af2-cf44-11e3-891c-001a4bcf6878.html.

10. Anderson 2004, p. 72.

11. Interestingly, when a third agenda item was raised at the end, that of having an affirmative action policy for women, the women present spoke against it.

12. Kim Forde-Mazrui 1992, p. 2.

13. Ibid., p. 3.

14. *Schuette v. BAMN,* 572 U.S. ___ (2014) (Justice Sonia Sotomayor dissenting).

15. I realize that the Michigan Law Review is run by students and may not, therefore, qualify as decision making by the state. I use the anecdote to raise the complexities inherent generally in considering any mechanism of affirmative action.

16. There are situations where the *state* constitution requires public education as a fundamental right. For example, in *McCleary v. State,* 269 P.3d 227 (Wash. 2012), the lawsuit for more educational funding has led the Washington State Supreme Court to require a particular level of funding for K-12 because of the "paramount duty" under the state constitution.

17. *University of California v. Bakke,* 438 U.S. 265 (1978).

18. Ibid., p. 290.

19. *Grutter,* p. 326.

20. Ibid., p. 324.

21. *Gratz,* p. 254. The consideration of "an applicant's alumni relationships" in making admissions decisions is worthy of note. Given that students of color were the ones "underrepresented" on campus, we can deduce that fewer students of color than white students go to Michigan and that there are therefore fewer alumni of color overall, meaning that, of course, this factor is likely to disproportionately benefit white students. Justice Sotomayor noted the use of an applicant's "legacy status" in her *Schuette v. BAMN* dissent.

22. *Grutter,* p. 318.

23. Ibid., p. 316.

24. Ibid., p. 319.

25. Ibid., p. 316.

26. Ibid., p. 320.

27. Ibid., pp. 312–313.

28. Ibid., p. 323.

29. Ibid., p. 324.

30. Ibid., p. 323.

31. Ibid., p. 325.

32. Ibid., p. 328.

33. Ibid.

34. Ibid., p. 329.

35. Ibid., p. 330.

36. Ibid.

37. Ibid., p. 343.

38. *Bakke,* p. 297.

39. *Grutter,* p. 324.

40. It may be worth mentioning that I am actually a fan of "traditional" (monogamous, vows exchanged, family unit first) marriage even though my spouse is female. I appreciate that there are varied views on the usefulness of the right to marry for the gay community (see Paula Ettelbrick's potent essay, "Since When Is Marriage a Path to Liberation?" *OUT/LOOK National Gay and Lesbian Quarterly,* Fall 1989), but I believe that marriage is an important structure for those who wish to partake in it (and no judgment on those who take a different path). Joking aside, I do not believe that Women's Studies and marriage are inherently antithetical.

41. As a white person in Niger, West Africa, I did experience being considered the "spokesperson" for the white race and the source of all knowledge on the United States. Of course, I had chosen to go to Niger and could choose to leave at any time. It is not the same situation as a person of color in the United States faces.

42. *Fisher v. University of Texas,* 570 U.S. ___ (2013).

43. Ibid.

44. Ibid. (Justice Kennedy majority).

45. *Fisher v. Texas,* 631 F.3d 213, 215 (5th Cir. 2011).

46. *Hopwood v. Texas,* 78 F.3d 932 (5th Cir. 1996).

47. Texas House Bill 588, codified as TEX. EDUC. CODE § 51.803 (1997).

48. *Fisher,* 224 (5th Cir. 2011).

49. Ibid.

50. *Fisher v. Texas,* 25–26 (5th Cir. 2014).

51. *Fisher v. Texas,* 645 F.Supp.2d 587, 599 (W. Dist. Ct. Texas 2009).

52. The United States District Court for the Western District of Texas granted summary judgment to the University of Texas in *Fisher,* 645 F.Supp.2d 587 (2009).

53. *Fisher,* 240 (5th Cir. 2011).

54. Ibid.

55. Ibid.

56. Ibid., p. 246.

57. *Fisher* (S. Ct. 2013).

58. Ibid.

59. Ibid.

60. Ibid. (Justice Ruth Bader Ginsburg dissenting).

61. Ibid.

62. *Fisher v. Texas,* (5th Cir. 2014).

63. Ibid. (Circuit Judge Patrick E. Higgenbotham for majority).

64. *Schuette v. BAMN,* 572 U.S. ____ (2014), (Opinion of Justice Anthony M. Kennedy).

65. Ibid.

66. Ibid. (Justice Sonia Sotomayor dissenting).

67. *Bakke,* p. 298.

68. *Fisher v. Texas,* (5th Cir. 2014).

69. *Schuette v. BAMN* (Justice Sotomayor dissenting).

70. Justice Sonia Sotomayor uses the term "race-sensitive admissions policies" over the term "affirmative action." *Schuette v. BAMN* (Justice Sotomayor dissenting).

71. See, for example, Coates 2014, p. 54.

72. *Schuette v. BAMN* (Justice Sotomayor dissenting).

Bibliography

Anderson, Terry H. 2004. *The Pursuit of Fairness: A History of Affirmative Action.* New York: Oxford University Press.

Coates, Ta-Nehisi. 2014. "The Case for Reparations." *The Atlantic* 313 (5).

Ettelbrick, Paula. 1989. "Since When Is Marriage a Path to Liberation?" *OUT/LOOK National Gay and Lesbian Quarterly* (Fall).

Forde-Mazrui, Kim. "Affirmative Action." Memo to the Michigan Law Review Editorial Board. March 23, 1992 (on file with author).

Forde-Mazrui, Kim. 2013. "Does Racial Diversity Promote Cultural Diversity?" The Missing Question in *Fisher v. University of Texas*. *Lewis and Clark Law Review* 17: 4.

Goode, Steve. "Washington: Anti-White University Gets Its Comeuppance." *White Genocide Project*. April 24, 2014.

Shepard, Bruce. "What Do You Mean by Saying, 'If We Are as White in Ten Years as We Are Today, Western Will Have Failed as a University?'" *Bruce's Blog*. January 28, 2014.

Stone, Brandon. "Western Washington Students Rally for Diversity." *Western Front Online*. April 28, 2014.

Legal Cases and Legislation

Fifth Circuit Court of Appeals. *Fisher v. Texas*, 631 F.3d 213 (5th Cir. 2011).

Fifth Circuit Court of Appeals. *Fisher v. Texas* (5th Cir. 2014).

Fifth Circuit Court of Appeals. *Hopwood v. Texas*, 78 F.3d 932 (5th Cir. 1996).

Texas House Bill 588, codified as TEX. EDUC. CODE § 51.803 (1997).

U.S. District Court for the Western District of Texas. *Fisher v. Texas*, 645 F.Supp.2d 587 (W. Dist. Ct. Texas 2009).

U.S. Supreme Court. *Fisher v. University of Texas*, 570 U.S. ___ (2013).

U.S. Supreme Court. *Gratz v. Bollinger*, 539 U.S. 244 (2003).

U.S. Supreme Court. *Grutter v. Bollinger*, 539 U.S. 306 (2003).

U.S. Supreme Court. *Schuette v. BAMN*, 572 U.S. ___ (2014).

U.S. Supreme Court. *University of California v. Bakke*, 438 U.S. 265 (1978).

Washington State Supreme Court. *McCleary v. State*, 269 P.3d 227 (Wash. 2012).

Chapter 16

The Beauty and Burden of Historically Black Colleges and Universities and the Extant Challenges Confronting These Institutions

F. Erik Brooks

Depending on one's perspective, the evolution and current state of historically black colleges and universities (HBCUs) could be cast as a treasured beauty or a troublesome burden. The beautiful truth about the original mission of HBCUs is that they sprang out of necessity to fill a void of educational opportunities for black people who had been freed from enslavement in the United States. Today, these colleges and universities' doors are opened to all races, colors, and creeds; moreover, they continue to fill their historical core mission of serving those with limited opportunity and access to higher education.

The American higher education system commenced in the early 17th century with the founding of Harvard University in 1636, the College of William & Mary in 1693, and Yale University in 1701. The original mission of Harvard University was to educate uneducated white male clergy. During Harvard's initial years, the majority of its courses were focused on religion and ministry. While, Harvard University, the College of William & Mary, and Yale University were created to train white clergymen, prior to the Civil War, there was not a structured higher education system for people of African heritage. In many parts of the United States, to educate anyone of African heritage was prohibited by law. The infamous "separate but equal" doctrine was upheld by the U.S. Supreme Court with its ruling in *Plessy v. Ferguson* 163 U.S. 537 (1896). This erroneous ruling reinforced the practice of educating former slaves in educational facilities that were undoubtedly separated and unequal from those facilities used by whites. This ruling was used as permission to continue with the discriminatory practices that provided blacks with only a rudimentary and second-class education at best.

The "separate but equal" doctrine was a travesty in practice; many of the state entities that operated separate educational facilities had no intention of providing equal facilities nor did they have any intentions to provide the financial backing to upgrade facilities designated for blacks and make these facilities as good as those designated for whites only. Instead of these state governments focusing on upgrading historically black institutions located in their states to make them equal, they focused on governing with an iron-fist to strictly enforce policies and traditions to ensure educational facilities would remain unequal. The application of these regressive policies served as a method to reinforce the concept of inferiority of black people. The *Plessy* decision in 1896 and its unjust application legalized dual racially defined educational systems. When the question arises, "Why are there historically black colleges?" the simple answer is at the time these colleges were founded and with a few exceptions, there was nowhere else for black people to go college because they were not welcomed at predominately white colleges. It was out of necessity that these colleges were founded with the fundamental mission of providing educational opportunity for disadvantaged black people immediately after the end of the Civil War. The preceding question presents an interesting paradox of the beauty and the burden of HBCUs.

This chapter provides a historical analysis of the development of HBCUs in the United States. It also examines the benefits (beauty) and the liabilities (burdens) of HBCUs and their current state of affairs. The chapter concludes with a discussion and recommendations for the future status of HBCUs.

The Creation of Historically Black Colleges and Universities

There are 105 federally recognized HBCUs, which are 3 percent of the colleges in the United States. The Higher Education Act of 1965 delineates a historically black college or university as

> any historically black college or university that was established prior to 1964, whose principal mission was, and is, the education of black Americans, and

that is accredited by a nationally recognized accrediting agency or association determined by the Secretary [of Education] to be a reliable authority as
to the quality of training offered or is, according to such an agency or association, making reasonable progress toward accreditation.[1]

The first historically black college was the Institute for Colored Youth
(now Cheyney University). It was founded in Cheyney, Pennsylvania, in
1837 when Richard Humphrey, a Quaker philanthropist, bequeathed large
amount of his estate to establish a school to educate the descendants of
the African race. After the founding of Cheyney University, two other institutions would be established when Lincoln University was founded in
Lincoln, Pennsylvania, in 1854 and Wilberforce University in Wilberforce,
Ohio, in 1856. Though these schools were technically called colleges, they
did not begin to offer college-level work until some years after opening
their doors. They relied heavily on the philanthropy of religious denomi-
nations and private organizations to sustain operations. During the early
years of these schools, the main mission was significant but narrow in their
scope. The mission of these colleges was to provide elementary and secondary education for newly freed slaves. The mission also centered on training
more black teachers and preachers. These colleges were operated as private
educational entities. Public historically black colleges would not take shape
until the federal government passed the Morrill Act of 1890 (also called the
Second Morrill Act), which required states that operated racially segregated
systems of higher education to establish land-grant institutions for blacks.
It was not until the passage of the second Morrill Act in 1890 that public
higher education of African Americans was designed to deliver scientific
education for African Americans.

The Morrill Act of 1862 also known as the Land Grant College Act gave
annual appropriations for general academic programs in agriculture, home
economics, and mechanical arts. Senator Morrill's intent was to make sure
that higher education would be accessible to all social classes. When Congress passed the Morrill Act of 1862, it authorized payment for 30,000 acres
of public land for every member to its congressional delegation based on
the 1860 census.[2] The proceeds from the sale of the land were put into an
endowment which would provide financial support for the colleges in their
state. In the beginning, not everyone benefited from the land-grant system.
Kentucky and Mississippi were the only two states to establish black colleges based on the Morrill Act of 1862, so a second act was enacted. The
Morrill Act of 1890 was passed to expand higher educational opportunity

for all people but in particular African Americans. Unfortunately, the Morrill Act of 1890 was used to strengthen the "separate but equal" doctrine in Southern states, and therefore, the Morrill Act of 1890 was created to provide blacks with the same opportunity as whites.

As a result of the second Morrill Act, funding to establish black colleges increased and black colleges expanded across the Southern region. The second Morrill Act of 1890 stipulated continuous federal appropriations for education for African Americans; this detail caused some opposition to the legislation and almost derailed its passage. Vermont senator Justin Smith Morrill presented the legislation to Congress multiple times before it passed and became law. Fearing losing an uneducated and exploited labor force, congressmen from the South attempted to block the legislation because they recognized that it would benefit black people and aid in financial support of black colleges.[3] The major impasse hinged on the mandate that appropriations would not be dispersed to any state or territory for the support and maintenance of a college where a distinction of race or color was made in the admission of students. Another factor contributing to this congressional impasse was the enabling legislation directing that funds received in a state or territory be equitably divided between black and white colleges. The enabling legislation of the 1890 Morrill Act provided for a permanent appropriation of $15,000 per annum to be increased by $1,000 per year until it reached $25,000 annually in 1900 to serve every state.[4] The provision of the Morrill Act (1890) that established black land-grant colleges became known as the separate but equal doctrine policy.

Many of the black colleges that had been operating privately were transferred to state governments and others were created through this legislation. The Morrill Act (1890) with federal assistance helped create 18 black land-grant institutions. Those institutions that were already in operation prior to the Morrill Act (1890) also received federal funding. These Southern state governments received federal funding under pretense that they would create "separate but equal" colleges. The Southern state governments were deceptive in their practices and their rhetoric was not congruent with their actions. Southern state governments partnered with the federal government to gain appropriations but did not do it in good faith. Many of them planned to receive federal dollars and provide scant financial backing or none at all and continue to keep black institutions inferior to white institutions. During the time the second Morrill Act (1890) was enacted, many of the private historically black colleges, notably Fisk, Howard, and

Hampton, were controlled and operated by white administrations that subscribed to the industrial model of education.

Liberal Arts Education Model versus Industrial Education Model

Any discussion of the history and direction of HBCUs must revisit the age-old theoretical debate between scholars W.E.B. DuBois and Booker T. Washington, addressing the mission and scope of historically black universities. DuBois and Washington specifically debated the question of whether African Americans should be educated in liberal arts curriculums or if they should pursue vocational curriculum. Washington's view was that newly freed enslaved people should prove themselves through self-reliance and an industrious spirit. Washington prescribed to a gradualist approach to higher education and civil rights. In essence, he wanted to prepare African Americans for the careers that were most available to them. During this time, many black and white leaders turned toward industrial education for black people. Washington and other proponents of the industrial model of higher education argued that African Americans should concentrate on training in manual labor and honing vocational skills in preparation for the employment opportunities that were available to them.

Opponents of industrial education believe that both the liberal arts and scientific ideals should be aligned with the study of black culture, and curriculums based on the preceding objectives should be the aim of higher education for black people. Chief among the opponents of Washington and the industrial model of education was W.E.B. DuBois. DuBois was critical of the industrial model of education because he believed that they were thwarting the intellectual ambition of black people. DuBois thought that blacks were compromising progressive civil rights and appeasing to white people to gain acceptance of white Southern educators and politicians. This debate would rage on through the decades and the critics of industrial education gained influence. DuBois continued to publically denounce the industrial model of education. He stressed that the liberal arts approach and importance of studying black culture and his relentless and rational rebukes of industrial education swayed public conversations about the best method of educating blacks. By the end of World War I, many African American leaders and educators had denounced Washington's educational theories and industrial model of education as best practices for educating blacks. These provocative public conversations resulted in student protests against the white administrations at Fisk, Hampton, and Howard in the 1920s. As a result of such protest, Mordecai Johnson was named the first black president of Howard in 1926.[5] Activism would be a constant thread of the beauty at most HBCUs.

Public HBCUs versus Private HBCUs

The most significant difference between private and public HBCUs is the way they are funded and operated. At the establishment of historically black colleges, most were privately operated. After the second Morrill Act was passed, public black colleges were created. Most public black colleges were founded by state governments and the bulk of these schools' funding has come from their state governments while private black colleges were founded by private organizations and many of them continue to operate more independently of their state governments. Funding for private HBCUs vary. Some private institutions such as Tuskegee University in Tuskegee, Alabama, and Howard University in Washington, D.C., continue to be heavily subsidized by state and federal financial support. Even with the reduction of government support, Tuskegee University continues to receive financial support from state government. The state of Alabama recognizes Tuskegee University's value to attract national and international attention. Howard University continues to receive subsidies from the federal government because of its location and unique arrangement with federal government at its founding. Congress chartered Howard University. In general, higher education has been receiving less funding from federal and state governments over the last few years. This reduction in funding has forced many public universities to function more like private colleges having to seek more independent funding. Since the economic crisis began in 2007, many private and public HBCUs have found themselves searching for new revenue streams and innovative fund-raising to remain financially solvent.

At a glimpse, governance of public and private HBCUs may not look very different; however, there are subtle differences between public and private black colleges. Like most public organizations, public historically black universities' governance is convoluted because they have more constituencies to answer. Because these schools receive public dollars, they have to maintain strong relationships with local, state, and federal entities. For example, public historically black colleges are overseen by their state governments by appointments of members to these schools' boards of trustees. In many cases, these schools can become easy targets in political battles, especially in states that have been historically conservative on race issues. In 2014, Elizabeth City State University, a historically black college in North Carolina, staved off an attack from its state government when the state senate proposed $21 billion budget reduction to higher education and suggested that the University of North Carolina system close down "small, unprofitable" Elizabeth City State University.[6] Also in 2014, the governor of Alabama removed two board of trustee members at Alabama State University over alleged conflicts of interests. In Alabama, the governor by state law serves as the head of the boards of trustees at historically black Alabama State University, at Alabama A&M University, and at predominately white University of West Alabama and Athens State University which enrolls only juniors and seniors. Contrarily, the governor does not wield such power over the state's premier predominately white universities, the University of Alabama and Auburn University, where he does not have the power to remove board of trustee members.

Historically and recently, black colleges in Maryland, Georgia, South Carolina, and Louisiana have borne the burden of fighting off closures and mergers. While private colleges still interact with state governments in the states in which they reside, they can usually avoid being used as political fodder as long as they maintain good relationships with key members of state legislatures, in particular the executive branch. Governing is made less difficult because their boards most often are independently chosen with little input from state government. Private colleges usually seek input from their alumni and sitting governing board members in choosing members of their boards.

In further comparisons of between public and private HBCUs, there is a vast difference in magnitude in terms of overall size and scope. In general, the overall size, student enrollments, and student bodies at private historically black institutions are smaller than historically black public institutions, which is significant because it usually results in a smaller professor to student ratio in the classroom. Traditionally, a smaller professor to student ratio usually correlates to better instruction and student learning. In private college classes, some undergraduate lower-division classes can have as little as 10 students in the class. *U.S. News and World Report* has provided rankings for undergraduate education at historically black colleges. The *U.S. News and World Report* used data from administrators at peer institutions, student graduation and retention rates, faculty resources, student selectivity, financial resources, and alumni giving. In their ranking system,

HBCUs are compared only with other HBCUs classified by United States Department of Education. While the *U.S. News and World Report* rankings have become a major part of the marketing machinery of higher education, HBCUs exposure in this magazine may increase name recognition and reputation among potential students.

Another prevalent difference between black public and private colleges is the cost of tuition and name recognition to the larger society. Some HBCUs are recognized by mainstream America. Perhaps, schools like those of Morehouse College, Spelman College, Howard University, Tuskegee University, and Fisk University have been popularized in main stream America. They have seemingly transcended to being "just universities," thereby encouraging some whites and African Americans to view them through a color-blind lens. These schools appear to resist the negative social and cultural forces that suggest that an education from a HBCU is subpar. Perhaps these universities are being judged on "the content of their character," so to speak, and they have escaped the web of prejudicial social biases. Perhaps, their excellent academic reputations of these universities have allowed them to avoid racial classification based on the racial make-up of their faculty and students. Because Spelman College is the nation's oldest liberal arts college for African American women, Tuskegee University was founded by American hero Booker T. Washington, and Howard University is located in the nation's capital, perhaps these factors have allowed HBCUs to become high-profile institutions that have transcended race and even become viable options for white high school students applying for college admissions. Howard, Tuskegee, Spelman, and Morehouse have been able to utilize their recognizable brand and market them to the mainstream. The recognizable brand-named institutions along with their private status enable them to charge higher tuition and also serve as gateway schools for Ivy League institutions and elite public institutions. In general, tuition is more expensive at private colleges than public colleges. This remains the case for historically black colleges, especially the elite ones. Public historically black colleges also charge out-of-state students more money for tuition and room and board than in-state residents. In doing a cost comparison, the difference in the sticker price of tuition can be clearly seen between private and public HBCUs.

U.S. News and World Report ranked the top private and public HBCUs and the cost of their tuition per year. Using objective and subjective measures, a comparison of top black public and private college was constructed. The comparison reveals that the highest-ranking colleges were private and their tuitions were far more expensive than the public black colleges that made the list. Despite the steady rise in the cost of college over the past 25 years, public HBCUs can be a great value for parents and students seeking a college education.

The Beauty of Historically Black Colleges and Universities

There are many aspects that are beautiful about HBCUs; one of the most notable features of their beauty is that these schools are steeped in history and their graduates have been the torchbearers for the African American community. The literal meaning of the phrase "Beauty is in the eyes of the beholder" is the perception that beauty is subjective. The beauty or merit of white institutions is often viewed through a lens of a traditional paradigm that values parameters like student enrollments, endowments, library holdings, and acreage of campus; many scholars and policy makers error by failing to witness the beauty of HBCUs. The beauty of HBCUs, however, is frequently measured within a different paradigm: (1) prevailing traditional missions and storied individual histories; (2) championing social justice and civil rights; (3) underscoring the vast contributions of their outstanding alumni; (4) providing a sense of community on campuses; and (5) offering classroom experiences that provide both traditional and alternative curriculums. The 1960s were the highpoint of many of these universities and often they along with the black church were the centerpiece of the African American community. During this time, these schools had booming enrollments and their campuses were the heart of intellectual activity and the pulse of political action for the African American community. Traditionally, these institutions and their students have been important agents for change. Historically black colleges have established a tradition of providing intellectual exchanges that allow students to master a particular discipline but also stir up cutting-edge innovation, intellectual curiosity, and social antagonism, all while embracing diversity of other cultures. These towering traditions are the fulfilment of DuBois's vision for the educational mission of black colleges.

Among the beautiful aspects of HBCUs is its historic mission to uplift the race. HBCUs began with the noble mission to provide education for newly freed slaves. Their goal was to bridge the cultural and educational gap between the races. The founders of many of these colleges believe that if former slaves were educated they could eventually become full citizens of the United States. These schools were not only tasked with providing rudimentary education until their students were prepared for college-level work, but they also taught former enslaved people the social graces of the time. With the practice of segregation, historically black colleges continue to provide educational opportunities for the descendants of former slaves. It was the hope of the founders of these colleges that blacks would advance the race socially and politically. The desegregation of higher education forced these universities to change and expand their mission. They have expanded from their original missions; however, they also have stayed true and continue to serve less affluent populations, first-generation college students, and underprepared college students. Most historically black college students are eligible for and receive financial aid. Students who receive financial aid usually need more interaction with faculty and support staff. Students on financial aid usually are also the first to attend college in their family, which also contributes to their need for additional support, mentoring, and encouragement. Faculty interaction is an area in which black colleges receive great marks. This close interaction between faculty and student correlates with the greatest gains in student learning and retention. Students who receive financial aid usually need and benefit greatly from close interaction with faculty. HBCUs usually take pride and have built their reputations on providing this support. This is the spirit in which these universities were founded.

The beauty of HBCUs should be trumpeted in the annals of American society because in many cases historically black college students and faculty were champions of social justice and conducted boycotts and sit-in movements in Southern cities during the civil rights movement. Many of the faculty members at historically black colleges inspired students through teachings on social justices, American history, and black culture which encouraged students to become active leaders in the civil rights movement. Faculty, staff, and students at black colleges became advocates for the African American community. Their faculty and students have been at the forefront of many social and political movements in the United States but often the remarkable contributions of black colleges and their students have been understated in the annals of American history. HBCUs were often the epicenters of activities for the civil rights movements in the South. Many of these students used their residence hall rooms as spaces to refine plot strategies on how they could participate in the larger civil rights movement in the United States. Many of these students were the conduits in a system of college students' social networks and became leaders in the civil rights movement.

While all of the contributions of historically black colleges and their graduates are too numerous to delineate in a single chapter, a few notable examples must be showcased. Outstanding graduates include the following:

- Diane Nash, a student at Fisk University, was central in leading the "freedom rides" and integration of facilities in Nashville, Tennessee.
- Stokely Carmichael honed his leadership skills as a student at Howard University.
- Franklin McCain, David Richmond, Joseph McNeil, and Ezell Blair Jr., students at North Carolina A&T University, led the sit-in movements in Greensboro, North Carolina.
- Jo Ann Robinson, a professor at Alabama State University, and the students called for a boycott when Rosa Parks, graduate of Alabama State University, was arrested for challenging a system of integration in Montgomery, Alabama.
- Charles Hamilton Houston transformed Howard University's Law School into a place to train lawyers to become social engineers and advocate for social justice.
- Out of Hamilton's social engineers' experiment at Howard University emerged Robert L. Carter and Thurgood Marshall. Marshall went on to become the chief legal counsel for the National Association for the Advancement of Colored People, United States Solicitor General, and an associate justice of the U.S. Supreme Court. Lloyd Gaines Murray, Donald Gaines Murray, Ada Lois Sipuel, and George McLaurin were lead plaintiffs in lawsuits challenging de jure segregation at predominately white universities.
- Martin Luther King Jr., a graduate of Morehouse College, became a renowned figure for social justice and peace.

HBCUs showcase their beauty through a sense of community and the betterment of the black community. With a few exceptions, prior to integration of white colleges, African American athletes attended HBCUs. At HBCUs, these black athletes were properly mentored and nurtured and they were coached by legendary black coaches. With the advent of big-time college athletics and television monies, black colleges could not compete with amenities provided to athletes recruited to predominately white colleges. During the 1950s through 1970s, many of the most prestigious athletic programs at predominately white institutions began to recruit more African American student athletes and this hurt athletics at black colleges. Northern universities were first in recruiting and playing black student athletes. Because of Southern tradition and racism, white universities in the South were slower in accepting black athletes. After seeing black athletes flourish at college athletics in the North and West, Southern predominately white universities began to recognize that black athletes were a goldmine to their athletic programs and gave them a competitive edge. In 1966, Texas Western University was the first predominately white institution to start five African American basketball players in an NCAA championship game. Texas Western matched up against perennial basketball powerhouse the University of Kentucky who did not have any black student athletes on its team. Texas Western won the national championship, after which many black student athletes became much sought after by predominately white universities and they were lured away with better scholarships and other benefits. These student athletes would have otherwise attended and become athletes at HBCUs and received coaching and mentoring from legendary college hall-of-fame coaches such as Eddie Robinson at Grambling, Marino Casem at Alcorn State, W.C. Gorden at Jackson State, Jake Gaither at Florida A&M, Earl Banks at Morgan State, and John Merritt at Tennessee State. Instead, many African American athletes began to choose predominately white universities with big-time sports programs and refused to consider attending HBCUs because of their perceived inferiority in college athletics.

At the beginning of integrating college athletics in the South, it was customary for predominately white schools in the deep-South to usually solicit only two to three athletes to try out for their football and basketball squads. In 1970, when the University of Alabama played against the University of Southern California (USC) at Legion Field in Birmingham, Alabama, black running back Sam Cunningham and the integrated USC football team beat famed coach Paul "Bear" Bryant and the Crimson Tide. USC's victory made the rabid football fans in the deep-South realize that without African American players their athletic programs would become second rate and they would no longer be contenders for national championships in football, basketball, and track. As a result, they began to poach athletes who attended HBCUs, and some argue that this has led to the demise of quality athletic programs at HBCUs. Even with the prevalence of elite African American athletes attending white schools, HBCU sporting events remain a strong link and the centerpiece of many social events in the African American community.

Another beauty of HBCUs is the linked fate philosophy that prevails at most of these institutions. Because of the traditional mission, HBCUs maintain a commitment to the black community. Most are located in black neighborhoods and communities, and therefore, they should be strongly linked to this community in their research, service, and teaching. HBCUs cannot wholly divorce themselves from black communities. The African American community and HBCUs are wrapped in a single garment of destiny and neither can be all that they can be without the other. In general, most faculty and staff at black colleges subscribe to a "link fate" philosophy and in doing so they motivate students to be their best intellectually and socially. Linked fate is a political theory that argues that African Americans believe that their own self-interests are linked to the interest of the race. Simply, African Americans are connected by the virtue of being black.[7] This subscription to link fate philosophy may be conscious or unconscious but it is very evident at most black colleges. The "linked fate" philosophy also allows faculty and staff to have a vested interest in seeing students graduate. These faculty and staff members also serve as role models for black students who attend these institutions. Students get opportunities to observe examples of African American professors and researchers. HBCUs have long been thought as positive learning environments, and students have more opportunities to engage their professors in and out of the classroom with purposeful educational activities. Linked fate theory can also explain why many black college graduates opt to choose careers that serve low-income urban communities and black colleges have traditionally encouraged this type of service to the African American community.

Various extracurricular activities are another beauty of the historical black college experience. Participation in extracurricular activities and deep social interaction are critical to the success for all students. These factors contribute to a sense of belonging and connectedness that some African American students do not find in predominately white institutions. Sporting events such as the black football classics and the conference basketball tournaments are just two beautiful extracurricular events taking place at black colleges. Social events such as homecomings, concerts, fraternity and sorority community service, and Greek shows remain beautiful aspects of extracurricular activities at black colleges. Often activities at HBCUs are the social and intellectual centerpiece of the African American community.

Often historically black colleges offer a culturally sensitive curriculum in concert with the traditional curriculum to a discipline. A culturally sensitive curriculum and utilizing a "constructivist" and "holistic student-centered" approach can combat the cultural and intellectual imperialism that is often found at predominately white institutions. Intellectual imperialism can stifle intellectual growth and curiosity. At some predominately

white institutions, professors fail to provide students with alternative perspectives, scholarship, and scholars in examining phenomena. This failure
to examine plausible alternatives or to offer additional background information through a narrow perspective may cause African American students
to disengage from the content presented in courses. For example, an African American student might be interested to learn that while Greeks are
credited with many of the ancient intellectual discoveries, the higher education system in Kemet (Ancient Egypt) is older and more profound than
the Greeks' educational system.[8] Greek scholars used the scholarship and
teachings from teachers in Kemet to expand and deepen their knowledge.[9]
At HBCUs students may also learn of the work of black intellectuals such
as Frances Cress Welsing, John Henrik Clark, Carter G. Woodson, Cheikh
Anta Diop, Maimba Ani, and Amos Wilson, which is often omitted from
mainstream scholarship in their disciplines. These alternative perspectives
in instruction and scholarship may motivate better academic performance,
generate greater social involvement, and fuel higher occupational aspirations for African American students. Alternative curriculums and information will assist students in having greater self-efficacy and self-agency. Style
and delivery also contribute to positive learning experiences at HBCUs.
Knowledge and the style which is transmitted has been discounted in student learning. Some scholars contend that greater sensitivity to style issues
and culturally sensitive curriculum will make meaningful contributions
to future pedagogy for educating African Americans.[10] Combating intellectual and cultural imperialism may assist HBCU graduates in being for
full functioning individuals with a greater sense of self and greater confidence. In the classic psychological study conducted in 1947, African American children were shown black and white dolls. Overwhelmingly in the
Clarks' study, black children chose the white doll as the most attractive doll.
Being taught alternative perspectives may assist African American college
students in valuing racial differences and embracing the achievements and
contributions of blacks to the world. At the least, the alternative perspectives offered at HBCUs can contribute to better self-concept in black college
students. Most HBCUs foster environments where African Americans may
feel more comfortable with self-expression and exploration of thought and
ultimately excel academically. The environments at elite historically black
colleges enhance student confidence and the intellectual ability to excel
and graduate and pursue graduate and profession degrees after undergraduate studies. Historically black colleges also offer an environment of acceptance to students. Generally, African American students do not experience

social isolation at black colleges that can be experienced at predominately white colleges.

The Burden of Historically Black Colleges and Universities

The beauty of historically black colleges is evident by their storied and celebrated histories. These histories represent past and future burdens for them as well. Some burdens of HBCUs are that they (1) face many fiscal challenges, low enrollments, and inadequate state funding; (2) attract a challenging student population consisting of first-generation college students and underprepared low-income students; and (3) are often forced to spend time and resources trying to justify their existence. While some historical and current burdens overlap, many of the historical burdens have increased because of many years of poor funding, institutional racism, and adverse impact from court decisions. Both historically and currently, these colleges are still faced with providing higher education for students who are often underprepared for college. These burdens coupled with contemporary challenges and systematic impediments will continue to be detrimental to the future of black colleges.

Adept fund-raising continue to be a burden for most HBCUs. HBCUS are frequently plagued by small endowments and systemic poor funding. Because many of their graduates are first-generation graduates, they tend not to generate as much wealth from multigenerational alumni. Consequently, their graduates do not tend to contribute to their alma maters. In addition, most historically black colleges have yet to develop a strong culture of financial philanthropy. Howard University ranks first with the largest endowment among historically black colleges with $513 million in its endowment. Spelman College in Atlanta, Georgia, ranked second with $327,171 million in its endowment, followed by Hampton University in Hampton, Virginia, with $254,103 million in its endowment. Meharry Medical College in Nashville, Tennessee, with $124,965 million, and Florida A&M University in Tallahassee, Florida, with $111,281 million rounded the top five historically black college endowments.[11] On the surface these amounts appear substantial, but in comparison to other private and public predominately white institutions these numbers are pale in comparisons. Data suggests that the top 10 endowments of predominantly white colleges equal $154.7 billion, while the combined value of the top 10 historically black college endowments equals $1.5 billion.[12] Poor philanthropic giving by alumni remains to be a burden for HBCUs.

Like all American universities, HBCUs are faced with the operational and programmatic goals like ensuring that their graduates are gaining appropriate knowledge, skills, and abilities while enrolled at their universities; however, HBCUs are disproportionally faced with educating first-generation and low-income students, which can make these goals more difficult. In 2009, President Barack Obama issued a clear-cut call for more college graduates in the United States. He also called for better retention and graduation rates at America's colleges and universities by 2020. These calls were not aimed specifically at black colleges, but they will probably motivate many more first-generation, low-income, and minority students to seek higher education. In many cases, this means more underprepared students will enter college. This presents a unique challenge for historically black colleges whose mission has always been to educate first-generation, low-income, and underprepared students. While this is a noble mission, it is also a burden. According to the Pew Research, parents' educational attainment is the greatest predictor of student college success. First-generation college students are more likely to drop out of college than students' parents who obtained a degree. Many first-generation college students come from families of low socioeconomic statuses and graduated from under-resourced high schools located in low-income urban neighborhoods. Indeed, there are many factors that contribute to the poor quality of education provided in low-income and urban K-12 school settings. It has been long understood that greater financial resources correlate to greater student achievement. Evaporating tax bases in poor communities and economic inequality contribute to poorly funded schools with fewer resources. The best teachers usually prefer to teach at schools that rank high in student achievement measures on standardized tests. In turn, students in low-income and urban settings are usually taught by new teachers, low-skilled teachers, or burned-out teachers, which can be compounded by frequent turnover of teachers. These factors lead to poor academic success at urban black schools. Poorly rated high schools in urban black communities are a major reason why students are not well prepared for college-level work, and when they attend college, they usually need remediation in reading, mathematics, and science. Unfortunately, HBCUs typically have limited resources and very few, if any, lack graduate assistants. More often than not, at historically black colleges, bringing these students up to college level becomes the burden of professors.

Another burden that historically black colleges face is justifying their existence to their opponents and critics. Unlike white institutions that serve specific populations, HBCUs are often forced to spend valuable time and resources just trying to justify their existence. Religious and women's colleges are not faced with these same burdens of continuously justifying their existence in today's society. Do colleges and universities such as Wellesley College, Agnes Scott, Smith College, Simmons College, Mount Holyoke, and Stephens College stave off their critics and justify why they are still relevant and a necessity? Rarely do these colleges have to justify reasons for holding to their original mission to train women leaders to assume leadership roles. Colleges with a women-centered focus continue to produce women leaders, and the academic environments offered at these institutions allow women to excel without having the institution's rigor and relevance questioned.

Are religious institutions such as Notre Dame University, Boston College, and Brigham Young University saddled with the burden of having to justify their relevance? No! It is simply understood that these institutions provide environments that allow students with specific religious affiliations to excel without having their religion beliefs questioned. These colleges and universities foster environments that allow students to feel comfortable in expressing their religious beliefs. Rarely are these institutions weighed down with questions about the benefits their institutions provide for students attending their colleges. Similarly to women's colleges and religious-affiliated colleges, HBCUs allow students to excel in academic environments in which they may be more comfortable. The effort that HBCUs are required to spend justifying their existence hinders them from devoting their time and energy from recruiting the best talent. Having to consistently justify their relevance and existence indeed causes a chilling effect in recruiting and retaining elite students and faculty at historically black colleges. These negative arguments have caused some misinformed people in the African American community to question the need and relevance of HBCUs and the quality of education. The question should be raised, "Why do HBCUs have to justify their existence while other institutions of higher learning do not?" Part of the answers lies in the fact that HBCUs continue to wrestle with a perception problem caused by racialized assumptions. While society values white institutions and their missions and work, many HBCUs are undervalued and underappreciated because of their traditional missions and service to the African American community. These perceptions also add to the erroneous assumption that HBCUs are second-class institutions and those who are enrolled as students and employed as professors are incompetent.

Current State of Historically Black Colleges and Universities

Historically black colleges have been experiencing increasingly difficult times since the 1990s. Many events have contributed to the beginning of the downturn in funding and student enrollments at historically black colleges. There are three key reasons why many historically black colleges are currently experiencing difficulties: (1) HBCUs are disconnected from youth and the larger African American community; (2) there have been changes in Parent PLUS loans and reductions in state and federal funding; and (3) many historically black colleges have experienced infighting and mismanagement among their leadership teams.

Over the years, historically black colleges have been proud transmitters of tradition and builders of African American communities in the United States; however, many historically black colleges have become disconnected from the youth and communities in which they are located. Historically black colleges cannot only be consumers of the resources of these communities; they have a duty to be the intellectual epicenters of these communities and educate them on issues pertinent to African American community at large. Many of these communities and neighborhoods have been built around the activities held at the HBCUs in their neighborhoods. Many HBCUs have failed to maintain their "town and gown" connections and tackle issues of the communities in which they serve. From the Middle Ages at European universities, the town and gown moniker has been used to describe the relationship between colleges and the towns that were located there. In the beginning the two maintained a clear wall of separation and the separation was the cause of tension between the two entities. The town and gown tension was carried into the modern era of higher education; however, modern universities have realized that tension and adversarial relationships with the communities that they are located are detrimental. It hinders not only the future progress of the town but the university as well. HBCUs must realize that the town and gown relationship is very important and service to their surrounding community is paramount and at the core of the traditional mission of their institutions by providing essential services for their communities. For example, Michael J. Sorrell, president of Paul Quinn College, a historically black college located in Dallas, Texas, in the Highland Hills neighborhood, in his 2013 TED Talk at Southern Methodist University noted that the average family income of the school's immediate community is $23,000 a year.[13] Sorrell also noted that this community did not have grocery stores where people in this neighborhood could get fresh fruits and vegetables. Paul Quinn College and its administration decided to turn its unused football field into an organic farm. President Sorrell is pushing a new historically black college model or perhaps returning to the traditional black college model where the university follows the institutional ethos "We over Me" by making a commitment to serve its immediate community.[14] At Paul Quinn College, Sorrell is endorsing a model of servant leadership where the needs of the community outweigh the wants of an individual. The school donates 10 percent of the product that is grown on the school's organic farm. It sells its foods to local restaurants and sports organizations. Paul Quinn College is a sterling example of historically black college engaging its immediate community and meeting some of its needs and tackling its pertinent issues.

Finding ways to finance college has always been a nightmare for African American and white parents alike and most low-income and middle-class families have relied on loans to finance college. Recent changes in federal loan requirements and procedures hinder many from attending college. HBCUs have been disproportionally affected by the changes in the Parent PLUS loan and reduction in federal student Pell Grants. The changes in Parent PLUS loans also have been detrimental to historically black colleges and smaller predominately white colleges because of less affluent and first-generation students who typically attend these schools. Higher education has increasingly become an expensive investment for all families. More and more families are seeking loans to pay for college, but the potential accumulated debt and high interest rates of student loans have caused some to put off college or not attend college at all. In 2011, the federal government made changes to policies in its lending guidelines for universities.[15] Prior to 2011, parents were approved for loans if they did not have in delinquent payments over 90 days, no foreclosures, bankruptcies, or defaults. The changes expanded the definition to include debt that was more than 90 days and debts that had been sent to collections. The changes eliminated numerous low-income and middle-class families from financing their children's college educations.

Unlike in previous times, the federal government also began checking for any unpaid debts that had been referred to collection agencies. Applicants are judged only by their credit histories. These loans are available to both graduate students and parents of undergraduates. Many of the students who attend historically black colleges use loans to meet the costs of their education. Changes in the federal Parent PLUS loan program especially have hurt HBCUs. Stricter regulations in these loans have caused a reduction in student enrollments because students are being denied loans because of poor credit histories. Many of the students' families have used PLUS loans to supplement the financial gap with the cost of tuition and the limit federal loans will provide. Since PLUS loans do not have a cap amount that can be borrowed, many lower-income families can borrow the entire cost of attendances which includes tuition fees, room and board, textbooks, and expenses. The average cost of attending a historically black college ranges between $15,000 and $45,000 per year depending on the college that the student chooses. Low-income families would find it difficult to make monthly installments on loans of this magnitude. If the changes to the Parents PLUS loan remain, historically black colleges and small white colleges that service students from less wealthy families will find themselves in a continuous conundrum. The economic crisis of 2007 paired with the federal government's changes in the Parent PLUS loan has caused many black colleges find themselves struggling to keep financially afloat. HBCUs continue to face problems such as declining enrollments, aging facilities, the loss of students and faculty to competing white schools, online institutions, declining state and federal resources, and apathetic alumni.

Some HBCUs are monetarily weak and others are dealing with accreditation concerns. In 2014, Wilberforce University was issued a "show cause" order by the North Central Association of Colleges and Schools Higher Learning Commission.[16] The accrediting body cited its struggles to keep up student enrollment and public confidence following several controversies with board and presidential leadership, inability to reconcile issues with finance and governance, and the physical breakdown of campus facilities. Wilberforce has one year to prove why its accreditation should not be revoked. Adding to the tensions at historically black colleges are financial, cultural, and political uncertainties. Several historically black colleges have faced downgrades in the credit ratings due to heavy debt, declining enrollments, and cash flow difficulties. In 2013, Alabama State University and Howard University were downgraded.[17] Alabama State University's credit rating was downgraded because of the institution's inability to cut its operating expenses and its stagnant revenue.[18] Howard University's credit rating was reduced because of declining admissions and a loss of revenue and weak fund-raising. Fort Valley State University's credit rating was downgraded because it had low cash in reserve and decreased student enrollment. In 2013, Morehouse College and Alabama A&M University's credit ratings also were downgraded because of declining enrollments and tuition revenue declines and cash flow problems.[19] Also in 2014, Alabama State University and South Carolina University were given an accreditation warning by the Southern Association of Colleges and Schools in part because of their issues of governance of their boards of trustees and debt.

Problems have not only emanated from external forces; internal strife at some HBCUs has hindered their progress. Struggles with governance have continued to stunt the progress of some HBCUs. In recent years, infighting among leadership teams and mismanagement at numerous historically black colleges have burdened them and crippled their effectiveness. It is uncertain if these incidents of infighting and controversies in governance are more prevalent at historically black colleges as compared to predominately white colleges, but it appears that there is an increased level of scrutiny for black colleges by accrediting bodies, legislative bodies, local and national media, and, to some degree, the African American community at large. Incidents of infighting on governing boards at predominately white schools such as Penn State University, DePauw University, George Washington University, University of West Alabama, and the University of Virginia have been documented, but only the infighting at Penn State gained media attention because it was also attached to scandal and football. The highly publicized infighting and the public exposure of discord within HBCUs contribute to the unfair perception that HBCUs are poorly managed and governed. Several squabbles at HBCUs have become public and spilled onto the pages of local and national newspapers and other periodicals that chronicle happenings at historically black colleges. Disagreements between governing boards and university presidents at Howard University, Tuskegee University, Alabama State University, South Carolina State University, Norfolk State University, and Southern University have been chronicled in national media outlets. These episodes of negative exposure to the infighting as chronicled earlier can have long-term adverse consequences.

If these institutions do not resolve the issues with their governance, they will continue to be burdened by these unremitting problems. The negative publicity exacerbates fears of incompetence or mismanagement and creates reluctance among potential donors and prevents them from making large financial donations to HBCUs. To resolve some of the governance issues, HBCUs should focus on annual and by-annual training for all members serving on their boards and clearly define and delineate distinction on governing issues and management duties. Taking these measures eliminates or at the least curtails many of the issues at the center of conflict and the infighting.

Recently, turnover in presidential leadership appears to be a perpetual theme at HBCUs. There has been an exodus of HBCUs presidents leaving their post over the past three years. Changes in presidential leadership have taken place at Howard University, Tuskegee University, Benett College,

Morehouse, LeMoyne Owens College, Saint Augustine, Kentucky State University, and Cheyney State University. Traditionally, university presidents have been male and 55 years of age or older. These changes in leadership at black colleges has resulted in a trend of seeking presidents under age 50 to move historically black colleges forward. In an effort to keep up with the changing times, HBCUs are turning to younger university presidents because of the shifting landscape of higher education. Some believe that younger presidents may be more in tune with the needs of current college students, updated pedagogy, and diverse curriculums and can move HBCUs in a more progressive direction. Hopefully, these younger presidents can harness positive energies and push stagnant institutions to meet the unique challenges of the 21st-century institution of higher education.

Conclusion

HBCUs were created to formally educate a former enslaved people so that they would receive an opportunity to become productive citizens in America. Their histories are replete with beautiful and burdensome examples of institutions that have successfully provided educational opportunities for African Americans. Despite the ongoing challenges to these institutions, they have consistently and persistently provided a space where African Americans could pursue higher education and a place where their educational dreams would not be obstructed and could be nurtured. HBCUs continue to face the challenge of fulfilling the noble and demanding mission of providing higher education for nontraditional students who are often underprepared for college. These burdens coupled with numerous contemporary challenges and systematic impediments threaten the future of black colleges. Currently, there are 104 HBCUs operating in the United States. Many of the non-state-supported HBCUs are in danger of becoming financially insolvent because of the skyrocketing costs of delivering quality higher education in the 21st century. Just like the African American community, HBCUs are not monolithic. They all have unique elements that make each of them special treasures. HBCUs remain a viable college option for many African Americans seeking a rewarding social and cultural experience and an excellent college education. With the demographic projections for future censuses, there are opportunities for HBCUs to increase their enrollments, revenue, and visibility. Despite all of their challenges, HBCUs have retained a steadfast noble mission of educating underserved students.

Notes

1. The Higher Education Act of 1965.
2. Carleton 2002, pp. 27–30.
3. Jeynes 2007, pp. 193–194.
4. Chapman 1999, pp. 385–404.
5. Mckinney 1997, pp. 70–72.
6. White 2014.
7. Dawson 1994. p. 118.
8. Milner and Lomotey 2014, p. 36.
9. Ibid.
10. Hilliard 1989, pp. 21–23.
11. National Association for College and University Business Officers Data 2014.
12. HBCU Digest 2014.
13. Sorrell 2013.
14. Ibid.
15. Bidwell 2014.
16. Hansen 2014.
17. HBCU Digest 2014.
18. Moon 2014.
19. Selingo 2013.

Bibliography

Bidwell, Allie. "Change to Loan Qualifications Hurt Students at HBCUs, For Profit Colleges." U.S. News, January 8, 2014. http://www.usnews.com/news/articles/2014/01/08/change-to-loan-qualifications-hurt-students-at-hbcus-for-profit-colleges.

Brooks, F. Erik, and Starks, Glenn. 2011. *Historically Black Colleges.* Santa Barbara, CA: Greenwood Press.

Carleton, David. 2002. *Student Guide to Landmark Congressional Laws on Education.* Santa Barbara, CA: Greenwood Press.

Chapman, Bert. 1999. "The 1907 Admission of Land Grant University Depository Libraries: A 90-Year Perspective." *Journal of Government Information* 26 (4): 385–404.

Dawson, Michael. 1994. *Behind the Mule: Race and Class in African American Politics.* Princeton, NJ: University of Princeton Press.

Hansen, Amy. "Ohio's Wilberforce University Faces the Possibility of Losing Accreditation." State Impact National Public Radio, July 1, 2014.

HBCU Digest. "Moody Downgrades Alabama State, Howard Credit Ratings." July 4, 2014. http://hbcudigest.com/howard-university-alabama-state-university-moodys-credit-downgrade/.

Hilliard, A.G. 1989. "Cultural Style in Teaching and Learning." *The Education Digest* (December).

Jeynes, William. 2007. *American Educational History: School, Society, and the Common Good.* Thousand Oaks, CA: Sage Publications.

Kenneth and Clark, Mamie. The Doll Test in Brown v. Board of Education of Topeka, 347 U.S. 483, 74 S. Ct. 686, 98 L. Ed. 873 (1954). http://www.naacpldf.org/brown-at-60-the-doll-test.

Mckinney, Richard Ishmael. 1997. *Mordecai, the Man and His Mission.* Washington, DC: Howard University Press.

Milner, Richard, and Lomotey, Kofi. 2014. *Handbook of Urban Education.* New York: Routledge.

Moon, Josh. "Moody Downgrades Alabama State Credit Rating, Montgomery Advertiser." July 3, 2014. http://www.montgomeryadvertiser.com/story/news/local/2014/07/03/moodys-downgrades-alabama-states-credit-rating/12196121.

National Association for College and University Business Officers Data. 2014. http://www.nacubo.org/Documents/EndowmentFiles/2013NCSEEndowmentMarket%20ValuesRevisedFeb142014.pdf.

Preer, Jean. 1982. *Lawyers v. Educators: Black Colleges and Desegregation in Public Higher Education.* Santa Barbara, CA: Greenwood Press.

Selingo, Jeffrey. 2013. "Colleges Struggle to Stay Afloat." *New York Times* (April 12). http://www.nytimes.com/2013/04/14/education/edlife/many-colleges-and-universities-face-financial-problems.html.

Sorrell, Michael. "New Urban College Model: Michael Sorrell at TEDxSMU 2013." http://tedxtalks.ted.com/video/Michael-Sorrell-New-Urban-Colle;TEDx SMU, 2013.

White, Herbert. 2014. "Budget: Elizabeth City State, N.C. Senate Proposal Targets Unprofitable Campus." *The Charlotte Post* (May 29).

Wechsler, Harold, Lester Goodchild, and Linda Eisenmann. 2007. *The History of Higher Education.* Upper Saddle River, NJ: Pearson Publishing.

Chapter 17

Mentoring Matters: A Proactive Approach for Mentoring Black Men for Collegiate Success

Ronald C. Williams and Adriel A. Hilton

In recent years, many scholars and practitioners within the field of higher education have examined the likelihood of equal access and opportunities for students of color, particularly African American men. Although a greater focus has been placed on this issue, many barriers continue to exist on American college and university campuses for students of color; and many institutions are grappling with the rates at which men graduate, specifically African American men. In 2003, the six-year graduation rate for African American men was 28.5 percent compared to 47.1 percent for African American women.[1] As colleges and universities become more concerned with its black male persistence rates, many institutions have developed and implemented mentoring programs that provide effective strategies that promote student success and persistence through the concept of student engagement. Such programs, if implemented properly, can create supportive campus community environments, deconstruct negative stereotypes about African American men, and raise the academic profiles of many of the participants. The next section highlights relevant literature related to this topical area. Also, terms such as "African American" and "black" will be utilized interchangeably within this chapter.

This chapter provides some insight on the need for mentoring programs geared toward African American men, based on historical underrepresentation in higher education, and on student and faculty experiences related to mentoring effectiveness. This literature provides a critical review of how mentoring programs have impacted black male collegians' success on

American college and university campuses in academic and social contexts. It contains specific details of the national shifts for support for students of color, as well as general narratives of student and faculty mentoring experiences at four-year colleges and universities throughout various regions of the United States.

The purpose of this chapter is to examine the impact as well as the experiences of African American male collegians who were mentored as a part of an effort to increase retention rates. This work may assist administrators, faculty, and staff to identify methods in which higher education institutions can implement more effective methods for positively impacting persistence toward baccalaureate degree completion for African American men. In an effort to appropriately contextualize the experiences of black male students, this chapter seeks to provide a comprehensive overview of their overall K-12 educational experiences, which may provide insight into their preparedness for college-level studies.

Historical Perspectives of Black Men in Education

Although the most salient methods for removing barriers to retention and persistence for black male student populations are mentoring and advocacy, it is imperative that researchers examine the historical factors that contribute to issues that have plagued black students in America since the 19th century. The comprehensive literature that is available on this issue provides relevant examples of desolate circumstances that African American boys, and ultimately men, faced (and in many cases continue to face) in educational environments.[2] Unfortunately, adjectives such as dangerous, dysfunctional, endangered, menacing, and uneducable are often utilized to describe African American men. According to Jackson and Moore (2006), these biased characterizations of African American men are well positioned within the social domain of education. Despite some negative perceptions of African American people, it is clear that people within the African American community have valued education for many years.[3]

During the Civil War era, many state laws prohibited black people from being educated, and in most instances, these unjust laws prohibited anyone from teaching persons of African ancestry to read. Despite the challenges, many students of color persevered and learned to read and write. In a few cases, some free blacks and newly freed slaves attended newly established black colleges during the mid-19th century. After slavery was abolished, newly emancipated people of color were able to complete secondary school. Many continued their educational pursuits by expanding their studies at postsecondary institutions. As time progressed, the importance of education became central to the lives of persons of color. This sentiment is well documented in the memoirs, papers, and teachings of African American leaders, such as Drs. W.E.B. DuBois and Benjamin Elijah Mays, Mary McLeod Bethune, George Washington Carter, and Mordecai Johnson.

Early prominent African American leaders helped design frameworks that promoted the importance of education in black communities. However, educational opportunities for black people were limited, and access to quality education was scarce due to the United States Supreme Court's decision in *Plessy v. Ferguson* (1896), which legalized separate but equal facilities between African American and white people in the United States. These and many other injustices, ultimately, led to the establishment of the National Association for the Advancement of Colored People (NAACP), which focuses on equality for all persons regardless of race (NAACP.org). During the civil rights movement, the work of Attorney Thurgood Marshall along with organizations such as the NAACP successfully argued against the "separate but equal" decree of the *Plessy* decision in the famous 1954 *Brown v. Board of Education of Topeka* decision. This landmark case set a new precedent by declaring that separate but equal educational facilities promoted inferior conditions for the education of African American youths. The next section highlights the success of black male students through various interventions.

Intervention Needs for Black Male Student Success

According to Jackson and Moore (2006), many African Americans have the desire to earn a college education. However, the enrollment numbers for black men in higher education are lower than the enrollment for other populations, and this is particularly true when comparing enrollment numbers to women. Currently, African American men account for 4.3 percent of the total enrollment at four-year higher education institutions in the United States.[4] This relatively low enrollment percentage for black college men is at the same level as it was in 1976.[5] According to Harvey (2008), only 33.8 percent of the 73.7 percent of black men who graduated from high school in 2000 attended college. These data are alarming when considering that 43.9 percent of the 79.7 percent of black women who graduated from high school in 2000 attended college.

In recent years, higher education has experienced an increasing gender disparity, as the number of females participating in postsecondary education continues to outpace that of males. While this gender gap is not endemic to particular racial and ethnic groups, it is more pronounced for African Americans. For example, while there were 116,624 African Americans who earned a baccalaureate degree in 2001–2002, there are noticeable differences in college attendance rates between African American women and men.[6] Currently, African American men account for only 4.8 percent of the total enrollment of four-year higher educational institutions in the United States.[7] While marginal gains have been made by African American men enrolled in colleges and universities, most face difficult challenges in their pursuit to attain their baccalaureate degrees.[8]

The American Council of Education (2010) reported that the six-year graduation rate for black men was 35 percent. Although this 35 percent graduation rate is 6.5 percent higher than it was in 2003, it still represents the lowest graduation rate of any other student population demographic in the United States. Due to this disparity between black male persistence and completion and white male persistence and completion, it is essential that faculty, administrators, staff, policy makers, and other stakeholders focus on persistence and completion for black males pursuing baccalaureate degrees at four-year institutions. Further, to make matters worse, Cuyjet (2006) indicated that the national data suggests that two-thirds of all black men who begin a program of study at a college or university will never finish.

The educational challenges of African Americans have caused major concern among stakeholders in higher education, particularly after the turn of the 21st century. Numerous studies have been conducted to investigate the success of black males in higher education environments. Research suggests that academic bias, particularly in K-12 settings where stakeholders have lower expectations for black males to attend college than their expectations for white male students to attend college,[9] has negatively impacted the educational progress of African American men. Unfortunately, these biases are present early in the education of African American boys and impede their educational progress, ultimately in some instances impacting their ability to graduate from high school. Academic bias is evidence in a number of ways. Also, data suggests that black males are also more likely to receive excessive discipline, which means that black men, typically, are expelled more often, subjected to harsh and unnecessary punishments, and suspended for longer periods of time and more frequently than white students.[10] In addition, many black males do not perform academically at the same or higher levels than that of their female and white counterparts; this is particularly true at the elementary and secondary levels.

Similar to black men in higher education settings, African American men are more likely to be underrepresented in gifted and talented education programs, Advanced Placement, or honors courses.[11] In addition, Noguera (2003) indicated that in some educational environments, African American men are more likely than other racial and ethnic groups to be marginalized, underrepresented, stigmatized, and labeled with behavioral problems. Many black men are disproportionately tracked into classes designed for students who have limited academic ability, which impedes challenging learning opportunities than high-ability tracks, while their white peers are being placed in honors or Advanced Placement courses that are designed to prepare students for college placement examinations and collegiate-level work at colleges and universities.[12] These truths make intervention programs necessary for black men who are fortunate enough to be accepted at and ultimately enroll at four-year colleges and universities.

Although early intervention at the K-12 levels for black male students can promote academic and social integration to educational environments, it does not eliminate the need for intervention at the college level. Many black males who attend college often continue to be challenged by the damaging effects of their negative experiences prior to enrolling in higher education institutions. Many faculty members at American colleges and universities assume that all of the students who have been admitted to their institutions stand ready to successfully complete a college-level program of study. As a result of these faculty members' assumption that all students are academically prepared for college-level work, students who are in dire need of intervention programs may not have access to these opportunities. This next section examines contemporary barriers that are present within the academy. These barriers prevent a significant number of students of color, particularly African American males, from succeeding against odds and obtaining their four-year degree.

Contemporary Barriers

Since the beginning of the 21st century, parents/guardians and students have become responsible for paying a larger portion of the tuition and fees assessed for higher education than what was previously required. Rising out of pocket costs, racial tensions, campus experiences, and, in some cases, lack of academic preparedness may leave many African American male students vulnerable to failure in educational environments. Furthermore, social pressures, cultural shifts, negative self-efficacy, and feelings of inadequacy exacerbate this issue, which negatively impacts the retention rates of black men on many four-year college and university campuses. In order to address the low retention rates of African American students on college campuses, many institutions have developed various programs to meet the needs of students of color. Retention and development programs have been designed to focus specifically on the black male student population, many of whom need extra support and encouragement.

Students who are not able to advocate for themselves must have persons who are willing to develop mentoring relationships to assist them in becoming successful in college. Arguably, three of the primary goals for public higher education are access, equity, and quality. Williams (2005) reported that these goals are constantly under attack by forces external to public colleges and universities. Access, equity, and quality in public higher education have become increasingly difficult to maintain and in some cases to achieve as a result of limited state resources and rising instructional and operational costs. The rising cost of higher education coupled with the challenges that many black men endured during their K-12 educational experiences has created significant barriers to degree completion. These barriers have caused intuitional personnel to identify best practices regarding the development, management, and sustainment of mentoring programs that are specifically designed to enhance the success levels of African American men attending American colleges and universities.

Mentoring for Student Success

Astin (1993) and Pascarella and Terenzini (2005) indicated that faculty-to-student mentoring is an effective method to remedy the disparity problem. However, many black students tend to seek mentoring from black faculty members, and the limited number of black faculty members at predominantly white institutions (PWI) reduces the number of opportunities that are available to establish these desired mentoring relationships. Hurtado (2001) indicated that the racial disparity between black students and white faculty is widening as more black students are participating in higher education while the number of black faculty is not increasing at the same rate. In addition, the lack of black faculty members may be one of the contributing factors to the negative experiences that many students of color face at PWIs. Other factors include the lack of campus environment/ culture, support resources, affinity groups, student organizations, and faculty–student interactions. While the issue of black students identifying same-race mentors at PWIs remains problematic, the issue is more prevalent for African American men because black men have been and continue to be underrepresented and considered low-performing students on many college and university campuses.[13] Consequently, many black men continue to face barriers and greater obstacles for baccalaureate degree completion than the majority student population and black women.

If institutions intend to focus on addressing retention and low attrition among black male students, a special emphasis should be placed on developing, enhancing, and sustaining mentoring programs that will positively impact black men's success in college. Not only does ensuring black males' success improve conditions for colleges and universities, it also has the potential to positively impact society because earning a baccalaureate degree can improve one's ability to become gainfully employed and contribute positively to the economy. As Harper and Harris (2012) noted, black men's underrepresentation in the higher education arena causes their underrepresentation in professional environments as well. For example, the average income for African American men was $30,000, as compared to $37,100 for all men in the United States. The $33,000 median income of African American families was lower than that of all American families at $50,000. The percentage of African Americans in poverty (25%) was more than twice that of the total population (12%). The next section discusses mentoring models utilized to retain black males.

Mentoring Methods for Students' Success

Mentoring is a shared process wherein learning occurs when relationships are developed over a period of time between persons who are more experienced in various subjects and contexts (mentors) and persons who are less experienced in specific areas and contexts (mentees). The development of this relationship is crucial because it is necessary to build trust and understanding between both parties. Most notably, the mentoring process is most effective when the mentoring is voluntary for all parties. This process works best when the mentees trust the mentors, and vice versa. Once barriers have been removed (or in some cases lowered) and mentees have been strengthened with the knowledge that is needed for success (within the various contexts), the mentors are able to serve as positive role models who have the authority (which must be given by the mentees) to motivate students to continually improve.

An analysis of the current data on student success revealed that many personnel at American colleges and universities are defining student success narrowly. Most studies indicated that high retention rates are indicative of student success. However, the dialogue on this issue should not begin and end with retention. There are many salient qualitative factors that should be considered when examining mentoring and its effectiveness on student success. Although rising retention rates indicate that there is some level of student success, an emphasis should be placed on a number of factors that impact how well our students are acclimating to collegiate environments. Further, students' ability to acclimate well, especially black men, is largely predicated on the campus culture and climate. Stakeholders ought to examine stereotype threat and racial micro-aggressions. In addition, institutions must be intentional about creating third spaces (social catalytic) for their black men to succeed but more importantly to express themselves. Finally, personnel ought to develop meaningful mentoring programs on college campuses.

Fortunately, in recent years many colleges and universities have developed programs where faculty and staff have been designated to work with black male collegians to help them navigate academic spaces. According to York College at the City University of New York, the institution established the Male Initiative Program that supports underrepresented male students there. In addition, Florida Memorial College designed the black Male College Explorers Program to assist black male high school students to improve their likelihood of being admitted to and successful in college. Both programs are designed to assist black male students to be successful in educational environments; however, the foci of the programs are different to accommodate the individual needs of the students based on age, academic status, college-readiness, and classifications in school. We have highlighted briefly two successful mentoring programs because these programs have helped both institutions increase the number of black men who are persisting in and being admitted to college. But a host of programs are present in the academy; some effective strategies employed in thriving mentoring programs include

- conducting focus groups to understand the lived experience of students on campuses;
- identifying and ensuring students have access to key on-campus resources;

- establishing and supporting quality and trusting mentor/mentee relationships;
- pairing students with key stakeholders that want to see them succeed;
- developing cogent maps for academic success through advisement;
- advocating for students (e.g., sponsorship to relevant academic or leadership conferences, exposure to unfamiliar cultural or social environments);
- prioritizing self-worth through practicing and reflecting on "presentation of self."

In recent years, due to the achievement gap, based on race and ethnicity and gender, many efforts to mentor young black males have been implemented in middle and high school. For example, mentoring programs that are designed to help black males in middle and high school to improve their grades and prepare for college entrance examinations will invariably be designed differently than programs that focus on strategies and initiatives that assist black men who are already enrolled in higher education institutions. There are various types of mentoring programs, and what may be successful at one institution may not be successful at another. Student focus groups have proven to be an effective way to identify specific needs of students who may be potential mentees. In order to identify the needs of the student population for which the mentoring is intended, college and university officials may need to conduct student focus groups with said student population. For example, a focus group that is structured to give the mentees the space to express their frustrations and share their experiences (whether positive or negative) on campus provides mentors with insight into issues that need to be addressed. These groups will provide students with an opportunity to engage in dialogue with mentors regarding many topics which include their apprehension about unfamiliar academic and social environments, concerns about their finances, and fears about their own safety or the safety and well-being of their families. Most notably, micro-aggressions have been the most common topic that is discussed during the focus group meetings. Students are regularly commenting on how negatively micro-aggressions are impacting their ability to excel in their studies. Although in most instances the prejudice and discrimination that black collegiate men are experiencing tends to be latent, the lasting effect on their experience as students on college and university campuses is significant. Therefore, college and universities should design mentoring programs that equip students to handle these problems professionally and appropriately. Connecting students with institutional personnel who can address their concerns is critical to retaining black men who have academic profiles and will graduate and make positive social and economic contributions to the workforce. Collegiate environments must be conducive for all students' learning, not for a select few who are privileged. (Mentoring programs may have a litany of activities or components that strengthen black men's ability to be successful in college, such as workshop series that place an emphasis on academic achievement and self- and community empowerment, tutoring services, advocacy sessions, team- and community-building activities (community service/service above self), and motivational speaker series that acknowledge the past while emphasizing a great future".)

Ideally, mentors are more effective if they have some understanding of what mentees are experiencing. Many studies on this issue suggest that African American male students respond best when their mentors are black men. However, arguably, black male collegians may be mentored by anyone who displays reasonable concern and care for their situation and their success. Mentees may benefit from various role models from diverse backgrounds and experiences. For example, if mentors are selected, said mentors can help mentees identify resources that may be useful depending on the situation. Typically, institutional mentors are well equipped with the information needed to help black male collegians navigate the college environment.

Academic Mentoring/Coaching

Typically, academic acumen is the primary focus of mentoring programs for black men on college and university campuses. Ensuring African American men's success in the classroom contributes to their overall success in collegiate environments. Earning high grade point averages may result in scholarship offers, college or university honors/acknowledgment, and greater access to graduate or professional school acceptance on completion of baccalaureate-level programs of study. In addition, increased academic success may result in greater self-efficacy and confidence in one's own ability to succeed in various facets of life. This confidence may result in increased socialization and positive experiences on collegiate campuses.

In many cases, academic interventions are needed to support black men's success in college. If a black male college student's academic performance is poor, it is incumbent upon the mentor to help determine why his academic performance is poor. It may take time for the reasons to be revealed. Collegiate mentoring programs for black males often pair the students with faculty mentors who can assist them with academic matters and have similar backgrounds, experiences, and interests. Mentors frequently provide students with additional tutoring encouragement and motivation. Sometimes, simply talking with faculty mentors helps students develop a sense of belonging at a college of university. Increased comfort in the college setting may result in higher grades and greater student engagement in cocurricular activities. Students who find a niche in college beyond the classroom tend to be more successful in class and more likely to benefit from the total college experience.

Academic advisors also play an important mentoring role by helping students develop cogent maps for academic success. In addition to assisting students to select courses, plan their schedules, and locate tutoring and learning resource centers, advisors spend copious amounts of time helping students develop socially and professionally. Some advising models include intensive advising, major and minor exploration based, and career search and preparedness. Arguably, advisors who provide services beyond course search and registration assistance can be considered academic mentors, even if they have not been officially designated as such. Intrusive advising requires meaningful conversations with students, which may include dialogue about their desires, fears, hesitations, and other salient factors that may be contributing to their academic success or lack thereof. Committed advisors who also serve as mentors can significantly add to the success of mentoring programs. Other factors are also crucial to the success of mentoring initiatives. The next section highlights relevant interventions employed in successful and relevant mentoring programs.

Relevant Interventions and Advocacy

Mentoring African American men for collegiate success is largely dependent on relevant interventions at the institutions. Mentors must be prepared and have the necessary support to intervene when specific problems and issues arise. These interventions must be problem focused and designed to address the needs of the mentees. For example, a student may share information about external pressures or conditions that are negatively impacting the student's ability to succeed in college. While colleges and universities cannot address all external pressures, institutions may have the ability to address the more common pressures that may impact student success. Frequently, mentors are called upon to help students to manage personal or external problems. A mentor's ability to successfully direct these situations and act appropriately, professionally, and competently within these opportunities is crucial to the success of the overall mentoring program and the degree of persistence of their mentees.

As noted previously, many black men have been disproportionately mistreated, misjudged, and negatively labeled throughout their educational journeys (K-16). They need people who are willing and able to advocate on their behalf. Advocacy for college students is not a new concept. However, historically, many black male college students, especially those who attend predominately white universities, have not had institutional personnel, especially faculty members, who have advocated for equal treatment and access to greater educational opportunities for them as have other student populations. Black men need advocates who will speak for their needs and protect their interests at higher education institutions.

Professional Mentoring and Career Preparedness

Another challenge that many students face, particularly African American men, involves readiness for and confidence to enter the professional work environments. Although black male students may be performing well academically, they may need assistance with the concept of "presentation of self." "Presentation of self" refers to how individuals are dressed and groomed, how they speak and write, and otherwise how they conduct themselves. Typically, when students have high academic profiles, especially those who are the first in their families to attend college or pursue professional fields, they scoff at the importance of how they present themselves. They do not value or know how to present themselves in a professional manner that is conducive to formal work environments. Mentors can help black male collegians understand and accept the value of dressing for success. Often times, many black men believe they should be allowed to express themselves without fear of judgment. The reality, however, is that people are judged by how they present themselves.

The purpose of professional mentoring is to share information that will help African American collegians present themselves in a professional manner based on generally accepted principles and norms. For example, gentlemen may be taught how to wear a suit that fits properly with an appropriate shirt, tie, socks, and shoes. If mentees are wearing earrings or other socially unacceptable jewelry for men, mentors may encourage them to remove the jewelry. Other traditional topics include professional speech, résumé building and interviewing skills, meal etiquette, and the appropriate utilization of socially media in a technologically advanced global society.

Institutional Resources and Motivation

The decision to develop mentoring programs to support black male students should be taken seriously and with care. Depending on the mentoring model chosen, program vision and mission, the services offered, and the level of expected activities, mentoring programs may be costly and difficult to manage at institutions with significant budgetary challenges. However, arguably, the benefits of a mentoring program outweigh the human and operational resources that may be necessary. Mentoring programs are most effective when institutional officials make a philosophical and financial commitment to developing, maintaining, and sustaining a successful mentoring program geared toward the positive academic and social acclimation of black men on their campuses.

Mentoring programs that are well positioned and highly visible on college and university campuses create and enhance positive experiences for African American men in college. Even though most universities provide advising and academic service centers, counseling centers, student activities offices, recreation and student health centers, multicultural centers, orientation activities, and residence hall staff who focus on student development and campus integration to all students, it is often helpful if mentors conduct individual or small-group orientation sessions to highlight these resources for students who feel disconnected from campus life. Because of past biases and neglect experienced in their earlier educational environments, African American men frequently perceive that the campus is not a welcoming and supportive environment. In order to counteract this perception, mentors must emphasize and demonstrate to their African American male mentees that institutional resources are for all students. Unfamiliar environments naturally create some hesitancy. Mentors can lend extra encouragement by motivating students to take advantage of institutional resources available to them.

Conclusion

Mentoring programs have proven to be an effective method for assisting African American men to successfully navigate collegiate environments. A comprehensive examination of institutional initiatives for black males in higher education has revealed that mentoring programs have contributed to decreased attrition, increased grade point averages, and greater social acclimation to campus life. However, much thought and consideration should be given to the type of mentoring program that is needed based on student demographics, enrollment trends, and the average academic profile at a particular college or university. The complexity or simplicity of the mentoring program is not as important as institutional commitment and campus support. Specialized initiatives that are geared toward a specific student demographic must be vetted by the faculty and other institutional stakeholders who will have a significant impact on the program. Key persons should be responsible for garnering campus-wide support for mentoring programs that are designed to enhance the overall experiences for black men on college and university campuses in the United States.

Notes

1. College Results Online 2005.
2. Strayhorn 2008.
3. Allen et al. 2007.
4. Strayhorn 2008.
5. Ibid.
6. National Center for Educational Statistics 2005.
7. Horn, Berger, and Carroll 2004.
8. Schwartz and Washington 2002.
9. Ogbu 2003.
10. Hale 2001.
11. Jackson and Moore 2006.
12. Jones 2001.
13. Harper and Harris 2012.

Bibliography

Allen, W.R., J.O. Jewell, K.A. Griffin, and D.S. Wolf. 2007. "Historically Black Colleges and Universities: Honoring the Past, Engaging the Present, Touching the future." *Journal of Negro Education* 76 (3): 263–280.

Astin, A.W. 1993. *What Matter in College: Four Critical Years Revisited.* San Francisco, CA: Jossey-Bass Publishers.

Barker, M.J. 2007. "Cross-Cultural Mentoring in Institutional Contexts." *The Negro Educational Review* 58 (1–2): 85–103.

Brown v. Board of Education, 347 U.S. 483 (1954).

College Results Online. 2005. http://www.collegeresults.org/aboutthedata.aspx#section-1.

Cuyjet, M.J. 2006. *African American Men in College.* Indianapolis, IN: Jossey-Bass.

Davis, J.E. 2003. "Early Schooling and Academic Achievement of African American Males." *Urban Education* 38 (5): 515–537.

Engle, J., and M. Lynch. 2009. "Charting a Necessary Path: The Baseline Report of Public Higher Education Systems in the Access to Success Initiative." Education Trust, Washington, DC.

Florida Memorial University. www.fmuniv.edu. Accessed August 29, 2014. http://www.fmuniv.edu/blackmalecollegeexplorers/.

Hale, J. E. 2001. *Learning While Black: Creating Educational Excellence for African American Children.* Baltimore, MD: The John Hopkins University Press.

Harper, S. R., and F. Harris III. 2012. *Men of Color: A Role for Policymakers in Improving the Status of Black Male Students in U.S. Higher Education.* Washington, DC: Institute for Higher Education Policy.

Harvey, W. B. 2008. "The Weakest Link: A Commentary on the Connections between K12 and Higher Education." *American Behavioral Scientist* 51 (7): 972–983.

Horn, L., R. Berger, and C. D. Carroll. 2004. *College Persistence on the Rise? Changes in 5-Year Degree Completion and Postsecondary Persistence Rates between 1994 and 2000* (NCES 2005–156). U.S. Department of Education, National Center for Education Statistics. Washington, DC: U.S. Government Printing Office.

Hurtado, S. 2001. "Linking Diversity and Educational Purpose: How Diversity Effects the Classroom Environment and Student Development." In *Diversity Challenged: Evidence of the Impact of Affirmative Action,* eds. G. Orfield and M. Kurlaender (pp. 187–204). Boston, MA: Harvard Education Publishing Group.

Jackson, J. F. L., and J. L. Moore III. 2006. "African American Males in Education: Endangered or Ignored." *Teachers College Record* 108 (2): 201–205.

Jones, L. 2001. "Creating an Affirming Culture to Retain African American Students during the Postaffirmative Action Era in Higher Education." In *In Retaining African Americans in Higher Education: Challenging Paradigms for Retaining Students, Faculty, and Administrators,* ed. L. Jones (pp. 3–20). Sterling, VA: Stylus.

National Association for the Advancement of Colored People. naacp.org. Accessed August 28, 2014. http://www.naacp.org/pages/our-mission.

Noguera, P. A. 2003. "The Trouble with Black Boys: The Role and Influence of Environmental and Cultural Factors on the Academic Performance of African American Males." *Urban Education* 38: 431–459.

Ogbu, J. U. 2003. *Black American Students in an Affluent Suburb: A Study of Academic Disengagement.* Mahwah, NJ: Lawrence Erlbaum Associates.

Pascarella, E. T., and P. T. Terenzini. 2005. *How College Affects Students.* 2nd ed. Vol. 2. San Francisco, CA: Jossey-Bass.

Patton, M. Q. 2002. *Qualitative Research and Evaluation Methods.* 3rd ed. Newbury, Park, CA: Sage.

Plessy v. Ferguson, 163 U.S. 537 (1896).

Ryu, M. 2010. *Minorities in Higher Education: 24th Status Report.* American Council on Education.

Schwartz, R.A., and C.M. Washington. 2002. "Predicting Academic Performance and Retention among African American Freshmen Men." *Journal of Student Affairs Research and Practice* 39 (4): 351–367.

Strayhorn, T. 2008. "The Role of Supportive Relationships in Supporting African American Males' Success in College." *NASPA Journal* 45 (1): 26–48.

Williams, R.C. 2005. "Higher Education Stakeholders' Perceptions of Tennessee's Current Performance Funding Policy." Doctoral dissertation. Retrieved from ProQuest Dissertations and Theses.

York College, City University of New York. york.cuny.edu. Accessed August 29, 2014. http://www.york.cuny.edu/student-development/mens-center.

Index

Note: *Italicized* page numbers indicate a figure on the corresponding page. Page numbers in **bold** indicate a table on the corresponding page.

leadership, 21–22; in education policy, 15–19; elimination of racial oppression, 11–13; experiential knowledge, recognition, 9–10; as interdisciplinary and eclectic, 10–11; introduction, 3, 4, 10; marginalized students, 72–73; meritocracy, 6–7, 218; narrative analysis/counter-storytelling, 222; Next Generation Science Standards and, 216–22; origins of, 195–96; racism as endemic, 5–6; skepticism toward neutrality, objectivity, color blindness, meritocracy, 6–8; teacher education, 22–25; theme one, 5–6; unifying themes of, 218. *See also* Disability critical race theory

Critical Resistance and A New Way of Life Reentry Project, 165

Crosscutting concepts (CCs), 222–25

Cultural capital and hegemony, 170–72

Cultural mismatches, 101–2, 171

Cultural racism, 56, 125

Cunningham, Sam, 386

Dasgupta, Partha, 300

Decriminalization of schools, 137–40

Deficit ideology, 75–78, 81

DeGaetano, Yvonne, 337

Delpit, Lisa, 170

Denver Police Department, 105

Denver Public Schools (DPS), 95, 96

DePauw University, 395

Desegregation, 15–16, 48, 221

Deservingness and worth, standards, 322–25

Diop, Cheikh Anta, 388

Direct eye contact concerns, 170–71

Disability critical race theory (DisCrit): conceptual framework tools, 199–200; conclusion, 204–5; CRT origins, 195–96; disruption of pipeline, 202–4, *203*; literature on, 194–95; origins and tenets, 196–99; overview, 191–92; reframing the pipeline, 195; school-to-prison pipeline, 192–94; traditional views of special education, 200–202

Disciplinary core ideas (DCIs), 222–25

Disciplinary double standards, 137

Disciplinary policy and practice, 82

Discrimination, 8, 45, 124–25. *See also* Implicit bias; Racism; Reverse discrimination

Disorders of Infancy, Childhood and Adolescence (DICA), 135

Dissonance, 54, 72, 74, 217

Diversity in Mathematics Education Center for Learning and Teaching, 239

Dominant *vs.* nondominant groups of students, 228

Dorsey, Tompson, 221

Douglas, Fredrick, 192

Dread Scott v. Sandford (1856), 70–71

Dropout rates: arrest impact on, 133–34; increases in, 131, 132, 195; reduction attempts, 107; school demographics and, 98; suspension and expulsion impact on, 132; zero tolerance impact on, 178

DuBois, W.E.B., 33, 141, 192, 379, 401

Dysconscious racism, 57

Ecological systems theory, 172

Economic marginalization, 301

Economic Opportunity Act (1964), 46

Educational controversies: care and respect in schools, 316–18; CRT and, 313–14; deservingness and worth, standards, 322–25; elite universities, 318–22; merit and worth considerations, 312–13; overview, 311–12; special funding, 314–16

Educational leadership, 21–22

Education policy: assessment in, 16–17; CRT in, 15–19; desegregation, 15–16; school funding, 17–19

Elementary and Secondary Education Act (ESEA), 46–47

Elite universities, 318–22

Elizabeth City State University, 381

Ellison, Ralph, 241

Emotional disabilities among students, 194–95, 199–200

Enculturation, 172

English Language Learners, 18

Environmental contextual impact, 73–75

Equal Protection Clause, 357

Equity and Excellence Commission, 304

Ethnicity paradigm, 37–38

Exclusionary discipline practices, 94

Experiential knowledge, recognition, 9–10

Expulsions. *See* Suspensions/expulsions

Federal Housing Administration (FHA), 151

Female-single-headed households, 50

FemCrit. *See* Critical race feminism

Feminism, 10

Ferguson, John H., 40

422 Index

About the Editor and Contributors

Editor

Lillian Dowdell Drakeford, PhD, is retired from the Dayton Public Schools, Dayton, Ohio, where she served as a teacher of the deaf and hard-ofhearing, intervention specialist for children with special needs, curriculum and instruction intervention coach, high school assistant principal, and associate director of curriculum and instruction. Dr. Drakeford completed a bachelor's degree in education of the hearing impaired from the School of Speech at Northwestern University and a master of education degree in curriculum and supervision from Wright State University. She holds a doctorate in leadership and change from Antioch University.

Contributors

Ayana Allen, Ph.D. is an Assistant Professor of Urban Education and Educational Policy at Drexel University. She completed her Post-Doctoral Fellowship at *The Urban Education Collaborative* at UNC Charlotte. She was previously a teacher and literacy specialist in the Houston Independent School District as well as a Director of College Counseling and Alumni Programs at YES Prep Public Schools. Her research interests include urban education, identity construction in school contexts, and broad issues of access, equity, and achievement.

Subini Ancy Annamma, Ph.D., is an Assistant Professor of Special Education at the University of Kansas. Her research and pedagogy focus on increasing access to equitable education for historically marginalized students. Through an interdisciplinary approach, she examines the interdependence of race and ability, and how their mutually constitutive nature impacts students' education experiences.

F. Erik Brooks is professor and chair of the Department of African American Studies at Western Illinois University. He is originally from Montgomery, Alabama. Dr. Brooks earned a doctor of philosophy from the L. Douglas Wilder School of Government and Public Affairs at Virginia Commonwealth University. He holds three master's degrees. He earned a master of science in counseling and human development from Troy State University, a master of public administration from Auburn University Montgomery, and a master of education from Alabama State University. Dr. Brooks earned a bachelor of science in journalism and art from Troy State University. He is a sought-after speaker and he is often called upon to speak at public events discussing African American history, historically black colleges and universities, popular culture, multiculturalism, and diversity.

Terah T. Venzant Chambers, PhD, University of Illinois, is associate professor of K-12 educational administration at Michigan State University. Her research interests include post-Brown K-12 education policy and urban education leadership. Venzant Chambers has published in journals such as the Journal of Negro Education, Educational Studies, and the Urban Education.

Cherese D. Childers-McKee is a doctoral candidate, teaching assistant, and Holmes Scholar at the University of North Carolina at Greensboro in the Department of Educational Leadership and Cultural Foundations. She is also affiliated with the Urban Education Collaborative at UNC Charlotte. Cherese has a master of education in Teaching English as a Second Language from UNC Charlotte and a bachelor's in Spanish from Wake Forest University. Cherese is National Board Certified with 13 years of experience as a middle and high school teacher of English as a Second Language. Her research interests include youth of color interracial/interethnic relations, critical literacy, and women's and gender studies.

Dana N. Thompson Dorsey is assistant professor in Educational Leadership and Policy at the University of North Carolina at Chapel Hill. Her research focuses on critically examining education laws, policies, and practices and their influence on P-20 educational equity and access and/or opportunity for students of color and other marginalized groups.

Donald Easton-Brooks is dean in the Colleges of Education and Business at Eastern Oregon University. His research is on the impact of educational policy and social factors on students in urban and ethnically diverse communities; he has published several articles and book chapters on this topic. Dr. Easton-Brooks's work has been cited nationally and internationally. His work on educational policy has been cited in letters to senators, the U.S. secretary of education, and educational initiatives in Africa and Australia. He has consulted with local, state, and national agencies on issues related to urban education and teacher quality.

Aysha Foster is a social science researcher whose research interests are psychosocial factors that influence academic achievement, including parental involvement, motivation, and cultural identity. She received her PhD in health psychology from Virginia State University. Prior to graduate school, Dr. Foster also taught in an elementary school for three years.

Alexi Freeman, JD, is director, Public Interest, and lecturer, Legal Externships, at the University of Denver Sturm College of Law. She previously worked at Advancement Project, assisting grassroots organizations on racial justice advocacy campaigns. Freeman graduated from the University of North Carolina at Chapel Hill and Harvard Law School.

Laurie Garo is a doctoral student in Curriculum and Instruction for Urban Education, specializing in school-based interventions for children exposed to gang and gun violence. She uses Geographic Information Systems as a research method to evaluate discipline disproportionality and to explore neighborhood violence indicators that may impact child well-being.

Elizabeth Gil is a doctoral student in K-12 Educational Administration at Michigan State University. Her research interests include family involvement, culturally responsive educational practices, and post–high school educational access and success. She taught in New York City public schools for over 10 years, working with children, parents, and teachers.

Ramon M. Griffin is a PhD student in K-12 Educational Administration at Michigan State University. His research interests include emotional and mental health wellness in African American males K-8 and the intersection between open enrollment charter schools, race, gender, and disability, as well as special education reform and law. A Southside of Chicago native, he earned his bachelor of arts degree in sociology and criminal justice from Dillard University in New Orleans.

Victoria M. Hand, PhD, is associate professor of mathematics education at the University of Colorado Boulder. She is interested in the relation between how children learn mathematics and broader social and cultural structures and processes. Her research examines—and is committed to narrowing—participation gaps in mathematics classrooms, or differences in mathematical participation between groups of students.

Nancy A. Heitzeg is professor of sociology and director of the interdisciplinary Critical Studies of Race/Ethnicity Program at St. Catherine University, St. Paul, Minnesota. Professor Dr. Heitzeg has written and presented widely on issues of race, class, gender, and social control with particular attention to the color-blind racism, the prison industrial complex, and the school-to-prison pipeline. For the past four years, Professor Heitzeg has also been coeditor of an online blog series, Criminal Justice, which is devoted to encouraging public education, dialogue, and action on issues of mass criminalization and incarceration.

Julie A. Helling teaches with the Center for Law, Diversity and Justice at Fairhaven College of Interdisciplinary Studies, Western Washington University. She received her BA in English from the University of Iowa, served as a Peace Corps Volunteer in Niger, and graduated from the University of Michigan Law School.

Adriel A. Hilton is assistant professor of College Student Personnel and director of the College Student Personnel program at Western Carolina University. Dr. Hilton previously served as assistant vice president for Inclusion Initiatives at Grand Valley State University. His responsibilities included consulting, advising, and providing support to all levels of administration, faculty, and staff.

Muhammad Khalifa is assistant professor in the Department of Educational Administration at Michigan State University. Having worked as a public school teacher and administrator in Detroit, Dr. Khalifa's research examines how urban school leaders enact culturally relevant leadership practices. Dr. Khalifa has recently published in the Urban Review, Educational Administration Quarterly, the Journal of Negro Education, and the Journal of School Leadership. He is coeditor of the forthcoming books, Exploring Critical Ethnographies in Education (SUNY Press) and Handbook on Urban School Leadership (Rowman & Littlefield). Dr. Khalifa is engaged in school leadership reform in African countries and has been helping U.S. urban schools perform equity audits to address achievement gaps and discipline gaps in school.

Chance W. Lewis, PhD, is the Carol Grotnes Belk Distinguished Professor and Endowed Chair of Urban Education at the University of North Carolina at Charlotte. In addition, Dr. Lewis is the executive director of *The Urban Education Collaborative,* which is publishing the next generation of research to improve urban schools.

Hui-Ling Malone is a California native. She received her BA in International Studies and Education Minor at the University of California, Irvine. Malone began her teaching career in Detroit, Michigan, and received her master's in education with a focus in urban pedagogy from the University of Michigan, Ann Arbor. She is currently a high school English teacher at Pathways Community School in south Los Angeles. Malone is passionate about social justice and working with the youth.

Mei-Ling Malone is an educator, grassroots organizer, writer, speaker, humanist, and mother. Dr. Malone teaches at Los Angeles Southwest College, UCLA, UC Irvine and in the Watts community. Her research critically examines the historical intersection between the prison industrial complex and discipline in urban schools in California.

Stefanie Marshall is a PhD student at Michigan State University studying educational policy. She is interested in understanding how policies can more adequately support science educational programming in urban contexts, specifically focusing on support for school leaders. Stefanie earned a bachelor of science in biology at Oakland University and a master's in educational studies from the University of Michigan with a concentration in policy and educational leadership.

Eileen Carlton Parsons is associate professor in science education at UNC. Her research investigates the role of race and culture in learning and participation of traditionally underrepresented groups in STEM fields, specifically the impact on access and attainment in K-20 STEM education.

Tennisha Riley is a doctoral student in the Developmental Psychology program at Virginia Commonwealth University. Her research interests include cognitive and emotional processes associated with aggressive and disruptive behavior both at school and in the community. She received her master's degree in psychology (Marriage and Family Therapy) from La-Salle University.

Dr. Theresa Saunders is assistant professor in education leadership at Eastern Michigan University. She has served as a teacher and administrator in urban school districts throughout the nation. Her research interests are leadership and social justice in school improvement and school finance; she is the convener of the African American Young Men of Promise Initiative in Michigan.

Zewelanji Serpell is associate professor in the Department of Psychology at Virginia Commonwealth University. Her research harnesses advances in cognitive science to develop and evaluate school-based interventions for optimizing African American students' learning and promoting their school mental health. She received her PhD in developmental psychology from Howard University.

Joi A. Spencer, PhD, is associate professor at the University of San Diego. Her work focuses on mathematics education and teacher education and reflects her deep commitment to educational equity and teacher development. Her research has examined mathematics learning opportunities in the poorest middle schools in Los Angeles, as well as the impact of video-based mathematics professional development on student learning and teacher.

Marcia Watson is currently an urban education doctoral candidate at the University of North Carolina at Charlotte. Her research interests include Afrocentric theory and educational philosophy, contemporary issues of black education, critical multiculturalism, and school discipline reform. She is the coauthor of *Unshackled: Education for Freedom, Student Achievement, and Personal Emancipation,* which was released in Spring 2014.

Gregory J. White is a PhD student in the Education Policy program at Michigan State University. His interests converge around equity, economics, and politics. A Detroit native, he earned his bachelor of education